Ma's Dictionary

Straddling the Social Class Divide

A Memoir

Milan Kovacovic

Greysolon Press
www.greysolonpress.com

Greysolon Press
P.O. Box 3073
Duluth, Minnesota 55803
www.greysolonpress.com

Ma's dictionary: straddling the social class divide

First Edition, 2011

11 12 13 14 15 • 5 4 3 2 1

Library of Congress Control Number: 2011931451

Softcover ISBN: 978-0-578-08168-7

Printed in U.S.A.

For Deb,

And for Paul, Laurie, Aaron, and Zach.

To Éric Vibart, friend and helmsman
on this voyage since its inception.

To Eva in Slovakia.

To the Ohmann-Krause family in Oregon.

The unexamined life is not worth living.

— *Socrates*

The unrecorded life is not worth examining.

— *Emerson*

Everyone who reaches the age of fifty should set aside
two or three weekends to write down their life story.

— *Bill Clinton*

Raconte-nous pas ta vie!
("We don't wanna hear your life story!")

—*A common French saying*

Dear Reader:

Every life, even the seemingly most sheltered or uneventful,
is an epic encounter with destiny, deserving to be recorded.
That said, I don't know whether or not you'll wanna hear my story.
All I know is it took me more than
three weekends to write it down…

— *Milan Kovacovic*
Duluth, Minnesota, USA

Contents

Prologue

Mother and Son, an Odyssey vii

Part I • Midwest Trilogy

1. Chicago Blues 3
2. The North Country 13
3. Ma's Dictionary 21

Part II • Saint-Aquilin, My Beautiful Village

4. Slovakia, a Shattered Idyll 43
5. Madame Mercier, Schoolteacher 64
6. Laundry Day 76
7. Payday at the Village Tavern 93
8. To the Source 103

Part III • Paris, the Bewitching City

9. Scholarship Student 119
10. Olga's Brother 141
11. 64 Avenue Henri-Martin 161

Part IV • U.S.A., a Jagged Journey

12. Americas 187
13. School Daze 210
14. Narrow Escape 218
15. Hobo Junction 228
16. Botch Your Life: the Brutal Way 239
17. Botch Your Life: the Gentler Way 251
18. U.S. Army 265
19. San Francisco Airport, Summer '67 286
20. Oxford-by-L.A., the Oasis at Claremont 304

Part V • Fast Forward

21. Disentangling the Psyche 317
22. Workin' at the U. 325

Acknowledgments 339

Mother and Son, an Odyssey

*M*y family, if one can call it that, was too dislocated and too poor to establish a household of its own. So I grew up in other people's homes, until the age of sixteen.

I was born in 1942 in rural Normandy, where my parents had been employed for more than a decade as foreign guest workers. My father died there of cancer when I was eighteen months old, in the midst of war and Nazi occupation. Meanwhile my sisters Olga and Eva—nine and six years older than me—were being raised since infancy by relatives, hundreds of miles away in my parents' native village in Slovakia.

In 1946, when rail travel to Eastern Europe was finally restored, my mother tried to restart her life by moving back to her homeland so she could be with her three children, two of whom no longer remembered her. But her resettlement plans foundered. Soon after our arrival in Slovakia, our family was split up again. She and I went back to France and remained there another ten years. Then, just before I turned fourteen, we emigrated to America. My sisters stayed behind in Europe, though in different countries.

Following our failed reinstallation among our kin in Slovakia, Olga, thirteen, had reluctantly accompanied us back to France. Faced with the loss of her familiar surroundings and an abrupt transition to a new language and culture at this vulnerable stage in her life, she became more and more estranged from our mother and endured a cruel destiny in Paris.

It had been expected that after some time ten-year-old Eva would also join us in France. Instead, face to face contact with her wasn't reestablished until seventeen years later, in part because the communist Iron Curtain soon slammed shut the eastern half of the continent; in part too because our precarious situation in the West shattered any prospect that our family would ever reunite. Maman worked as a live-in domestic, and therefore could not raise us herself.

I thus spent the first ten years of my life in a boarding arrangement with an elderly peasant couple in a village in Normandy, and became strongly attached to my aged, infirm, indigent guardians and to our "primitive" way of life that had scarcely evolved in centuries. At the same time, as a frequent visitor to my mother's place of employment, I often crossed the class divide into the sophisticated world of the *haute bourgeoisie*. Later, between the ages of ten and fourteen, I even became a direct beneficiary of the schooling prerogatives and other amenities of that milieu, including domicile in the mansion of her new employers, the Kapferers, at 64 Avenue Henri-Martin, one of the most prestigious addresses in Paris's exclusive Sixteenth District. Through observation and instinct, my uneducated but talented mother had become a valued practitioner of French cuisine, and I, her homeless son, was adopted as an extra member in a household of twelve that included a live-in domestic staff of six.

My upbringing thus took place at opposite extremes of the social scale. Against all odds, I was headed for a promising future by the time I reached adolescence, thanks to the support and hospitality of the Kapferers, complemented by the thoughtfulness of their cosmopolitan daughter Martine Wildenstein, who liked Maman's cooking and often visited for lunch during her extended stays in France. As an annual rite of spring, she made me the recipient of her son Alec's hand-me-down wardrobe. He was one year older than I, and heir, with his younger brother Guy, to the world's preeminent art dealing dynasty. His expensive suits, ties, and other fine clothes fit me just right. Though destitute and *sans famille*, I easily passed for a *petit Monsieur*.

As if to usher in this radical transformation, I also received at age ten an all-expense national scholarship from the French government, to attend an "elite" boarding school in suburban Paris. My placement on this unexpected educational path was due solely to the guidance and tutelage of Madame Mercier, my teacher for the preceding five years in the village one-room schoolhouse.

The luck that had brought me this conjunction of personal and institutional support vanished with my mother's stunning decision to emigrate to America when she turned fifty. I did not oppose her project, though it meant forsaking my school friends and my generous sponsors, as well as my beloved Paris. I had inherited her sense of adventure and her recklessness, along with her misleadingly placid disposition.

Contrary to Maman's deluded imaginings of a "better future" for us in the New World, the move proved disastrous. I fell into a drastic downward spiral for an entire decade, and she permanently. I recovered from my demise only because of a belated intervention by my disappeared surrogate father, the State. However, his reemergence into my life occurred for a less magnanimous reason than previously in France: Conscription, in January 1965, at the start of the Vietnam War.

I ignored my first draft call, but then yielded and wasn't prosecuted. Ironically, the Army rescued me from my dead-end civilian existence and enabled me to reinvent myself once more. My former good fortune returned after its prolonged lapse. The unfair, arbitrary, capricious ways of the military all played in my favor. I finished my tour of duty with an honorable discharge and a massive case of survivor guilt.

I now earn my living teaching at a university—an outcome attained by miracle, given that I barely managed to finish high school. Delinquency, multiple identities, family disintegration, divided attachments, linguistic and cultural uprootings, mutations in modes of living, disordered education, workplace alienation: My mother often said "Every family have story."

My sisters Eva (left), 10, and Olga, 13, in Slovakia shortly before our family's 17-year separation.

Part I

Midwest Trilogy

Mother and Son at Chicago's lakefront, a year after arrival in America.

Chapter 1

Chicago Blues

"One doesn't 'learn' another language. One falls into it."

— *Georges-Arthur Goldschmidt*

Okay, Miles, let's go through this pronunciation drill once more. Repeat the words after me, and make sure you put the stress on the right syllables. And remember, we're in the English mode now, not *Frahnsay*, okay? Also watch out for the cognates…you know, the words that look the same in both languages but are pronounced differently."

For what seems like the hundredth time, my high school speech correction teacher Miss Nelson pushes the recording button on her tape machine, and we go through her list again. First she hides each word with a ruler, and after I have imitated her pronunciation as best I can, she lowers the ruler to let me see the word. Then I repeat it once more, this time associating sound with spelling. Phonics, revisited in the tenth grade.

When we're done with the list, she rewinds the tape and we listen to the embarrassing results….

As evident from my speech correction lessons, I didn't "fall" into English. I floundered into it.

My struggles began when I first arrived in Chicago as a fourteen-year-old immigrant from France. I had studied the language at school in Paris before, with seemingly good results, but upon coming to America I faced surprising new challenges to my sketchy book knowledge.

At the same time, my native language was not my mother tongue. I knew only just enough of my mother's Slovak, and she just enough of my French, for basic conversation between us in fractured syntax, roughly equivalent to

"What time is?", or "Where you put mine bag?", or "Please pass to me sugar." We settled into a makeshift Franco-Slovak vernacular arrested at a pitifully low level, and made no progress from there.

Despite our frustrating verbal limitations, she and I managed to communicate fairly well, mostly about mundane matters of daily life. Still, shared fluency remains an inescapable necessity for meaningful exchange beyond the rudiments, even though it does not ensure mutual understanding. Under those conditions, how could I hope to truly know my own mother?

And now English, the language of the great Shakespeare, was superimposing itself on our fragile little Tower of Babble. In French, I called my mother Maman (which I pronounced Manman, in the proletarian way of my native village); in Slovak, I called her Mama; and in English, Ma. Unsettling, for at the core of identity.

Ultimately, thanks in large part to Miss Nelson, I think I have managed to resolve some of my most glaring English pronunciation problems. But my bilingualism didn't come easily. Usually, this condition of dual identity develops organically, by osmosis, through the circumstances of life, without conscious effort or deliberate study. One "falls into" the new language.

So, why didn't this happen for me? A learning disability? A lack of aptitude? Some other mysterious factor in my background?

Two years after arriving in Chicago, after a very difficult initial adjustment to America, similar in many ways to my sister Olga's tribulations in France, I was settling into a life radically different from the one I had known in Paris. Among the group of teenage friends I took up with, I found myself the only one still attending school. The others had marched defiantly into the principal's office on their long-awaited sixteenth birthday, and confronted him, the secretary, and the truant officer with a gleeful "I'm outta here, man! You're never gonna see my face again!" which I suspect was reciprocated with a silent but equally gleeful "Good riddance!"

For some obscure reason, I persevered, but attended classes only just enough to avoid failure or expulsion, and *not once* took a book home. I was now a high school student hanging out with high school dropouts. I again straddled two worlds, juggled two identities, but this time in a reversed context, riding the social escalator down, at full speed, to No Future—albeit with some desperate momentary thrills in the process—instead of up, as before in Paris. There, fanciful yet quite conceivable career prospects awaited me, including, at the end of my studies, likely becoming a sort of "liege man" or trusted aide for the Kapferers, to whom I felt indebted with everlasting gratitude and loyalty for having taken me into their home during my four years of French secondary schooling.

Maman, whose artful cooking and exquisite Slovakian pastries had delighted the most discriminating palates in Paris, got a job in Chicago on an assembly line in a canning factory and later as a live-in housekeeper; and I, having lost all moorings, became mildly delinquent. I never achieved my American friends' "prestige" of having to report to a probation officer or serving some jail time.

One day, despite my having no blatant academic or behavior problems except general disinterest in school, I was called in to the principal's office:

"Miles, this is Miss Nelson, our speech therapist. Your teachers think you would benefit greatly from her professional help."

"Professional help? Me? What for? I don't need any!" I protested, shocked to discover that I had been the subject of some discussions, that my shield of anonymity had been violated.

"Oh, yes you do, young man! Have you had a chance to hear your English pronunciation lately? Miss Nelson will record you on her tape machine and let you find out for yourself what you sound like. We'll notify your Mom by mail. She needn't worry about the cost, remedial services are free."

The principal might as well have given the letter directly to me. In our dislocated family unit, with Maman knowing no English and only sketchy French, I had been the one in charge of administrative matters for a long time already. I liked the fact that American schools mentioned only mothers. Fathers were left out of the picture, as if they didn't exist.

In France with the authorities at the *lycée*, it had been the opposite: "You will bring a note signed by your father." I always had to remind them that mine was deceased. "Okay then, from your mother or your guardian."

At such times, I proceeded to write the note myself, and included in the signature, to clinch authenticity, the accent marks and "ová" spousal ending that Maman continued to use from her Slovak native tradition: Eva Kovačovicová. After thirteen years of married life and fifteen as a widow, she also still wore her wedding band, now razor thin.

In French, the pronunciation of our lengthy foreign last name posed no problem. It was just a matter of patiently aligning one syllable after the other, with equal stress on each. In English, however, even without the "ová" ending, the reaction was usually either patronizing befuddlement "How in the world do you say *that*?", or outright butchery.

So I began a rigorous program of speech correction under the direction of Miss Nelson, who normally worked with stutterers or other speech-impaired students, not immigrant aliens like me. My program of orthophonic therapy lasted an entire semester, one hour twice a week, face-to-face in a tiny windowless office with Miss Nelson and her tape recorder. I attended those sessions faithfully, unlike my other classes.

At the time, I thought I had a fairly good grasp of English grammar, because of—or despite—my previous studies of the language in France, including the method that emphasized memorization of individual sentences, beginning with "My tailor is rich." But correct pronunciation eluded me. And yet I had no difficulty overcoming some problems that seemed to bedevil my American classmates, for instance the distinction between "its" and "it's," or between "lend" and "borrow," as in "Hey man, can you borrow me two bucks 'til next week?"

I had given up trying to understand the difference between the relative pronouns "that" and "which"—nobody could explain it anyway—but I certainly knew the distinction between "that" and "who," the former denoting things and the latter people. It seemed straightforward and obvious enough, yet I routinely heard sentences like: "Everybody *that* ditched school yesterday went over to Chuck's house 'cause his ol' man and ol' lady are both working."

I kept these grammatical observations to myself, for fear of appearing preoccupied with things that maybe didn't matter much in the totality of life. I probably saw my adeptness at this kind of nitpicking as a comforting, secret compensation for my other linguistic shortcomings. I let go of "My friends and I…" and opted instead for "Me and my friends…" in order to better fit in, after one of my buddies said I talked like a book.

Part of my difficulty with spoken English was that words had to be learned individually, like Chinese ideograms. Furthermore, identical scripts could often be pronounced differently, with no apparent logic. Like the quaint but incoherent Anglo-Saxon system of weights and measures, with its pints, pounds, ounces, feet, and inches (i.e. thumbs—twelve thumbs to a foot), this defied any sense of order or clarity for someone steeped in the rationality of the metric system.

Here's a cursory sampling of the oddities I was encountering in English pronunciation: "Elvis Presley will *record* a new *record*." Or "It's a *minute* problem which (that?) I can solve in a *minute*." Another one: "I will *read* from the *red* book that (which?) I *read* once before."

How about "gotcha" series like "Ear/near/pear/fear/bear/shear/tear/tear— as in 'Don't shed a *tear* for this *tear* in the fabric. Or: lean/mean/Sean. Also, what to make of "colon, colony, colonial, colonel (kernel!)?" Not that other languages, including French, don't have their share of endearing eccentricities, but spoken English certainly presented enough of them to drive anyone crazy. Pity the poor American school children when they first learn to read.

Similarly, I knew how to pronounce "Kansas" and "Ar," but put the two together, as in the name of the state that had been much in the news because of racial integration problems in Little Rock, and you ended up with something completely different, "Arkansaw!" Same thing with "famous" and "in-famous."

The stress patterns within words gave me a lot of grief as well. For instance, I could not figure out how to correctly pronounce such seemingly simple words as "salad" or "syllable."

And even after the problem of stress pattern within words was resolved (you had to be a musician to replicate the sing-song characteristics of words like "nationality" or "azalea"), cognates presented perverse additional idiosyncrasies. I continued to pronounce "psychology" with a "p" and "sculpture" without, like in French.

Another error of mine, caused by interference from my native language, was that I didn't pronounce "h's" at the beginning of words. "His house" came out as "is ouse." I also tended to omit "s's" at the end of plural nouns, as in "I ave many problem." My English was heavily anchored in French.

Miss Nelson didn't disagree with me about the difficulties of English pronunciation. To make me feel better, she even mentioned an example cited by the playwright George Bernard Shaw:

"'Ghoti,' she declared, "can be pronounced in English 'ghoti (goatee)' or ... 'fish'."

"What?" I objected. "Fish? That's impossible!"

"No, it's not," she replied. "*F* as in enou*gh*; *i*, really wild this one, as in the plural of woman: w*o*men; and *sh* as in na*ti*on. So, there you have it, ghoti and/or fish."

But, difficult as they were, words proved to be child's play compared to individual sounds. She drilled me through the complete inventory of English phonemes, so complex with its diphtongs and what not, before focusing on my main problem: I was pronouncing the American "th" like a French "d," "t," "s," "f," or "z," depending on the context. It startled me to hear how bad I sounded on the slowly winding reel, compared to her prompts. I hadn't been aware of that before I started the speech correction lessons:

"Thirty" : "Dirty"

"Thirty first" : "Dirty thirst." Damn, for once that I get the "th" right, I put it in the wrong place.

"Thirty second" : "Dirty seconde." Ouch, French intonation on that one.

"Thirty third" : "Dirty turd"

"Thirty fourth" : "Dirty fort"

"Miles, do your classmates ever make fun of your pronunciation?"

I enjoyed hearing her call me Miles, a version of my name she had Americanized a little (the other teachers called me Milton). If I had been musically talented at all, I would have loved to be a jazz musician like Miles Davis. He had been one of my American idols in France, along with James Dean, whose collar-up leather-jacketed look I continued to cultivate. But to my surprise the revered horn player seemed less well known in Chicago than in Paris.

"No, I don't think they make fun of my pronunciation, except they sometimes call me Frenchie."

"Okay, Miles, let's try again. This time let's focus on the contrast between voiced and voiceless fricatives. Look at me and listen carefully. Tongue between the teeth: 'Thank you for this thing.' Please repeat."

"Sank you for zis ting," I muttered, unable to reproduce the oral articulations demonstrated with such facility by my model. My "thank" came out as a perfect French "5," *cinq*.

"No, no, young man, you have to push your tongue between your teeth, but you must also pull it back right away. Like this, look!" And she'd point her lacquered fingertip at her glistening lips, through which emerged the pink tip of her tongue, sending shivers down my spine: " 'Thank you for this thing.' See, it's easy."

Observing her through these countless repetitions, it finally dawned on me why, in an American movie I had seen in Paris dubbed in French, Marilyn Monroe looked so odd saying *merci* with her tongue peeking out like that.

Miss Nelson had infinite patience. She was very attractive too, and looked completely out of place, like a hibiscus flower, in this dreary windowless room with its clanging radiator. She often wore angora sweaters in pastel colors, directly on her skin. From deep within their soft texture flowed wafts of luscious fragrances that contrasted mightily with the prevailing smell in the school's hallways—a vague odor of sweat and chlorine from gym clothes festering in crammed lockers, tinged with chalk dust and hormones oozing through Clearasil-caked pores.

I felt ill at ease feigning clinical detachment while having to observe those slippings of Miss Nelson's tongue between her teeth, as she repeatedly demonstrated how to produce the "th" sound. With the fatigue and concentration of unrelenting phonetic drills weighing down on me, I often succumbed to flashes of delirium: by constantly pushing forward with my tongue for the "th's," wouldn't I develop buck teeth, and then have to wear braces, with rubber bands and all, like some of my better off American classmates? Good luck trying to pronounce "th's" with those contraptions in my mouth! Instead of an orthophonist I'd wind up needing an orthodontist.

The mocking voice of Charleau, the raunchiest of my former boarding school classmates in Paris, also taunted me during those moments of torpor: "Look at her tongue, Kovaco, it's going in, it's going out, it feels so good, it's an invitation. You're a chickenshit if you don't slip her the tongue too, all the way to her tonsils."

Charleau was being his usual vulgar self, but his ideas did leave some lingering temptations in my mind. A woman of thirty-something could probably teach me a lot, without my having to take her out to the movies, or to the ice cream parlor, or any of that teen-age dating stuff. "Miles, let's do some *fricatives* today" was my cross to bear, but I also heard it as a possible gateway to paradise. It sounded like a word Charleau might use...

Once, a rare tinge of impatience in Miss Nelson's voice startled me from my libidinous reveries:

"You know, Miles, it's pretty unusual for a young man your age to resist so much. You should let yourself go! Don't hold back! Surrender!"

Surrender? I recoiled in embarrassment, then panic, my face turning red. To what? To whom? To her? Was this my dream come true, or some bad joke being played on me?

I didn't know where to hide in our suddenly oppressive hothouse cubicle. Was she reproaching me for not daring to make amorous advances in our intensive phonetic encounters? I felt that since she was older, it was up to her to take the initiative. Still, no question about it, Charleau was right: I was a chickenshit.

"As-sim-i-la-tion, young man," she hammered. "That's what you're resisting: as-sim-i-la-tion! You're now living in the U.S.A., aren't you, so why don't you just start accepting this new reality. Look, you've been in this country two years already, you're only sixteen, you're still young enough to lose your accent completely. And you're Caucasian, so you can assimilate fully. People won't be asking you where you're from anymore. Wouldn't you like that?"

"It's not my fault if I can't pronounce the 'th's'," I blurted out in a dis-ingenuously pleading voice, relieved that it was my pronunciation, not my manhood, that had been questioned. And I didn't correct her on the geo-graphical mix-up. My ethnic origins were not from the Caucasus, as she seemed to imply, but from Czechoslovakia, which furthermore often got confused by Americans with Yugoslavia. But what did that have to do with, anyway? And yes, I would have loved to be able to blend in and not be asked where I was from.

"Listen, Miles," she continued, "your case is very puzzling. You seem to have a good ear for English, you pick up on a lot of things, so theoretically you should also have good pronunciation. I discussed this with a psycholo-gist friend of mine. We both agree that your strong French accent is probably the outward sign of an equally strong, perhaps pathologically strong attach-ment to your native language, and an unwillingness to move away from it despite your immigrant status. It's as if you wanted to stay on the sidelines and remain an observer instead of plunging fully into your new culture. There might be a rejection of America buried deep down under this at a subcon-scious level. You like it here in Chicago?"

"Yes," I lied brazenly..."Except that...hmm...it's...hmm...too...too...flat, too flat and windy."

I didn't know what to say. I didn't want to offend her by telling her that it had been a huge catastrophe for me to emigrate to her country and lose the protection of my two powerful French patrons, so essential for somebody who was "alone in the world" like me. It seemed plausible and innocuous enough to attribute my blues to the commonly disparaged landscape and weather of the

Windy City. I didn't want to come off as a whiner or a smart aleck, whereas in fact I was mourning the disappearance of my scholarship and my friends from boarding school, as well as the Kapferer/Wildenstein support and the streets of Paris that had provided me so much solace in the past.

"And what do you plan to do later in life, Miles?"

She seemed to take a genuine interest in my future. We gladly pushed aside the phonemes for this more interesting drift in our conversation.

"I don't know. Hmm....Travel maybe. Yes, that's what I'd like to do, travel. I want to see hmm...some...hmm...HILLS!"

In her presence, I wanted to dazzle and shine, but instead my brain shut down. I discouraged her with my ineptitude, and we returned to our phonemes. She gave up trying to know me better. I felt like a nincompoop, ruining every opportunity as soon as it turned up. Damn it! Not only chickenshit, but stupid too!

Those were some of my predicaments with the English language and sundry other matters many years ago. After five decades in the U.S. with part of me still in France due to lasting attachments there compounded by professional endeavors here, I relish the American idiom and feel at home in it, but I still occasionally trip myself up and mispronounce words by placing the stress on the wrong syLLAble. "Your dad sometimes talks funny" is how a six-year-old playmate of my children once put it. I may also now and then commit an inadvertent Gallicism, especially when I'm tired. For instance, "Please extinguish the TV." Or the reverse, with an Anglicism sneaking into French, such as *"L'eau était pollutée"* ("The water was polluted"; should be *"polluée"*). Nothing is worse, in those embarrassing moments, than a zealous interlocutor reminding you of your lapses, which you hoped might slide by unnoticed. This danger of "contamination," feared by language purists, is the reason why the Russian writer Solzhenitzin made no attempt to learn English during his twenty-year exile in Vermont. Ditto for the French aviator Saint-Exupéry during his wartime stay in Washington D.C., where he wrote *Le Petit Prince*.

I have no idea what language I dream in, nor whether I do so in black and white or color. However, I continue to count in French. Surprisingly, numbers seem to trump words in the deepest recesses of the mind, even though personally I much prefer the ambiguity of words to the precision of numbers, especially in dealings with creditors and such.

Bilingualism, with its dual perspective on the world, is enormously enriching, but it is also a heavy load to carry, especially when it pertains to French and English, two languages that convey a particularly vast and compelling cultural production: books, magazines, newspapers, films, recordings, a veritable deluge, compounded by a proliferation of inexpensive new media erasing time and distance—the internet, satellite radio and television, e-mail, telephone, the cup runneth over.

The truly bilingual person being bicultural as well, a vital need and desire to keep abreast of this cornucopia sets in. A daily "global awareness-local action" diet consisting of, for starters, the local newspaper followed by *The New York Times* and *Le Monde*. To neglect or abandon one or the other pole of this duality would be equivalent to psychic amputation.

It's difficult to stay centered when you're thinking about "over there" while you're "here" and vice-versa. A constant tug-of-war, a perpetual dilemma, yet admittedly a "rich people's problem" undeserving of empathy, as I once was reminded by a colleague envious of this condition.

Irony of fate, just like the neurotic destined to become a psychiatrist, or the acne sufferer a dermatologist, or the convict a self-taught lawyer, I'm constantly faced with those linguistic conundrums in my professional activities—teaching French language, culture, and literature in America.

But this may all be moot. With the mishmash of verbal and sensory overload, my family fears that in my dotage I'll revert back to my dormant first language—Slovak—and they won't be able to understand anything I say.

While troubling enough, this perspective pales in comparison to the view expressed by my friend Roland H. Simon, who teaches at the University of Virginia. When I asked him how he felt about his bilingualism, he said: "I'm equally at ease in French or English, but what I fear is to fall in the crack between the two and become mute."

Chapter 2

The North Country

"Autobiography is a quest for identity."

— *Joseph Ohmann-Krause*

*L*ake Superior Dental Clinic, Duluth, Minnesota. Mid-morning on a bright, very cold January day. You can tell from the plumes of steam rising straight up from the chimneys that the temperature outside is well below zero. But inside it's nice and warm, and that's what counts.

Comfortably installed in the contoured dental chair, I'm undergoing an annual teeth cleaning. This procedure has literally saved my teeth, which were ravaged early. When I was drafted into the U.S. Army in 1965 at the age of twenty-three at the start of the Vietnam escalation, I was already missing five, three on the right side, two on the left. No big deal, I thought. The front ones were okay.

At the time, war or not, I didn't project much into the future. Certainly not past age thirty. Within a few years after arriving in America, I had deteriorated from "chosen youth" of the French Republic and James Dean wannabe, to a bleak mental and physical state. The gaps in my mouth showed a little when I smiled, a bit more when I laughed. A definite class marker for us white trash, as I discovered at induction. Along with the Appalachian recruits who presented even worse cases than mine, I was fixed up by the skilled military dentists who spared no effort or expense to get us ready for war with perfect teeth, insisting on the importance of yearly prophylaxis to preserve their handiwork. If we survived.

I did survive, through pure luck, despite myself. In fact the Army saved me, way beyond my rehabbed smile or any other expectations, but that's another story. It's ironic that a near-pacifist like me would end up celebrating the military. Sadly, it's the only social development program we've got.

Wearing surgical gloves to protect herself from AIDS and other infections, a mask covering her mouth and nose, goggles shielding her eyes, dental hygienist Karen Vukonich embarks on her meticulous task. She has just the right touch, at once firm and gentle, inspiring confidence. The slight pain feels beneficial. After these annual visits over more than two decades, she knows how to humor me, especially about having X-rays taken. And from one year to the next, I also see her as a mirror to my own evolution, I mean... hmm...aging. I suppose she sees the same in her patients. Time has been kind to her. I find that reassuring. But I'm also beginning to apprehend the day when, inevitably, she will announce she's retiring.

Meanwhile, disconnected as I am from the cares, concerns or deadlines of ordinary life, and insulated from the Northern Minnesota deep freeze by the triple-paned bay window decorated with cheerful stained glass hangings, I drift into a pleasant doze to the sound of FM Lite, wishing this blissful lull would never end. A fleeting thought, immediately dismissed, does however cross my mind: *"Man, your life must be pretty hectic and lopsided if this is the best you can conjure up for escape and relaxation."*

Koyaanisqatsi! "Life out of kilter!" the Navajos would say. But right now, under the glare of the overhead light and in the midst of this sterile environment of chrome and steel, I'm experiencing utter peace and contentment. Nirvana, or Satori, in Zen parlance.

A wave of self-satisfaction sweeps over me: *"You've come a long way, man. Hell, you've got a great job with benefits, you're able to modestly house and feed your family, you've handily surpassed the average life expectancy of 58 for men in post-communist Russia, and so far, knock on wood, your health falls into the relatively tolerable 'petits maux, grandes misères' (little ailments, big miseries) category. Plus you've also lucked out in the love and friendship department. Not too bad a balance sheet for a life that could have ended up wretched."*

If my jaws weren't stuck wide open at that moment, I'd sigh with contentment. Another negative thought bubbles up in my mind, but it too evaporates before it has a chance to spoil my euphoria: *"Watch out, this is too good, it can't last, some disaster must be lurking."*

My friends in California, where I lived for thirteen years, can't understand how or why I have ended up here, on the northern edge of what they call "Flyover Land." Like much else in life, it's the result of happenstance. I let them feel sorry for me. Even if I had the opportunity, I wouldn't trade places.

Anyway, things are never perfect. It's true we have occasional blizzards and arctic spells here, along with slippery hills testing one's bravery and driving skills (serves me right, after my complaints to Miss Nelson about the flat Chicagoland), and it's true that spring arrives a bit late in our region, but I'll take those drawbacks over the tornadoes, hurricanes, wild fires, floods, earthquakes, unbearable heat, and other calamities afflicting other parts of the nation.

Duluth is home. It's where after much roving and many twists and turns in Europe and the U.S.A. my roots have finally taken hold—in part through my branches, my two adult and two younger children, who have been and are being raised here, twenty years apart, with a strong attachment to this beautiful place rated one of the most livable cities in the United States by *Outside* magazine. A well-deserved ranking, with clean air and abundant water, spectacular views from hills overlooking Lake Superior, and nature amazingly close for an urban setting. I once saw a mama bear stretching up on her hind legs to pick treats for her two rambunctious cubs from the gnarled old apple tree in our backyard. Another time, a solitary moose made its way across our garden in the morning mist, like an apparition. Not to mention the deer wandering throughout the neighborhoods. This in a metropolitan area of 130,000 with a vibrant cultural life, a large medical complex, four college campuses, international shipping from the harbor's towering grain silos, a still active manufacturing base especially in aviation, and plenty of other aspects—including some neglect and dilapidation—that make it a genuine urban center as well as a favored tourist destination.

From the political standpoint, as important as the physical setting, I'm also fortunate to live in Duluth, the city with the highest voter turnout in the nation in the 2004 presidential election. With its progressive tradition, personified by the late senator Paul Wellstone, a long-time friend, the state of Minnesota is to the U.S. what Scandinavia is to Europe—at the leading edge on many fronts. Social conscience and solidarity seem to fare better in northern climes. I hope this enlightened tradition survives, despite the increasing right-wing attempts to destroy it, and the huge void left by Paul's absence.

Boosterism aside, I'm staying put, I'm not moving any more. I feel the need to leave only to see friends and family in Minneapolis-St. Paul, or further out on the West Coast in Oregon and California, or in the other direction in France and Slovakia, with a stopover in New York if possible. That's my little world, my little slice of the planet, from East to West along roughly the 40th parallel. It's the narrow but deep furrow I have dug for myself, a pattern since childhood, when I first got a bicycle at age six and began wandering out of my village in Normandy, or going to Paris alone on the bus, but always repeating the same routes. I'm at the core a sedentary nomad.

At any rate, the only real travel is the voyage of no return, one-way, to an entirely new life, in a new place, which could be far or near, and I've had my fill of that. In fact, the longest journey I've ever undertaken is the forty-five miles from my native village to boarding school when I turned ten.

While these thoughts run through my mind in a stream of consciousness induced by the tranquility in the dental office, I'm aware only of my own breathing unfettered by the gurgling contraption in my mouth, and I gaze at the valiant birch trees standing firm outside in the icebox. I can almost hear their silvery bark crackle and snap against the pure blue sky.

After scraping with intense concentration at a particularly resistant spot on my teeth, Karen rolls back her stool to catch her breath. Pulling her mask aside, she startles me from my inner musings with an unexpected question, setting off the turbulence I was fearing in my restful flight in the armchair:

"Milan, I've been meaning to ask you this for a long time: What's your nationality? Are you Serb or Croat?"

"Why?" My response is accompanied by an instinctive, regrettable, slightly paranoid recoil, one eye focused on her nametag, *Vukonich*, the other on the needle-sharp pick in her hand.

"Because I have a friend who has the same last name as yours, and she's Croat."

"Well, Karen, I'm neither Serb nor Croat, because I'm neither Orthodox nor Catholic. Thank God for that, given what's been going on over there."

She seems taken aback by the vehemence of my reply. Its defensive tone is due to a cover story I read in the *New York Times Sunday Magazine* describing the war crimes trial at the International Court of Justice of a Bosnian Serb official named, too close for comfort, Dr. Milan Kovačevic, same age as me. The article was called to my attention by a jokester friend who saw there an obvious explanation for my long silence in our usually prompt exchange of correspondence.

Milan Kovačevic/Kovačovic, as common a name in the Balkans as Bob Anderson/Andersen in Minnesota. Innocence under the protective cover of numbers, or guilt by association? Nikola Kovačovic, yet another Serb tried and sentenced in The Hague. I continue my response to Karen with an ex-culpation:

"Actually, my family is from Slovakia, from a village where some of my relatives still live, and where our name is pronounced a bit differently than in Serbo-Croat, Kovačovic, with a "tch" sound in the middle, and "vits" instead of "vitch" at the end. And although I don't practice their religion, my kinfolk there are Protestant. They're untainted by the horrors inflicted on each other by our Catholic, Orthodox, and Muslim brethren further south in the Balkans."

There, I have spoken my piece, in answer to a touchy question about ethnicity that I've been asked before, in this Northern Minnesota region inhabited by many descendants of Yugoslav immigrants. But I know my contrary tone doesn't sit well in ecumenical, tolerant America, where you can profess any creed you want, but are considered a subversive or a misfit if you lack any religious affiliation at all.

Thus, for instance, back at the time of my induction in the Army, after the soldier on registration duty had blam! stamped my name, serial number US 56391035, and blood type A into my dog tags, he had offered in a monotonous, tired voice three alternatives—"Protestant, Catholic, or Jewish?"—for the last item to be punched in: my choice of last rites. And then, without waiting for my reply, as my hesitancy was holding up the line, he had blam! stamped the only other option available—NO PREFERENCE—into my indestructible metal i.d., to be worn around my neck for the next two years, and stuffed in my mouth in case I became a H.R., a Human Remains.

In Minnesotaspeak, the language of humorist Garrison Keillor, the inscription would have come out as "WHATEVER." And that would have been fine with me. After all these years, I'm still not accustomed to America's religiosity.

It's not that I'm hostile to organized religion, which is to spirituality what formal schooling is to education: potentially great, potentially very bad—and I've seen both. In my personal experience, though, secularists have tended to be more moral, and often even more "spiritual," than pious people. And certainly less prone to kill and oppress in the name of God, or Allah, or Whatever.

Poor Karen, she glances at the clock, realizing she has opened a Pandora's box by asking her patient such a seemingly simple question. She has forgotten that

outside the dental office he is by trade a professor, in other words a specialist
in making short stories long. She resigns herself to a lecture, her mask now
dangling from its elastic string.

"But you're right," I continue, on a roll "Kovačovic is a Yugoslav name,
Serb however, not Croat, at least that's what I've been told by people in the
know, who on the other hand have been contradicted by others, equally credible, including a historian of the region. There have been, and continue to
be, all kinds of migrations and displacements in Central Europe, and maybe
some day I should undertake more thorough research about my origins, perhaps in the global population archives of the Mormons. Or is it better not
to know? To further complicate matters, my father was born "on the road" in
Croatia, where his mother was traveling as an itinerant seller of tablecloths
embroidered by the women of her village in Slovakia. And what about you?
...Vukonich... Are you Serb or Croat?"

"Neither," she answers, savoring the opportunity to one me up. "I'm Irish.
It's my husband who's Croat."

Interestingly, Karen used the word "nationality" instead of "ancestry" to refer
to her ethnic roots and mine, as is often the case with Americans. I've observed a similar tendency among students in the Beginning French classes I
occasionally teach—a level I enjoy, unlike many of my colleagues, because it
allows great opportunities for tangents and play. In order to defuse any apprehension about the nosiness of my elementary talk-making interrogations
("What is your name? Do you have any brothers and sisters? What did you
eat for breakfast? Where do you live? How much do you pay for rent?"), I tell
the students that the course counts as adjunct training for one of the most
popular majors on campus: Criminology.

The answers to my interrogations, using the limited vocabulary at hand,
are usually fairly circumscribed and predictable. But to the question "What is
your nationality?" deviously posed to elicit *only* a strictly controlled grammatical response, whose sole purpose is to differentiate masculine from feminine
("Je suis améri*cain*," in contrast to "Je suis améri*caine*"), the class invariably
falls into chaos:

"How do you say Welsh, Russian, and Greek? And how do you say 'one
third?' I'm one third Welsh, one third Russian, and one third Greek."

One third? I give out the requested information, including the fraction
that thankfully goes by unchallenged, but I silently wonder (my field is not

mathematics) whether procreation is possible in odd-numbered configurations...

I conclude these sessions, in which everyone is uncharacteristically eager to participate, with an anecdote about Mark Twain. Apparently, during his travels through France, the celebrated writer was invited to a reception during which his host set out to tease him:

"Mistère Clémence, I have heard zat you Americains are obsessed with ze généalogie, and zat you are always asking to yourselves ze same question: 'Who, who was my grandfazer?'"

"That's true, Monsieur," replied Twain, "but I've heard that you Frenchmen are also very preoccupied about your origins, and that you are constantly asking yourselves: 'Who, who was my father?'"

Innocent as it was, Karen's question about my ethnic background left me with a disturbing quandary. Having established for her that I wasn't Serb, Croat, or Protestant, I still had to define for myself *who* I was, or at least *what* I was—*who* being perhaps unknowable. In addition to my overriding preoccupation about social class, to what human group, to what tradition, to what concrete, necessary, intermediate earthly way station in the transcendent cosmos did I belong? I sensed that this quest for identity would prove enormously complicated, but I was comforted by the fact that unambiguity and purity exist only in matters of religion, where despite sectarianism and heresies, you can only be one hundred per cent Catholic, or one hundred per cent Protestant, or one hundred per cent Jewish, not one third each.

The most logical starting point on that quest for identity seemed of course to be the person who has known me the longest, shared all my peregrinations, and probably defined me more than I even realize: my mother. I was ready to leave the dental chair and head out into the cold to visit her at the nursing home.

Mama Bear and her cubs heading for our old apple tree in Duluth.

Chapter 3

Ma's Dictionary

We are all ignorant, about different things.

— *Mark Twain*

*D*AT NOT IT! Dat not same one again! Letters was different! You throw mine dictionnaire away, like everyt'ing dat belong to me!"

Slumped in her wheelchair, my mother pushes the shiny new *Thorndike-Barnard Illustrated Children's Dictionary* back into my hands. Her rebuke spews out from deep inside her chest in a raw, frightening tone. She no longer looks feeble. All her strength is concentrated in her accusation.

At the nursing home where she has been a resident now more than six years, and where I stop by to see her every Tuesday and Thursday evening—and longer on Sunday afternoons to do her laundry and such because otherwise those personal items tend to get lost—I have finally resigned myself to join the support group for "depressed caregivers." That's the name given to the family members who are burned out or have trouble coping with the plight of their loved one in the institution. "A good first step, Milan," says the geriatric psychologist who facilitates the meetings taking place after my Thursday visits, "It shows you're no longer in denial." With a bit of a feminist perspective, she has warned us dozen or so participants: "Let's face it, folks, these sweet little old ladies have been too nice too long. When they let go, look out! There's lifelong anger and resentment pent up in those women. Some of it will be aimed at you simply because you're there. Try not to take things too personally. At times you won't recognize your own mothers."

Nursing homes are largely a mother-daughter environment. The fathers are long gone, and I'm the only son in the group of middle-aged daughters, an uneasy intruder in the women's circle. We're the sandwich generation, taking care of growing children at the same time as invalid parents.

Ma has no assets. She forfeits her social security income except for a tiny monthly allowance, and her room, board, and medical expenses are free. But nursing homes, even the best like hers, are dreadful places.

Ironically, she ended up in one because of medical hubris. At 75, after a stroke, she had recovered enough to shuffle around with a cane instead of a walker. She lived in a comfortable studio with its own bathroom and cooking facilities built as an addition to our house. She got along well with my wife Vera, and doted on her grandchildren Paul and Laurie, for whom she always had a snack ready when they came home from school. She could shut her door for independence and privacy, or open it for connection, reciprocal visits, spontaneous sharing of meals. Friends envied our freedom to come and go at will without the need for a baby sitter, as well as the huge enrichment to our family life provided by an adult presence supplementing the sparseness of just "mom and dad." An ideal situation for everyone.

The only cloud over this little utopia was the severe arthritis of the hip that Ma endured for many years, until one day the joint literally locked up, with the slightest movement causing excruciating pain. The needlessly feared, long postponed hip replacement surgery became unavoidable. With the technical advances of the recent past and the magical skill of her orthopedic surgeon, the procedure went well, and she was freed of the pain that had plagued her for more than a decade.

As is routine following such surgery, she was then turned over to the Rehab Department. But the tough regimen of physical therapy to which she was subjected despite her objections and mine—we were both content with her shuffling around in house slippers—proved to be her undoing. The physical therapists determined that she could, should, and must walk straight and wear regular shoes. They claimed I didn't have her best interests at heart if we settled for less.

There was something grotesque about my poor mother striving to achieve good posture between parallel bars meant for gymnasts, or trying to squeeze her misshapen feet into the "regular" shoes assigned to her, which turned out to be the rigid, ugly, black leather type with half-heels formerly worn by WACs with their dress uniforms in the Army. Horrible shoes!

Not surprisingly, a sore developed on Ma's constricted heel, and it continued to fester due to poor circulation, to the point that her surgeon was called upon to undo all his good work by having to amputate her repaired leg at the knee, to prevent gangrene. Thereafter, predictably, things changed for the worst. She became afraid of remaining alone during the day, and home health care arrangements weren't available. She bravely tried but couldn't adapt to her artificial leg, and her lodgings in our house addition proved unsuitable for a wheelchair.

The only feasible alternative was a nursing home, where over time her physical condition deteriorated further, under the triple onslaught of age, ailments, and the force of gravity. From an already worrisome history of stroke, hypertension, arthritis, and amputation, she sank into a series of new ordeals and humiliations, among them heart attack, blocked carotid artery, incontinence, prolapsed uterus, dwindling eyesight, lost dentures. Cancer and diabetes seemed to be the only calamities that had not befallen her. She endured this avalanche of afflictions with fortitude, at least on the surface, and her mind seemed to remain amazingly clear throughout. But I began to experience a growing sense of despair and helplessness at each visit.

One never knew what to expect next, except that now, in her late seventies, Ma's physical condition would inevitably worsen. Still, several times, after being near death, she rallied at the last moment. The years passed, roommates came and died, she seemed indestructible:

Dying

Death is not natural, only inevitable.
It is not something we do with the grace and ease of the wind.
We are an amazing machine that embraces life.
A complex machine of extremes: strong yet fragile, rational yet passionate.
Our bodies resist even when the mind is no longer aware.
Each breath is a gift we do not relinquish easily.

— D.S.

I settled into an inertia of helplessness when, during the sixth year of Ma's residency at the nursing home, I finally joined the support group for depressed caregivers. I had been invited to do so earlier, as family caretaker for one of the residents with the longest occupancy, but I had repeatedly begged off, for lack of time or other pretexts. The facilitator had told me, though, that after about four years, equivalent to the duration of a U.S. presidency, any sentient caregiver had legitimate cause to be depressed, and that it was nothing to be ashamed of.

Ironically, my decision to join the group was precipitated by a seemingly trivial event, compared to Ma's physical degeneration: an episode of roommate incompatibility! But it also signaled a major change in her mental attitude, ushering in new behavior patterns and obsessions, among which her fixation on her long lost, and I thought forgotten, dictionary. Up until then, not wanting to be a burden on anyone, she had been cooperative, uncomplaining, grateful for every little thing, polite to a fault. "Tank you very mach" was her most frequent expression. Her only request to me was that I occasionally bring her fries and real coffee from McDonald's to compensate for the insipid prevention-possessed nursing home fare. I of course obliged.

Just as an easy child gets better care than a difficult one, she too had become a favorite of the staff, and had at one point been honored as "Resident of the Year." She was this nice elderly woman who made no demands, until one night, at eleven p.m., I received a phone call from the nursing home: "Milan, please come over right away, your mother is completely out of control. We can't calm her down. She's yelling and screaming at her roommate and it's not in English, we don't know what she's saying. We'll to have to move her into another room."

As I sped to the nursing home, my first reaction, after being thankful that I lived in a town with everything located fairly close, was to rail against the absurd two-beds-per-room arrangement, which inherently invites trouble. Even under the best circumstances, even in independent dwellings, elderly people tend to be cranky, set in their ways, needing peace, quiet, and solitude for reminiscence and reflection. That's the true meaning of "retirement." In nursing homes, however, they are dehumanized first and foremost by the loss of privacy.

Privacy is more necessary there than anywhere, and synonymous with dignity, in view of the irritating symptoms of dementia and failing health that have to be endured from others, or inflicted on them. Why not have smaller individual rooms, with a shared toilet between? It would not cost more, and socialization, when wanted, could take place in the hallway, like in French campus dorms.

When I got to the nursing home, I found Ma in a new room, alone, disheveled, still agitated from the commotion.

"What happened?" I asked her as calmly as I could.

"*Ona je puta!* " ("She's a whore!") she shrieked, mixing French with Slovak, in an ugly, vulgar voice I had never heard before, while pointing angrily in the direction of her former room down the hall, which she had been sharing for the past few months with a sweet octogenarian named Helen. *"Ona je puta,"* *"Ona je puta,"* she kept yelling with that shocking tone in her voice. I couldn't believe I was hearing my mother talk that way. She, the model of self-denial, always so discreet, so self-effacing, so unassuming.

"Why do you call her insulting names like that, Ma?" I asked sternly.

"You not can see what dey do? I know what dey do! Are you blind or idiot?" Her voice now expressed contempt, as if she was ready to disown me.

"Ma, all they do is sit on the bench in the hallway every afternoon from 1:00 to 3:00, and then he goes home. They just sit there hardly talking or doing anything, except for the swig of whisky they have at 2 o'clock. What's wrong with that?"

"Mine God, you *are* idiot! You not can see she is *puta* and she is *alcoolique* too!"

Ma's explosion against Helen had been simmering for some time, but I never imagined it would take such proportions. I sensed hostility ever since she first used the word "they," with visible disdain, to refer to Helen and her "Prince Charming." That was the nickname the staff had given to Helen's daily visitor, a gentleman also in his eighties. Although Helen's suitor was as frail and wispy as she, he still managed to drive, a big Buick sedan that he berthed each time in the same spot near the main entrance, so he wouldn't have to walk too far. He always wore a suit and tie, his shoes were polished to a bright shine, and he kept his hat on during the entire length of his visits. He and Helen would sit side by side on the bench in the hallway, exchanging a few words now and then, mostly about the weather outside. They didn't look at each other but straight ahead together in the same direction, he with his hands folded over his cane, she with her elbows resting on her walker. During each visit, at exactly 2 o'clock, he pulled out a small flask of whisky from the inside pocket of his suit coat. He unscrewed the cap, barely larger than a thimble, and served Helen a swig from it, followed by a similar one for him. And that was all until 3 p.m., when they hugged and said goodbye. Nothing there for Ma to get so riled up about.

When I introduced myself to the support group "I'm Milan, and my mother has been here more than six years," I drew gasps of admiration, tinged with anguish and pity. "Oh my God, six years!" exclaimed one of the participants with less seniority than I, probably panicked that the same fate might befall her. When I explained that Ma's outburst had caused me to finally join the group out of desperation, the consensus was that my mother had reached the breaking point with being nice, and that her flare-up had been a pure unadulterated fit of jealousy, her reptilian cortex green with envy, unrestrained by decorum or the veneer of civilization. The group was both shocked and fascinated by her primal reaction, her total loss of inhibition, so out of character, yet revealing of so much vital energy left hidden in that slumped listless body.

The nursing home staff, saints all, maintained a non-judgmental attitude in the aftermath. I feared that Ma might get expelled for being unmanageable, and if so, where would she go? To my great relief, she was allowed to stay *alone* in her new room. She relished her solitude and never again behaved too badly, but she did exercise newfound assertiveness. Whereas before she never stated her opinion about anything, she now began to forcefully express immediate likings or aversions. Every time President Reagan appeared on the TV, she'd yell "Why somebody not shoot him!" She also dumped the Lutheran chaplain who had been ministering to her soul, which was heavily burdened by her failure to bring me up in the Protestant religion of our kin "back home" in Slovakia. She found him too unctuous and patronizing; she hated the way he held her hands when he talked to her. Instead, she turned her conscience over to Father Brennan, the quadriplegic Irish Catholic priest who himself was a long-time resident in the institution. And she hounded me during my visits, about how I should wear nicer clothes like I used to as a teenager in Paris, or presently about how I was responsible for her missing dictionary.

Two

"Okay, Ma, Okay." I try to placate my mother, mindful of the geriatric psychologist's advice not to take our elderly mothers' recriminations too personally. "I'll return this one too, the bookstore manager has agreed to exchange it if needed. Don't worry, eventually I'll find the exact same dictionary as the one we lost."

"**You** lose it, not me."

"Okay, Ma, Okay."

Hell, there are only so many children's illustrated dictionaries being published. I should be able to find the one she wants. I don't remember throwing away her old dictionary (was it a Random House, a Webster, an American

Heritage? they all look the same) but I don't have a clear conscience either. I know that periodically I succumb to violent impulses to throw things out, only to regret those rash actions later. I shall forever pine for my leather schoolbag from the lycée in Paris, stored away as a useless object soon after our arrival in America, then dragged along in my every move from Chicago to San Francisco to Los Angeles and finally Duluth, only to be discarded two and a half decades later, in a fit of housecleaning frenzy.

Ma's dictionary had fallen apart over the years. She had mended the torn pages with tape, and patched up the binding with needle and thread and a strip of cloth. A touching labor of skill and love, but in my barbarian compulsivity, I could well have mistaken that book for junk, and subjected it to the same fate as my schoolbag.

The quirks of heredity are amazing. Ma and I share at least one trait for sure: a weird attachment to dictionaries. I still have my old *Larousse Illustré*, faithful companion during my entire last year of primary school, now worn coverless—I didn't inherit her patience and savvy for repairs.

Pangs of guilt. Ma's reproach is probably justified. I must resolve the situation and find the right dictionary. What other editions are left? MacMillan? Yes, I'll try that one. What a puzzle, this mother of mine! Why her sudden fixation on her lost dictionary? But wouldn't I feel the same way if my old *Larousse* disappeared?

Three

Of thought, in relation to Françoise, one could hardly speak. She knew nothing, in that absolute sense in which to know nothing means to understand nothing, save the rare truths to which the heart is capable of directly attaining. The vast world of ideas did not exist for her. But when one studied the clearness of her gaze, the delicate lines of her nose and lips, all those signs lacking from so many cultivated people in whom they would have signified a supreme distinction, the noble detachment of a rare mind, one was disquieted... and one might have been led to wonder whether there may not be, among those humbler brethren, the peasants, individuals who are as it were the élite of the world of the simple-minded, or rather who, condemned by an unjust fate to live among the simple-minded, deprived of enlightenment and yet more naturally, more essentially akin to the chosen spirits than most educated people, are members as it were, dispersed, strayed, robbed of their heritage of reason, of the sacred family, kinsfolk, left behind in infancy, of the loftiest minds, in whom—as is apparent from the unmistakable light in their eyes, although it is applied to nothing—there has been lacking, to endow them with talent, only the gift of knowledge.

    — Marcel Proust, translated (magnificently!) by C.K. Scott Moncrieff, et al.

I was deeply moved by this portrait of the servant Françoise in Marcel Proust's great autobiographical novel *Remembrance of Things Past*. Proust's geography had long evoked vivid personal memories for me. The lilacs, the hawthorns, the poppies, the flowering apple trees etched so brightly in the landscape of his family's country home in Combray had reawakened in me those same radiant blossoms that had illuminated my own childhood in the village of Saint-Aquilin. The water lilies dotting the surface of Proust's gently flowing Vivonne had also conjured up before my eyes the lush palettes glistening on my cherished river Eure as it meandered along a row of poplars through the luxuriant meadows of Normandy, in a valley bordered by thickly wooded hills. In Paris too, at the Kapferers' mansion on Avenue Henri-Martin, I had observed many aspects of the upper class life portrayed by Proust, and during a subsequent trip to Venice, I had experienced the aesthetic euphoria he describes in "Place Names." I knew the *social* and *physical* environments in Proust's work; but here suddenly, I was also recognizing in Françoise an *individual* who seemed utterly familiar.

    Whenever I teach Proust at the university, I like to linger on this passage. I ask the students whether they have ever met anyone like Françoise, who despite her inherent distinction and obvious intelligence "knew nothing, in that absolute sense in which to know nothing means to understand nothing, save the rare truths to which the heart is capable of directly attaining." They shake their heads, unable or unwilling to imagine total ignorance. I have to provide an illustration:

    "Okay, let's say, for instance, someone who has demonstrated an incredible sense of adventure, as well as unusual initiative and resourcefulness, by moving during her lifetime from Slovakia to rural Normandy, then to Paris, Chicago, San Francisco, and finally Duluth without having any idea where those places are located on a map, nor any desire to find out."

    "Impossible!" they reply. "How can anyone supposedly so smart be so ignorant?"

    My example is not hypothetical. The world traveler I have described is none other than my mother, an uneducated peasant woman whose most startling endeavor, among others, was to emigrate *twice* in her lifetime, first from

her native Slovakia to France in 1930 at age 25, and then, with utter recklessness, to America at 50, for no apparent reason, with her teen-age son as her
not very responsible guide.

Like Proust's Françoise, Ma's luminous intelligence was evident. In
France she had become an expert cook and pastry maker, simply by observation and instinct. She used neither measuring cups nor recipes, and she
disdained the authoritative cookbook that her employer, Madame Kapferer,
had provided her for reference and menu selection. To pay for our one-way
ship passage to America, she devised a clever stratagem, of which Madame
must have surely been aware but feigned no knowledge of: In the weekly
budget entrusted her for the food purchases of the Kapferer household,
Ma listed the prices of produce sold in nearby Rue de la Pompe's exclusive
shops, while in fact she purchased those items at the much cheaper, but one
kilometer distant, Rue de l'Annonciation street market. On week-ends and
during school vacations, when I stayed "home" at the mansion and helped
her with this daily task, she and I took turns lugging the two oilcloth shopping bags filled with leeks, carrots, artichokes, melons, apricots, or whatever
fruits and vegetables were in season. We paused at each street corner for a
brief rest: our aching arms and backs signaled we had legitimately earned
the difference in price. Her ploy required stamina and, even more, accurate
bookkeeping.

The graceful curve of Ma's forehead, her straight bearing, the poise and
confidence gained from living among the wealthy whom she served, all these
signs gave the impression that she was a woman of distinction. During our
voyage to America in March 1956 aboard the "Liberté," when most of the
passengers and a good number of the crew had been immobilized in their
cabins by a tremendous North Atlantic storm, and racked with nausea as
soon as they dared rise from their berths, she, normally prone to motion sickness in automobiles, did not miss a single meal throughout the entire ordeal.
Three times each day like clockwork she could be seen marching forward
resolutely along the mirrored vestibule leading to the ship's heaving dining
salon, where the place settings and silverware were bolted down to the tables.
Her right hand clutched the railing on the wall, her left arm was folded over
her purse. The pale headwaiter posted below the chandelier at the entrance
of the empty dining room greeted her with an admirative: *"Madame doit faire
souvent la traversée!"* ("Madame must often make these crossings!") Only ob-
sequiousness and decorum prevented him from exclaiming *"Chapeau!"* ("Hats

off") to this seasoned traveler. Little did he know that Milady was literally lost at sea.

Considering Ma's non-existent knowledge, her clarity of mind and powers of synthesis seemed all the more remarkable. Whenever I asked her advice or opinion on any problem, she could reduce the issue, no matter how complex, to three or four salient elements, and then conclude with an unnerving, detached, yet deeply philosophical and judicious "*Však, delaj si jak si myslíš*" ("Well, do as you think best").

She was a woman of few words, easily irritated by gabbing or wordiness. "*C'est une pipelette*"—"S/he's a chatterbox" was her most frequent judgment of people, along with "*ordinaire*," a dismissive term she apparently picked up from her first employer in France.

In my present academic world, where specialized knowledge is commonplace but clarity of thought and concision of expression somewhat more rare (myself included), I have seldom encountered Ph.D.s endowed with my mother's piercing intelligence. Unfortunately, as with Proust's Françoise, her "lofty mind was applied to nothing." Or at least to the "nothings" of knowledge that most people take for granted. She did, after all, manage to survive through the extraordinary complexities of her life—and that in itself should be considered an awesome achievement.

I could not anticipate how Ma's ignorance might manifest itself. For instance, my son Paul having written a musical composition at age seven, a friend once commented in her presence that he might some day become another Beethoven. After the friend departed, she asked me to clarify a point: Was this man named Beethoven an acquaintance of ours, and if so would he be coming over for dinner sometime?

Other times, her reactions were more predictable. Each Friday prior to her amputation, when I took her to the supermarket, in mid-afternoon so she wouldn't have to fight the crowds, I'd engage her in the same uninspired conversation, just to break silence, as we drove past the university:

"That's where I work" (I'd nod towards the campus).

"*Tam robíš?*" (with astonishment each time, pointing the head of her cane in the same direction). "You work there? In dis buildings?" (The Slovak verb *robiť* denotes manual labor, the only kind she knew and, I surmise, understood).

"*Ano.* Yes."

"*A jak to že nerobíš teď*? And why aren't you working now?" (again with renewed surprise each time).

There was no point using an abstract term like "teach" to describe my activities, which I suspect she didn't consider real work anyway; no point either trying to explain that my duty hours were somewhat flexible and I didn't have to punch in and out of those buildings, even if they might conceivably be mistaken for some kind of factory (a colleague calls it "The Plant"). Similarly, she could not understand why I might go to my campus office to complete something or other at 8 p.m., when everyone is supposed to be home, or conversely how I could drive her to the supermarket on Friday afternoons, when everyone is supposed to be at work. We lived together in completely different worlds. Once, as I was rejoicing over the news that an academic essay of mine had been accepted for publication, her deadpan response appeared as startling to me, as my answer no doubt was to her:

"And how mach maney dey pay you for it?"

"Nothing."

Ma's existence revolved around practical activities that kept her busy: cooking, baking, sewing, gardening, canning (for some obscure reason, she disliked knitting). She didn't know the meaning of boredom. She needed no entertainment, wasn't interested in listening to the radio, turned her TV on only for the afternoon soap operas, without my assistance at last, after I finally convinced her in a fit of exasperation that *she could do it by herself, damnit*! But she remained reluctant to change channels, preferring instead to leave her set permanently tuned to CBS, for fear she might not later be able to retrieve her favorite program, "Another World."

Later, I began to feel retrospective guilt about my outbursts of impatience when I realized that with the inexorable march of time and progress I myself had become as incompetent and helpless—and as dependent on my own children for anything beyond the rudiments on the computer and other digital gizmos—as she had been with the TV. And although I had gotten to be a clever enough food connoisseur, confident in my tastes and judgments and capable of waxing at length about gastronomic matters, I certainly couldn't brag about my actual repertoire in the kitchen, limited to three disparate specialties: *bananes flambées*; chicken prepared on the Spanek Vertical Roaster; and salad greens with an olive oil and balsamic vinegar dressing made with a touch of garlic, Grey Poupon mustard, and sugar—a pathetic tally in view of my extensive opportunities to learn the culinary arts firsthand as her frequent helper in the Kapferer kitchen. Wasn't paying attention, I guess...

Ma was not illiterate. She could write—in the agonizingly slow, awkward, laborious manner of someone whose fingers are not used to holding a pen— and the results, in her native Slovak, were unfailingly fascinating. For English and French, she resorted to the one-on-one Slovak phonetic spelling system to transcribe, accurately, whatever she heard, or misheard. "*Kol bek tu drajver lajsnis ofis*," for instance, was a message she once left for me next to the phone, to "call back to driver license office," where I had apparently forgotten my wallet. She was able to read, with intense concentration, the Slovak mail she received from my sister Eva and from our other relatives in the "old country." And she could decipher her English correspondence, tentatively with her index finger following the letters while her lips silently mispronounced the words. She made no attempt to absorb the meaning of those words anyway, her English mail consisting exclusively of Medicare, MediCal, or Medicaid insurance matters which she deferred to me, eliciting yet more rants on my part about all that "damned paperwork." But despite her ability to read, I can't remember her ever opening a book, a newspaper, or a magazine, except on three specific occasions.

The first of those episodes had to do with that famous, elusive dictionary. Soon after our arrival in America in 1956, her employer at the canning factory suggested she enroll in a night course of English for immigrants and refugees. A children's illustrated dictionary with large typeface and simple sentences was recommended by her instructor. She spent most of her spare time in her next job, as a live-in domestic in the Chicago suburb of Elmhurst, religiously poring over that dictionary, and continued examining it from time to time through the years.

Then, nearly a decade later, in 1965, when she turned sixty, there was the naturalization booklet that she studied to apply for American citizenship. I wanted her to obtain a U.S. passport so that, thanks to a free pass on the airline I was working for, she could hopefully reconnect with Olga and Eva in Europe.

Ma had entered the U.S. with a "stateless refugee" travel document, and she now needed to get her disjointed papers in order. As with bureaucracies everywhere, this would present some challenges. At the San Francisco

Immigration and Naturalization office, an intimidating examiner ("He was *ordinaire*, he look mean, he shout at me") made her so nervous and flustered that she reported back that she had confused Lincoln with Washington, forgotten that Eisenhower—not Roosevelt—had preceded Kennedy, couldn't remember the first amendment to the Constitution, or the length of a senator's term of office, or the minimum age for a presidential candidate (50, she thought).

"You failed the citizenship test, M'am," concluded her torturer.

"Vat can I do now?"

"Learn the material better, M'am, and take the test again. Minimum time before retake is two months. Next!"

"Mister, please, my son he bring me here and now he go to Army, maybe Vietnam. He not be able help me. Vat can I do?"

"I said, Next! You'll have to move on, M'am."

That was the only time I ever saw my mother cry, although she once confessed that she had shed many tears, in private, when we first came to America and were trying to hide our grief from each other.

Two months after her failure on the citizenship test, having relinquished her afternoon soap operas so that she could sear into her memory the facts of U.S. history, the articles of the Constitution, and the rules of government, she was tested by a more congenial examiner. This time, she passed with a perfect score.

That was the extent of her reading activity until twelve years later when, during the summer of 1977, at seventy-two, she suddenly plucked from my bookshelf a Czech translation—fairly close linguistically to her native Slovak—of Stendhal's nineteenth-century French novel *The Charterhouse of Parma*. She then plunged into a three-day round the clock reading binge from which she emerged only after she had devoured the entire book in total, manic absorption. I was horrified, as one would be in the face of a monstrous, unexplainable event. Might there have been a literary sensibility, perhaps even an intense passion for words and language, entombed under Ma's taciturn exterior? I tried to probe further into that seemingly far-fetched possibility, and as usual, ended up with more than I had bargained for:

"Well, Ma, pretty good book, eh?" (actually, professional shame on me, I had not read *The Charterhouse*, but only Stendhal's other classic novel, *The Red and the Black*).

"Yes, dat was very interesting story. But you know, every family have interesting story. *Bože moj, na priklad naša!* (My God, for instance ours!) You should to write book about it."

And then, whammo, her characteristically candid, disarming conclusion: "It be very *populaire* book. All your friends buy it."

Ma's prodding me, on the heels of her reading *The Charterhouse*, to write down our family's story, was induced in part by a prediction regarding the destiny of her three children, which she heard from a gypsy fortuneteller she consulted in Paris prior to our departure for America. Two of those prophesies had already come to pass. The seer had told her that one of her daughters would marry late, and the other die early, without specifying which one. That cruel uncertainty, along with the dire nature of the prediction, had been a painful burden for Ma. She placed as much faith in palm readers as in God, and though estranged from Olga, she eschewed favoritism in a visceral way.

Incredibly, tragically, Olga passed away from cancer, and three years later Eva married, both at 40. That was enough to reinforce Ma's belief in the all-seeing powers of her fortune teller.

The third prediction, regarding me, but with still no sign of fulfillment on the horizon in my early forties, was that I would become a writer. This of course explained Ma's interest in getting me moving in that direction: "When you write our story, when?"

For my part, I was a voracious reader and I loved literature, as did Eva, but up until then I had not seen myself as a "writer." Nor did others. When I once gingerly hinted to my mother-in-law, she a very lucid Czech survivor of the Holocaust, that with the advent of the Macintosh and word processing with a mouse, I might perhaps embark on an extensive writing project, she quipped, probably foreseeing the dangers to marital life inherent in that fantasy: "But Milan, you're a teacher, not a writer!" Perhaps she had also heard the poet Czeslaw Milosz's warning that "when a writer is born in a family, the family is finished." "Finished" because, damned if you do damned if you don't, some people object to being portrayed, even favorably, and others—often closest to the author—resent being left out: "Don't I mean anything to you?"

Actually, at about the same time, three other aspects were pushing me in the "writing" direction, more specifically a memoir, for which, as Ma repeatedly declared, our family's eventful journey provided abundant material.

One of those new developments was my sense of indignation about the emerging dismantlement of "Government" at the hands of the Reagan administration. In my personal experience, contrary to the condescending rightwing viewpoint, "Government" had not served as a nanny, nor even as a dad. It had been my *father*.

Ironically, the second event focusing me in the writing direction turned out to be the dreaded, fickle, harrowing tenure process at the university. Its only redemptive aspect, because of the detailed documentation required at the end of the six-year probation period, was that it forced me to look back on my jumbled educational past (undergraduate credits from seven different institutions, etc.) with utmost chronological accuracy, as if organizing photos from the hodge-podge of a shoe box into a coherent album. From that ordering process, subsequently extended to early childhood and other significant periods, a clear map of my life emerged, forming the structure of an eventual book.

The third push to write down my story was my frustration in answering, with any coherence or brevity, such seemingly simple questions as "Do you have any siblings?", "Where did you go to college?", "Did your parents come with you to America?", "How come your name isn't French?", "Did you move directly to Duluth?" And so on. An explanatory handout would be needed to answer such questions.

Although I never felt contemptuous of Ma, I was often irritated by her abysmal ignorance, which also caused her to suffer greatly, by her own admission ("*Já som tak hlúpa!*" "I am so stupid!" she lamented). Besides, it imposed drastic limits on our range of communication, tenuous already because of our various linguistic and cultural barriers. She depended on me, imposed on me, and in exchange accepted my outbursts of impatience. However, I began to suspect that her submission to ignorance was a convenient refuge of some sort.

I knew from personal experience that the mind is capable of working in peculiar ways. For instance, when I moved to Southern France in 1972-73 with my wife and toddler son for a year of graduate studies, our little nuclear family then on the skimpiest of budgets (thank you, staff of the Nice university restaurant, for doting on "*le bébé américain*" and feeding him free on the sly), I purchased an old Peugeot 403, one of those indestructible vehicles favored at the time by North African guest workers, the successors in France to my parents' Slavic generation. I soon discovered that the 403's transmission didn't engage into fourth gear. Faced with already plentiful financial and other difficulties, I convinced myself that the car had only three gears. I completely shut out the problem from my mind for that entire year! In fact, I was genuinely surprised, and reawakened from my self-induced hypnosis, when a mechanic who was considering to buy the car from us before our departure back to the States exclaimed upon returning from his test drive with the Peugeot: "Hey, *mon ami*, what happened? You realize this car is missing a gear!" Embarrassed, I let him keep the old workhorse for free... and probable resale to the next set of Arab owners.

Another experience which convinced me that the mind can behave in strange ways was Ma's stroke at 70, in 1975. At the time, she felt most comfortable expressing herself in her native Slovak, which remained surprisingly unadulterated despite almost half a century abroad. Her English was still minimal after twenty years in America, and she seemed to remember only a few words of the tentative French she had learned in her twenty-six years in Paris and Normandy. In both languages, for instance, she dispensed with the past, present, and future tenses of verbs, and left them all instead in the infinitive: "Yesterday we go to supermarket." "Today we go to supermarket." "Tomorrow we go to supermarket."

The stroke caused Ma's entire left side to be paralyzed. Nearly as frightening as the paralysis, however, and much more mysterious, were the linguistic upheavals triggered by the seizure. Slovak and English both vanished from her registry. Poof! Gone! Instead, her pidgin French of two decades earlier resurfaced, intact, frozen in its mispronunciations and scrambled syntax. The hospital staff couldn't communicate with her and needed me to interpret. To hear her fractured French felt as if her voice was now transmitting live an earlier recording of itself, or as if a mummy suddenly began to talk in an extinct language. Then, over the next several weeks, as the paralysis thankfully regressed, her language too returned to "normal." French disappeared, and Slovak and English reemerged in their former configuration.

The conjunction of those bewildering experiences, along with Ma's onetime Stendhal reading binge, her infantile attachment to her dictionary, and my fascination with the Proust excerpt about Françoise, prodded me to delve further into the mystery of her bizarre intellectual development, or lack thereof. Accustomed to the unrelenting candor of the depressed caregivers support group, I am steeled in my resolve to unearth an explanation.

Four

"Ma, why is it you never want to read? Why is it you don't know anything beside cooking, baking, sewing, and gardening? Why, Ma, why? These things are important for sure, but what about knowledge, what about books, what about learning? Did something happen to you when you were young?"

"*Pretože já som bola Popelka!*", she blurts out. "*Já! Som! Bola! Popelka!*" ("Because I was Cinderella! I! Was! Cinderella!")

The floodgates open. She straightens up in her wheelchair, visibly relieved of a long-kept secret. Why didn't I ask before?

She recalls for me the fateful day during her childhood in Slovakia, when Mr. Sedláček, the schoolteacher of her native village of Bzince pod Javorinou, paid her father a visit:

"Please, Mr. Stano, I beg of you again, let Eva continue with her schooling. She learns so well. She always ranks first in class. She could still help you at home in the evening and work in the fields during harvest season."

"Look, Mister Teacher, enough of this. I'm her father, and I already told you NO before, so don't insist. Leave my house this minute and don't come back!"

And so Ma's schooling ended on her fourteenth birthday, June 30, 1919. Like Cinderella, she became her family's servant, envious of the independence and the small wages that her four older brothers and sisters earned from working the fields of the village's three landowners.

Her father had survived the carnage of World War I, turned in his rifle, put away his spiked helmet. Borders in Central Europe were reshuffled, the new nation of Czechoslovakia carved out from the dismembered Austro-Hungarian Empire. But in the timeless village, life remained unchanged.

Although Ma deplored her fate, she herself would probably not have agreed to continue her studies and thus feel singled out and favored, inevitably she thought at the expense of her siblings. Her egalitarian instincts imprisoned her as much as her father did. Finally, at twenty-five, unable to withstand her condition any longer, she heard of employment opportunities in France and fled there.

Before the War, in 1909, my grandfather Stano had returned to the village empty-handed and embittered after a three-year stint looking for gold in Alaska. He claimed he had been robbed on the way back. That had been his first and last attempt at earning a living. Following his return to Slovakia, he spent his days sitting by the window, smoking cigarettes, bantering with passersby, and otherwise directing the household. Meanwhile his wife crisscrossed the heart of Europe like a gypsy, from Prague to Budapest to Bratislava to Vienna, hawking lace tablecloths embroidered by the village women.

Popelka! From her days at school, Ma had acquired a passion for reading stories and novels. At every opportunity during her housekeeping duties at home, she tried to sneak in a few pages, only to be rebuked by her father, who didn't hesitate to tear books from her grasp, and fling them to the ground. "You're supposed to work, not loaf around!" Finally, defeated, she shut down and stopped reading.

Five

"Well, Ma, what do you think? Is this the one?"

I hand my mother the *MacMillan Illustrated Children's Dictionary*. She straightens up in her wheelchair, puts on her glasses, leafs through the pages, hones in on a detail. Her eyes light up with a gleam I haven't seen in years.

"Oh, yes, dat is it! Dat is it! I am so happy. Tank you very mach."

Six

A few weeks later, I receive a phone call from the nursing home social worker:

"Milan, have you noticed a change lately when you visit with your mother?"

"Yes, she seems depressed. She says that now she's losing her memory."

"She says the same thing to the staff. She no longer complains about her lost dictionary, thank God for that, but now it's her declining memory that she's obsessing about."

"Well, aren't loss of memory and some dementia normal with old age?"

"Loss of short-term memory, yes, but dementia covers a wide spectrum. So far we haven't seen any evidence of full-blown Alzheimer's in your mother. Her complaints about phantom pains in her amputated leg have nothing to do with that, it's the body's memory, it's to be expected, even after several years. She remembers your name, she recognizes you. I'd say she is doing reasonably well from the mental standpoint, considering her age and condition."

Seven

"Ma, how do you know your memory is going bad? You seem able to remember the smallest details from your childhood."

"It's mine dictionnaire."

"How so?"

"I not can remember words."

"What do you mean?"

She tenses up, puts on her glasses, angrily reaches for the dictionary in the side pocket of her wheelchair, opens it up at the letter "F," where she has inserted a piece of cloth as a marker.

"See, I not can remember more than here."

Suddenly, it dawns on me. I recoil in shock and disbelief: "No, Ma, No, No, No!"

She's been attempting to *memorize* the dictionary.

With my parents at Moulin–Sagout, a year before my father's death.

Part II

Saint-Aquilin, My Beautiful Village

Maman and Eva in Slovakia, shortly before her return to France.

Chapter 4

Slovakia, a Shattered Idyll

I've always thought that because my daddy died before I could ever know
him, he became a more formidable memory, a greater influence, and a
more palpable presence than he would ever have been had he lived.

— *Harry Crews,* A Childhood

*I*n my memory, no trace of my father. He died at thirty-eight of throat
cancer, when I was only eighteen months old. Everything I know about
him is what I've heard from others, in snippets that are always too short to
give me a complete picture. Their recollections and a few photographs are
the only vestiges of his passage on this earth, aside from his three children—
none of whom remembers him.

My parents were born the same year, 1905, and grew up near each other in
the peasant village of Bzince pod Javorinou in Slovakia. They together had
nine siblings, eight of whom remained there or close by all their lives.

In 1930, at 25, Maman left Bzince after hearing of openings in France
for foreign guest workers. This in the midst of the economic depression that
had created widespread unemployment in that country, apparently without
diminishing its reliance on imported labor to fill jobs that the French couldn't
or wouldn't do, a situation similar to today's across much of the "developed
world." She was to be employed as a live-in domestic for the Lavril family,
wealthy resident owners of a dairy/flour mill/pharmaceutical lab complex
forming the hamlet of Le-Moulin-Sagout in Normandy.

Once there, she arranged for my father to be hired by the same employer,
as a laborer. They married soon after his arrival in France. For over a decade,
until my birth in 1942, they were lodged in the master's house, plantation style.

Although coupled, my parents did not attempt to establish an independent household in France. Like the unattached foreign workers employed with room and board at the Moulin-Sagout compound, they wanted to save as much of their wages as possible so they could return to a decent existence in their native country—that is, purchase a small plot of land, two or three pigs and a cow, plus some bricks and mortar to build a modest dwelling. Family life in France would have entailed expenses for autonomous housing and compromised this project.

Also, since old-age pensions did not yet exist, my father felt responsible to help out his parents financially. He accomplished this by paying them to raise his children, not an uncommon temporary arrangement among foreign guest workers at the time, except that in our case it became permanent.

Maman returned "home" alone to Slovakia at the end of her pregnancies to deliver my two sisters, Olga in 1933, Eva in 1936. She then left them in the care of our paternal grandmother and went back to work in France, in each instance three months after their birth. I was born in Normandy instead of Slovakia only because at the time of my arrival the turmoil of war and the German occupation of France precluded rail travel to Eastern Europe.

During his thirteen years abroad, my father returned home only once, briefly, during the pre-war summer of 1938, when Olga was five, and Eva two. That's why they too don't remember him, and why they had no recollection of Maman either when she returned to Slovakia in 1946 with yet another stranger from their immediate family, me.

Because he died before I could know him, I have constructed in my mind a somewhat vague but mythical image of my father, this mysterious figure whose absence has perhaps marked me even more deeply than would have his presence. Having heard only praise about him, I idealized and secretly worshipped him. Although Maman also remained strongly attached to his memory, throughout my childhood she seemed reluctant to talk about their life together. I attributed this reserve to her stoicism and general reticence to express her feelings, especially after such a devastating loss, which she must inevitably have perceived as a form of abandonment. She conveyed her emotions in conduct and selfless actions rather than in words, even though the Slovak language lends itself particularly well to the expression of feelings—no doubt a subjective notion of mine (the writer Vladimir Nabokov, when asked about his relationship to the three languages in which he felt at home, said that Russian spoke to his heart, English to his head, French to his ear).

I didn't realize that Maman's reluctance was also an attempt to shield me from information that might damage my hallowed view of my father. Many years later, she revealed that not all had gone well between them. After Eva's birth she had considered staying in the village in Slovakia, rather than leave her daughters again. She hoped he would also return from France to join them. While she anguished over this decision, he sent her an ultimatum by telegram: "If you don't come back, I will find another woman." She yielded. Proud as she was, even if she loved him, which I believe she did, she could not avoid feeling resentful and humiliated by his intransigence.

In the Lavril compound at Moulin-Sagout, employing about two dozen "guest workers" from Poland and Slovakia, my parents enjoyed favored status, as evidenced by their housing situation within their employer's home. This arrangement made Maman conveniently available for her never-ending domestic duties, yet it was unusual for a working couple to be billeted that way.

When Father died, his casket was set up for the wake in the Lavrils' living room. His identity must have been more complex than his social standing as a common laborer seemed to imply. He had actually established a French connection earlier, in 1924, by escaping there for some time to avoid the draft in Czechoslovakia. He was probably a *déclassé*, basically proletarian, yet able to function comfortably among different levels of society. It must have been difficult for those closest to him to fathom his harsh, abstract stance toward paternity and family life, whereas in all other realms of character and personality he seemed so well-liked and respected, not only by the bosses, who trusted him enough to keep him in their home, but also his fellow workers, who looked up to him to settle conflicts or handle administrative matters on their behalf. I imagine he was, like most people, a web of contradictions—at the same time a good son, a tyrannical husband, an indifferent father—nonetheless esteemed for his integrity, candor, and sense of humor. I once heard him characterized as "transparent in an opaque world." I can't help but wonder how my relationship with him would have turned out if he had lived.

He enjoyed a close friendship with Maurice Lavril, eldest son of his employers, student of medicine and pharmacy, and heir apparent to the expanding pharmaceutical branch of the Lavril dairy enterprise. Its Lactoserum and

Lactacyd products would become celebrated in the field of dermatology and, subverted by Maman for cosmetic use, leave her face completely smooth and wrinkle-free well into her sixties.

Maurice often accompanied my father on his early morning rounds to gather milk from the outlying farmhouses in the Sagout valley. What did they talk about, on the jostling wagon? Or, content to direct the team of horses on the familiar trail in the morning mist, did they just commune in silence, as peasants often do?

Maurice's sister Alix once described my laborer father to me in startling terms, echoed by her sister Thadée: "*Jan, c'était un seigneur*" ("Jan was a lord"). Be that as it may, in thirteen years of employment at the Lavrils, he never sought promotion to foreman, choosing instead to maintain solidarity with his fellow workers. I surmise he had a strong aptitude for leadership, but no interest in it. Or did he simply lack ambition? I have heard that said of me too...

After I was born, my parents continued to work under the same room-and-board arrangement, but they moved out of the owner's house into separate quarters in the compound.

Father's death would again thwart Maman's maternal instincts and deprive her of the opportunity to raise her own children. She had to continue her live-in employment and therefore could not take care of me. So she resorted to the only feasible solution: a private "*en nourrice*" foster care arrangement. People who were aware of our circumstances did not judge her harshly for that.

I was boarded in the nearby village of Saint-Aquilin-de-Pacy-sur-Eure (the longer the name, the smaller the village) with an elderly peasant couple, known there as Old Man Lepais and The Widow Vermot, who became my Pépère and Mémère, my Grandpa and Grandma. This placement turned out to be the first of several instances of good luck and determinant encounters in my otherwise unpromising future. Except for the brief interlude of our botched return to Slovakia two years later when I was four, I lived under this couple's warm affection until the age of ten.

From my guardians' dwelling, I could walk back and forth, a distance of about half a mile, to visit Maman at work at the Lavrils during the day. She also often accompanied her employers to their other residence, a vast apartment located fifty-five miles away in Paris at 5 Avenue Emile Deschanel, at the foot of the Eiffel Tower. I occasionally went along for the ride. I would stand on the floorboard on the passenger side next to Monsieur Lavril, with my hands on the dashboard and my nose to the windshield, and prod him to race other automobiles on two-lane Route Nationale 13, the conduit between our village and Paris. He liked to drive fast and was only too glad to indulge me, while Maman and Madame, petrified in the back seat, closed their eyes or tried to look down at their shoes instead of the tree-lined roadway zipping past us. What scared them most was when he passed cars that did not take his challenge to their honor lightly. Instead of maintaining speed, some drivers would accelerate and try to keep us from merging back into our lane, with oncoming traffic closing in fast, head-on. But Monsieur would call their bluff and not slow down. An excellent driver, he always found the punch in his powerful cars to pull us through at the last moment. I felt exhilarated riding up front with a full view of the road, but would have gotten car sick, like Maman often did, if I had been jostled back there like the ladies.

We crashed only once, into a wall, with hardly any damage to the car and only a bump to my forehead, when Monsieur Lavril miscalculated a short cut through narrow streets in the town of Mantes-la-Jolie. He was trying to shake off a sports car that had been chasing us on the open stretches of the road.

Each trip to and from Paris with Monsieur at the wheel was for me a thrilling adventure, starting or ending under the breathtaking height of the Eiffel tower. At the foot of that celebrated monument, on Iena Bridge, I spent hours watching the street athletes diving from the parapet into the Seine flowing below.

Awakening

My "real" life, the one of which I am conscious, as opposed to my gleaned prehistory, began nearly a year after my father's death, when I was two years and four months old. I even know its exact starting date, because of a recorded event that marked it indelibly: the U.S. Air Force bombing raid against the Nazi occupiers of our region. This first remembrance is engraved in my memory by a *smell* that I can still conjure up, the smell of moss and lichens in a damp underground cave.

The night of August 20, 1944, I emerge into consciousness, hurled by the scruff of the neck and kicked by a soldier's hobnailed boot onto the dank compacted floor of the storage cave at Sagout. It's actually a tunnel dug into the hill overlooking the Lavril compound. Previously used to stockpile the dairy's production of Camembert cheese, it now serves as a bomb shelter. A loud human bark (*Rein? Schnell?*) propels me into existence, and simultaneous first feeling of separation: my companion, a white dog with black markings, is left behind, never to be seen again.

Candles flicker in the dimly lit cave. Gathered there are people already familiar to me, although my sensory memory begins only with this moment. They are lined up on benches against the wall, like a fresco: Maman, Pépère and Mémère, the Lavril family, the workers of Sagout, the inhabitants of Saint-Aquilin. From outside, sounds of apocalypse reach us in the shelter, earth-shaking thuds vying with the rageful "Ack! Ack!" of anti-aircraft salvos.

Roaming

My early childhood, from the time of the air raid until the age of four when we returned to Slovakia, unfolded in a sort of melancolic enchantment, of continual wanderings and reverie.

Although I lived with Pépère and Mémère in the village of Saint-Aquilin, I spent a good part of my days at the Moulin-Sagout compound whenever Maman was there instead of Paris, fulfilling her duties as a live-in housekeeper doubling up more and more often as a cook. From morning to evening—except for the mandatory afternoon nap at my caretakers'—I roamed freely along the road to the hamlet, and through the fields, meadows, and wooded hills forming the Eure River valley with its numerous brooks and the tributary stream activating the wheel of the flour mill at Moulin-Sagout. I most often wandered alone, or on occasion with other children from the vicinity. The beautiful countryside of Normandy provided a spectacle of infinite richness and variety, sometimes tinged with an indefinable sadness, as if something was missing from this otherwise perfect setting. The slightest detail could trigger that wistful yearning, or on the contrary provoke unbounded elation. I alternated frequently between those opposite feelings in the course of a single day. Adults commented about my "precociousness and emotionality." I had no idea what they meant by that.

In the evening, when feasible, Maman accompanied me back to the village at Pépère and Mémère's. I liked it best when she was delayed in her work past twilight. It meant we would walk hand in hand in the dark along the country road under the starlit sky.

Amidst those solitary wanderings between my two "homes," I registered a harsh preliminary lesson: the protective aura of my deceased father, which I imagined hovering over me in my peregrinations, proved to be only an illusion. An excruciating sting on the back of my hand, so sharp that I thought my days were ended, convinced me of that: I had *not* inherited his legendary ability to charm bees. I had heard that they covered his entire body and allowed him to reach into their hives to gather honey with hardly any protective gear. Despite all the warnings to stay away, I tried to do the same, once and only once, but didn't even get close before being attacked. The beehives at Moulin-Sagout continued to fascinate me, but I kept at a reasonable distance after this sobering lesson.

One day, not long after the bombing raid, I was crawling with a girl my age through tall grasses and wildflowers. We wanted to observe the mesmerizing swarms of bees from a safe place and also, thus hidden, play doctor and engage in reciprocal examination of our anatomies, when the buzzing of bees gave way to a louder, even more ominous sound. From our hiding spot on the ground we heard—coming closer on the road and then passing us by— the familiar, frightful din of hobnailed boots hammering the pavement. The German soldiers stationed in our vicinity were marching out of Sagout for a last time, in a semblance of formation. "Auf Viderzène, Krauts, go to hell!" Pépère kept saying lately, in reaction to the Nazis' jitteriness. A few days earlier, when he was coming home from the fields for lunch, they had unleashed a barrage of machine gun fire at him, for no reason, and fortunately missed him before he took cover behind a wall.

With the sound of those horrible studded jackboots fading off in the distance, and the whirring of bees rising again downfield, I felt a broken twig from an apple tree tickle my neck, and the warm sun caress my naked butt. An indescribable happiness overtook me at that moment.

Soon after the Germans departed, the Americans soldiers arrived in our region, and handed out their delicious mint chewing gum to the village children. I had never tasted anything so exquisite; it literally made me drool, with beads of saliva dripping from the corners of my mouth. But this new discovery confirmed in my mind that, as with the beehives, pleasure and danger are often linked. Maman had cautioned me, while scraping with disgust a piece of gum that had stuck under her shoe: "If you svallow this, you get sick, it block your intestins." Her warning seemed logical. I tried not to chew, and instead carefully sucked on the flavorful sticks that I cut into small pieces so the taste would last longer.

After the disappearance of my companion dog following the bombing raid, I didn't roam as much as previously, or so I was told. Apparently, he was a sort of mascot who belonged to no one and everyone, and was welcomed in all corners of Moulin-Sagout, much like myself. For some reason, maybe because he had perceived that similarity between us, the dog had latched on to me and had a tendency to lead me astray in the surrounding countryside, causing Maman and others in the hamlet much worry, including on a couple of occasions having to form search parties, before he brought me back to our starting point.

To Maman's great relief, my unaccompanied wanderlust was now limited to a smaller perimeter, about a kilometer long and half a kilometer wide. I covered this territory every day tirelessly in all directions. The only disruption to these repeated tours was the compulsory after-lunch nap at my caretakers'. Mémère tried to counter my protestations: "Don't fight it! Take advantage of sleeping now! Later you'll regret not being able to rest like this in the afternoon."

Lying impatiently on my straw mattress in the bedroom that I shared with my elderly guardians, I gazed at the shadows filtering in through the shutters. Then, imperceptibly, the cackling of the chickens below the window took on the rhythm of a lullaby, and despite my attempts to stay awake, I sank into delicious sleep. But no matter how pleasant the drowsiness, I deplored wasting my time that way. There were so many interesting things to discover or revisit in the beautiful valley!

My wanderings showed little imagination. I was starting my lifelong pattern of digging a furrow. But everything fascinated me. I didn't tire of ceaselessly undertaking the same circuit. And I had those immediate, unexplainable feelings of attraction or aversion for different places.

The cemetery of Saint-Aquilin, where my father was buried without a tombstone, and the abandoned German pillbox, at the crest of the hill, marked the northern edge of my territory. I didn't venture beyond that boundary onto the vast Evreux plateau, with its chalky soil that felt sticky underfoot when wet.

To the east, about two hundred yards from Sagout, I did not push into the woods farther than the abandoned limestone quarry. My anxiety in this sector was caused by the only frightening situation I ever experienced in my rovings: the encounter earlier on with a forest vagrant. He appeared suddenly on the path through the woods, in shoes that were cut out at the tips to free up his toes. He wore no socks, and carried a rucksack on his shoulder. The purple skin of his swollen ankles seemed ready to burst, and despite the summer heat, he was wearing a black overcoat whose tails fell into tatters. His face, hidden under a thick, dirty beard, looked almost as grimy as that of the chimney sweep from Pacy.

I never saw the vagabond again after that startling encounter, but the memory was strong enough to make me stay away from the area. When I came across him on the path, I was too surprised and too scared to jump out to the side. He grunted and stared fixedly ahead without acknowledging my presence, despite the narrowness of the trail. I wondered afterwards whether he had set up his living quarters inside the cement structure housing the electric transformer on the road below. It was also a gathering place for swallows, perched up by the hundreds on the transmission lines overhead. A sign with a drawing of a skull and crossbones, and illustrations showing how to give first aid to someone who had been electrocuted, sought to discourage entry into this possible makeshift of an abode.

As if to confirm my anxiety, much farther to the east in the same direction, thankfully way beyond my perimeter, was a place I had never seen, but which made me shudder each time I heard its name: *L'équarissage*, the rendering plant.

The Eure River marked the southern edge of my territory, and to the west, the village of Saint-Aquilin, composed of about twenty houses. Later, on the occasion of my sixth birthday, Madame Lavril offered me a beautiful blue Peugeot bicycle, which became my new companion and extended my radius of activity almost two kilometers further west, to the hamlet of La-Noë-du-Bois, fully deserving of its poetic name.

During those pre-school years, I arrived mornings at Sagout after already a pleasant amble through the countryside, where I could feel the dew and admire the peacocks strutting in the meadow below the walnut trees. Maman then prepared for me, following the recommendations of soon-to-be doctor Maurice Lavril, a bowl of *bouillie*, unctuous mixture of milk and flour, accompanied by, phooey, a bitter swig of Quintonine fortifier, or worse, a spoonful of cod liver oil. "If it tastes bad, it's good for you," said the adults who tried to convince me of the efficacy of those potions. Sometimes this supplementary breakfast consisted of raw egg yolks, freshly gathered from the chicken pen, and whipped up with some port wine.

"I'm going around Sagout" I would then tell Maman, before heading out for another tour of the domain, which I can still see vividly:

In the tributary stream turning the wheel of the flourmill, a wire mesh prevents the fish from entering the churned up zone. They are forced at that point to turn back against the flow, and can easily be caught with a net:

gudgeons, trout, crayfish, and a multitude of minnows wriggle and bump into each other in the clear sweet-smelling water; sometimes even a mean-looking pike appears, or an eel curled up under a stone on the sandy bottom among the graceful stems of aquatic plants hugging the banks. But we have been warned to be careful. There's a danger of drowning. It has happened before, and it's a big fear for the Sagout children, and even more for their parents. I don't fret about it, though. I can't swim, but I'm able to wade across the stream with my neck just above the water.

On the other side of the small bridge, on the tennis court of red clay surrounded by a high fence, two houseguests of the Lavrils swat a ball back and forth, their outfits so white they almost hurt the eyes.

Back across the bridge from this more recreational side of the compound, on the unloading dock shaded by the weeping willow tree, tall gleaming milk cans are lined up in a row, necklaces of foam pushing through their lids. On the outside of the building, the creaky winch lifts flour sacks to the attic; and inside, the cheese maker turns the delectable Lavril camemberts on their individual nests of straw at the just right stage of ripeness, before sprinkling them with a few pinches of salt.

In the administrative office, located in the middle of the compound, the accountant, hunched over his table with a ruler in one hand and a green visor over his eyes, writes down numbers and draws neat lines and columns on ledger sheets.

But already the blacksmith calls me over and hands me the bellows. I love to fan the fire while he hammers the metal. Near the anvil, the gentle Percheron waits to be shod. He is my favorite horse to ride.

Next in my rounds is the hayloft, where rectangular bales of straw form tunnels for children's games of hide and seek. Stray cats live there too, and birds nest among the beams.

Then the pigpen, which I can't pass by without feeling sickened by the remembrance of the slaughter I once witnessed there. Two professional butchers wearing long aprons and rubber boots had been hired for the task. With precise movements and no visible anguish, despite the animal's piercing cries, they had slit his throat, crucified him to the wall, scalded him, and then skinned and quartered his flesh with knives that sank into his belly as easily as if it had been a slab of butter.

Near the pigpen, the fenced-off kennel houses the pack of dogs for the hunt in Sologne, a distant region near the Loire River famous for its wild game. The dogs are not the petting kind. They stink like wild beasts. Turbulent and snarly, they seem ready to tear each other apart when their daily ration of swill and bones is thrown at them. During hunting season, the captive horde is loaded aboard the old Saurer truck and transported to Sologne, where, finally freed, they chase a hapless deer or wild boar until its heart explodes.

While awaiting that periodic expedition, the Saurer stands ready for its next trip to Paris, in the garage adjoining the kennel. I climb aboard, sit behind the steering wheel, and roll down the window. The upholstery has the feel and smell of dry, cracked leather stuffed with horse hair.

Behind the truck sits the Volkswagen amphibious jeep abandoned at Sagout by the Germans, along with artillery shells, hand grenades, machine gun belts, and other munitions strewn all over the hills when they fled from our area. Luckily for us, they didn't plant any land mines.

I arrive next in the beautiful garden surrounding the Lavrils' residence. The pathways are covered with freshly raked white gravel. The gardener moves the sprinklers, pschitt pschitt, across which it's so much fun to run during hot summer days. He trims the hedges, mows the patches of grass, prunes the raspberry bushes, thins out the vegetables, devotes his closest attention to the flowerbeds planted throughout in geometric patterns.

My inspection tours usually end with a visit to the lab where pharmaceutical products derived from milk are concocted. I like the fragrance of the finished Lactacyd ointment, but its fabrication gives off a slightly nauseating smell. Still, it's fascinating to watch the process, with its gurgling alambics, vials, and beakers.

Work activity at the Sagout compound would not last much longer. One night, a huge fire destroyed the main building containing the flour mill and the dairy operation, across the grounds from the masters' house, which remained untouched. No one was hurt, and the animals were spared, but sparks and flames rose high into the sky.

Grieving

My father lies buried in the cemetery located on top of the hill overlooking the village of Saint-Aquilin. From this vantage point, one can see the Eure River meandering through lush meadows between two rows of poplars.

Throughout my childhood, I came to pay my respects at his grave every Sunday, and sometimes more often still, spontaneously, when games of tag or hide-and-seek took place on the hill with children from the village or from the nearby town of Pacy. My sadness in front of his resting place arose in part from the contrast between the beauty of the site and the disturbing presence of death and eternity. The cemetery was at the center of my universe.

Although he had lived and worked in France for more than thirteen years, my father did not intend to settle there permanently. For proof, the Slavic first names of his children, defying assimilation: Olga, Eva, Milan. During the same period, other guest workers installed themselves for good in their adopted country, established true households, named their offspring Monique, Cécile, or Jean-Pierre.

The return "home" to Slovakia, always postponed, as when he refused to join Maman following Eva's birth, had in Father's case become a myth that sustained him during his many years abroad. Paradox less rare than might appear, he had accepted to live and work in his host country, more or less indefinitely, but not to settle or die there.

Fate saw it otherwise. As the only consolation in his eternal exile, he rests in a position he probably would have liked, on an incline, facing the valley, in a site that was familiar to him. In his rounds to collect milk for the Sagout dairy from outlying farmhouses, he drove his horsecart on the trail past the cemetery daily. Saint-Aquilin resembles his native village of Bzince pod Javorinou enough to appease his peasant's soul.

At the end of my meditations in front of my father's grave, I would hear him exhort me, in a blank voice whose tone or accent I could only imagine: "All right son, enough of this, you run along now."

I would then jump over the wall of the cemetery, and hurtle down the hill at full speed, risking a fall at every stride, or a crash against a pine or a juniper tree. I reached the road at the bottom in complete exultation, my tears already dried, reconciled with my fate, until the next visit. I missed my unknown father deeply.

Slovakian Idyll

In summer 1946, when peace returned and it became possible to travel eastward again, Maman decided to resettle permanently in her native village. From being a solitary child raised until then "*sans famille,*" I would suddenly turn into a privileged four-year-old doted on not only by Maman under these favorable new conditions, but also my sisters, grandparents, eight aunts and uncles, and a bevy of cousins. The only shadow on this appealing prospect was the wrenching separation it entailed from Pépère and Mémère and my cat Zaza.

The entire village of Bzince pod Javorinou seemed inhabited by our relatives or their extensions. I didn't know the Slovak language, but would soon fall under the spell of its mellifluous sound, which has since remained associated for me with the euphoric warmth of Bzince.

There, my paternal grandmother ruled. Although dirt poor, she held, without realizing it, skewed aristocratic values. For this diminutive but powerful matriarch, that strange attitude took the form of an inordinate preoccupation about lineage and descendants.

According to Maman, *Babička* (Grandma) Kovačovicová exerted a not so subtle pressure on her three sons to produce at minimum one male heir each, in order to transmit the family name, absent any fortune. This demanding expectation of hers was tempered by a more reasonable but potentially contradictory edict: that they not produce offspring in "excessive" quantity, lest their family become an institutional enterprise, or worse, a nightmare for their wives. She herself had given birth to ten children, four of whom died in infancy, including a set of twins. The survivors lived in the village of Bzince or nearby except for one daughter who had emigrated to America. Maman's four siblings had also settled in the village.

Given Babička's well-intentioned but domineering attitude, I'm glad to have been her grandson and not her son. Yet, ironically, I probably owe my existence to her concern about succession. Every birth occurs in a context ranging from desired, to accidental, to fatalistic, to unwanted, with many gradations within this spectrum. At the time of my birth, in 1942, Maman was thirty-seven years old. For her to have a child at that age—in the chaos of war, under our disjointed family circumstances, with her husband showing emerging signs of a fatal illness—must have been far from ideal. Assuming my father was able to communicate the news of my birth to his mother, which I doubt in view of the disruptions caused by the war, he would have basked in her approval for only a few months before his death.

As an infant I was wheeled around Sagout in a rakish pram, and outfitted in hand-knit clothes and booties, with ruffled collar and gold neck chain and bracelet. And I was fed with a silver spoon and a silver goblet no different than Xavier Lavril's. He was the youngest child of Moulin-Sagout's owners, a year and a half older than I. We became frequent playmates and roamed freely throughout the compound along with the foreman's son, Alain Debel. Distinctions of social class between us would be held in abeyance until schooling began. Then Xavier attended a private institution in Paris in the Lavril family tradition, while Alain and I enrolled in Madame Mercier's one-room schoolhouse in the village. Ironically, the latter turned out to be vastly superior. Immanent justice was at work there.

As evidenced from the few photographs that remain, my sisters also wore fancy clothes, even miniature folk costumes, during the three months Maman stayed with them after their birth. The impoverished people of Slovakia placed great emphasis on representation at the very beginning and the very end of life, at the risk of neglecting the intervening period. They put a considerable part of their meager resources into *"comme il faut"* ("proper") infant outfits and tombstones. That's why, in addition to the post-war travel difficulties, Maman could not bring herself to leave France for Slovakia without first purchasing a full-length gravestone for Father's burial site. She did this nearly three years after his death, as I was shocked to discover from a funerary invoice I found among her papers at the time of her own passing, forty-one years later.

The voyage by rail to Slovakia proved to be an erratic, seemingly endless affair. The train moved as often backward as forward, with long periods of waiting in the middle of the countryside for no apparent reason. The hissing of brakes and the clanging of wagons coming to a complete stop were as frequent as the whistle blast before each grade crossing, or the chugging of the steam engine eager to get somewhere, anywhere. Our train limped through the stark ruins of the bombed-out German cities, where only the skeletal outer shells of some buildings remained standing. The rest had collapsed into mounds of brick and rubble.

Contrasting with the grim journey, Bzince glowed in the radiance of its simple, gaily-painted houses. In the whirlwind of arrival, it took me some time to learn who was who among our numerous relatives. Soon, I was invited to join family expeditions to hunt mushrooms in the nearby forests, and I was entrusted, with a long willow stick, to herd an aunt's flock of geese along the stream that ran the length of the village. I also often accompanied the teams of oxen to the fields, on a country road lined with plum trees bursting with fruit.

Oxen were used as beasts of burden in Bzince, whereas in Saint-Aquilin's farmsteads, horses fulfilled that role. Curiously, although the oxen seemed more primeval and archaic than the horses, Bzince felt more modern than

Saint-Aquilin. This impression was perhaps due to the contrast between my cheerful new surroundings, and the world of old age and cemeteries I had left behind.

Everything in Bzince seemed festive! The oxen sometimes wore bouquets of flowers on their yoke. Men and women headed out to the fields in the morning with scythes and pitchforks on their shoulders, singing heartily along the way. At work, they took frequent pauses, sitting on the ground under the shade of fruit trees. During those breaks, they passed around a heavy loaf of rye bread, from which everyone sliced off a piece with a big folding knife. They washed down this savory fare with ladles of cool water from a milk can wrapped in wool. For dessert, they just reached up and grabbed some luscious plums or apricots overhead.

On special occasions, people wore colorful folk costumes. One of my more distant relatives—I could only identify grandparents, aunts, uncles, and cousins—was a cobbler. Although my feet were growing fast, and the results of his labor would not serve very long, he made me a pair of knee-high boots from the finest leather, to wear with the traditional outfits stitched by the village women.

I fell very smoothly into the Slovak language. More than any other language I know, Slovak expresses feelings openly, even gushingly, through an unabashed use of diminutives and terms of endearment. In Bzince, I was never called Milan, but Milanko, Milko, Zlato, Zlatko, Zlatičko, Zlatinko. I basked in this effusiveness and affection.

At the same time, a stoic tradition persisted in this agrarian culture, especially in communication from children to parents. The language offered itself up as a unique tool of emotional expressiveness, but its use was another matter, dependent on individual personalities and other factors that I did not fully understand. Olga and Eva, for instance, continued to address our mother formally, as did all the village children in speaking with their parents. I didn't follow that path, because it hadn't been the custom in France except in rare instances among upper-class families including, if I remember right, the Lavrils.

My adaptation to Bzince was proceeding smoothly, when a cataclysm shattered this newfound paradise: Maman discovered that the paternal clan had "borrowed" the savings that she and my father had entrusted to them before the war, in the form of cash they were supposed to keep at home under a proverbial mattress. She was counting on this money for her reinstallation. She wanted it reimbursed in full immediately, not at some indefinite later date or, in her mind, perhaps never. Dismayed by this betrayal, she resolved to leave for France again, and this time take her three children with her. Olga was thirteen, Eva ten, I four. The families intervened. They judged her plans insane. Finally it was decided that Eva would remain two more years in Bzince and join us after that.

In retrospect, I think Maman suffered from impulsiveness and wounded pride. I can well understand my relatives' rationale for using the "idle" money during the eight years of her last absence, especially under the mitigating circumstances of a seemingly endless war and the upbringing of two of her children. I cannot cast stones. In my adult years, I once also "borrowed" a sum that had been sent to me for safekeeping and had for a long time lain fallow, with little likelihood it would ever be claimed. When the funds unexpectedly became due, I was rescued by a providential bank loan, an option not available to my kinfolk.

Maman, Olga, and I headed back to France. For the return journey through the ruins of Germany, my maternal aunt Anna filled one of our suitcases with several days' supply of my favorite treat: delicious plum and apricot dumplings. That's also when I realized that during the two months of our Slovakian stay, I had learned to speak the language of my family but had *totally* forgotten French.

Although my paternal grandmother Babička had initially, quarrel of paupers, opposed my parents' marriage, judging Maman too impoverished a party for her son, she had finally accepted her daughter-in-law, raised my two sisters, and become strongly attached to Olga. She died soon after our departure, no doubt in large part from heartbreak.

Eva, who had been left behind, underwent yet another traumatic experience at her guardian-grandmother's funeral. No one stepped forward to take her in. She stood there forsaken, grieving, and dejected among all the relatives surrounding the coffin laid out in front of the house, until kind maternal aunt Anna clutched her hand and said, "Well, girl, it looks like you're coming home with us."

The subsequent political events of 1948, when the communist Iron Curtain closed off Eastern Europe, followed by the Cold War of the 1950's and the vicissitudes of our life in France, caused Maman to relinquish little by little her intention to have Eva join us in the West. Our family settled into permanent separation. Face to face contact wasn't reestablished until seventeen years later.

When we returned to France, I was placed back at Mémère and Pépère's, and Olga joined me there. I quickly relearned French and just as rapidly forgot Slovak...again (I assume it had been my primary language as an infant, until Father's death).

Maman resumed working for the Lavrils, this time in Paris, with only occasional forays to Sagout. After the flourmill and dairy burned down, the main house in the compound became their "country estate." She remained in their employ four more years, until her final separation in 1950, after two decades of faithful and devoted live-in service.

In the "upstairs/downstairs" world of the bourgeoisie, discord often reigns among the staff, and the relationship between master and servant can become exceedingly complex. "Our maid is a full-fledged member of the family" is a statement often heard. And it is true that Maman had grown more attached to Madame Lavril than to her own mother.

Madame had taught her everything about the French culinary arts and transformed her from a Central European peasant girl into a still uneducated, but in many ways sophisticated Parisian woman who, no doubt mimicking her employer, was prompt to label people she didn't like as "*ordinaire*." In fact Maman had become not only Madame's willing slave, but also her confidant. And although there was only a small difference in age between them, their relationship had taken on many mother-daughter characteristics.

It is undeniable that lacking independence and generally not inclined to emancipation, domestics are as much in the charge as in the service of their masters. However, after twenty years of loyal service, Maman felt compelled to leave the Lavrils, for a variety of reasons. Notable among those was a hiring decision by Monsieur for the household staff. It reflected in a blatant way his previously more discreet abuse of *droit de cuissage* with younger female employees. He was installing his current mistress at home.

His wife perhaps didn't care; after all, this was the French bourgeoisie. But Maman, ever protective of Madame, could not endure having knowledge of the situation. Another example of immanent justice: Employers of live-in domestics forfeit their right to privacy.

An even more troubling event than Monsieur's philandering occurred at the same time. In Paris Maman had become less isolated than at Sagout, through contact with other domestics when she did the household's daily food shopping at a nearby outdoor market. She discovered she was being paid less than the prevailing wage for her duties. Armed with this new knowledge, she confronted Madame, who professed surprise and ignorance, and immediately agreed to bring her up to the standard rate.

But the trust between them was irrevocably broken. Madame apologized profusely for her negligence, which she attributed to the overwhelming complexity of running dual households in Paris and Sagout. "Please, Eva, I beg of you, forgive me, it was an oversight!" is how my mother described her employer's pleading. Although she genuinely empathized with Madame's travails, Maman perceived the salary discrepancy as an inexcusable breach of faith, and evidence she was being taken for granted. Patient to a fault, as behooves a domestic, she could also be headstrong. After making a decision, she did not look back. Twenty years earlier, at the time of her first emigration to France, she had fled from her native village with similar determination, and had shown the same resolve again when she discovered the disappearance of her savings following our return to Slovakia.

The breakup with Madame was extremely painful for both of them, and for me too. I had grown very fond of the Lavrils. Along with Maman and Olga, plus Pépère and Mémère, they were my family. Madame's gift of the Peugeot bicycle had been one of the peak events of my childhood. And I held vivid memories of Monsieur indulging me during those rides to and from Paris in his powerful cars, when he and I felt like "Kings of the Road."

Those were my perceptions at age eight. I can trace my passionate adult belief in egalitarianism and the necessity of labor unions to Maman's wage incident at the Lavrils.

Redemption

Our failed reinsertion amongst our kin in Slovakia, the disconcerting comings-and-goings between languages and cultures, the multiple losses suffered since infancy, including most recently the vanished paradise of Bzince, had no doubt severely affected my psyche, because during the intervening year between our return to Saint-Aquilin from Slovakia, and my enrollment in Madame Mercier's one-room schoolhouse at five, I behaved in an abominable manner, without fetters, without self-restraint. Whereas before I had been a calm, cooperative, obedient child, I became chronically churlish and angry. I had undergone an unexplainable transformation.

I indulged in horrible tantrums. Though nearly blind, Mémère tried to sew, and she always asked me to thread needles for her. When mending the holes in my socks, she often nicked her fingers despite the thimble. Not only her yelps of pain, but also her clumsiness and her inept results made me bristle. After trying on the mended socks, I flung them to her face, yelled, screamed, stamped my feet. I rolled on the floor, cried big tears: my poor toes couldn't withstand the discomfort imposed by her "shitty stitching" or her loose threads and dangling knots. Her reaction: "It's not nice to talk like a horse carter. Where did you learn such foul language? It's not from school, you haven't been there yet, but I can't wait for it to start. Maybe Madame Mercier will know what to do with you. Me I'm at wit's end."

Pépère and Mémère put up with my loutish behavior, and persisted in raising me with kindness. I was never beaten or spanked, nor even harshly reprimanded. In their long experience of raising other people's children, my elderly guardians ignored the meaning of the word "punishment." They simply waited for their boarders' difficult stages to pass. "How many kids I've raised during my life, how much brattiness I've endured!" sighed Mémère.

Pépère could have flattened me with a flick of his hand. For the Sunday stew, forsaking his walking stick, which he used as both a cane and a club, he knocked the rabbits out of their misery with a mere whack of two fingers behind their neck. He next took out one of their eyes and held them upside down over a bowl, where their blood, mixed with some vinegar, splashed on his wooden clogs. The neighboring cats, roused up by this sacrifice, drove themselves wild in raucous sarabands around the hapless victim. With a single yank, Pépère then tore the rabbit's skin from its ears to its hind legs. "That'll be some nice fur for winter gloves," he exclaimed, before nailing the pelt inside out on the wall of the shed.

He could have inflicted the same fate on me to put an end to my tantrums. I loved animals too much to consider myself in any way superior or different from them.

One day, I overstepped the threshold of tolerance. Olga was staying in the other side of the house, in the "nice room," the one with whitewashed walls, a real mattress on the bed, and a coal heater that was left unused because we feared it might leak poisonous gas. Maman called it the "clean room," to distinguish it from the one I shared with Pépère and Mémère, and which she considered a hovel. She wanted me to be installed in the better room too, but we were accustomed to our former arrangement and Olga, understandably, preferred to stay alone. I didn't see the point of making any changes.

In the middle of one of my worst tantrums, Olga, unable to withstand my screaming any longer, came flying from her room into the kitchen and hurled herself between Mémère and me. She was nine years older, she towered over me, she pushed me back with both arms. I was overtaken with such rage that my words went far beyond my intention: I insulted her. My irritating litany since our return from Slovakia, "I'm bored, I'm bored, what can I do, I'm bored, I'm bored, I'm bored" suddenly switched, like the needle of a broken record, to "You're not my sister, leave me alone, go back to your country, you don't even speak French, you're not my sister, leave me alone, go back to your country..." Upon which, blinded with fury, thinking that Olga was about to strike me, I bit her like a mad dog, leaving a bloody gash on her wrist.

In the burst of tears that followed, hers of pain, mine of stupefaction and remorse, I collapsed on a chair, overcome by an illumination. The gaze of our father, from high up in the cemetery, bore down on me, pierced me like a bolt of lightning, condemned me, revealed how grotesque, hateful, and mean I was.

I felt immeasurable shame. My conversion was immediate. From now on, I would be calm, patient, considerate. Promised, it was an oath. I would help Mémère and Pépère, I would show them each day my filial affection, I would no longer enjoin them to relieve me of boredom, I would not complain about Mémère's sewing, I would take care of all the chores, I would not mock Olga for her French mistakes.

Soon after this incident, my long awaited schooling began. Madame Mercier found in me a pupil intensely receptive to her teaching, particularly of morals. I ardently wished to make amends. I was eager to apply my new-found desire to "be good." I had undergone a spiritual conversion.

This transformation had nothing to do with religion, which was alien to my upbringing. After Madame Mercier taught us how to read, I did manage to locate a copy of the Lord's Prayer, and I learned it by heart, on my own initiative, with superhuman effort and the written text always nearby for a peek, because my otherwise satisfactory brain was deficient when it came to memorizing *verbatim* anything longer than a sentence or two. But my use of that formal incantation was a superstitious crutch rather than the sign of a newly discovered religious faith.

Top: My father's funeral at the Lavrils.

Bottom: Ten-year-old Eva at her guardian Babička's funeral in Bzince pod Javorinou

Chapter 5

Madame Mercier, Schoolteacher

Your work and your efforts, and the generous heart you put into them,
are still alive for one of your little schoolchildren who, despite the
passing of years, has never ceased to be your grateful pupil.
I send you all my love.

— *Albert Camus, in a letter to his primary-school teacher
Monsieur Germain, upon receiving the Nobel prize for literature.*

My two youngest children—Aaron born in Duluth in 1994 and Zachary in 1997—complained bitterly every single day upon returning home from grade school, about the confinement they endured in the classroom. This despite having wonderful teachers, who themselves deplored this state of affairs imposed by the "system."

It pained me to hear my sons' litany: "Dad, it's horrible, no recess!" And right they were. A forty-minute period for combined lunch and "recess" was their only free time during the entire day, unrelieved by other opportunities to socialize, do unstructured activities, or move their bodies—what with merely forty-five minutes of Physical Education every fourth day! I tried to raise awareness in the community about this situation and encountered general agreement, but inertia prevailed. A new "normal" had set in, hugely detrimental to kids. My indignation was fueled in part by the contrast with my own grade school experience, in what today would be considered an archaic substandard environment.

Saint-Aquilin's one-room schoolhouse was located about half a mile from the home—a fifteen-minute walk along a tree-lined road meandering through the countryside of Normandy. But for us children, getting there often took longer. We were easily distracted, especially during springtime, by the brooks bubbling across the meadows into the gently flowing Eure River, or by the frogs, butterflies, rabbits, partridges, porcupines, and other creatures scampering in the ditch below the hedge of hawthorns bordering the road.

Since meals weren't served at school, we returned home for lunch and covered this pastoral route, *le chemin de l'école*, at least four times each day—rain, shine, frost, or snow—from the beginning of October to mid-July. This repeated jaunt over the same terrain enabled us to savor the beautiful landscape and capricious but temperate climate of our sector of *"La Douce France"* ("Sweet France") in their subtlest variations.

The first day, Pépère offered to accompany me to school, even though during her monthly visit from Paris at the end of August, Maman had already introduced me to the teacher, Madame Mercier. At his age and in his wooden clogs, walking longer distances was difficult for him, but I was glad he wanted to come along, for I'd feel less alone, and I'd have someone with whom to share my excitement. I knew from having traipsed with him in the past to the nearby town of Pacy-sur-Eure, that he could manage this sort of effort by stopping for a pause on each of the small stone bridges that spanned the brooks along the way every hundred yards or so. "Let's park our arse here for a while!" he'd say.

Twenty-five pupils attended Saint-Aquilin's school in 1947, the year I enrolled. They ranged in age from five—like me when I began—to thirteen-year-olds in their last stretch of compulsory schooling, including my sister Olga who was then just beginning to learn French. What an overwhelming challenge it must have been to teach this class, when I reflect on it!

The gravel yard surrounding the classroom buzzed with tag games and other spirited play before the start of the school day and during mid-morning and mid-afternoon recess. But when our teacher blew her whistle to get us back inside, we immediately fell into two ranks, without pushing or shoving, girls on the left, boys on the right, and quietly proceeded to our benches and desks, where we never sat long enough to get bored or antsy, thanks to those timely breaks outdoors, under the covered *préau* when it rained. The schooldays unfolded in a pleasant, active, orderly way.

Madame Mercier's overriding goal was to teach us how to read—fast, before Christmas in our first trimester! She subscribed to the view that children should learn to read so they can then read to learn. Therefore, during autumn, she focused most her energies on the new batch of pupils entering her classroom. But that didn't mean she neglected the other children, less needy of her attention by then. They could help each other, always older to younger in order to avoid humiliation, she saw to that, or they could work independently while she concentrated on the beginners during this crucial phase of their development. She knew her students well, and she handled these teaching complexities and delicate pairings with great deftness. Sometimes she created a silent, studious atmosphere, with all the pupils absorbed in their specific tasks. Other times she clapped her hands and demanded the group's undivided attention. Occasionally, she allowed the class to get fairly animated, without letting this interfere with the individual concentration of those who might perhaps later become the sort of adults who prefer to do their work in the hubbub of a café. Whether or not her pupils would go on to intellectual occupations, as a number of us did, she provided all her charges with an equally solid foundation, attuned as much as possible to their personal interests as well as their abilities and temperament. Without being aware of it, was Madame Mercier applying the vaunted Montessori method?

With our teacher's gift of reading by Christmastime, the world of knowledge opened itself up early to our eagerness and our curiosity. She based her approach on intensive phonics: "**BA, BÉ, BI, BO, BU,**" leading, as a reward for our efforts, to richly evocative words like "*baobab*" or "*abracadabra*." And all of a sudden, as if by magic, after those initial attempts we found ourselves uttering...whole sentences! I experienced the same feeling of exhilaration mixed with surprise when I first learned to ride my bicycle: "Look, I can do it!"

Following the winter vacation, we went on to writing, first in cursive, then block letters. For each penmanship session, we practiced with freshly sharpened pencils that gave off a wonderful smell of wood shavings. But these tentative, erasable markings were considered appropriate only for drafts.

For the next step, we switched to the traditional purple ink and blotter of school writing, symbolizing neatness, confidence, and commitment. We dipped the nibs of our penholders in the inkwell built into our desks, and carefully traced the thin upstrokes and fuller down-strokes of each letter on the pages of our notebooks imprinted with small squares for accurate spacing. Madame Mercier modeled the same forms for us on the blackboard marked with horizontal lines, like a musical staff. We winced and laughed when her chalk screeched on the upstroke. The use of newfangled ballpoint pens was prohibited by the Ministry of Education. It was thought their advent would mean the end of penmanship, one of the mainstays of instruction in the early grades. Along with reading and writing, we learned to count during that first year devoted to the development of basic skills.

Madame Mercier sought to arm her pupils for the struggles of life, with knowledge and civic virtue. Her profession was for her a vocation, in the secular tradition of the Republic. Her living quarters with her husband and their daughter Josette—a classmate of ours—adjoined the schoolroom in a small brick building which also served as a community center. She literally lived and breathed her work but refused to be considered a role model; she recognized that her family life suffered greatly from her professional absorption. She belonged to that exalted and much admired corps of primary-school teachers, *les Instituteurs et Institutrices*, veritable missionaries of the State. In France, starting at the end of the nineteenth century, they had instilled fervor for social justice and wrested the people's allegiance from the Catholic Church, which until then held a tight grip on schooling and was perceived as siding with the rich. Above all, she was deeply conscious of the determinant impact of *primary school* on a child's future: It's there that basic knowledge and love of learning are nurtured, or on the contrary blunted.

Because public funds were limited after the war, she fulfilled her teaching and administrative responsibilities without any assistance, except from family members on two specific occasions. Her husband, employed in the town hall of nearby Pacy-sur-Eure, walked home for lunch everyday. Since he knew how to play the clarinet, she sometimes enlisted his help in the classroom to make up for her acknowledged deficiency in the musical arts. And her retired father, who was missing an arm like so many veterans of World War I, and who had inspired her to follow in his footsteps as an educator, also lent his pedagogical expertise during his yearly month-long winter visit from Brittany.

Madame Mercier attended not only to our minds and character, but also our physical health. She had a rope-climbing portico installed in the schoolyard, and on the gravel grounds, under the linden trees, she taught us complicated group calisthenics for the annual Fourteenth of July celebration, when she paraded her brood—exceptionally spiffed up in white that day—to the stadium of Pacy-sur-Eure (no small feat to achieve such uniformity of clothing for a single occasion, as any parent today will attest). Also, by relentlessly

tracking grime on our bodies, and demanding that we prod our families to corrective action, she fostered progress in the rudimentary hygiene of the village.

Our teacher adamantly maintained that full, productive days at school
provided sufficient academic learning, and that her pupils or their often
barely literate families should not be burdened with homework—she had
deep respect for "*les gens simples*" ("common folk"). She felt that children's
time after school should be spent doing chores and other practical activities,
or playing, or reading for pleasure, or simply observing the world, especially
nature. She even accepted that kind of "idleness" during the school day. Windows ran the full length of the wall on two sides of the classroom, and I spent
many moments at my desk watching clouds float by in the ever-changing
Ile-de-France sky.

The successes of Madame Mercier's pupils in various external exams
brought her great satisfaction, and served to reaffirm her convictions and
validate her methods. Her remarkable results year after year helped instill the
notion that effective schooling, especially in the early grades, could in fact
compensate for "disadvantaged" home environments. Reflecting after retirement on her long career, she said that one of the most important factors in
achieving these outcomes was the total trust she enjoyed from her pupils'
families. I was extraordinarily lucky to have landed in her classroom, where
I remained for five years, until the age of ten—when she arranged for my
transfer to boarding school in Paris with a full scholarship for the then highly
selective academic track in secondary schooling. Needless to say, she had a
tremendous impact on my education and destiny.

After initiating us during that first year to the intricacies of reading, writing, and counting, our teacher expanded our horizons during the rest of our
time under her tutelage with progressively deeper discoveries. She taught
us spelling, sentence analysis, composition (though we often found it hard
to think of anything to write about), arithmetic (with emphasis on mental
calculations without pen and paper), history, geography, and some biology.
She valiantly tried to make us sing, without much success, until her husband
stepped in. Music wasn't my forte either. She assigned art projects, although,
again, she herself did not know how to draw or paint very well, and neither
did I, but some students were talented in that realm, and served as mentors
for the rest of us. I particularly enjoyed the art project not requiring drawing that she asked us to undertake for Mother's Day one year. We were each

given a clay pot, which we had to decorate with putty embedded with pieces of earthenware that we salvaged from the village dump and broke into small fragments with a hammer. I think Maman liked the results.

Spelling, a core subject in our program, came easily to me. Words simply looked right or not, and I almost always received a perfect score on dictations. On the other hand, I failed miserably at another central part of the curriculum, *récitation*—learning a poem or piece of prose by heart. All the while I marveled that some of my classmates seemed to have no difficulty with this daunting task. I remembered all the details of the texts we were supposed to memorize, and the page numbers where they appeared, but I could not "for the life of me" reproduce the words verbatim.

Because Madame Mercier knew us so well, she showed forbearance for our various idiosyncracies. In a sense she was helping us discover and develop our interests and aptitudes, and encouraging us to circumvent or ignore obstacles rather than confront them—a wise pedagogical stance, in my opinion. Before the term was invented, she put into practice in her classroom the concept of "multiple intelligences." If we were discouraged by some deficiency or other, she reminded us in a self-deprecating way of her own limitations in art and music. She also knew better than to attempt endeavors beyond her reach in physical education, for instance rope climbing. For that, she showed us the diagrams she had received from the Ministry of Education, and told us to figure things out ourselves. We did, although at first we had some difficulty understanding how to use our legs for support. Even more than a strength exercise, rope climbing was viewed as a lifesaving skill, to enable us to get out of a burning building if we ever needed to.

We were surprised to find the rope-climbing portico installed in the schoolyard when we returned from summer vacation one October. It became the central monument of the grounds, and a magnet at recess time. All the children, boys and girls, would learn how to climb rope that year. It was an objective established in Paris by the authorities, and considered as important as learning to swim, which unfortunately was left by the wayside—too complicated and expensive. Eventually, Madame Mercier had to separate the children under the portico, because the girls complained that the boys looked up their skirts when they climbed, and teased them that they saw their underwear.

Perhaps most important, our teacher instilled in us principles of lay morality and indignation against injustice. She heightened our consciousness regarding equality, but also cautioned us not to succumb to the poison of hate. To this day, I can hear the question she raised to explain the inevitability of the French revolution of 1789: "Do you find it acceptable that some people be endowed with privileges, by law, just because they are members of the aristocracy or the clergy?" Posed in such a compelling manner, her question elicited clear thinking, emotional commitment, a taking of sides. My response was an unequivocal and immediate "No!"

Upon filing into the classroom in the morning, we put on our protective smocks, grey for boys, red gingham for girls. On rainy days, we spread our outer clothes to dry around the coal stove in back of the classroom, with steam soon rising from those clumps of wet woolens.

The oldest boy's first task was to fill the inkwells to the brim, his fingertips soon stained purple. On our desks we found our notebooks, those sacred single repositories of all our work that Madame Mercier had corrected the night before.

There followed about twenty minutes of individual review, with our nose buried in those notebooks where mistakes, if any, had been marked in red for contrast. "Sit up straight, children, if I can't pass my ruler between your desk and your forehead, you'll become nearsighted or hunchbacked" repeated our teacher, as she walked between the rows and assisted the pupils who raised their hand to catch her attention. She trained us to use silent signals, and explained that these strict procedures were necessary to maintain order in the busy classroom—chaos being deemed acceptable only during recess. One time a boy in the back snapped his fingers to call her over. "I'm not your servant," Madame Mercier snapped back, without trying to identify the perpetrator. She went on to explain to the class how disrespectful that gesture had been.

After the perusal of the notebooks, we continued with the first and most important collective lesson of the day, the most interesting too, the one I awaited with great anticipation each time: Morals, ushered in with a summons: "All right everyone, stop what you're doing and listen to me."

From the fables of La Fontaine and other literary texts, or from personal stories and anecdotes, Madame Mercier extracted stirring lessons about virtues and vices, which she preferred to call, less solemnly, "qualities" and "shortcomings." The ethical principles under consideration, often in opposite pairs—for instance generosity contrasted with miserliness—were described with great clarity by our teacher.

Although she repeated these lessons year after year, I never tired of them. I waited in anticipation, if not ambush, to see how she'd present her familiar material each time. She didn't alter the themes, and barely modified the variations, but she added or changed a few details here and there. Through these repetitions, the lessons firmly anchored themselves in our hearts and minds, and taught us patience and perseverance. She was also developing our sensibility to literature, storytelling, and the importance of detail. She said we would continue to appreciate La Fontaine's fables, even as adults, for their freshness and artistic charm. To convince us of that, she compared them to Aesop's versions, from which they were derived. They were the same stories, but told much more vividly by La Fontaine.

Our teacher wrote precise lists of character traits on the blackboard, and expounded on these with examples of good and bad conduct. She presented morals as knowledge: we were being taught to *know* right from wrong. Most distinctions were clear-cut. Very few fell in the gray zone.

I can remember only two ambiguities. One pertained to ambition, which could be viewed as good or bad depending on the context, and the other had to do with pride and vanity. Vanity was an obvious shortcoming, since it did not rest on any worthwhile foundation. Pride too was a shortcoming (*orgueil* in French), but at least, based on admirable or noteworthy achievements, it wasn't empty like vanity, and could therefore be considered acceptable, or even dignified (and in that case be called *fierté*). But excessive or arrogant pride of any kind was deemed reprehensible. Madame Mercier agreed that those distinctions were sometimes difficult to parse.

On the way to school one morning during my third year I was dragging my foot along the hedge of hawthorns, and watching the pearls of dew fall to the ground. Suddenly, in the ditch below, I couldn't believe my eyes, on a spot where the grass seemed trampled, I saw a wet banknote! Instantly, as if by reflex, I lunged down the embankment and put my foot on the bill to keep it to the ground, even though there was no wind. I wanted to hide it from my classmates on the road, and then pick it up discreetly, as if it were an insect or a slug, and decide how to proceed from there—namely keep it, or turn it in.

The answer to my dilemma emerged quickly. With my foot locked on the bill, I heard Madame Mercier's morals lesson on property and honesty echoing in my mind: "This money doesn't belong to you. You must return it." And I also felt my father's gaze bearing down on me from the cemetery up on the hill. The power of those combined judgments wiped out the fleeting desires the windfall had triggered in me, such as the purchase of a bag of marbles, or some comics, or a few tablets of Chocolat Poulain to complete my collection of animal pictures from the wrappers. I decided to turn in the money to Madame Mercier.

When I arrived at school, I stopped in front of our teacher, excitedly gave her the bill, and told her where I had found it. She paused, sucked on her teeth—the characteristic sound she made, a tic really, when she was mulling over something—and then she said:

"In the ditch? Must be some drunkard who lost it there while sleeping off his wine. Since it's impossible to find out who this money belongs to, we'll put it in the school's piggy bank. You'll get an extra point for today."

Madame Mercier's teaching of morals inculcated a code of conduct. For the rest, it was enough to learn how to read, write, and count. We received a clear education, firmly dispensed: "You must, you must not."

"You must maintain a neat notebook. You must not snitch for trivial things." She applied this attitude to spelling. "Be a conformist in the small things, and a rebel in the big ones," is what she said to those who complained. Many years later, she was distressed to hear her adored grandson Jérôme, who was experiencing some difficulties in that sacrosanct subject, quip: *"Mémé, l'orthographe c'est la science des ânes!"* ("Granny, spelling is the science of dunces!")

Another image she employed to describe rules as a form of freedom had to do the emergence of traffic lights in some of France's bigger cities, a new phenomenon she described for us in her geography lessons: "Stop at the red, cross at the green."

In the village, boys wore short pants held up by suspenders, year-round until the age of seven. They also often wore a barrette to keep their hair from flopping down over their eyes. Home haircuts were rare in the village, and visits to the Pacy-sur-Eure barbershop a luxury. After turning seven, as a sign of greater maturity, boys chucked their suspenders for a belt, discarded their barrettes, and could wear long pants if they wished.

Girls didn't go through these major transitions in clothing. They wore skirts or dresses year round, with knee-high socks from November through March, anklets otherwise.

In winter, a thin layer of ice covered the ponds dotting the meadows along the way to school. We must have looked funny during that season, bundled as we were from the waist up, our heads and necks enswathed in woolen "mountain crossing" caps that resembled medieval knights' helmets with slits for the eyes and nose, our hands stuffed in mittens sewn from the fur of rabbits skinned for the traditional Sunday stews. But our legs remained bare like stilts planted in oversized galoshes. Fortunately, since we didn't carry anything, our hands stayed free. We could run or veer off course easily.

One day, American soldiers from the nearby U.S. Air Force base of Evreux appeared at our school for a public relations operation of…delousing. They lined us up in the schoolyard under the linden trees, and an officer nonchalantly handed out to each pupil an entire pack (not one stick but five!) of Wrigley Doublemint gum, the best chewing-gum on earth, sweeter even than the Spearmint tablets the soldiers threw to us from their trucks and jeeps when they passed through the village in long convoys.

That day in the schoolyard, the wealth and generosity of the Americans surpassed all expectations. We would be able, supreme luxury, to chew two, three sticks at once, puff up our cheeks, dislocate our jaws, gladly risk choking on that gum, so great was the pleasure it provided.

After allowing us to masticate for a while, the soldiers ordered us, with easily understood gestures, to spit out our gum and trample it into the gravel-covered ground. But before our reluctance to obey their command could evolve into a mutiny, they changed tactics and demonstrated how to temporarily save that precious delicacy, by sticking it to the collarbone, under our clothing. Then they ordered us to close our eyes and mouth, squeeze our nose shut, and hold our breath while, with a hand pump, they sprayed us from head to toe with a fine white powder resembling talcum, a miracle cure for lice they said. They called it in their language "*DiDiTi*," whereas we pronounced it "*DéDéTé.*" For good measure Madame Mercier was sprayed too, and the soldiers themselves ended up looking like the breadmaker of Pacy, covered with flour as he worked around his brick oven on top of which his companions, a multitude of crickets, warmed themselves.

Lice disappeared after this procedure, but returned several months later. We expected another chewing gum and powder session, but the American soldiers didn't repeat their wonderful visit.

There was another event of note at our school, this one occurring on a yearly basis during the fall term: the medical exam. It had an unpleasant beginning, consisting of various vaccinations administered by a nurse, but also a pleasant yet embarrassing finish. Boys were checked in the morning, girls in the afternoon, every year by the same woman doctor dressed in white. We waited for our turn single file, naked except for our socks and briefs, in the drafty community center reeking of ether that day. Each time, it was the same wordless procedure in the private consulting room at the end of the line, for myself and I presume the other boys too, although we didn't talk about it.

After having checked various parts of my body with her stethoscope and other instruments, and written on my chart as I could observe from the corner of my eye "Insufficient weight—Protruding shoulder blades," the doctor looked away to the side, as if suddenly disinterested by my presence, and in a one-two motion, pulled forward on the elastic waistband of my underwear with her left hand, while with her right hand she reached inside and cupped my testicles. I knew it was probably impolite, but each time, as soon as she pulled on the waistband, my zizi stood up. She pretended not to notice and so did I, but I felt a bit embarrassed.

Inside the classroom, the big political map of the world featured two predominant colors: pink for the French colonial empire, yellow for the British. The continent of Africa was almost entirely covered in these two shades. We learned the names of the rivers, major towns, tribes, and languages of *Afrique Occidentale Française* and *Afrique Équatoriale Française*, but none of us had ever actually seen a black person.

And then one day, on the sidewalk in front of the school grounds, an African man appeared, in colorful native clothing, and just stayed there, apparently waiting for something. He was wearing a long robe embroidered at the neck, and a bright fez on his head. We were mesmerized, and we all gazed at him from a distance, as if he was a Martian. Madame Mercier told us to stop gawking and instead continue on with our recess activities. She then asked me to run to the gate and convey a message to the man: "*Milan, va dire au monsieur que l'arrêt d'autobus pour Paris est plus loin sur la route, près de la mairie de Pacy.*" ("Milan, go tell the gentleman that the bus stop for Paris is further up the road, near the town hall of Pacy.")

"*Va dire au monsieur*" ("go tell the gentleman"), her use of that term completely erased the alien perception I had of the stranger, and instead turned him into someone no different than any Frenchman named Dupont or Durand, despite his charcoal-black skin and his exotic accouterment.

Unbeknownst to me then, I had just learned from our teacher a great civics lesson that I would remember all my life, about respect and consideration. Also implicit in her attitude was a veiled condemnation of colonialism, an ideology as abhorrent to the enlightened values of the Republic as the American founders' acceptance of slavery. Like these hallowed figures, though, we were prisoners of our times.

Madame Mercier parading her spiffed up brood through Pacy-sur-Eure on Bastille Day (Olga in back tallest; me in 3rd row middle). Photo courtesy Josette Le Bon.

Chapter 6

Laundry Day

"Richness of poverty!"

— *Sister Emmanuelle*

*I*n the space of ten short years, roughly 1955 to 1965, the rural France in which I grew up changed radically, some say more than during the previous five centuries. At midpoint in that decade, Jean-Pierre Chabrol, a chronicler of peasant life, encapsulated our generation's experience in two sentences: "We knew those who still knew how to make soup. We will know those who will go to the moon." Echoing this view, Jean Malaurie, publisher of the *Terre Humaine* anthropological collection, told researchers in his field that the vanishing peasant culture so close to home deserved their attention fully as much as distant Amazonia.

The transformations brought about by the sudden advent of modernity into the archaic world of my childhood were mostly for the good (I greatly appreciate indoor plumbing, adequate heating, and improved medical care, among other creature comforts), but some paradoxical outcomes have also ensued. For instance, we now generate appalling amounts of garbage compared to that period, and we utilize more and more labor-saving devices, yet we seem to have less and less…Time, which seemed to be an infinite commodity back then.

Never mind that we don't *wash* clothes anymore; we can barely find the time to *load* our programmable washing machines. Whenever I encounter that predicament, I am transported back to a particular laundry day in the household of my elderly guardians in Saint-Aquilin:

"Milan, today I'd like to wash the sheets. It's a big job. Do you think you can help me?"

"Oh yes, Mémère, yes, yes."

Something to do at last! I've been oppressed by boredom ever since summer vacation began, three long weeks ago, at the end of third grade.

"Okay then, get the washtub from the shed. I'm going to boil them."

"But it's got a hole in it."

"No, it's been fixed. The potmender came through Saint-Aquilin while you were still in school."

In the shed connecting the house to the chicken coop, I find my tabby cat Zaza sprawled out on a bale of straw under a ray of sunlight crisscrossed by tiny specks of dust. She stretches and purrs to acknowledge my presence, but, too comfortable or lazy, doesn't bother to open her eyes.

Our other cats, less domesticated than Zaza, are roaming the fields. Sometimes they vanish for several days in a row. Sometimes too, new toms appear from nowhere, install themselves in the shed, and stare at me defiantly when I discover them curled up in a corner, as if I were the intruder. All those vagabonds manage to find their way to the front of our house, though, every Thursday. They gather there in fretful, meowing anticipation—as if a lookout had alerted them—to await the arrival of the butcher from Pacy-sur-Eure. His delivery van stops weekly at our doorstep after wending its way through the village; but we seldom buy anything from him, relying instead on our chickens and rabbits for meat.

"So, The Widow Vermot, what can I get for you today? Do you want me to cut you up three nice little slices of steak, tender enough even for you to chew? If your wallet's a bit thin, no problem, I'll put it on your tab and you can pay me next week, or when your old man gets a hold of some money."

And to amuse himself while his elderly client tries to decide, the butcher throws out a few pieces of lung meat to fuel the frenzy of the cats. In the past, two of them, overeager or distracted, already lost their lives under the wheels of the departing vehicle.

At our house, we never feed the cats. It's a rule. "Otherwise they get lazy and stop chasing mice," says Pépère. Occasionally, though, I sneak a saucer of milk to Zaza, the survivor, my favorite. She ensures continuity and permanence in our menagerie, and she alone is allowed to enter the house, only during the day. The other cats come and go, disappear, give birth in the shed to kittens who, no sooner discovered, their eyelids still closed, are executed by Pépère, when not already murdered by the marauding toms. He hurls the poor little beasts one by one against the wall of the house, our wall of lamentations, or else drowns them all together in a potato sack tossed in the river. Among the litters, a few chosen individuals are sometimes spared, for replacement. But woe onto the sick, lame, or wounded cats. Pépère's merciful club soon puts them out of their misery: "Animals shouldn't suffer," he says.

In the shed, amidst the jumble, I rescue the galvanized washtub with its banged up sides and patched bottom, buried under a mound of fragrant alfalfa. We use the tub not only for laundry, but for my baths too, when we feel up to it, every couple of weeks or so, depending on the season. In summer, I just soap up in the river.

Personal hygiene at our house is limited to the bare essentials. For me, a splash of water on the face, at the hand pump outside in the morning, even in winter when I have to break the icicle that has formed overnight at the spout. From time to time, a quick wipe behind the knees, at the crease of the elbows, and inside the socks down to the ankles. At school our teacher Madame Mercier occasionally inspects those strategic parts of our bodies for grime. Good thing she doesn't ask us to remove our galoshes to check between our toes.

Mémère usually waits till afternoon to wash. She can't endure the cold water at the pump because of her facial neuralgic pains. Instead, she warms it up on the coal stove in the kitchen, removes her bonnet and glasses and runs a damp washcloth over her face. Then she pats her cheeks and forehead dry with the thin waffle cloth towel, lights up a cigarette, and, blinking to avoid the smoke, unfurls her bun to comb her long white hair, which at that moment gives her a strange, demented look, like a benevolent witch.

Pépère's ablutions consist mainly of soaping up his face and neck with a shaving brush on Sundays. Installed on his chair at the end of the kitchen table around which we spend most of our waking hours, he sharpens the blade of his straight razor with the whetstone nestled inside the bull's horn hanging on the wall. It's the same sharpening stone that he carries on his belt to the fields with his scythe. He twists his mouth, puffs up his cheeks, cranes his neck, tests the blade against his throat, which he pretends to slash across in order to provoke the usual, nervous "Careful! Don't cut yourself!" from Mémère. Soon, prickly white stubble floats at the surface of the bowl that only moments earlier contained his morning chicory.

How fresh and prim he looks when, the ceremony completed, he reaches from his chair to open the window and dump the contents of the bowl on the sidewalk. He then inspects himself one last time in the mirror before hooking it up on the wall until the next Sunday.

But Pépère's weekly procedure also involves a second phase, much more dramatic than the first. After a brief pause and a swig of applejack brandy to strengthen his resolve, he proceeds to change the bandages wrapped around his legs from the ankles to the knees, like the infantrymen of World War I. He has three large varicose ulcers, two on the left calf, one on the right. When he rolls up his heavy twill pants, he notes that the bandages from the preceding Sunday are as usual stained with pus. "Damn it, those bastards are oozing again. If it makes you sick, don't look," he warns Mémère and me.

Pépère curses while he slowly unfurls the bandages. He then insults and cajoles the lesions and gnashes his teeth at the fateful moment when he must tear the gauze away from the raw flesh: "You slut, you bitch, you whore, easy now sweetheart, easy honey, gently, there, there, we've got it, it's done." After a sigh of relief, he leans down and blows softly over the wounds to appease the flaming pain, while I stand at the ready with the bottle of applejack in case he signals with an impatient gesture to give him "Another shot, quick!"

Thanks to the small monthly money order from his eldest son Pierre, who is a career enlisted man in the French Navy, Pépère doesn't have to save the bandages and reuse them after a difficult washing. With his long reach, he disposes of the soiled dressings directly into the kitchen stove, where they ignite with a crackling sound on the glowing embers. Following another brief respite, he cleans his calves with absorbent cotton soaked in ether, taking great care not to brush against the gaping flesh, else he would scream with pain. The kitchen takes on the smell of a hospital, not so much unpleasant as disturbing, a sensory reminder that matters of grave medical consequence are at hand.

All three of us having recovered from the initial shock of this weekly procedure—in my case with the help of a few sugar cubes imbibed in apple-jack—Mémère, Pépère and I closely examine those calves gnawed to the bone. We then express our collective assessment: No, the size of the ulcers hasn't changed since the preceding Sunday. This observation, the same every week since my earliest recollections, discourages us once more, but reassures us at the same time. A cruel legend has it that a decrease in the size of the wounds means that the Grim Reaper is lurking nearby.

Except for those horrible ulcers and other aches and pains that keep him awake at night, Pépère is in reasonably good health for his age—which means he's still able to keep working. There is no such thing as retirement in our peasant world. You work until you can't, and then you die.

After extracting the washtub from the shed, I take it to the pump under the lilac tree to rinse out the cobwebs. I then bring it to the kitchen and place it on the stove for Mémère:

"All right, son, now please fill it to about half. Me, I'm going to stoke up the fire."

I scurry back and forth between the pump outside and the kitchen, carrying the water in half-filled buckets to avoid splashing on the floor.

When the boiling point is reached, Mémère dunks the sheets in the washtub and pokes at them with Pépère's old walking stick. She has salvaged it from the shed, and uses it to lean on and feel the ground in front of her when she walks in the garden. She doesn't see well, and it makes her dizzy to raise and lower her eyes to look where she steps. Pépère has cut a newer, stronger cane for himself, from a branch he found on the path up the hill after a thunderstorm, near the cemetery.

The kitchen fills with steam. "Quick, Milan, open the window, but don't make any drafts."

Mémère swallows a few breaths of fresh air, coughs, wheezes, hungrily relights her cigarette butt to reward herself for our accomplishments thus far: "Say, son, let's make us some coffee, the real stuff, not chicory. You can also take a jar of it to Pépère out back in the field. He is hoeing potatoes. It'll do him good to drink some java and plop down on his butt for a while."

The "field" is the potato patch, located just behind our vegetable garden. Its owner, Madame Bricout, rents it out to us, along with the house, for a symbolic annual fee, more like charity. It's a godsend for Pépère to be able to grow his potatoes so close to home and in large enough quantity for the whole year.

In the field, I find Pépère working on his knees. Tall, strong, and straight like a tree when he is standing in his wooden clogs ("It's not Old Man Lepais we'll ever see as a hunchback" they say of him in the village), he nonetheless has lost all his flexibility. He tries to avoid bending to the earth for long stretches of time because it's hard for him to straighten up afterwards. That's why he works on his knees whenever possible. Mémère has given him an old burlap bag to protect his pants from the wear and tear of direct contact with the ground. She no longer sees well enough to mend his clothes.

When I arrive with the coffee, the giant raises himself up slowly, takes off his cap, wipes his brow with his sleeve. A sharp horizontal line runs across his forehead, tanned leathery skin below the groove, clammy white above. We sit on the collapsed stone wall separating our potato patch from the property of the neighbors, a rich Parisian family whose country residence in the village is tended by Monsieur and Madame Bourlat, a live-in gardener and housekeeper couple. Pépère sips his coffee, still burning hot in the mustard jar wrapped in a handkerchief, while I admire the shiny white Jaguar sports car parked on the other side of the crumbling wall, next to the terrace with a colorful parasol over it.

Without a word, in the good heat of this summer morning, the air cloudless and still, birds chirping, insects buzzing, a dog barking in the distance, Pépère and I share a moment of peace and contentment, tinged with sadness about the huge tragedy that recently befell the Bourlats. Their son Jacques had come home on leave from military service in Indochina, after a month-long voyage to the seaport of Toulon, through the Indian Ocean, the Suez Canal, and the Mediterranean. During his stay in Saint-Aquilin, I saw him many times working side by side with his father in their garden. He had an excellent reputation in the village as someone who helped others and caused no trouble. And then the horrifying news: in Toulon, on the way back to the colonies in the Far East, before he even got on board ship, Jacques had been stabbed to death by a fellow soldier in a barroom brawl. Everyone in the village was shocked and repulsed by the horror and absurdity of it all.

After he finishes sipping his coffee, Pépère pulls from inside the stained rim of his cap the plug of chewing tobacco that's always lodged there. He cuts off a piece, wedges it under his gum, spits, rubs his hands vigorously, grabs his hoe. "All right, son, now back to the taters. Thanks for the java, it did me good."

When I return to the house, Mémère announces that we will wait till afternoon to take the sheets to the wash house by the river for the soaping, brushing, beating, rinsing procedure: "We have to let the water cool off anyway; meanwhile, you can get the wheelbarrow ready. Me, I'm going to make the beds."

In the bedroom adjoining the kitchen, where our two beds are set up—a regular one for Pépère and Mémère, a cot for me, both with with straw mattresses—Mémère opens the creaky door of the massive wardrobe. A stack of neatly folded sheets is piled in there, remnants of her ancient Norman bridal trousseau, I suppose. Made of rough linen, hard wearing and tinted with minute particles of grey and brown fibers, they hardly ever show dirt.

A flutter of wings: the ruler of the henhouse, an uppity rooster, appears on the ledge of the open window. He struts back and forth, surveys the inside of the bedroom, turns away to scrutinize his cackling brood pecking at the ground below. His crest looks iridescent in the sunlight. Fortunately for him, he doesn't dare enter the room. It's bad enough that he wakes us up at dawn. Nothing unusual about that: we go to bed at about the same time as the chickens, especially in winter. So, why shouldn't we also get up with them in the morning? By habit, though, Pépère always swears at the irritating beast: "You bastard, if you don't shut up, I'm gonna twist your neck, you'll see." Mémère intervenes: "Leave him alone. It's not his fault, it's nature's way. Besides, I like to wake up to his *cocorico* better than to the ringing of an alarm clock. With the shutters closed, we don't know what time it is."

Pépère's ire at the rooster doesn't run deep. I saw him lose his temper only once, on a Sunday morning when he wanted to sleep in a bit longer. That day, succumbing to irritation, he leaped up from bed as if he had forgotten his aches and pains, and, flinging the shutters open, he emptied the chamber pot on the head of the astounded bird.

The trek to the washhouse will distract me today from the tedious routine since the start of vacation. Usually, after I finish my morning chores of feeding the chickens and the rabbits, and helping Mémère air out the bedding on the windowsill, I climb up to the highest branch of my apple tree to daydream and contemplate the village. It's divided in half by two-lane *Route Nationale 13* meandering like a river through the surrounding hills and meadows on its way to Paris, 55 miles to the Southeast.

I know the exact distance, having covered it several times already aboard the Citroën bus. Twice a year or so, I spend a few days with Maman in Paris at her new place of work. The first time she waited for me at the end of the line, Porte Maillot, but since then, I manage from there by myself, "like a big boy," the adults say. I stay with her at the mansion of the Kapferers, the employers with whom she hired on following her breakup with the Lavrils. They live about a twenty-minute walk from Porte Maillot, at 64 Avenue Henri-Martin. When I get there, I have to stretch to reach the doorbell at the entrance: three short rings, two long ones, and the concierge, Monsieur Allais, recognizing the Morse code for household members, releases the front gate from his lodgings.

Maman always awaits me with my favorite snacks, in summer a slice of Parma ham from Signore Rossi's Italian delicatessen on nearby Rue de la Pompe, served with a trace of tarragon vinegar and followed by the sweetest Cavaillon melon. But for me the height of luxury is not so much her exquisite food, nor the unusual features of the mansion, such as the dumbwaiter from her ground-floor kitchen to the dining room above, nor the antiques in the various salons, nor the paintings from Monsieur Kapferer's collection of great masters, Van Gogh, Renoir, Bonnard and others adorning the marble main staircase. While these things are nice, they don't compare to the fourth-floor bathroom, which is all mine the first night of my stays. Not only does it have running water, but hot and cold as well. Heaven on earth! The walls, floor, and ceiling are covered with gleaming white ceramic tile, and the claw foot bathtub is surrounded by a waterproof curtain. The showerhead can be hand-held or hooked up high, and its flow adjusted from a trickle, to a fine spray, or a downpour like I imagine Niagara Falls would be. I'm also given a large terry cloth towel, incredibly thick and absorbent compared to the skimpy waffle cloth in Saint-Aquilin. I can use as much water as I want, and wallow in the tub as long as I like. If, impossible dream, I could transpose Pépère, Mémère, and Zaza to 64 Avenue Henri-Martin, life would be perfect...

Paris is so enticing! I feel irresistibly drawn to the city. I love to walk aimlessly along its narrow streets and wide boulevards, or plunge into the labyrinth of the métro and exit anywhere I want to explore. The possibilities seem infinite. But what an ordeal, the three-hour trip on the slow bus between my village and the spellbinding metropolis. Each time, it never fails, I get motion sickness. I don't know why. The fumes maybe. I didn't have that problem when riding in front in Monsieur Lavril's car.

During one of my previous journeys on the bus to Paris, a quick-thinking kindly priest in long black robes, seated next to me, mercifully extended his beret at the desperate last moment when I could no longer hold back my nausea. Everyone around us laughed at his charitable gesture and the loss of his beret, which he tossed out the window without showing the slightest sign of disgust. That day, awed by my seatmate's saintly act, I vowed never again to caw defiantly like a crow when I encountered a priest on the road, as Pépère had taught me to do, in the anticlerical tradition of Saint-Aquilin. The village church was destroyed during the Revolution, but the religious name remained.

In my daily routine of vacation, after the interlude of daydreaming in the apple tree, I climb back down to earth and begin to inspect anew the mysterious roll of film I found in the ditch on the way home from school the last day of classes. The roll was lying there, half unfurled in wet grass below the hedge of hawthorns.

Since then, I have been trying to pierce the secrets of photography, to extract an image, a glimmer, a shadow, anything, from this enigmatic roll. In vain. Each day, I dunk it, first in cold water drawn from the pump, then in a slightly warmer bath from the barrel set up under the gutter dangling from the roof. We no longer use that rainwater since Olga left for Paris, where she works as a live-in housekeeper. During her two years in Saint-Aquilin, she washed her hair with it. She said the soap foamed better that way.

Sometimes, I dry the film on the clothesline under the sun, sometimes I hang it in the soft shade of the lilac tree. I've even tried adding a little vinegar for a rinse, like Olga did with her hair. Nothing works, the surface of the film remains shiny on one side, opaque on the other. I'm beginning to accept that there are some things I'll never understand. I sense that I'll soon stop these futile experiments, and that I'll chuck this damn roll of film where it belongs, on the dung heap in the garden. And yet there are people who manage to extract pictures from these long strips of plastic marked "Kodak." How in the world do they do it? What is their secret?

Abandoning the impossible, I usually proceed, on these idle vacation days, to a more rewarding endeavor that erases my frustrations and rebuilds my confidence. In the hallway, near the door to the cellar, I fling my beautiful blue Peugeot bicycle—the gift from Madame Lavril on my sixth birthday—upside down on its saddle and handlebars. Its lion's head insignia is similar to the emblem of my family's country of origin, Czechoslovakia. I learned to ride it quickly, soon with no hands, but nearly killed myself one day when I braked hard and landed on my head after flipping over the handlebars. It's only when I was questioned about the accident by a passing motorist who stopped by to help, that I learned you're supposed to brake first with the right hand, and then the left.

Despite this early mishap, I love my bike. I have now figured out all its innards. Almost daily, armed with the wrench and screwdriver that came in a leather pouch hooked to the saddle, I take apart the marvelous machine. Nuts, bolts, chain, wheel bearings, mud guards, crank arms soon litter the floor of the hallway. The frame looks naked and grotesque, with its arms and legs paying dumb homage to the ceiling. I then proceed to clean, oil, and re-install the parts, simply for the renewed pleasure of verifying each time their precise mechanical arrangement.

And that's all, until evening chores. Meanwhile boredom assails me, at once sweet and oppressive.

I have only one real friend in the village, Jeannot, but he's a year younger than me. Furthermore, he is not interested in what fascinates me most: classification, a quest for order and clarity in all things.

That quest can be easy: Is the Nile longer than the Amazon? (Yes, by 258 km). What is the biggest city in the world? (New York, U.S.A., pop. 8,343,000). Etc. The answers to those kinds of questions are clear. I simply looked them up in the dictionary at school.

Or the questions can be much more complicated: "Who's the strongest animal in the jungle?" I say the lion, of course; my friend Jeannot says the tiger; and neither of us can prove he's right.

Another impossible question that preoccupies me, and completely stumps Jeannot: "When he was named commander in chief of all allied forces in 1918, did Marshall Foch usurp the glory owed to Joffre?"

Although we're now in 1950, *my* war is the old one, the great one, the First World War, 1914 – 1918. Pépère talks about it sometimes, with reluctance at first, but with increased animation when I prod him. He was an artillery gunner in a 75mm battery: "You know, son, war is hell, but your learn a lot of things in the Army."

The war had brought about Pépère's only visit to Paris in his lifetime, when he was drafted at the age of 33. The front was another story: "Our cannons pounded the Krauts, but they hit us hard too. The only factor in all that was luck, pure and simple luck. At least our situation wasn't as bad as that of the infantry grunts in the trenches. There, they had to endure the butchery of shrapnel, and the mud, and the rats, plus on top of all that the clouds of mustard gas. Those who didn't die lost their minds, or their arms and legs, or their faces. Just look around at all the cripples and the disfigured *Gueules Cassées*. Our motto was: 'They will not pass.' Finally we won, but at what cost? And when you see what happened twenty years later! What a disgrace! It's clear, in 1940 France was sold out by its corrupt politicians, a lazy breed that doesn't know what real work is. They spend their lives making speeches and attending banquets. We should make them toil like us, with a pick and a shovel. That would straighten them out. And if they start wars, they should be the first to go to the front."

I love to hear Pépère's rants and pronouncements. His negative attitude toward reading ("You're going to ruin your eyes") is the only source of tension between us. It's too bad, because otherwise we get along great. I would love to head out with him like two vagabonds, carrying a bundle on our shoulders— the way we did when we once went to visit his clan in the town of Dreux.

At school, Madame Mercier has introduced me to the *Petit Larousse Illustré* dictionary, which has become my favorite book. But there is only one copy of it, and it has to stay on the premises. At home, the place where I can relax and read is the attic. There, one floor above the kitchen stove around which Mémère shuffles all day, I open the shutters to let in the light, and sit back comfortably against the mound of German artillery shells and machine-gun belts stored there by Pépère. He gathered these abandoned munitions from the surrounding hills after the American advance through Normandy in 1944, and then piled them up in the attic for "safe storage," and the eventual resale value of the brass casings. Since then, he hasn't gone up there and has seemingly forgotten about this arsenal amassed under our roof. Accompanied by Zaza who purrs on my lap, I plunge yet again into a new reading of my stack of *L'Illustration* magazines, fabulous trove of images discovered in a corner of the attic long ago, and rediscovered with magnified pleasure after I learned to read in Madame Mercier's classroom. Verdun, the Marne, the Somme, the Poilus, the Dragoons, the Tommies, the trenches, the Dardanelles, Big Bertha, the Krauts with pointed helmets—I know by heart the entire 1914 – 18 saga. The dreaded Uhlans, descendants of Attila the Hun, can charge with sabers high, I have no fear, they will be repelled by our brave cavalry. The French are invincible. It's enough to look at Pépère's fists, big like bludgeons.

My military folklore thus constructs itself in the glorious pages of *L'Illustration*, sanitized of any gore in spite of their exclusive war content. The sight of a porcupine run over on the road haunts me for days, but a photograph of a squad of soldiers ensnared in barbed wire, and mowed down by machine gun fire, is somehow made to look heroic in the pages of the magazine.

The most disturbing objects in the mishmash of the attic are not the mounds of live munitions piled up there, but the three gas masks lying in a corner. I hate the stifling airless feeling you get when you wear them, but I sometimes put one on anyway, to scare myself, and because it feels so good when I take it off. Pépère says that although these ugly contraptions weren't used in 39-45, we should keep them around for the next war, just in case. "Never two without three" he declares, and predicts that the next time it'll be the Russians and the Americans who'll fight each other, with us getting tangled in the middle.

When I take the wheelbarrow for Mémère's laundry out of the shed, I see Pépère in the potato patch shielding his eyes to check whether the sun is at its peak. "Lunchtime!" he shouts, and pulls out his pocket watch to confirm the call of his stomach. He leans on his fists and pushes himself backwards off the ground, like a powerful gorilla. With a stiff gait, he heads for the house. His wooden clogs resonate on the dry path. At the garden hedge, he grabs a handful of currants, and swallows them in one gulp. With a few swings of the pump handle, he fills the bucket and plunges his craggy paws into it. He admires the graceful plume unfolding from his loam-covered fingers into the clear water. When the spiral has dissolved, he vigorously rubs his palms, splashes his face, emits loud snorts like a walrus.

In the kitchen whose shutters are half closed to hold back the noonday heat, flies buzz around until silenced by the sticky strip hanging from the ceiling. While Mémère serves up the stew, I go down to the cellar to draw a bottle of cider from the barrel. It's not real apple cider, but a slightly sour beverage, a mixture that Pépère concocts every month. It would probably be better to drink clear water from the pump, but that idea doesn't even come to us, as if drinking water was a bizarre notion. Once a week, though, I fill up our two bottles of red wine at the village grocer's, where I love the acidic smell floating around the cask. On special holidays we treat ourselves to hard cider, the champagne of our region.

Pépère yanks open the iron blade of his faithful Opinel knife, and cuts three slices from the crusty loaf of bread on the table.

"Not for me," says Mémère, "I don't dare eat any, because of my loose stump."

"Do you want me to pull it out with the pliers? Like that you'd be rid of it quickly," replies Pépère.

"No, anyway, it's my last one, I'd rather wait till it falls out by itself."

"As you wish."

To finish the meal, we savor a piece of camembert cheese, with "two fingers" of red wine. "Too bad we don't have strawberries or cherries anymore," says Mémère, "but pretty soon we'll have apples again."

I love the seasonal unfolding of fruits and vegetables, even in winter, when Belgian endives and Jerusalem artichokes still grow in the garden. Maman also occasionally sends us packages of bananas and oranges on the bus from Paris, along with Slovakian pastries and caramel candy that she makes from melted sugar. Thanks to the vegetable garden, the potato patch, the rabbits, the chickens, and Maman's treats from Paris, Pépère says we can survive on very little money.

While Mémère puts our chipped earthenware plates and warped tin forks in the dishpan, Pépère pulls his tobacco pouch from the drawer and rolls two cigarettes. They're neither smooth nor round because the tobacco is of the cheapest kind, with twigs sticking out.

The paper at the hollowed end of Mémère's cigarette bursts into flame at the touch of her match. She winces: "Nothing against you, Old Man, but I much prefer my store-bought Gauloises or Caporals, when I can afford them."

Like Pépère, Mémère has long ago given up on doctors, who are powerless against her ailments. Her chain-smoking habit results from her last medical prescription, when Pacy's physician, Dr. Mollard, visited her at home:

"Old Lady Vermot, to appease your neuralgic pains, since nothing else seems to work, why don't you try smoking. I would recommend a pipe."

"Me, smoke a pipe! No way, doctor! Never! What would I look like? But I'll try cigarettes, indoors only, in private."

Thick blue clouds stretch lazily across the inert kitchen air. Smoking looks so relaxing.

"All right, I'm going back to the potatoes, see you later," says Pépère, pushing his chair from the table. "But first, to pamper my feet, I'm going to stuff my clogs with fresh straw. While I'm at it, I can change the mattresses too. We'll sleep better tonight."

Mémère interrupts: "I've already made the beds and put on clean sheets. We'll change the straw in the mattresses next time. Let's all instead take a nap. The sun out there is beating down pretty hard. Better not go out before two o'clock."

"You're right," says Pépère, "we're not used to this kind of heat in Normandy."

I'm never eager to take a nap, but this time, no sooner said than done, we literally hit the hay. Pépère removes only his wooden clogs. He lies straight on his back, his hands folded on his chest like a mummy. Mémère curls up as usual on her side of their bed.

The stiff clean sheets at first offer a welcomed resistance over my sunken straw mattress, but the rough linen soon loses its rigidity. As I begin to doze off and lose sight of the moving shadows on the wall, Mémère's voice breaks the quiet:

"Pépère, you're snoring. Roll over on your side."

"No, I'm not snoring. Stop nagging."

"Milan, can you believe that? He's not snoring!"

I chuckle, and attempt not to take sides in their squabble, the only one they ever have. I'm so used to Pépère's snoring that I no longer even notice it.

"Turn over on your side," Mémère asks him again.

"No, I can't, it makes my shoulder sore," he protests.

Attracted by the exchange, the rooster leaps up on the window ledge again. He proceeds with his usual routine, examines the room from his favorite perch. The hens cackle below. I drift into sleep.

When Pépère snores and Mémère complains, at least I'm reassured that at that moment they're not thinking about the "damned pains" that assail them in the silence and immobility of night. They say they are partially delivered from these torments only by the reemerging activities of dawn. They envy me for sleeping so soundly even in the midst of thunderstorms. Along with our early-to-bed habit, this release from pain is probably one of the reasons we get up so early, except on Sundays and holidays.

On those special days, after opening the shutters, we grant ourselves an extra snooze for an hour or so. And when we do finally rise, holidays are marked only by the simplest rituals of embrace and good wishes: "Merry Christmas," "Happy New Year," "Happy Easter," "Happy Bastille Day." That's all, no rigamarole, no exchange of gifts, just plain, genuine, strongly felt affection. Pépère insists: "You have to keep life simple." Maybe that's why we don't bother to celebrate birthdays, in addition to the fact that it would be presumptuous: "Who do you think you are?"

At Christmastime in the village, the town crier of Pacy gathers everyone with a solemn drum roll, and distributes food packages to the poor and the elderly. The hot wine served to the morning visitors—according to an ancient protocol, the "ambulatory people" stop by to pay their respects to the "old folks and invalids"—and the rabbit stew at lunch, with a bottle of hard cider, are our only other traditions on festive days.

When I awaken from the afternoon nap, I glimpse Mémère's silhouette on the yellowed mirror of the massive, slightly leaning oak wardrobe. She has let her hair down to comb it. Pépère is already gone to the potato patch.

"Milan, Pépère loaded the tub and the sheets on the wheelbarrow before he left. Are you all set to go to the washhouse? I don't think you can take your fishing pole, we already have too much to drag along. It's too bad because there are plenty of maggots for bait in the piece of cheese I set aside for that."

Our journey gets under way. A distance of about three hundred yards separates us from the washhouse, starting with the path across Pépère's potato patch. I have a hard time balancing the wheelbarrow, with Mémère following me and clutching my shoulder.

"Don't walk too fast, it's hard to keep up with you," she mutters. She is wearing house slippers and she drags her feet against the clumpy edge of the path. Because of her bunions and twisted toes, that's the only footwear she tolerates.

"Mémère, walk in the middle. You're going to fall or sprain your ankle." I try not to sound too much like a scold.

"I can't," she pleads, "if I walk in the middle I'll stumble into your feet and trip you."

As we pass by him, Pépère yells out in a mocking tone: "Are you sure you don't need a horse and a cart to haul your laundry?" We laugh at his remark and continue on our way.

All of a sudden, just as we're about to reach the main path to the washhouse, Mémère grabs my arm:

"Stop. I can feel it breaking off."

"What? What's the matter?"

"My stump," she says. "Don't move, it's coming out."

She reaches into her mouth with her thumb and index finger, rocks her head back and forth:

"There, there it goes, I've got it, it's gone."

She extracts a brownish tooth from her mouth, brandishes it victoriously, brings it to a few inches from her glasses, inspects it with a mixture of joy, pride, and disgust, and throws it away with a shrug. "Ah, good riddance. What a relief. No more teeth, it's over. Now I'll have peace, at least in that department. Can we sit down somewhere?"

I lead Mémère towards an old tree trunk collapsed on the side of the path. She pats the smooth, comforting bark, clears her throat, spits out some blood, reaches instinctively for the cigarettes in her apron, changes her mind: "No, I'm not about to start smoking outdoors, like some floozy. Are we still far from the washhouse? Let's keep going."

Mémère sees only up close, thanks to her triple-thick glasses. She never reads, though it's not clear whether that's due to her poor eyesight, or because she doesn't know how. For that and for writing, she defers to Pépère. She can't make out the row of poplars that, about a hundred yards away, marks the tributary stream where the washhouse is located.

After crossing the narrow stone bridge, we arrive at our destination. Struggling down the wash house steps, we pull, tug, drag the heavy metal tub with the wet sheets, and I go back up to the wheelbarrow for the brush, the paddle, and the brick-sized bar of Marseilles soap.

Mémère is glad that we're alone down there today. She's not a talkative person, although she doesn't mind hearing village gossip, mostly from her sister, the Widow Samson, who lives down the street from us at the opposite end of Saint-Aquilin.

"All right, now I'll manage by myself," she sighs. "You can go for a walk and return in a while."

I climb back up the washhouse steps, and seeing no trace of the fearsome Delagoutte bull that we Saint-Aquilin children are supposed to avoid at all cost even if we don't wear red, I crawl under the fence to cross the meadow separating the Eure River from its gentle confluent. Three cows are standing in a huddle, motionless except for their tails shooing flies away in lazy strokes. They watch me pass by while they placidly chew their cud. A fresh, grassy smell rises from the cow pies splattered here and there on the ground. I dodge around them on my way to the river, and avoid the thistles, whose prickly stems cast bluish hues against the emerald sheen of the meadow.

On the bank of the Eure, the clump of hazel trees leaning over the water offers me the familiar shelter of its tangled branches. From this leafy vantage point, I watch the current flow below. At once beguiling gurgle and dark depth, the stream mesmerizes and frightens me. If I should fall, I risk, says the legend, to be sucked in and disappear forever in one of the whirlpools whose imprints disrupt here and there the smooth surface of the river. At the bottom of the water, among the reeds, a large pike illuminated by a ray of sunlight remains immobile against the current, its fins taut, as if rising from the depths of time. Dragonflies frolic in joyous zigzags towards the raft of water lilies anchored near the shore. Ploop! A frog dives in, limbs outstretched to pierce the water without splash. On the other side of the small island hiding the mysterious "beach" of Pacy, where I have never gone, a boy shouts:

"Look, *Papa*, look at me, I'm floating, quick, look at me!"

His yells remind me of another enigma, as mysterious as the roll of film: How does one learn to swim?

When I return to the washhouse, Mémère has already finished her work. Seated on the bottom step of the stone stairwell, she puts out her cigarette and stashes away the butt behind her ear. Dragging the heavy tub back up, one step at a time, proves even more strenuous and cumbersome than going down.

We reload everything onto the wheelbarrow, and head back home. Just before we cross the small bridge, Mémère stops to take a breath. She grips my arm, tighter than usual:

"You know, Milan, today was the last time. It's too hard. We won't be going to the washhouse anymore."

Pépère and Mémère.

Chapter 7

Payday at the Village Tavern

"There are two or three men in the village who normally don't drink,
but who go on a binge once or twice a year... For five or six days, you see
them amble from village to village...And suddenly they stop drinking, they
return to their homes and their jobs,...faultless heads of household, until
the next bender. And they're probably right to purge their heads through
their stomachs. Others have been known to leave home one day without
warning, carried away by who knows what latent nostalgia or despair their
excessive sobriety hadn't managed to overcome. Those don't return."

— *Pierre Jakez-Hélias, The Horse of Pride*

Seated at the kitchen window, Mémère pulls aside the curtain and anxiously scrutinizes the street. Through the haze of her thick eyeglasses, she tries in vain to detect the silhouette of her man. She cups her hand over her ear, listens intently for the sound of his wooden clogs on the pavement. Nothing. Our tabby cat Zaza, standing on Mémère's lap with her front paws on the window sill, stares in the same direction and with the same worried look as her mistress.

"Milan, it's getting late, before we know it, it'll be dark. Can you go get Pépère at the tavern? I'm afraid he'll let himself be dragged into some trouble if we don't pull him out of there pretty soon. You'll see, those drunkards will be carrying on late into the night again."

"Okay, Mémère, I'll bring him back right away."

Pépère frequents the village tavern, across the street from our house, only on payday, the last working day of each month. Otherwise, he stays clear of the place. And each time, Mémère sends me there to fetch him. It has become a ritual at our house.

In Saint-Aquilin, payday is a time of celebration for the men, but of anxiety for the women. Despite his age Pépère still works as a casual laborer, so he always grants himself that day off. He devotes the morning to the computation of his hours for the month, and the afternoon to the collection of his due from his various employers. His tongue purple from the colored pencil he uses only for this special occasion, he adds up out loud the numbers listed in his dog-eared notebook, which he carries at all times in his twill jacket.

Pépère works by half days—never less than two hours, never more than four—Mondays through Saturdays, for whoever wants to hire him in the village, mostly the farmer Delagoutte who also employs our neighbor Brossaud as a full-time horse carter. His other main employer, The Widow Bricout, owns our house as well as several parcels of land around the village. When he's not working for these two or someone else, he tends our vegetable garden and potato patch. Sometimes, for more extensive projects, such as the mowing by hand of Delagoutte's alfalfa field, he is hired in a lump-sum payment because, though his strength and availability are valued, he is old and has become notoriously prone to granting himself more and more frequent—and long—pauses.

Thus, for instance, during the past month, one could see him take the road up the hill to the alfalfa field that borders the woods nestling "*Le Nid de Chiens*" ("The Dogs' Nest") farm, a name acquired in the sixteenth century, when the earthy, much-loved king Henri the Fourth is said to have slept there amidst his pack of dogs before winning the battle of Ivry. Nobody remembers exactly why that battle was fought, except that it had to do with religion, Catholics and Protestants at each other's throat, with king Henri finally switching faiths just to keep the peace.

On the way to the alfalfa field, Pépère's left hand balanced the scythe on his shoulder, and the walking stick in his right hand marked the rhythm of his stiff gait, like a sergeant major leading a march with a slight limp. As he walked, drops of water spilled on his clogs from the rim of the bull's horn tied to his belt for the whetstone.

In the middle of the hill he would stop for a moment to sit on the red and white road marker with its glistening black letters: "Évreux: 13 km." I could imagine his words in the conversation he often held out loud with himself when he worked alone: "Say, I'm going to park my arse on that stone for a while." Then, after the pause, a deep breath, a defiant glare at the alfalfa field: "All right, let's have at it." And he waded into the green expanse. From the village, only his cap and the tip of his scythe remained visible above the embankment.

Whenever I accompanied Pépère to the alfalfa field to help him with a sickle, I liked to walk in step with him, and imitate his stride. I was eager to grow up so I could also balance a scythe on my shoulders. After working side by side for a while on those wonderful days, he'd send me home, much to my disappointment: "Don't overdo it, son, you've got your whole life ahead of you to toil like this after you turn fourteen and finish school."

The handling of the scythe, half standing half leaning, was especially hard on him: "I'll get another damn backache, you wait and see." The best relief from his working pains was when he laughed out loud at the rabbits and partridges that occasionally popped up in the tall grass and scurried out ahead of him: Ha! Ha! Look at that son of a gun run! Ha! Ha! Look at them wings flap!"

After counting up his hours for the month, and shaving off his stubble to mark the occasion even though he usually does so only on Sundays, Pépère heads out to collect his wages. Then he proceeds to the village tavern, "*Le Relais des Routiers.*"

The French farm hands and road workers of the region, as well as the foreign laborers from the Lavril dairy, work as usual that day. But after pocketing their hard-earned money, they celebrate at the *Relais des Routiers.*

Our village has two drinking establishments, located kitty corner from each other at the intersection of two-lane *Route Nationale* 13, and narrower *Route Départementale* 14. On the right side, "*L'Auberge de Saint-Aquilin*" ("The Inn of Saint-Aquilin"), and on the left "*Le Relais des Routiers*" ("Truck Stop"). But we village people refer to those two places as, respectively, "*Chez Guida*" and "*Le Bistrot.*" Two totally different worlds, a few meters across from each other.

The local inhabitants go to *L'Auberge de Saint-Aquilin* only to buy postage stamps, cigarettes, and smoking or chewing tobacco. Otherwise, it's the exclusive domain of rich Parisians, or British visitors, or sometimes American tourists, who stop there for lunch, dinner, or refreshments halfway between the capital city and the beach resorts or the fancy thoroughbred farms and horseracing tracks of Normandy. One of my favorite pastimes is to inspect their shiny cars in the gravel parking lot. The French automobiles, Delage, Delahaye, Bugatti, whose speedometers go up to 210 attract me more than the English ones, Jaguars, Aston Martins, Rolls Royces, marked GB, with steering wheels awkwardly placed on the right side and speedometers that only go up to 160; or the big American cars, Cadillacs, Packards and such, that top off at a disappointing 120, and that you have to be careful of when you walk or bike on the road, because they're so quiet.

I like the cozy, muffled atmosphere at *Guida's* but Pépère feels it's not a welcoming place for peasants like us. He doesn't appreciate the stares of the city people when he enters, except if it's a woman, in which case he tips his cap to her. He says we're forced to go in there for tobacco and postage stamps, but otherwise he wouldn't set foot inside that place.

When I think of it, he has a point. It's difficult to imagine Pépère getting in and out of any car with his big wooden clogs, or even going to Paris at all—in fact, I've never seen a peasant like him in the city. Still, I love the smell of expensive perfumes and blond tobaccos inside the inn. According to Pépère, rumor has it that some of those cigarettes for courtesans, "Lucky Streek" or "Chtestairefiel," he has forgotten which, contain opium!

Behind the cashier's nook where Monsieur Guida presides, are piled dozens of cellophane packs containing cigarettes imported from the U.S.A. and England, much more colorful in their wrappings than the lowly Gauloises or cheaper still Caporals that Mémère sends me to fetch for her when she has enough money for ready-made cigarettes. With these bright packages, the Anglo-Saxons rise back in my esteem, previously undermined by their puny speedometers.

It's well known in the village that the American tourists love colorful things. Their older people are sometimes even dressed in sherbet hues, instead of grey or black. We in Saint-Aquilin find that amusing, along with the fascinating singsong pattern of the English language, of which we don't understand a word. But deep down inside, although we sometimes find them strange, we realize the Americans are superior. Their dollar rules, and they have all the chocolate, cigarettes, and gasoline they want. They won the war. Their wealth is so immense that their soldiers can wear a fresh shirt every day.

My favorite American things, in addition to chewing gum, are the empty bottles that the soldiers throw out from their convoys, and that we find in the ditch on the way to school. The most beautiful ones are the Smirnoff vodka bottles, made of sparkling glass cut like crystal, with all kinds of royal crowns and coats of arms on the label. Those, I treasure and collect. Seven of them are lined up along the wall inside the shed, like an altar. Once in a while I run them under water at the pump and polish them with Mémère's Sunday dishtowel, made of lintless rough linen. They shine like diamonds.

One thing I don't understand is how, with the name ending in -*off*, plus the medals from Saint-Petersburg, the tsar emblems, and all the Russian stuff, those bottles could come from America. But I've heard that Americans love vodka and even manufacture it in their own country. And I thought they hated the Russians! How can you figure that out?

At *Guida's*, the facade of the inn is covered with ivy, and the tables, decorated with bouquets of flowers, are set with white linen cloths, porcelain china, and gleaming silverware. At the bar, under the beamed ceiling, you can hear ice cubes clinking in stubby cocktail glasses, and patrons often sip their drinks with straws that Monsieur Guida gleans from the surrounding wheat fields, like wildflowers, during his morning walks with his big German Shepherd, who then takes up his position for the rest of the day sprawled on the floor just inside the entrance, ignoring the poodles and other lapdogs who visit his domain. And every time a car leaves, Monsieur Guida claps his hands, signaling to the busboy, who wears a black vest and a long white apron, that he should drop whatever he is doing and scurry outside to rake the gravel smooth again.

In *our* tavern, nothing fancy, only bare electric bulbs dangling from the ceiling. Mémère nonetheless suggests that I run a wet comb through my hair to look presentable before setting out to fetch Pépère. "Also put on your barrette to keep your mop out of your eyes, and look both ways before crossing the street. We don't want you to get run over, your mother would never forgive us. Sometimes the trucks barrel down the hill very fast."

Trucks drive through our village, one every ten minutes or so, but they seldom stop at the *Relais*. Where they do sometimes come to a halt, though, is at the curve at the bottom of the hill, flipped over in the ditch, merchandise spread out all over the place, when by misfortune their brakes have failed. The last one contained a load of Camembert cheeses, hundreds of them littering the road in their flattened little wood boxes. Luckily there are no trees in that spot, only a crumpled hedge, so I've never heard of any driver being badly hurt.

In front of the tavern today, there are no cars or trucks, only a few bicycles and two mopeds. My dream is to have one of those when I'm older, a zippy Mobylette.

In the countryside, people still walk along the roads from hamlet to hamlet, and bicyclists seem to move in slow motion, sitting like penguins on their rusty machines, knees out, clumsily pushing down on the pedals from side to side, never standing up in the saddle like the Tour de France racers who once passed en masse through our village. Instead, the regular people dismount at the slightest incline.

Two women wearing headscarves and aprons stand in animated conversation at the tavern's entrance. They have leaned their bicycles against the wall and probably come from Pacy-sur-Eure, because I've never encountered them before. They, however, seem to know me. As I pass by them, one says to the other:

"The Widow Vermot should be ashamed. I don't care if she's old, lame, and half blind, she shouldn't send her boarding kid in there to get her old man out."

I repress a strong urge to tell the woman to mind her own business. I don't want to hear any criticism about Mémère, and I don't dislike my monthly visits to the tavern. On the contrary!

In the large smoke-filled room Pépère stands a good head above the crowd and the hubbub. He is carrying on in a louder voice than usual, turned toward the audience with his back against the counter, his walking stick in one hand, a glass of red wine in the other. His cap is half cocked on his head. He taps it lightly with his cane for each salutation.

Between fragments of dialogue and outbursts of noise, I hear the usual topics being discussed: The weather; the aches and pains associated with it ("My damn rheumatisms acting up again"); crops; farm and small-game animals; children ("Can't wait for them to turn fourteen so they can earn their own living"); current events, summed up in one sentence: "It's the government's fault." Never mind that the government changes continually.

I wind my way through the crowd to Pépère the giant. He greets me with a wink:

"So Mémère sent you in here to get me out, eh? Don't worry, I won't be long." Then he turns to the proprietress: "But first, Madame Lady Boss, a round of red to all the gentlemen at the counter. And a glass for the boy too. It'll do him good. It'll give him strength and color."

Proud to be treated like a grown-up, I long for the day when I'll be able, like Pépère, to lean with my back against the bar. For the time being, if I stretch on my tiptoes, my glass of wine is just within reach on the counter. I could prop myself up a good ten centimeters higher by standing on Pépère's wooden clogs, but, afraid to look childish or ridiculous, I dismiss this easy solution.

At home, I'm not particularly fond of wine, although I like its acidic smell when I fill our two bottles each week from the wooden cask at the grocery store; but here, in the warm and noisy atmosphere of the tavern, the usually sharp liquid is transformed into a smooth elixir, and I understand why, once inside, the patrons are reluctant to leave. I feel the same way.

At the first swallow, a tingling sensation spreads through my entire body, from scalp to toes. I feel my muscles swell. It's true that wine makes you stronger! It also makes you more talkative, but at the same time hard of hearing. In fact, everybody seems to be yakking simultaneously, then yelling louder and louder, often repeating the same thing twice, and if you stop to listen—but nobody does—the whole place seems engulfed in a deafening din. Maybe because of the sudden burst of energy provided by the wine, it's not unusual for patrons, even after a hard day's work, to get into arguments, and go outside to "settle it" man to man. They throw out insults, threaten and jostle each other, their friends intervene and try to hold them back despite their rageful rants: "Let me go! Let me go! I'm gonna kill that bastard!" Then, no sooner released: "Hold me back! Hold me back! Don't let me strangle him!" The bystanders intervene and separate the foes, who then reconcile and return inside arm in arm to booze some more, with gushy toasts to everlasting friendship, and slobbering, hiccupy proclamations that you can't "trussht hic anyone who doesn't hic drink."

Among the drunkards, says Mémère, you can distinguish four types: the "mean winos," the violent ones who get carried away in terrifying fits of rage; the "sad winos," who lament and cry in their glass; the "happy winos," who laugh about everything without knowing why; and the "deaf winos," who shout and yell themselves hoarse and think they're just speaking at a normal level. However, according to her, the souses all share a common taint: their pay is swallowed up in drink. "Wine should only be consumed with meals, and in moderation," she says.

With the violent boozers, one can expect frightful scenes when they return home. They kick in the door, tip over the furniture, break the dishes. The family, terrified, takes its usual precautions, hides the kitchen forks and knives, barricades itself in the children's room. The best one can hope for is that on the way home this kind of drunkard will collapse in the ditch, and spend the night there sleeping off his wine. He offers a sorry sight the next day, when the schoolchildren encounter him on the road, dirty, disheveled, bareheaded, his cap lost somewhere, his hair tangled and gnarled. Still too haggard and woozy to saddle up, he walks his bike, his fury at least dissipated.

Although Pépère is incredibly strong, he is very gentle. Independently of the drunken violence problem, many kids get slapped around or beaten by their parents, but this has never happened to me. The abused children probably get their revenge when the parents grow old, though, because we also hear a lot of talk about the mistreatment of elderly people.

Except for the owner's wife and the waitress, there are only men in the tavern. "A drunken man sure is an ugly and shameful sight," says Mémère, "but a drunken woman is worse." Still, it's well known that some women drink, but they hide it, at home. Not Mémère, for sure. She never touches alcohol, she is allergic to it, like Maman and Olga.

On payday, some wives, like the women from Pacy, wait for their husband at the tavern's exit. Fruitless hope. After standing there for a long time, they go away empty-handed. Their presence at the door has had the opposite effect: as long as they wait there, he will not leave.

Other wives, even more brave and rare, try to intercept their husband before he enters the tavern, where he is eager to settle his primary debt, the only one he truly respects: his tab from the previous month.

"Give me some money for the household, before you spend it all in there."

"Out of my way, shrew! Don't come 'round here to humiliate me in front of my colleagues."

"Colleagues! In the tavern, Monsieur acts like a big shot, eh! He buys rounds for his cronies. But at home he's not even able to decently feed his kids. This month we're only gonna eat sardines and canned food again, eh, wino, scumbag, zero."

"Buzz off! I'm fed up with your bullshit. If you don't shut up, I'm warning you, I'm gonna let you have a taste of this." And he raises a menacing fist. "You wait and see, we'll settle this when I get home tonight."

"If I didn't have the chicken coop and the garden plot, we'd all croak of hunger."

"Big deal. You have nothing else to do. I'm the one who's slaving like a mule."

"And who takes care of the kids and the household, eh? You think that's nothing? I'm fed up, fed up."

"Yeah, well I'm fed up too."

She blocks his entry into the tavern, but with a sharp jab of the elbow, he pushes her aside, and slams the door shut behind him without looking back. Stunned, she remains speechless in front of the entrance for a long while, her hands on her hips, not daring to follow him inside.

So go the diverse households. When we talk about them sometimes at the kitchen table, because in the village everything ends up being known, Mémère concludes with a weary tone: "Why don't some of those people just get divorced."

Pépère hates to hear that word. He quickly changes the subject whenever it comes up. After being a widower, he himself was divorced—a rare and shocking thing in our region—before he took up with Mémère, without them bothering to get married.

Through the din of the tavern, dampened in my head by a cloud of fog, a voice with a Slavic accent stands out:

"Really, Old Man Martcel, you have to drink vone more red. Madame Lady Boss, you fill up Père Lepais glass vone more time before he go home wit boy." And as if to conclude the offer with an exclamation point, a massive, calloused hand lands squarely on the shoulder of Père Lepais' comrade, me.

"Slabo, I really shouldn't," says Pépère, "but I won't say no. All right, then, cheers." And they clink their freshly refilled glasses.

Pépère empties his in one gulp, smacks his lips, wipes his mustache with the back of his hand. I'm not the only one who has gained some color; his complexion has also taken on a rosy glow at the cheekbones.

"Well, bye till next time everybody," trumpets Pépère. "I wet my whistle nice. Forward, son, let me lead the way."

With his walking stick, Pépère cuts a path through the crowd and pulls me by the hand. My eyes are burning from the cigarette smoke. We bump into the waitress, who is holding high over her head a tray filled with empty glasses. She is pleading for some space: "Coming through, gentlemen, coming through, please make room, coming through, watch out please."

Suddenly, Pépère's hand lets go of mine and, as if moved by an invisible prod, lands squarely on the waitress's butt. Only the precarious balance of the glasses on her tray spares him a spontaneous slap on the face.

"Hey," she fumes, "what's with you, dirty old man! What do you think you're doing!" Then, in a taunting tone: "Besides, if I was you, I wouldn't embark on things I might not be able to finish."

Pépère seems startled by her remark. I hear him mutter "You wench!" under his bristling white mustache. Before we know it the waitress has disappeared with her tray in the back room.

Outside, a blast of crisp evening air clears up my head and lungs. Pépère seems tired but content, strangely serene, relieved.

"You know, son, after all, I'm glad you came to get me out of there. I'm glad to be going home, but don't tell anyone, especially Mémère. You'll understand those things later."

I'm puzzled that this is the secret he wants me to keep, not the incident with the waitress. Across the street, Mémère, still waiting for us behind the window with Zaza on her lap, gets ready to ladle out her thick steamy potato soup. Time to eat. We're all hungry, very hungry.

Our house across from the tavern.

Chapter 8

To the Source

"One day, I was studying alone in the room next to the kitchen.
The servantmaid had laid out Mademoiselle Lambercier's combs on a
board to dry. When she came back to get them, she found one in which
an entire side of teeth was broken. Whom to blame for this damage? No
one besides me had entered the room. I was questioned.
I denied having touched the comb. Monsieur and Mademoiselle
Lambercier consulted each other, exhorted me, pressed me, threatened me.

I maintained my innocence...Were it not for the risk of boring the
reader with so many puerile details, how many examples could I not give
of the impact that the slightest childhood events can have on determining the most prominent traits in an adult's character. I dare say that
one of the most deeply engraved in mine is an indomitable aversion for
injustice...Who would ever believe that this
invincible feeling originates from a broken comb?"

— *Jean-Jacques Rousseau (1712-1778) describing an episode from
his childhood under the foster care of the Lambercier family.*

*W*hat, as an adult, is the source of my allergy to injustice, my instinctual indignation, ready to ignite at any moment for the slightest
reason? Why this "righter of wrongs" attitude, these quixotic struggles, this
perpetual agitation? Why can't I just mind my own business, as I've often
been enjoined to do?

The discovery of Rousseau's text about the broken comb was for me a
revelation in self-knowledge. It provided a direct answer to those nagging
questions: I too had been the victim of a false accusation during my childhood.

Although Rousseau admitted that in the course of his life he had (like all humans?) done a number of regrettable or shameful things—for which he was never accused, much less punished—he vehemently denied until his death having broken Mademoiselle Lambercier's comb. For perplexing reasons, perhaps childhood integrity, he was never able to forget this false accusation, nor accept it as a modest price to pay for his unexposed transgressions.

With the same unyielding immaturity as this illustrious figure, I have held on to a fierce resentment about a seemingly trivial childhood event—except that in my case the upshot has been insignificant, whereas in his, it became a determinant cause of the French revolution! In Rousseau's own words, the incident stoked a lifelong "fire" in his belly. Hence the incandescent power and persuasiveness of his social and political ideas that otherwise might have remained less passionate or compelling.

One fine April morning, a week before my tenth birthday, as my classmates and I were leaving the school grounds to return home for lunch, Madame Mercier held me back at the gate:

"Milan, wait here until everyone is gone, I want to talk to you."

What was this about? It sounded ominous. She had taken on the stern look that came over her when she meted out a reprimand.

It seemed to take forever for my schoolmates to leave. They jostled up to the bottleneck at the narrow gate, then exited single file to the street and ran free, while I stayed imprisoned in the courtyard. When they were all gone, Madame Mercier looked me straight in the eye and said:

"Listen, Milan, I've received complaints that you're pushing kids in the ditch on the way to school."

I was stunned. This was a lie. "It's not true. I never pushed anyone. Who complained? Bouquet?"

Bouquet's name spontaneously came to my lips because he was the only classmate toward whom I felt any kind of antipathy, for having called me "carrot top" a couple of times in the past. His father ran the gas station and auto repair shop at the crossroad in the village, so the whole family acted sort of standoffish from the common people. But Bouquet was older and bigger than me, so it would have been ridiculous to think that I could have pushed him in the ditch.

"I can't tell you who complained," Madame Mercier replied to my protestation, "because that would create still more problems. You know I don't like tattling, but the accusation seems founded, so I have to intervene and do something. It's no fun to get pushed in the ditch, you know, especially with these April showers forming puddles everywhere. The only solution I can see is that you'll leave school ten minutes after the other children from Saint-Aquilin. That way, even if you run like crazy, they'll be in the village before you can catch up with them. And for the return, I want you to do the opposite and get to school ten minutes ahead of them. Is that understood? You'll do that until the end of the school year. It's only a couple of months away, it's not so bad, and besides May is full of holidays."

"But it's not true, *Madame la maîtresse*, I didn't push anyone."

"Listen, don't give me a hard time. I've given careful thought to this. I don't see any other solution. And these few minutes are not such a big deal."

With twenty five pupils from kindergarten to eighth grade under her tutelage, Madame Mercier worked under constant pressure from dawn till night. She had no time to hem and haw. Her decisions were final.

> *"Try to imagine a shy and docile personality in ordinary life, but ardent, proud, indomitable in passions; a child always governed by the voice of reason, always treated with gentleness, fairness, leniency, who doesn't even know what injustice is and who, for the first time, experiences such a horrible one from the very people he loves and respects the most. What a reversal of ideas! What a disorder of feelings! What an upheaval in his heart, in his head, in his entire small, moral, intelligent being."*

— Rousseau

Madame Mercier's punishment felt like a betrayal, something I had never experienced. I had been brought up with utmost kindness, at home and at school, never struck, nor even severely scolded, although during my difficult period of re-adaptation from Slovakia I probably deserved to be chastised on many occasions.

I had boundless respect for Madame Mercier. My only reproach was that she imposed finicky standards in penmanship, while not applying them to her own writing— always so hurried, except for the texts of the dictations that she carefully wrote out at night on the flipover blackboard for the following day. She maintained strict discipline in the classroom, and seemed tense all the time, but behind her firmness, one could sense a deep undeclared affection for each of her pupils. For five years, I had been particularly moved by her teachings in morals, civics, and history, through which she instilled in us her passion for social justice. Quietly sitting on my bench, listening to her exalted words, my index finger stained from purple ink, I chewed the tip of my wooden penholder and felt outraged by the misdeeds of the aristocracy and the clergy. Down with privilege, yes to the Revolution! But my indignation stopped short of advocating—like Robespierre and his extremist faction—the guillotine for these villains, or the sacking of their castles and churches. The enemy remained abstract: our teacher, a true humanist, sought to develop in us an appetite for lofty ideas, and a rejection of hate.

And now, with this cruel punishment dealt out for a false accusation, Madame Mercier—the embodiment of fairness—was committing the gravest injustice. I was devastated.

A child's character is whole. I allowed her no excuse, nor did I try to understand her reasoning. I felt no forbearance for her perpetually stressful situation, her right to make mistakes or show occasional impatience. I raged in silence and endured her irrevocable sanction.

"This marked the end of my childhood's serenity. From that moment on, I stopped enjoying pure happiness, and even today I feel that the memory of my childhood's charm stops there."

— Rousseau

With that punishment, the sweet meanderings of my childhood ended. The walk to and from school, up until then so idyllic, became for me a solitary race punctuated with curses. I no longer stopped along the brooks in the meadows to pick watercress for Mémère's salads and wild herb soups, and the occasional sight of a porcupine run over on the road now triggered only revulsion, instead of the deep sorrow I felt before.

Although I had never attended church and wasn't drawn to organized religion, I had been sustained by a number of superstitions gleaned from the smidgen of theology that survived in our secular region. Those beliefs also vanished from my registry. I stopped signing myself with a discreet movement of the chin when passing by the wayside crucifix. I abandoned my silent recitation of the Lord's Prayer at the curve on the road before reaching the village, to elicit God's assistance in finding our house intact. Before, I feared that my nearly blind Mémère had burned down our abode by dropping her ever-present cigarette butt, and that my elderly parents had been pulverized along with our dwelling by the explosion of the German artillery shells stored in the attic, leaving me alone on this earth, with no home, no family, Maman and Olga working in faraway Paris.

But now all those fears disappeared. Madame Mercier's unjust treatment enraged me so, that it purged me of my excess emotionality.

I now looked forward to only one thing: the entry exam into secondary school. Until then, I had dreaded taking this test—not from the academic standpoint, which Madame Mercier had told me not to worry about—but because of the painful breakup it would entail from Pépère and Mémère. Though I was powerfully attracted to Paris and felt euphoric, sheltered like in a womb anywhere within the magical city, I was unsure I'd have the strength or will power to leave my guardians.

By her unjust treatment, Madame Mercier toughened me up for the great departure. Otherwise, I might have caved in to Pépère's pressure, whenever we talked about my future: "Why would you want to leave Saint-Aquilin? Do you think you'll be better off in Paris than here? You could stay and obtain your *certificat d'études* without all these upheavals. You could then be an apprentice in the village or in Pacy. It would be better for you, and for us too. We could all stay together. Wouldn't you like that?"

Of course, I would have liked that. I loved my elderly caretakers and the village, but I also felt a need for adventure, for a new beginning, for broader horizons, and Paris fulfilled those desires to the ultimate degree. For the first time I experienced real tension in my relationship with Pépère; in comparison to this, his negative view of reading ("You're gonna ruin your eyes") seemed like a mere quibble. He was expressing the opposite of what I desperately wanted to hear from him. I hoped he would be supportive, or at least neutral in the matter of my schooling. Instead, my revered mentor—the giant who towered over the crowd when I proudly fetched him from the village tavern on payday—was now blocking my way to Paris, like the oak tree that he was, planted in the middle of *Route Nationale 13*, my umbilical cord to the city.

Before the false accusation at school, I didn't think I'd have the courage to go against or around Pépère. Mémère, always quiet, didn't intervene in such matters. She seemed resigned to whatever happened. Maman, the third adult involved in this situation, had been convinced by Madame Mercier that the move would be good for my future. She had not been hard to persuade. She felt that my living conditions at Mémère and Pépère's were deplorable and, though cheap by any measure, the cost of my room and board consumed nearly half of her wages as a live-in cook in Paris. Her monthly visits felt more and more like inspection tours disturbing our routine. Her criticisms were difficult to bear for Mémère and Pépère, and forced me to grapple with divided loyalties. My intellectual development and emotional well-being were in the hands of others. The two don't necessarily coincide.

Maman had no idea how the educational system worked, nor any awareness of the stakes involved. From her experience as a domestic, she thought that boarding school was only for the sons of the rich, but Madame Mercier had told her that in my case money wouldn't be an obstacle, because she had checked with the authorities and, based on my school results, she was sure I could get an all-expense national scholarship from the French government. In addition to the financial incentive of free room and board, Maman vaguely sensed that my going to a residential lycée would clarify and enhance her status. Raising me as she had until then in a private foster care arrangement—a mode of upbringing that usually pertained to the children of unwed mothers or Parisian prostitutes—might have been considered shameful by people unaware of her widowed condition and live-in employment.

In order to bring about this new beginning, there remained only one additional step: the all-important entrance exam, at a time when only ten percent of a generation in France graduated from high school. I had no idea what the test entailed, but Madame Mercier repeatedly stated I would pass without any problem.

And now, my teacher's unjust accusation hardened me. It made me feel ready to take the exam and leave Saint-Aquilin. My childhood thus ended at age ten, with this unwarranted punishment and the prospect of a wrenching separation from my native village and the elderly couple who had raised me there since infancy.

While I seethed over the unjust sentence, Madame Mercier and my classmates continued to act as if nothing happened. My "banishment" was to be self-monitored, and it pertained only to the walk to and from school. I decided, instead of sulking, to do whatever I could to persuade my teacher that she was wrong. The best opportunity would come through the exam, which I took by getting myself on the bus to our county's main town of Évreux, about eight miles from the village. I had never ventured in that direction, opposite from Paris. I went in without apprehension, but breathed a sigh of relief when the test was over, and treated myself to a cup of hot chocolate in a café before returning home.

Madame Mercier received the results at the end of June, two weeks before the end of the school year. A score of 85 points was required. She told me I passed with 145, and she expressed great satisfaction with this outcome but made no mention of lifting my sanction. I felt jubilant at having validated her long-standing support and confidence, but disappointed that it didn't lead to a pardon.

If any credit is due for the test results, it belongs entirely to my teacher. Without her instruction and guidance, I would never have taken or passed this exam. No one around me knew of its existence, much less its stakes. The disadvantaged are even more intimidated by the privilege of knowledge than by wealth. They censor themselves out of schooling: "Education is not for people like us."

In order to enroll in the selective academic track to which the results entitled me, I would have to go away to boarding school. From an external viewpoint, this relocation appeared to pose less of a problem in my case than it might for children brought up under normal circumstances, in families reticent to let their offspring leave home at such a young age. From the outside, it appeared I had grown up in a deprived environment, without strong attachments.

This perception could not have been further from the truth. I was in fact extremely close to my guardians Mémère and Pépère, under whose affectionate care I lived a life made rich, ironically, by our destitution and our archaic mode of living. This paradox can be viewed as the revenge of poverty, which magnifies sensory perception and makes one forever appreciative of the smallest satisfactions, including creature comforts taken for granted by more privileged people.

After being informed of the test results, Madame Mercier undertook the necessary procedures to place me in a residential lycée in the Paris area, as well as obtain a scholarship to cover my expenses. I also needed an age waiver, because I was one year younger than usual for this transition to sixth grade, the beginning year of the academic track in the secondary cycle. She handled all the red tape herself, no doubt a considerable endeavor beyond her already overwhelming workload.

She thought I was ready for the exam even the preceding year, and had approached her district inspector regarding the possibility of a two-year age waiver, but her request had been categorically denied, thankfully so when

I look back. Since I had already completed the primary school curriculum, she allowed me to spend my entire last year in her classroom poring over one of the most enthralling books I have ever read, the *Petit Larousse Illustré* dictionary. She had offered me this treasured volume at the previous year's school awards ceremony. I was interrupted from my concentrated study of the words and encyclopedic knowledge contained in the dictionary only by her occasional requests to help younger classmates with specific problems of grammar or arithmetic.

Madame Mercier thus provided the foundation, direction, and structure of my education, and the *Larousse* filled in the rest. I could not have hoped for a better primary school experience, the most determinant for any child. And I was not, by far, the only one to have benefited from her teaching. Her pupils did consistently well in the various exams and hurdles that confronted them in their schooling.

The paperwork undertaken by Madame Mercier to place me in a lycée and obtain the needed scholarship seemed to be moving forward at a normal pace, when an unexpected problem arose. The Ministry of Education authorities, perhaps skeptical about the nationality of applicants with foreign-sounding names, had contacted her to ask that a certificate of French citizenship be added to my dossier.

Panic! We were already past Bastille Day in late July, with the new school year only two months away. Nobody had given any thought to the citizenship question. After all, except for our brief sojourn in Slovakia when I was four, I had spent my entire existence in Saint-Aquilin, where everyone knew me as a local child with a Slavic name but a deep and genuine anchoring in the village.

Madame Mercier's husband, accustomed to solving administrative problems in his job at the Pacy-sur-Eure town hall, looked into the citizenship matter, and explained to us the difference between *jus soli* (the law of the soil) that prevailed in France and the U.S.A., and *jus sanguinis* (the law of blood) pertinent to West Germany. But he also learned that to acquire French nationality, if you were of foreign parents, it was not enough to simply have been born on French soil; you also had to step forward and officially declare and request that citizenship. It was a mere formality, but it needed to be done. Time was short, we had to move quickly.

Maman came down from Paris a few days earlier than usual for her end-of-the-month visit, so that she could appear with me before the Justice of the Peace in Pacy-sur-Eure. She was then in the beginning phase of her third complicated, employer-sponsored renewable ten-year permit to live and work in France, the notorious *carte de séjour*.

I had until then considered myself not only French in nationality, but also, in fanciful extrapolation, Norman and even soon-to-be Parisian in specific identity. How more rooted in France could anyone be?

The declaration process turned out to be my first direct contact with the great master of all things, BUREAUCRACY, which would, after this hectic initiation, fall by default under my purview in our household. But the avalanche of legal terms and concepts bombarding us at once (declaration, naturalization, *jus soli*, *jus sanguinis*, affidavits, *carte de séjour*, etc.) remained for some time jumbled in my mind. Pépère, who was by then grudgingly accepting my departure, teased me about this confusion: "I told you you'd have been better off staying in Saint-Aquilin."

On July 30th 1952, the day of my declaration for French citizenship, I left the otherwise banal proceedings in the Justice of the Peace's office ("Are you *the* mother?" he tersely asked Maman) in a state of elation, because I sensed this was a defining event in my life. Up to that point fatherless and vulnerable, I had now been formally adopted by the most powerful of any protector, the State, who would henceforth guarantee my future, by way of the scholarship. The anonymous, distant nature of this support made it all the more significant to me. And when I needed to hang on to a more concrete, personalized image of this abstract intervention, my teacher Madame Mercier embodied it. Those two forms of help, *personal mentorship* and *institutional aid* were in fact inextricably linked, and as I would later learn in America, ineffective or even useless when not *both* present.

The prospect of the scholarship made me feel independent, secure, and potentially carefree. Until then surrounded by old age or ignorance, I had considered myself "in charge" of a myriad of things, and felt burdened by that mantle of responsibility. On the other hand, true to my ambivalent nature, I didn't entirely dislike that state of affairs, because it made me feel needed and helpful. Although I was very young, I of necessity took care of my infirm elderly guardians as much as they took care of me. Yet, despite our deep mutual love, this situation could not last. I had to break out and make my way to Paris.

This prospect of adventure and discovery in the big city made me both euphoric and overwhelmed with sadness. In leaving Saint-Aquilin, I was rejecting my filial duty and abandoning Mémère and Pépère at the threshold of their very old age, she seventy-four, he seventy. But to stay in the village when fate was calling me so imperiously, almost ordering me toward the vast external world, would have been a form of suicide. Life is a sequence of ruptures. Some, one never fully overcomes…

I was thus forsaking the totality of my childhood in one fell swoop: my adored old parents, my cat Zaza, my beautiful village. Later, the memory of this radical break would make subsequent upheavals difficult to envisage, although it confirmed that, despite my acute emotionality, I was capable of astonishing harshness and decisiveness. I was capable of closing an entire chapter of my life without so much as looking back. Or so I thought.

Finally, the awaited letter arrived, confirming that I had been awarded a full scholarship for tuition, room, board, and laundry. It also stated that I had been assigned to the lycée for boys at Saint-Germain-en-Laye, a public institution housing about four hundred boarders in grades six through twelve, plus an equivalent number of day students.

The town of Saint-Germain-en-Laye, an affluent suburb of Paris, had the reputation, like its neighbor Versailles, of being favored by the prevailing westerly winds with healthful air still unscathed by the sprawling metropolis. I remembered that detail from one of Madame Mercier's geography lessons, with blue arrows denoting air currents blowing eastward from the Atlantic coast on the wall map of France and Europe.

At first I was disappointed: I hoped to be assigned to a school within the Paris city limits. But I soon got over my initial letdown and accepted this choice established entirely by fate and circumstance. Madame Mercier said that I should consider myself lucky, that the lycée of Saint-Germain was a sought-after institution, and that anyway, to the best of her knowledge, there weren't any boarding schools for boys my age within Paris proper.

I already knew the town of Saint-Germain a little, having passed through it on the bus during each trip between the village and Paris. I remembered especially the road sign on the plaza next to the moat of the medieval Château, with the inscription "Paris Notre-Dame 17 km," signifying that my three-hour ordeal, trying to repress motion sickness in the crowded, jostling bus would soon be over. My heart exulted in finally reaching the excitement of the city, conveyed by the appearance of the first subway station at Porte Maillot, but the suburbs appeared wan in comparison.

"It's now been nearly fifty years that this incident took place...
Well, I declare to the Heavens that I was innocent, that I had neither
broken nor touched the comb, that I had not come near the board,
and that I had not even thought of it."

— Rousseau

Forty years after leaving Saint-Aquilin, and following numerous visits to my native village over those several decades—during which Madame Mercier and I have had the opportunity to share fond memories without my mustering the courage to spoil our reminiscences by bringing up the ditch episode—I have come from Paris to spend a beautiful June day at her house, and place some flowers at my father's grave. The tombstone is in an advanced state of deterioration, but at least it offers a place of remembrance. Pépère and Mémère on the other hand have suffered the supreme indignity: they are buried in an unmarked plot for indigents.

Madame Mercier is now eighty-four years old, I am fifty and have been living in America since the age of fourteen. Monsieur Mercier, who still drives, has picked me up at the train station in the nearby town of Vernon, home of one of my favorite painters, Bonnard, and a few kilometers distant from another cultural shrine, Monet's house at Giverny. As we drive through the gently rolling countryside, I realize how fortunate I am to have been brought up in such a beautiful environment. No wonder those celebrated artists chose to settle there.

I am a man fulfilled. I love my new hometown of Duluth, on the shores of Lake Superior in Minnesota. It has become the native landscape of my children, whose roots are as firmly planted there as mine in Normandy. I think it is the greatest gift I could give them—roots *and* wings, a combination sometimes difficult to achieve. Pépère had certainly given me roots. I only wish his resistance to my leaving had not cast an unresolved shadow on our otherwise wonderful relationship.

This time I have brought a tape recorder, and Madame Mercier and I have spent the entire morning talking on the terrace of her house, with Monsieur Mercier joining us in the conversation and bringing treats and refreshments periodically. In the garden, a multitude of flowers explode in full bloom, and intoxicated birds sing ravenously in the cherry tree bursting with fruit. Madame Mercier and I are discussing her experience of teaching for twenty-five years in the one-room schoolhouse of Saint-Aquilin.

After a scrumptious lunch under the canopy, accompanied by good wine and followed by a cup of espresso coffee and locally distilled applejack brandy, I gather the courage to bring up the subject of my long-standing wound. Monsieur Mercier has just commented that he can't get over how his wife's former pupils, now in some cases already grandparents, revert back to behaving in her presence like the little schoolchildren they once were. He knows us all. The Merciers and their daughter Josette lived upstairs in the combination schoolhouse and community center of Saint-Aquilin during the whole time Madame Mercier taught there.

After her retirement they moved to Pacy-sur-Eure. Their house is located next to the small hospital where I was born, and where my father, Mémère, and Pépère died, all three without my knowledge: my father because I was too young, my caretakers because I was by then a teenager sowing wild oats in Chicago. My entire childhood is thus concentrated in this tiny microcosm on Rue Aristide-Briand. Monsieur Mercier says that a few days before, my former schoolmate Alain Debel stopped by on his way back to Brussels where he is a business executive. I remember how I envied Alain's way with animals. He could call hares, moles, or ferrets out of their burrows into the open. We enjoyed seeing their startled reaction when they realized they had been tricked and then scurried back into their holes. Alain didn't use his power to harm the little beasts, just to have some fun at their expense.

Monsieur Mercier says that those visits from her former pupils bring great joy to his wife. He marvels at how they've remained attached to their teacher over several generations. I was with her between the ages of five and ten, and Alain stayed even longer. Many of our classmates did quite well in life despite entry into the working world at fourteen, thus attesting to the quality of our primary education. After our batch went through, the postwar French economy soared, compulsory schooling was extended to sixteen, formal credentials became increasingly important, and our teacher finally obtained an assistant.

"Madame Mercier, do you remember the punishment you inflicted on me at the end of my last year at school? I had to leave the grounds ten minutes after everyone else. You said that somebody had accused me of pushing them in the ditch. But it wasn't true, I want you to know that, it wasn't true."

There! Primed by the glorious lunch and the applejack brandy, I have at last spoken my piece. After forty years, I'm finally unburdened of a weight I've been carrying around all this time.

"Punishment?" She looks puzzled. "Ten minutes after the others? No, I don't remember anything like that. In fact I don't remember having ever punished you. You know, I tried not to show favoritism, because everyone needs to be loved and be treated fairly, but I sure was proud of your schoolwork."

Loved!!?? She never allowed herself to use words like that during her career. She did not *express* love, she *showed* it through her selflessness and devotion. But now, retirement has transformed her. She falls in that category of people who, by her own admission, are better grandparents than parents. She is relaxed and serene, not tense and preoccupied as she always seemed to be during her years in the schoolhouse. Her universal affection now reveals itself openly, without the reserve and egalitarian attitude formerly imposed by her duties. Her most cherished possession is a medal inscribed "Mother to All the Children of France" awarded to her by the French government at the end of her career.

"But you know, Milan," she says, "I've often wondered whether I didn't make a mistake by sending you off to Paris so soon. I couldn't figure out what else to do with you in the classroom, and I didn't want to hold you back, so at the time I thought that was the best solution. But maybe I was wrong because I know from experience that for boys especially, emotional and intellectual development are often not the same. But the principal at the lycée of Saint-Germain-en-Laye had heard about your test results, and he had written me that he wanted you to come to his institution, and that you would get a scholarship and also an age waiver. So you can imagine how flattered I felt from a professional standpoint."

I can't believe it! She completely sidesteps my allegation. She has absolutely no recollection of the ditch incident. Zip! Zero! I can tell by her reaction that her surprise is genuine. For her, this determinant event in my life had gone by unnoticed, one of the multitude of problems she had to solve daily during her long and distinguished career in the one-room schoolhouse of our "remote and archaic" village.

"Remote and archaic" relative to the mindset and living conditions prevailing at the time of my childhood in rural Normandy. Again, to think that Mémère had never been to Paris, only fifty-five miles distant, and Pépère only once! We were on the cusp of the unprecedented transformations that took place during the decade after I left for America.

With the economic boom of the 1960s, Saint-Aquilin became a sought-after exurb for affluent Parisians, who could drive to and from the city in less than forty-five minutes on the newly built tollway that ran parallel to my old two-lane *Route Nationale 13*. And the talented daughter of one of my grade school classmates commuted by train to Paris twice weekly for her music lessons. Our primitive abode without running water—basically a stone structure with peeling walls punctured by holes for the doors and windows—was transformed into a comfortable, modern dwelling with proper amenities, and the hovel next door into a fashionable antique shop with a gleaming plate glass window.

How presumptuous and egocentric on my part to think that, in the colossal march of time and events, Madame Mercier would remember such an insignificant blip as the ditch episode, whereas at the very moment of her memory lapse, I couldn't recall with absolute certainty which ones of my numerous aunts and uncles in Slovakia had died or were still alive.

At the conclusion of my "confrontation" with Madame Mercier that day on her terrace, I was swept by a wave of forgiveness, and I let go of the anger and resentment about the false accusation. But I noticed a simultaneous decrease of the fire in my belly, and was somewhat troubled by this sensation, similar to the disappearance of chronic pain from an ailment to which one has become so accustomed that relief, while hugely welcomed, feels at the same time almost like a loss.

Long live *La République* and its heroic primary school teachers!

Part III

Paris, the Bewitching City

Versailles, le 2 2 OCT 1952

L'INSPECTEUR D'ACADEMIE

à M⁺ *Kovacovic*

St Aquilin de Pacy (Eure)

J'ai l'honneur de vous faire connaître que le jeune *Kovacovic Milan*

vient de se voir attribuer une bourse nationale d'*Internat 6/6*

d'un montant annuel de

pour entrer au 1ᵉʳ octobre 1952 au *lycée de St Germain en Laye*

en classe de *6ᵉ*

Je crois devoir vous rappeler que pour les élèves déjà en cours d'études dans l'enseignement du second degré, dans l'Enseignement technique ou dans un Cours complémentaire, la bourse nationale n'est attribuée que sous réserve de l'admission du candidat dans la classe supérieure.

L'Inspecteur d'Académie,

N.-B. — Le boursier devra rejoindre le 1ᵉʳ octobre l'école désignée ci-dessus.
   Si, pour cause de maladie, un délai est nécessaire, la famille devra m'adresser une demande de congé avec, à l'appui, un certificat médical.
   Au cas où le boursier ne pourrait entrer à l'école où il a été affecté, la famille devra me demander le transfert pour un autre établissement, 15 jours au moins avant la rentrée des classes (en indiquer le motif).

VERSAILLES. — IMP. LA GUTENBERG. — 1A

A notice informing my father that I have been awarded a full scholarship for boarding school.

Chapter 9

Scholarship Student

"Anyone who has been to boarding school knows, at age twelve, nearly all there is to know about life."

— *Gustave Flaubert*

O n the afternoon the new boarders were expected to report at the lycée of Saint-Germain-en-Laye, Maman and I hurried to straighten up her kitchen after lunch at the Kapferers. It felt as if we were embarking on a momentous journey into an unknown world, only eight miles distant. I wasn't scared, but my stomach churned with excitement.

For this new stage in my life as a ten-year-old, I was equipped with a reddish-brown leather schoolbag that we had carefully chosen at the outdoor market in Levallois, from the luggage stand displaying its wares next to those of our Slovak friend Jaro Supatik, who sold rabbit and chicken meat, and even live poultry. The leather goods seller had convinced us of the quality of my schoolbag, and had overcome our shock at its price, with a scent test. First he brought up to our nostrils a less expensive one, made in Egypt. Its gamy smell made us recoil. "You don't want this one," he said, "nobody'll want to be near you." Following which, he let us sniff for contrast "the bag I want this young man to have." No comparison. "Believe me, Madame" he added in a conspiratorial tone to clinch the sale and counteract Maman's instinctive distrust of shopkeepers, "poor people can't afford to buy cheap things."

To carry the rest of my belongings, Maman gave me her suitcase—a scratched up, ill-closing affair tied with a belt. A model known as the "immigrant and refugee special" at the Clignancourt flea market where she had bought it. A mismatch to my nice-looking schoolbag. In the suitcase, despite my protestations—like most proletarian people, I preferred store-bought pack-aged things—she had placed a metal can filled with her homemade cookies and caramel candy. It was stashed under my brand new underwear marked "69" with two little red numbers, "6" and "9," that she had carefully sewn together. What teasing I would later endure from my classmates for this number that had been assigned to me by the authorities as the mandatory marking for my laundry!

The day before going to the lycée, I studied our itinerary and decided to go by train from Saint-Lazare station, rather than by suburban bus from Porte Maillot. I loved rail transportation, whether above or below ground, but disliked buses, except the open-backed ones in the city, which were great fun to ride.

"Nanterre," "Rueil-Malmaison," "Chatou," "Le Vésinet," "Le Pecq," the train makes its way through five stations before reaching Saint-Germain-en-Laye, half an hour from Paris. My eyes are glued to the window, but all I've seen so far are deserted streets lined with houses surrounded by a fence or a wall. Where are the people? What misery!

The spectacular leap over the Seine, as we near the end of the line, below the esplanade of the Château, revives me a bit. But except for one or two animated thoroughfares, the town of Saint-Germain—which we cross on foot, stopping often to rest our arms from the luggage—also has that wan provincial feel, so different from the pulsating energy of Paris.

How I would prefer at that moment to be in the heart of things, strolling in the lively streets of the capital, near the Halles central market for instance, or at the Printemps and the Galeries Lafayette department stores, where I can wander at will among the merchandise displays as if visiting a mu-seum of contemporary life, similar in many ways to the Museum of Man in our neighborhood; or walking down the teeming Rue de la Roquette in the Bastille district, site of my first inebriation at age seven when I accidentally drank too much wine during a visit there with my mother to a Slovak friend of hers; or simply standing at the métro station "Franklin D. Roosevelt," the one I prefer above all others for its luminous display windows, its modern vending machines, and its slight incline with a curve.

Once, I saw in that station a disheveled vagrant shake himself up from the bench where he was sleeping, and yell at the top of his lungs in the direc-tion of the empty tunnel, with that raucous Parisian verve, what everyone on the quay was mulling in silence: *"Alors, tu l'amènes ta ferraille!"* ("Come on, bring on that heap of iron!"). Not that he really cared about the arrival of the delayed subway train, because he proceeded to take a swig from a bottle of wine that he pulled out from the pile of rags forming his pillow. He then laid down again to continue his nap, this time on his side, with his back disdainfully turned to the crowd. It was such fun to see the sudden rush of latecomers, their burst of excitement, as they raced to beat the automatic door barring access to the quay when the "heap of iron" finally pulled into the station, and to watch how the passengers packed themselves into the wagons like sardines in a can.

Instead of getting on board with the overflow throng, I just sat out this departure and waited for the next train. My patience was rewarded with another show. A group of *loubards* (teen-age delinquents) entered the platform across the tracks from us, and started to heckle the old vagrant *"Hé vieux pédé, va cuver to pinard ailleurs."* ("Eh, old fag, go sleep off your wine elsewhere"). Awakened by these taunts, the old man sat up, rubbed his eyes, gazed as if through a fog in the direction of the hecklers, and promptly dismissed them with a pun on *"pédé"* that left them ridiculed and speechless:

"Ouais, pédé, parfaitement, j'suis PDG, et non seulement ça, mais en plus Peintre-Décorateur. Et vous, vous êtes tous comme des p'tits chiens, vous aboyez d'loin, p'tits merdeux." ("Yeah, *pédé*, that's what I am, *PéDéGé* (CEO) and not only that but also *peintre-décorateur* (painter/decorator). And you, you're all like little mutts yapping from afar, little shitheads.")

Upon which, he once more turned his back to the crowd and returned to sleep without acknowledging the spontaneous applause of the people who had filled the platform again for the next train.

In Paris, there's entertainment everywhere. It's limitless. No sooner have you left an attraction, another one appears. It's enough to simply open your eyes and look around while strolling at random wherever your feet take you.

When Maman and I finally reach the lycée, its walled-in appearance reminds me of one of the few places I don't like in Paris, the Santé prison. For the whole school, covering an entire block, there is only one access point, consisting of a large carriage entrance, which is closed, and a tiny door next to it, through which people enter and exit single file, like a procession of ants.

Inside the entryway, a reception hall houses the booth of the concierge, who supervises all comings and goings, and next to it the *"parloir,"* the visiting room, farthest point to which parents are allowed. With a heavy heart I kiss Maman goodbye in that room filled with somber-looking people.

Dragging my suitcase on the asphalt of the schoolyard, I head toward the *surgé*, the general overseer, a gruff man with a walrus mustache. He is dressed in a black suit shiny at the seat and the elbows and bursting at the seams. His enormous paunch protrudes out of his unbuttoned jacket. He is wearing a wide beret that flops down over his ear on one side. His barrel chest is cluttered with a watch chain, suspenders, a whistle, a necktie with soup stains. He stands in the courtyard barking out orders that reverberate throughout the compound. But I guess him to be possibly less mean than he appears. When he checks off my name from the list on his clipboard he mutters "Welcome to the lycée young man, I'm M'sieur Blau, but you know what, your name's too long, I'm gonna call you Kovaco." He points to the stairwell at the far corner of the yard and tells me to go choose a bed in the "fourth dorm."

"Oh, one more thing, Kovaco, don't drag that suitcase, pick it up off the ground."

At the bottom of the stairwell, I pause to catch my breath before the steep climb. An older boy comes running down the steps at full speed, one hand holding on to the banister to maintain his footing. Without breaking his stride, he yells at me with a smirk on his face: "*Fais gaffe, bizuth, t'as intérêt à pas t'gourer d'dortoir si tu veux pas t'faire enculer.*" ("Watch out, plebe, you better not get in the wrong dorm if you don't wanna get cornholed.")

What??? I infer, without understanding it fully, that his threat implies some sort of violence designed to scare the new students. Anxiety seizes me, the feeling that I have been thrown into a lions' pit, with no way out. I make an instant decision: I'll fight back with all my strength if I'm physically attacked, but I won't respond to taunts. I'll just ignore them.

Before climbing up the gloomy staircase, I go back outside for a gulp of fresh air to fortify my courage and determination. The asphalt courtyard is surrounded by the four wings of the brick building, and metal grilles protect the windows of the ground-floor classrooms. In the middle of the yard a few stunted trees shelter not a fountain, but the trickle of the outdoor latrines. Everything in sight reminds me of a sordid prison.

The dorm isn't much better. It looks like a sanatorium. About fifty narrow metal beds are lined up on each side of the cavernous room, which forms an entire wing of the lycée. Kids are sitting on the edge of their cots, silently unpacking their belongings. Some are shuffling cards and trying to start games of hearts or *belote* to break the ice with their neighbors.

The beds are all made up, with taut white sheets and grey blankets. There are no pillows, only bolsters. The walls are newly whitewashed, and the wooden floor polished to a bright shine. Despite the airing of the dorm by drafts from opposite windows, an ever so slight whiff of urine, coming from the thin mattresses, floats around the room, vying with the scent of floor wax. The temperature and the atmosphere chill me to the bone.

The dorm supervisor is a reluctant university student called a *pion*, a preceptor, who does this kind of work to defray his living expenses. He is housed in a central cubicle surrounded by a floor-to-ceiling curtain. As bedtime approaches, he comes out of his "room" to yell out an order:

"OK, tooth brushing time. This half of the dorm to the bathroom at this end, this half at the other end. No pushing or shoving!"

Everybody scrambles in the appointed direction, toothbrush in one hand, toothpaste in the other. I haven't yet encountered either of those objects. Empty-handed, I don't know what to do. So I just observe the bustle at the wash troth for a while, and decide to imitate an Arab kid who is swishing water in his mouth and vigorously rubbing his teeth with his index finger. I tell myself that the next time I have a chance to go into town, I'll get a toothbrush.

Before shutting off the lights, the *pion* gives us a brief orientation:

"You'll shower once a week, in the building across the yard, after the Thursday outing to Saint-Germain forest. You'll leave your laundry bags in the shower room that day. Make sure all your stuff is marked with your number. Also, no reading in bed after lights out. I don't want to see any flashlights under the sheets, or they'll be confiscated. Understood? Good night!"

My "refugee's special" suitcase sticks out compared to the luggage of the other students, made of leather and decorated with stickers from various resort hotels and steamship lines. I push it under my bed and decide to get rid of it at the first opportunity, even if it entails telling Maman it was stolen. She'll probably never have occasion to come back to the lycée anyway, and if so, she won't be allowed inside, I'll be called out to meet her in the visiting room at the entrance. I'll hear Monsieur Blau's thunderous voice echoing through the courtyard: **Kovaco, au Parloir!** ("Kovaco, to the Visiting Room!"). Wishful thinking...

The first weekend at the lycée stands out as one of the bleakest moments in my life. On Saturday afternoon the school emptied out almost completely, not only of its day students, but also of most boarders, who went home to their families in Paris for the weekend. There is hardly anything more depressing than being a leftover student at boarding school when the building is deserted.

And on Sunday, it was worse still. Besides the students from the French bourgeoisie, a number of my classmates came from prominent native families in France's increasingly restive colonial empire: Indochina, Arabic North Africa, Black Equatorial and Western Africa. The "Overseas," as those students from faraway places were called, also remained behind on Saturday, but they departed from the lycée right after lunch on Sunday, for an afternoon visit to their surrogate guardians in Paris. The only students then left at school were those held back on detention, plus the unfortunate *pion* condemned to supervise the forced "oxygenation" march to the Château esplanade, and forlorn me, who had no place to go.

Maman didn't want to impose on the Kapferers' hospitality, so we had decided that I would visit her only on the last Sunday afternoon of each month. And we hadn't figured out anything for the school breaks, approximately two weeks every couple of months, plus the entire summer, when it was mandatory to vacate the premises of the lycée. I could not imagine returning to live in Saint-Aquilin. That would be too painful, except for occasional day trips to stay in touch with Pépère and Mémère and at the same time visit my father's grave.

The *pion* tried to make the best of the Sunday outing to the Château Esplanade, with its panoramic view over the Seine and the Eiffel Tower in the distance. He even tried to ingratiate himself to us by relating some historical anecdotes about Louis XIV, going so far as to call him a "stubborn jerk" for having located his megalomaniac palace in low-lying, swampy Versailles, instead of high up here at Saint-Germain-en-Laye, where his more enlightened ancestors had built a hunting lodge at the edge of the royal forest. "He was insane, he wanted to control and dominate nature," the *pion* concluded. But our forlorn group couldn't care less about seventeenth-century King Louis, or the view from the esplanade. In fact the spectacular vista, admired by families out for a Sunday walk, felt to us like an additional affront, dangling before our eyes a freedom we couldn't have. We deliberately turned our backs on this impressive sight and looked instead in the opposite direction, towards the woods. The detainees, notorious troublemakers all, didn't even try to create a rumpus. Why oppose the *pion*, who was here too against his will, why trip people in the ranks? Why victimize anyone? A sense of dejected solidarity permeated the group.

The essential thing for me during that miserable start at the lycée was to not break down in tears. I was ashamed of my emotional collapse. The other boys, coming from wealthy backgrounds, seemed much more resilient than I. They were accustomed to Spartan institutional living. France did not coddle its "golden youth." Many of them had already spent extensive periods of time away from home, and even gone abroad, starting with linguistic stays in England at age seven or eight—considered in their world the "age of reason," when you begin to get weaned from overprotective nannies, and are propelled into the wider world. Compared to them, I was soft-skinned.

Furthermore, in Saint-Germain I was the "*benjamin*," younger by a year than all the other sixth-grade freshmen. While I easily passed for older with my classmates, this wasn't necessarily the case with the teachers. One of them wrote on my first report card "Adequate attention span despite his young age." And I was certainly the poorest, although I hoped none of my fellow students knew that.

When they returned to the dorm on Sunday night, my classmates often spoke of their plans to ski in the Alps at Megève or Courchevel during winter vacation, or go ice skating at the Molitor rink in Paris, or about concerts at the Olympia music-hall by the expatriate American jazzman Sydney Bechet, or about their record collections at home. I pretended I knew what they were talking about, but in reality had no idea. Up until then, I had only had access to an old radio plagued by the crackling sound of "parasites," and owning a record player seemed a luxury beyond my dreams. My preference went to accordion music, but I knew better than to admit that, sensing I would be ridiculed. However, I don't think any of my classmates knew or appreciated the streets of Paris like I did. The only thing we had in common, from totally opposite circumstances, was a feeling of divided loyalty and attachment toward parents and nannies, or in my case caretakers.

At the height of my despair, after two wretched week-ends spent in confinement at the lycée, a miracle occurred. Although I wasn't expecting to receive any letters, Mr. Blau blared out my name in three resounding syllables KO-VA-CO that silenced the deafening clatter of dishes and metal trays in the school's lunchroom, and signaled that the day's mail call had begun. It was a note from Madame Kapferer, expressing surprise that I had not yet returned for a visit, and inviting me to consider her house as my home for school breaks and vacations, as well as overnight every week-end. "It might be a little cramped, but for the time being you can sleep on a folding cot in your mother's room."

Thanks to my kind savior, a Jewish saint really, to whom I shall forever remain grateful, a huge pall was lifted. Not only would I now live in Paris, but at the most desirable location in the whole city, the mansion at 64 Avenue Henri-Martin in the 16th district. Upon reading Madame Kapferer's letter, I thought my heart would burst.

However, this stroke of good fortune did not mean the end of my travails. My adaptation to classroom work at the lycée also turned out to be extremely difficult. During the entire first year I felt helpless, whereas before I had achieved excellent results without effort. In academics, I went from self-assured big fish in a small pond, to disoriented minnow in a vast ocean.

What happened to my brain? It no longer functioned. Rosa, rosae, rosam, I didn't understand Latin declensions. Nor English grammar. Nor music theory. Pathetic in drawing. Mediocre in natural sciences and woodworking. Average in French, math, and history-geography. Only spelling held on, thanks to my photographic memory. And of course I ranked dead last in my nemesis, "*récitation*" (learning a text by heart), 34th out of 34.

I feared that I might lose my scholarship, but my anguish was unfounded. I managed to navigate through this harrowing first year with my woeful performance seemingly unnoticed by anyone except me. I was thankful the teachers and administrators at the lycée showed patience—or indifference—about my initial results, as attested by their recurrent, laconic, yet comforting evaluations: "*Peut mieux faire*" ("Can do better").

Yes, do better. But how? One thing was certain: I couldn't afford to fail. I considered the scholarship a salary of sorts for my schoolwork. I was earning my living. I had to. Maman couldn't provide for me.

I felt frustrated to have lost my scholastic confidence, derived from the amazing clarity of Madame Mercier's teaching, and also to have lost the joy of learning that had characterized my years in her classroom. I accepted my academic deficiencies—it's useless to try to develop a talent one doesn't have—and I was well aware of them, beyond the bizarre aspects of my memory. How many times had I heard Madame Mercier mention that I resembled her, in that I sang out of tune and didn't know how to draw. But I couldn't understand why my intellect had collapsed to such an extent. And there was no one with whom to talk about it. I was drowning.

In addition to my problems of dismal academic results, age difference, and social class adjustment, the daily life of a boarder proved to be very challenging at first. The direct violence I feared when I first arrived at the lycée never materialized, but I had to endure, like all freshmen, hazing and harassment from the more established students. For instance, we were often rolled out of bed in the middle of night by ghosts who disappeared as soon as their terroristic mission was accomplished. Or the snorers among us (fortunately I wasn't one) got the humiliating "toothpaste in the open mouth" treatment.

In the dining hall, students were seated at rectangular tables of eight, four on each side, in order of seniority, with a pair of sixth-graders like me across from each other in last position. Metal trays laden with eight portions were distributed for each course from a cart in the middle aisle. The freshmen had to settle for whatever was left after the other students helped themselves, more or less copiously according to their mood of the moment. It was out of the question to complain to the *pions*, who walked the aisle, book in hand, perpetually absorbed in their own studies. They didn't want to be disturbed. Also, ratting was viewed as a serious violation to the inner code of silence, punishable by a collective beating. The code was rarely broken. Although a climate of latent violence and pervasive hazing prevailed, I never witnessed nor experienced any outright brutality in my four years at the lycée. Nor any homosexual acts, although a few students overtly claimed to be gay, one of them even flouting his weekend visits to gatherings hosted by the famous playwright Jean Cocteau and his movie actor friend Jean Marais. Despite the crowded collective setting, "propriety" was adhered to, and I never saw any boy totally naked, including in the showers which were arranged in cubicles to ensure privacy.

Sometimes, swayed by the protestations or the laments of the abused freshmen, their tormentors would let on a glimmer of humanity: "Shut up, later it'll be your turn to treat others that way." And indeed the cycle of "tradition" seemed to follow that course, with the victims in due time becoming the next persecutors.

The food, or whatever remained of it when the serving trays reached the end of the table, was excellent. I especially liked the Monday lunch menu, consisting of stuffed tomatoes as hors d'oeuvre, followed by beef stew, then green salad, camembert cheese, and for dessert yoghurt or fruit (in the basket containing apples, bananas, and oranges, we at the end invariably wound up with the lowly apples). I also looked forward to the seafood dishes every Friday. For the afternoon snack at 4 p.m., we were served a *"pain au chocolat"* with one liter of pasteurized beer for each table. At breakfast, bread with butter and marmalade, and a bowl of café au lait.

And with each meal, unlimited amounts of bread, baskets of it, already sliced, that we could refill at will from a large barrel. Those cut up pieces of baguettes were also used as projectiles for food fights across the dining hall. I didn't participate. These outbursts of mayhem troubled me. I had been brought up to not waste food, and to value bread especially.

My morning queasy stomach from the village disappeared at the lycée. I attributed this wondrous improvement to my new diet, particularly the unrestricted access to bread.

At Pépère and Mémère's, we ate very little bread—complex food, impossible to make without a good oven, and requiring an elaborate transformation process from wheat to flour to dough even before the baking stage—unlike foods pulled directly from the ground in our garden, a small-scale cornucopia, and eaten raw or cooked on the stove top: strawberries, carrots, radishes, turnips, potatoes, rutabaga, onions, Jerusalem artichokes, cabbage, leek, spinach, lettuce, Belgian endives. Or picked from stems a little higher up from the soil: peas, string beans, tomatoes, currants, raspberries. Or gathered from tree branches in the manner of hunters and gatherers: apples, pears, apricot, quince, cherries, walnuts. Oranges and bananas were considered fancy, exotic fruit consumed only at Christmas time. For meat, Pépère simply ambled to the henhouse or the hutches to grab a rabbit or a chicken by the neck. I was in charge of collecting eggs.

In our self-sufficient mode of living, bread seemed needlessly expensive and impractical. When we bought some at the village grocery store, it had to be eaten right away. Otherwise, it quickly hardened, and by breakfast time the next morning it had become so crusty, especially for Mémère, that it had to be dipped in the bowl of chicory.

Because of this scarcity of bread, in Saint-Aquilin I seldom had a full stomach. This was a rather special form of malnutrition since in wealthy families, on the contrary, consumption of bread—considered proletarian, excessively filling, and of low nutritional value—was limited. They favored instead fresh garden vegetables, which we in the village took for granted. Another paradox of poverty! And another idiosyncrasy of mine! I often wondered whether other people too were afflicted with these kinds of mental and physical quirks.

After my miserable initial classroom results, I began during the second year to understand the structure of Latin, and to recover my former scholastic mettle. In the dining hall, I also moved up one notch. But above all, I discovered soccer.

I especially liked the pickup games in the asphalt courtyard after each meal, with whatever we could find to kick around, often only a tennis ball or a sardine can. My feet were growing fast, and after my stiff new shoes were broken in, and the protective metal cleats that Maman insisted on had dissolved from the sparks emitted at each kick, I could count on a period of relative foot comfort.

The absolute soccer king in our lycée was Zacharie Noah, two or three years older than I. Son of a Cameroon tribal chief, he would later become a professional soccer player, and father of the tennis and pop music star Yannick Noah, himself father of noted Chicago Bulls basketball player Joakin Noah.

Zacharie reigned over soccer not only in the lycée courtyard, but also at the Saint-Germain sports stadium. What a virtuoso he was! I lacked his supreme skills, but he appreciated my tenacity and often chose me to be on his team for the pickup games. I found this flattering. From the backfield, we had developed a strategy together. With his stunning dribbles, he would run up the courtyard and serve me on the right foot perfect passes that I only had to shoot, sometimes on the volley, onto the wall marking the opposite team's goalpost. The next time, it was my turn to pass to him, and at that point, everybody scrammed out of the way of his cannon shots, which sometimes shattered the classroom windows, despite the protective grilles.

Soccer in a regular field appealed much less to me than those pickup games in the schoolyard. This was due to another weird and unusual shortcoming of mine, which could remain hidden in the confined close-to-the-ground yard play, but became more obvious in the airy stadium setting: I never hit the ball with my head. I had done that once, and it had rattled the synapses inside my skull so much that I never attempted it afterwards. I used convenient pretexts, such as not owning shin guards or regulation shoes, to avoid stadium games and putting myself again in that predicament.

At the beginning of my third year at the lycée, we transferred to an attractive new campus located on a wooded hill not far from the Château. It no longer looked like a prison, but with the disappearance of our asphalt courtyard we also lost our "soccer field." I became interested for a while in handball, and then running. My favorite distance was the 400 meters race through the park of the new lycée with its big trees and various slopes. For this sport too, I was averse to the stadium track, flat and boring. I loved cross-country running, without pushing myself too hard, more for the fun of it than for competition. Physically and mentally, I now felt great.

That third year, eighth grade, when I was twelve, with also in my class several 14-year-old repeaters towards whom I tended to gravitate, was for me a period of flourishing. Imitating my classmates, I began to smoke, most often contraband American cigarettes, dampened during their transfers on the Mediterranean sea off the coast of Marseille or Sicily, and then dried again. The Arabs at school smoked the most. Their fingers stained to a dark brown, they owned whole cartons of those smuggled cigarettes, purchased cheap. In the fraternity of tobacco, following the precepts of the Koran, and in the manner of the street peddlers of their native lands, they occasionally sold them back to us one cig at a time, presumably for no profit. Following the normal progression, I also moved up to second in line at table in our section of the dining hall, almost as good as being at the head.

That year, I racked up first prizes in French, English, Spanish, and History-Geography, as well as certificates of merit in French to Latin translation and Physical Education. I did well in algebra too and loved geometry. All this with another upper-class trait I somehow absorbed: the eschewal of effort, perceived as unseemly. In my case this attitude went further than an elegant pose. It bordered on the kind of lazyness that, under the appearance of lethargy, nonetheless has a redeeming value: It leaves one available for whatever comes up. I was an idler, endowed with an infinite capacity to do nothing that even included an allergy to "killing time" with board games or card playing. Either consciously or unconsciously, I also censored myself out of extracurricular activities—requiring schedules, fees, and specialized training or equipment—that my classmates commonly engaged in, such as judo, jujitsu, fencing, tennis, ice skating, skiing, or horseback riding. Independently of obvious economic factors, those activities didn't enter my mind. They were for people "not like me." I did well at whatever came to me naturally and disregarded the rest. This made for a rather narrow sphere of endeavors, limited to kicking a ball around, strolling in the streets of Paris, or reading anything and everything, with a marked preference for poetry, comic books, and detective novels.

Regarding the French prize, I thought my classmate Larrose deserved it more than I did. He was the wordsmith in our class. But since he had peaks and valleys in his results, I finished slightly ahead of him overall for the year.

Our grading system resembled the Tour de France, with yellow jersey, members of the pack, stragglers, and injuries or accidents. In Latin to French translation, supposedly easy compared to the reverse in which I had done well, I crashed in that third year: 27th out of 34, whereas the preceding year I had received the first prize. In math, honorable result, 7th in the last stage, and in biology 3rd in the final sprint, but not very good in the first trimester: 22nd. In *récitation*, no surprises, always last. All in all, a satisfying tally, particularly in the humanities, the only subjects in which I held any semblance of competitive attitude.

When I first entered the lycée, I was placed in the Latin-Modern Languages track. This suited me fine. I discovered later that there existed other options with different emphases, such as Latin-Ancient Greek, or also a "Modern" track, and a "New" track, with a full complement of courses in every one of these alternatives, but varying doses of math, science, and languages in each. Except for my selection of Spanish as a second modern language, I had no input in any of these choices. Anyway, it would have been for naught. The differences, or their consequences, defied my understanding. By then, I was simply "there," fitting in quite nicely, not working hard, yet getting excellent results. The "can do better" comments continued to appear on my report cards, but now they were inscribed in the behavior and attitude column rather in than the academic one. Nothing drastic, though. I was simply coming out of my shell. My musical tastes also progressed, from accordion *musette* to a genuine passion for Miles Davis in jazz, and Georges Brassens or Léo Ferré in French *chanson*.

At the end of that otherwise wonderful third year, an unfortunate experience occurred. I had already returned home to Avenue Henri-Martin for the summer. There remained only to attend the school awards ceremony. On that morning, I prepared to leave from Maman's kitchen:

"Okay, I'm going now."

"Where you go?"

"Well, back to the lycée for the awards ceremony. I talked to you about it last week. It was on my report card. You even told me to go show it to Madame, and she mentioned that you could prepare a cold lunch and let the other domestics take care of things if you wanted the day off."

"Ah, yes, I remember. Is *obligatoire* I go with you?"

"Well no, it's not *obligatoire*, you don't *have* to go."

"You want I prepare something for you to take for eating there? I make sandwich with ham."

"No, don't bother. They're planning a special meal for the students and their parents in the lycée's dining hall." And then, gingerly: "Are you coming?"

"No, I not go. I do shopping in Montmartre in afternoon to buy fabric for sending to Slovakia. They have sale. I give you money for train and métro tickets."

"Okay, thanks. I'll be back later this evening. Since I'll be at Saint-Lazare train station, I'll go for a walk on the Grands Boulevards before returning home."

Damn, I hadn't anticipated this. Do I go or not go? I'll be all alone at the ceremony. None of my friends will be there. I feel dejected instead of happy for this occasion.

At Saint-Lazare station, to take my mind off my predicament, I buy the sports daily *L'Équipe* for the soccer section. At the Chatou stop, I think of my sister Olga, who was working there as a live-in housekeeper when I first started at the lycée. Once, we took the train together from Paris. We arrived at the station late, so we jumped on board when the wagons had already begun to move, and her high-heeled shoe got stuck between the quay and the boarding step. She lost the shoe but could have gotten her leg torn off. Afterwards in the train, we laughed about the incident, and discussed what would look more grotesque: return to her employer's barefoot, or limp along on only one shoe. She opted for bare feet.

When I arrive at the lycée for the ceremony, I find the overseer M'sieur Blau pacing up and down the hallway in front of the visiting room, his hands behind his back. His floppy béret pulled down as always to his eyebrows, he greets me with a friendly nod. I sense he sympathizes with me. Maybe he's aware I'm a scholarship student?

"Well, Kovaco, what's going on, you're all alone? No parents or guardians coming along? Don't worry, at lunch I'll sit next to you, and we can toast each other with a glass of red."

The reception hall is filled with students and their parents, or in the case of the "Overseas," their Paris guardians. The principal opens the session and the assistant principal calls out the names of the award winners, to whom he hands out books offered as prizes.

When it's our class's turn, my name is called several times in a row. With each trip to the podium, I return to my seat with a book. Soon, a whole stack is piled up on the empty spot next to me.

At the end of the ceremony, the principal invites everyone to the adjoining dining hall. M'sieur Blau, already installed there, waves for me to come sit next to him. For this occasion the tables are covered with white linen, and carafes of wine have replaced the bottles of pasteurized beer. As always, the food is excellent, but I don't pay much attention to what's on my plate.

The father of an older student shakes my hand:

"Congratulations, young man! You really racked up the prizes! But your name isn't French, if I'm not mistaken it sounds Yugoslavian. Are your parents by any chance involved with the diplomatic corps or UNESCO? You don't have a guardian here in Paris?"

"Yes, but he couldn't come."

"Listen, we're returning to the city right after lunch, to the Seventh District. If you want, we can give you a ride back with us. Where do you live?"

"In the Sixteenth, Avenue Henri-Martin, but no thanks, I was planning to take the train."

"As you wish."

Dessert barely finished, I bid M'sieur Blau goodbye and hurry to the railroad station with my cumbersome stack of books.

It's a hot day, so the windows on the train are rolled down. I sit in the last row. The few other passengers in the car have also taken preferred seats facing forward, so they all have their backs to me, and they're absorbed in their thoughts or reading newspapers.

In the middle of the high bridge spanning the Seine between Saint-Germain and Le Pecq, I'm seized with a sudden irresistible urge: "*Throw these damn books out the window!*"

And I act on it.

Relief is immediate, as if I had just vomited. I feel liberated by this spontaneous, crazy act, and find neither the strength nor the desire to watch the books that I imagine cascading down to the river like a flight of seagulls.

Back in Paris, I decide to take a walk on the Grands Boulevards, to the métro station Bonne Nouvelle. As always I feel revived by the liveliness of the city. The street peddlers are selling a mishmash of knickknacks piled up in large inverted umbrellas that they can fold in a jiffy in case the cops show up: ballpoint pens in four different colors, handkerchiefs, potato peelers, pocket mirrors, sample-size shampoo, chewing gum ("The real American stuff, ladies and gentlemen, not an imitation, come forward, don't be afraid, get some for your children"), spiral notebooks, shoelaces, a jumble of disparate merchandise that they thrust at passersby stupefied by the generosity of these magicians endowed with a dizzying gift of gab: "Not one, not two, not three, not four, but five, five, you heard me right ladies and gentlemen, five handkerchiefs, and I'll even throw in a pocket mirror for the same price, and why not, some shoe laces too."

Whew! I'm back in Paris, I can breathe again and forget the awards ceremony.

At the beginning of ninth grade, when I was thirteen and in my fourth year at school, our new literature teacher—a pale man with burning eyes who wore a cape and was imbued with the aura of leading a bohemian life in Montmartre— fulfilled our pent up expectations of explosive discoveries by introducing us to the long-awaited poetry of Baudelaire, Verlaine, and Rimbaud. My classmate Larrose seemed destined to become the new prodigy of French letters, the new Rimbaud, jaded beyond his years like his illustrious and infamous predecessor who had written *"Assez vu, assez eu, assez connu"* ("Seen enough, had enough, known enough") at seventeen. I can't even recall Larrose having a first name, as if he had already achieved a writer's fame.

Our class had had some nibbles of poetry before, but that year we plunged into the writings of the celebrated 19th Century trio. And there again, much to my lament, my faulty memory prevented me from learning by heart even the briefest poem—though the few lines I managed to remember gained by their dearth a special meaning:

From Baudelaire:

> *Sois sage ô ma douleur*
> *Et tiens-toi plus tranquille*
> *Tu réclamais le soir, il descend, le voici*

Une atmosphère obscure enveloppe la ville
Aux uns portant la paix, aux autres le souci.

So perfect it is best left untranslated, lest the dictum be confirmed that when you translate poetry what you lose is...the poetry.

Or the Baudelaire line I once relished throwing to Larrose to trump him in his affectation of *"ennui"* (tedium): *"La chair est triste, hélas, et j'ai lu tous les livres"* (this one translatable, as "The flesh is sad, alas, and I've read all the books") until he corrected me *"C'est pas Baudelaire, c'est Mallarmé."* ("It's not Baudelaire, it's Mallarmé.") I checked, and he was right. I could have put my hand in the fire that Baudelaire was the author of this line, so much did it seem in his vein.

Or from Verlaine:

Le ciel est par-dessus le toit
Si bleu, si calme
Un arbre par-dessus le toit
Berce sa palme.

Sublime in French for its musical and linguistic simplicity; corny if translated.

I discovered later in life that almost everyone has some sort of shortcoming, sometimes hidden, similar to my inability to memorize texts by heart, the most common being a deficient sense of orientation, or various lacks of aptitude, most notably in math, music, art, or languages; and in the physical realm, coordination.

Did my classmates in the lycée know I was a scholarship student? I don't think so, but I'm not sure. At any rate, they expressed no such inklings. My home address, on famous Avenue Henri-Martin, the street used in the French version of Monopoly to designate wealth, gave me cover. When I met with them on weekends in Paris, it was usually in some café or rendezvous point, as was common in France, instead of each other's homes.

One of the *pions* even nicknamed me *"L'Anglais"* ("The Englishman") alluding, with a tinge of mockery perhaps, to my proper table manners and polite demeanor. His misperception is easy to understand: although my upbringing had taken place at the lowest rung of the peasantry, I had also since infancy been closely exposed to rich people and their way of life, through Maman's employment. I had no doubt absorbed some of their traits. That's why a butler, who doesn't even have lodgings of his own, can easily pass for an aristocrat, while a plumber, who at least lives independently, is not likely to be perceived as upper class. This, along with my Alec Wildenstein clothes, explains why I could outwardly be (mis)taken for a *petit Monsieur*.

Among teachers and administrators, I assume my financial circumstances were known, but during my four years at the lycée I had an indication of that only once, in a French class. We were ranked all the time, publicly, at every turn, for everything, and in every subject, relentlessly. In that particular instance, the teacher praised me in front of the class for having turned in the best essay. He then launched into an embarrassing tirade:

"You all come from well-to-do families, and yet Kovacovic, whose parents are poor immigrants from Yugoslavia with no books or library at home I'm sure, passes you up in French. You should be ashamed. His father is a cook. It's hard work, you know, to always be leaning over a hot stove. Shame on you all."

I felt my face turning red. But nobody in the class ever spoke to me about the incident, as if I alone had heard the teacher's harangue, in which furthermore he had badly scrambled the facts.

Inside the lycée, one could reinvent oneself. The external world's social distinctions were to a large extent held at bay.

The initial year of adjustment had been excruciatingly lonely for me, not only due to my age, but also my peasant background even more dissimilar from the prevailing norm than race (the factor of skin color tends to become irrelevant for those who are situated high up on the social scale, as was the case for the indigenous "Overseas"). But after that difficult early period, I began to adapt to my new surroundings and to appreciate the positive aspects of lycée boarding life. It allowed for greater camaraderie, better study conditions (for those who cared about that), more fun, faster maturation, and wider autonomy than our day-school classmates could experience at home. Perhaps as a rationalization or a self-defense mechanism, we considered those students henpecked by their parents, and therefore inferior to us. In the internal hierarchy of the institution, they themselves accepted this subordinate status. It's as if for them too, who unlike us had a choice, the peer group had become more important than family.

If girls had been present, boarding school would have been utopia... maybe. An adolescent fantasy of heaven, or a hell on earth with unimaginable tensions, intrigues, and jealousies?

In my case, I had mutated in those four years from a shy loner ("docile" read several comments in my early grade reports), into a moderately misbehaving teenager with a newfound ascendancy that, I'm proud to say, I did not unduly exploit.

Concerning behavior, I had to be careful. I couldn't afford to heedlessly transgress the rules of the institution, like some of my hotheaded friends who didn't care the least about consequences I would have found devastating—for instance getting expelled from school, which would entail my losing the scholarship and ...what next? An apprenticeship back in the village? I couldn't contemplate that perspective, nor could I financially afford to attend private school, which at the time catered to students who had failed out of, or been expelled from, the more prestigious public sector, such as my lycée represented (Yeah wealthfare!). I marveled at the carefreeness and bravado of my friends who could throw all restraint to the winds. I walked on the thin ice of misbehavior with them, but remained mindful of the danger lurking at every step. I had no safety net to rely on, nor would I be rescued if I fell through.

Regarding social class, my background did not limit my horizons. Madame Kapferer had solemnly declared to Maman, in my presence, that she should not worry about my future: Monsieur would see to it that I'd be "well placed" after my studies. Since he was known to have important stockholdings in the Shell oil company, I fantasized I might travel the world over, from the Sahara to Indonesia, as the Kapferers' "liege man" based in Paris.

Or perhaps a researcher in pharmaceuticals? That notion derived from my early-childhood meanderings at the Sagout dairy complex in Normandy, where Lactoserum products were concocted. But I had some misgivings about science, associating it in my experience with the slightly nauseous smell prevailing in the labs at both Sagout and the lycée.

Those were the two hazy career prospects that occasionally entered my mind. I lacked sufficient imagination to contemplate any others.

At some fleeting moments the refined atmosphere of the various salons and boudoirs of 64 Avenue Henri-Martin did entice me. I enjoyed, on hot summer days, retreating from the burning mineral city to the fragrant shade of the chestnut trees lining the avenue in front of our windows, with its equestrian lane in the middle. There, each morning, ladies and gentlemen in jodhpurs, including the Kapferers' daughter Madame Legrand, rode their frisky thoroughbreds between the Eiffel Tower esplanade at Trocadero plaza and nearby Boulogne Woods.

True to my congenital ambivalence, though, I felt equally at home in the raucus working-class neighborhoods, Rue de la Roquette in the Bastille district, or Rue Rambuteau near the Halles central market, or the Nation district at the eastern end of the city. There, Maman sometimes took me along to visit Slovak compatriots of hers, confirmed bachelors lucky enough, given the severe Parisian housing shortage, to find lodgings in *hôtels meublés*. These consisted of cramped furnished rooms filled to the ceiling with neatly stacked suitcases and cardboard boxes, and only a sink and a hot plate for amenities. Toilet? Down the hall, Turkish style, a mere hole in the floor. And once a week, a visit to the public showers several blocks away.

These compatriots were either too indecisive or too poor to set up household or marry a widow with dependents. Woodworker, tailor, or produce handler at the Halles central market, they dreamt inveterately: this one, of the advent of communism in France; this one of starting up his own small business. Among workers, the unprecedented economic expansion of the "thirty glorious" post-war years hadn't yet manifested itself. And when it did, they were pushed out to newly-built housing projects in the suburbs, in order to make room for offices and a more affluent social class in the central city.

There was another realm in which I was a bit off from the "norm": religion.

My parents' native village of Bzince pod Javorinou in Slovakia was divided into two camps, Catholic and Protestant. My kin were Protestant. In Bzince, unlike in less fortunate regions of Europe, the antagonism between those two groups stayed within civilized bounds, limiting itself to the use of the distancing pronouns "we" and "they."

In France, following the religious civil wars of the sixteenth century, Protestants formed only a tiny minority, and their "temples" were few and far between. Maman gave up on religious practice, simply because of logistics, and felt guilty about my lack of Christian education. She considered enrolling me in Catholic catechism in Pacy-sur-Eure when I lived in the village, but I vehemently resisted that notion.

In Saint-Germain-en-Laye, there was a Protestant temple not far from the lycée. To please Maman, and also to have a legitimate excuse to get away from the confines of school, during my last year I enrolled for religious instruction on Thursdays, the day off from regular classes then "reserved" for such activities in the secular French educational system. Occasionally, to please her even more, I attended the Sunday morning service at the temple on Rue Cortambert, two blocks from the Kapferers, after helping her with the grocery shopping.

All of a sudden, Protestantism, so rare in France, and considered elitist, was at my doorstep. The congregations at Saint-Germain and Rue Cortambert were made up mostly of well-to-do people. I could see this by their serious manner and the quality of their clothing, but I was surprised they addressed God in the familiar "*tu*" form, instead of the formal "*vous*" used by Catholics.

My participation did not rise above a superficial level. I was an outsider and, deep down, content to remain so while at the same time saddened to not belong. I made no effort to integrate, and no one reached out for me. Had anyone done so, I probably would have resisted.

Notwithstanding my late flourishing at the lycée, there remained a major problem to solve, *the* problem that overshadowed all else. Those of us boarders who had not yet resolved it were reminded of our predicament by the chorus of chants taunting us when we returned to the dorm from Paris each week-end: "Another Sun-day/Sun-day / and sti-ill/sti-ill / cher-ries/cherries."

Sunday night around Saint-Lazare rail station, prior to taking the commuter train back to Saint-Germain, a dilemma confronted us novices. To resolve the problem or not? And where to go? To nearby Rue d'Amsterdam, brightly lit and where we might get brushed off by the streetwalkers because of our age, anyone below sixteen being likely to get turned down? Or a few blocks further, to Rue de Provence, more shadowy, and where looser rules were said to apply?

I was thirteen, but had always passed for older. The time came, one Sunday night, before the departure of the last train, to decide whether or not I was going to "go upstairs" in one of the dingy hotels.

I was prepared. I had "borrowed" some funds from Maman's shoebox of cash for the purchase of food for the Kapferer household, and had every intention to return the exact same amount at the first opportunity. End-of-year holidays were near, and I could count on a gift of some banknotes from Madame Kapferer. I would return the money to the shoebox instead of depositing it in my savings account at the post office, as Maman expected me to.

That first experience of real "*petite mort*" ("little death") turned out to be a scary, thrilling enough affair, but not memorable. On the intimacy scale, it rated a zero. I had to pay first, and was pushed back vigorously when, in the heat of consummation, I tried to kiss my initiatress on the lips. "That's the one thing we don't do," she said, with absolute determination and a feigned look of horror.

That night at the lycée, I could finally strut back to the dorm and participate in the bragging sessions.

Just before lights out, Durand, more experienced than me in these matters, came over to my bunk and slipped me a tube of ointment.

"What's that?" I asked.

"Penicillin," he said. "You better apply it for three days in a row if you don't want to catch the syph."

Chapter 10

Olga's Brother

"Through one of those bizarre quirks of fate that I often encountered
in the course of my life, I found myself at the same time above and
below my condition: I was both a disciple and a domestic in the same
house, and in my servitude I nonetheless had a preceptor of a rank
appropriate for the children of kings."

— Jean-Jacques Rousseau

Following our return to France after the failed reinstallation in Slovakia
when I was four, Olga attended Madame Mercier's one-room schoolhouse for two years, and during that time boarded like me at Mémère and
Pépère's in Saint-Aquilin. She turned fifteen in July at the end of that second
year. Madame Mercier, in a generous act of rule bending, simply kept her
on beyond the age limit in her program. She wanted to help Olga catch up
with her schooling, which had been ravaged by emigration when she entered
adolescence. All the while, Olga was struggling with the French language,
especially in view of the well-intentioned but impatient and unrealistic expectations of our mother, who wanted her to quickly become a clerk-typist,
symbol of female upward mobility among the domestic class.

When this project obviously failed, Olga began to work as a live-in *bonne
à tout faire* (literally a "good for everything" housekeeper) in a series of Parisian families. During her difficult teen-age years, she was left to fend for
herself in the city, without material or moral support. Among her employers,
only the last one, Madame Perret, showed any care or concern.

Olga's employment with the Perrets, at 51 Rue Raynouard, coincided
with my second year at boarding school. Since her place of work wasn't
far from Avenue Henri-Martin, I often came over to see her during my

weekend and vacation stays in Paris. The last of those visits, during the December holidays, stands out vividly in my mind:

Rue de l'Annonciation, the belly of Paris's 16th District, three days before Christmas. Olga leads me by the hand, single file, in front of the fruit and vegetable stands lining the sidewalk. Like every morning at this time, the narrow street is filled with shoppers making their daily rounds. Cars no longer attempt to get through. Their impatient horns and squeaking brakes have been stilled, replaced by the strangely muffled sound of feet shuffling on the pavement, with fragments of conversation or gossip overheard ("Have you heard that.... But don't tell anyone..."), and the calls of vendors competing for the customers' attention, like the barkers at the entrance of the nightclubs at Pigalle.

Exuding scents of expensive perfumes, wrapped in full-length mink coats with sumptuous Hermès scarves loosely draped over their shoulders, and followed by a maid who lugs the oilcloth grocery bags, the rich ladies of Passy lift their lap dogs off the ground to protect them from the crunch, or to defuse an occasional confrontation. Today, it's an ill-behaved toy poodle wearing a rhinestone collar and yellow sweater who is being scolded by his mistress—"You mean little terrorist you, you leave that nice boy alone"—as another mink-clad dog owner cradles her dachshund visibly frazzled by his encounter with the neighborhood bully.

The bejeweled ladies flit from one stand to another, squeeze, sniff, taste the merchandise: "Let me have a slice of that orange, would you, I want to be sure they're sweet, are they from Morocco?" They compose their lunch and dinner menus right there, on the spot, according to whim or inspiration. The street abounds in victuals: meat, fish, fowl, cheese, butter, eggs, in seemingly endless varieties. Half a dozen kinds of oysters, brought in to Paris on the night train from the Atlantic coast, and presented on glistening beds of ice and seaweed. White-skinned and yellow-skinned chickens hanging upside down from hooks, ready for the kitchen but with their crests still on, and with registry tags affixed to their feet to certify region of origin. Eggs for every conceivable purpose, the best ones for soft-boiling, with shells that are hard enough to be carried loose in paper bags, and ranging in color from white to brown, and even pale blue ones laid by guinea hens. Not to mention the overflowing fruit and vegetable stands, and the enclosed shops with their enticing displays of bread and pastries, confectionery, delicatessen, wines and spirits. What to choose from all this profusion? What to choose?

Today, Olga opts for simplicity, to contrast with the upcoming holiday feasts. She decides on bifteck-frites-salade for lunch, and meatless pasta for dinner. "Anyvay," she says, "Monsieur and Madame Perret not care what they eat when they very busy like now."

I walk behind her, my knees bumping at each step against her big shopping bag already filled to the half with…comic books. "This going break mine arm and tvist mine spine," she grumbles. Fabulously generous despite her modest wages as a live-in housekeeper for the famous architect Auguste Perret and his wife, Olga has just offered me an entire stack of my favorite titles at the corner news and stationery shop. What a treat! She even introduced me to the owner:

"Monsieur propriétaire, this is mine little brother Milan. He is one who be picking up *Lé Monde* newspaper for Madame Perret in afternoon today."

"*Lé* plural, or *le* singular, Mademoiselle? It's important to pronounce correctly, you know. The Perrets are prominent intellectuals, and they often reserve several copies of the newspaper, for their friends or for Monsieur's associates I presume. So, this afternoon, will it be *Lé* or *Le*?"

"*Lé*, only vone," answers Olga, tripping herself up in her French mispronunciations. Then, pointing to the comics on the rack, she tells me "Go ahead, Milanko, help youself, take all you vant."

Before her invitation is finished, I lunge with disbelieving eyes at this gold mine, grabbing on the way a special issue of the sports daily *L'Équipe* devoted to soccer. What a windfall! Except for the Monday morning issue of *L'Équipe* featuring the complete results of the Sunday sports events, I can't really afford much in the way of reading materials. Aside from my métro tickets and transportation costs to school, which I try to pocket by sneaking on board the train whenever possible, I only get a token allowance from Maman. If I need something, I have to ask her, and she always manages to rummage some funds from one of the shoe boxes under her bed, but my requests have to be for some useful purpose, for instance school supplies at Gibert Jeune in the Latin Quarter, my favorite store in all Paris. I can spend hours there, drooling over the display cases of fountain pens like those owned by my classmates, with brand names that are out of reach for me: Parker, Waterman, Mont Blanc. Or Maman gives me money for shoes at the Bata store, because I outgrow mine fast or wear them out playing soccer in the asphalt courtyard of the lycée. Outside of that, I don't cost her a thing, what with my free room and board at the lycée and at the Kapferers, my fancy clothes from Alec Wildenstein, and even a month of summer camp at Hyères on the Riviera, which Madame Kapferer arranged for me through the office of social services for the "economically disadvantaged" people of the 16th District, at the town hall across the equestrian lane from her mansion. But despite these misleading outward appearances, including my snobbish address at 64 Avenue Henri-Martin ("La Di Da..."—I try to keep it quiet to avoid the teasing), I have no money. And whenever I get a banknote from Madame Kapferer or Madame Perret, for New Year's Day or end-of-school or some other occasion, Maman expects me to immediately salt it away in my savings account at the post office, and not think about it anymore. "Like this, I have peace, I know you not be in street when you have majorité, when you be twenty one." Her obsession about not raising a future indigent must have spread to my benefactors too, because whenever they give me some money, they don't say "Here, it's for you," but "Here, it's for your savings account."

At the news shop on Rue de l'Annonciation, when Olga was about to pay for the comic books, the owner admired my haul:

"How lucky you are, young man, to have a sister who spoils you like that. By the way, how old are you? I know that Mademoiselle here is about nineteen or twenty, a wonderful age. What about you?"

"Eleven and three fourths, M'sieur, twelve in April."

"And how come you don't have a Chtecolovak accent like her?"

"Because I was born in Normandy."

"In Normandy? How so? Explain that to me. Or on second thought, no, you're probably in a hurry, I'm sure you young people have lots of errands to do. I won't delay you, I'll ask Madame Perret to fill me in on the details some other time."

I'm eager to return to Olga's kitchen in the Perrets' penthouse so I can read my comic books in peace, while she goes about her work. I'll peel potatoes for her, and slice them so she can make French fries, and after lunch, I'll dry the dishes. Except for those chores, I'll be free to read to my heart's content, provided Madame Perret doesn't interrupt me too much, which from past experience wouldn't be a surprise, because she's intolerant of idleness or of anything that isn't "educational" or "cultural." For the time being, I let myself be dragged by Olga along the fruit and vegetable stands, absorbed as I am already in the adventures of my favorite characters: Croquignol, Ribould-ingue, and Filochard—the Nickeled Feet trio.

"You can should wait when we get home to read. Look where you put feet" Olga chides me as I stumble against the curb.

Pavel Harmady reigns as usual on a platform behind his salad stand on Rue de l'Annonciation, two steps up from the sidewalk. He holds forth between a pyramid of neatly stacked Belgian endives to his left, and a similar pile of lettuce to his right. He is the street's most popular salad man. From a distance one can hear his stentorian voice veiled by the whizz of heavy smoking: "Come forvard, come forvard, ladies, not hesitate, not be scared, I not bite. Look at mine salad. Is not gorgeous?" And he proudly displays plump heads of lettuce in his extended hands. "Not hesitate, ladies, sqveeze it, kiss it, hug it, not hesitate!" As Olga and I proceed towards him, he comes down from his platform to give us a peck on the cheek, not twice, not thrice, but four times, following the custom of I forget which region, Brittany I think. His face, clean-shaven at one a.m. for his nightly rounds at the Halles central market, already feels bristly. His smile is highlighted by the gleam of several gold teeth. He is wearing bib overalls and a thick turtle neck sweater, a sailor's cap is cocked on his head, his feet are kept warm in furry après-ski boots, and the fingers of his right glove are cut out at the tips to enable him to return change to the customers.

"So, kids, you do shopping today, eh? Madame Perret, she stay home to write correspondance? You not cold, bare heads like this? Winter you must wear hat. Your mother been here already. She gone back to Avenue Henri-Martin with two bags filled."

He pulls a wad of banknotes from deep inside the zippered chest pocket on his overalls, and slips a crisp new bill into Olga's hand.

"Olinka, you and little brother Milanko go to café to varm up with hot chocolate or applejack vith sugar cubes."

"Thanks, oncle Pavel, " says Olga. "We go to Café La Muette to have something."

As we walk away from uncle Pavel after another series of pecks on the cheeks, she tells me in a conspiratorial tone:

"I like when Madame Perret have much *correspondance* to do at home, and she send me to do shopping. I take so much time like possible."

Pavel is from the same village as Maman in Slovakia, and he's a schoolmate of hers from the primary grades, so we call him "uncle" though we're unrelated. He has learned his French in Paris's central food market, the Halles. There, he is a wholesale buyer during the night for the fruit and vegetable merchant on Rue de l'Annonciation, where he works at the salad stand until half past noon.

Pavel and his wife Henriette, who is French, have no children of their own, but they dote on everyone else's kids, including Olga and me. They live right next to the Halles, which are quiet during the day, when Pavel needs to sleep. At night, in contrast, the entire area is overrun by a jumble of carts and trucks, with mounds of meat and produce brought in from all corners of France to feed the Paris population. The Halles then become a human circus as well, with revelers in tuxedos and evening gowns capping the night in one of the numerous cafés, and mingling in a natural and friendly way with the regular workers, or the streetwalkers wearing heavy makeup, or the bag ladies and the vagrants picking up discarded cabbage leaves from the pavement, or the strongmen in bloodstained smocks carrying entire sides of cattle on their backs.

"I can at least treat myself to taxi, instead of to go home by métro" is Pavel's justification for the special reward he grants himself for having risen in the middle of the night for his forays into Paris's chaotic core, where he invited me to tag along with him one unforgettable time. He occasionally hires a vagrant named Bébert as his gofer, provided Bébert can be located and is willing to work. When I accompanied Pavel, we searched for Bébert a good half-hour before we found him, sound asleep, half-buried in supreme comfort in a buoyant mound of lettuce, too drunk to even open his eyes.

Curiously, Pavel has taken on a bit of the regional accent of the truckers from the south, with whom he has frequent dealings in his work at Les Halles. They tease him, though, for his persistent inability, like all Slavs, to pronounce "*vin*" (wine) correctly. It comes out as "*ven*" (wind).

"Hey guys, I buy, let's go have glass of *ven*."

"Nothing against you Pavel, but we prefer something more substantial."

After the detour with Olga at the Café de la Muette, as we return to the Perrets' residence on Rue Raynouard with our load of groceries and comic books, we walk along the wall bordering the garden that surrounds Balzac's house, below us on the hill of Passy. I suck from between my teeth an exquisite last remnant of sweetness and applejack brandy. The radiant heat of the sugar cubes dipped in Calvados has warmed my stomach, and my ears still buzz from the frothing of the milk for Olga's hot chocolate under the steam of the majestic espresso machine: PSCHHHHHhhhhhhh. "One Spanish choco for the young lady with the beautiful chestnut hair, one!" the waiter called out to the espresso handler, who used every spare moment to polish his spectacular machine, like a railroader tending to his locomotive. "One Spanish choco. *Au lait!*" (With milk!) the handler answered, in a pun which took me a while to understand ("*Olé!*"). There, close to Olga, in the warm hubbub of the café, watching the passersby outside, and with my supply of comic books piled up on the table, my happiness was so complete I wanted time to stop.

Monsieur Perret's seven-story building in cast concrete fascinates me, but I am somewhat resistant to its deliberately austere style. What attracts me, I think, is the personal mark of the architect, his will, his obvious intent to break new ground and stand out against the "conventional" (says Madame Perret) luxury of the freestone apartment buildings on Rue Raynouard.

Not that Monsieur Perret is incapable of designing beautiful buildings in a more traditional Parisian style. For proof, his sumptuous Théâtre des Champs-Élysées, on Avenue Montaigne, my favorite edifice of his, featuring breathtakingly smooth, curvy lines from his Art Déco period, with collaboration from other artists. Every time I spend a day with Olga, Madame Perret corners me in the kitchen to talk to me about architecture and other cultural things. She must think I'm bored sitting there peeling vegetables or lost in thought, because she gives me subway tickets and sends me out on prescribed tours of Paris to visit Monsieur's creations. Petite, thin, fraught with all sorts of nervous ticks and twitches, her white hair cut straight across at chin level, she wears no makeup or jewelry and is always dressed in the simplest, most ordinary clothes. She speaks—no she spits out her words—in staccato volleys that leave me exhausted, while at the same time, with an agitated gesture, she pushes back the glasses that are constantly sliding down her nose. She is probably as old as Mémère, but she is so full of energy that I don't perceive her as an elderly woman. She can't stand to see me daydreaming on my stool in the kitchen, watching the clouds float by over the Paris rooftops, or worse, reading comic books.

One day, she erupted in the kitchen in a particularly agitated state while I was shelling beans for Olga, and she brandished a postcard featuring the Notre-Dame du Raincy Church, her favorite work of Monsieur's, all the

while badgering me: "My boy, you have your whole future ahead you! Be
an architect! It's the most beautiful profession in the world, the surest path
to immortality! Look at this! Look! Look!" And she propped the familiar
photo under my nose, the same picture she sent me at the lycée with a note
of encouragement for my work in Latin, which was then finally beginning
to click after the horrendous first year, the same postcard that she asked me
many times to drop off for her at the corner mailbox, addressed to one or another of her correspondents in Japan, Sweden, Brazil, U.S.A., Finland, India.
At the Perrets, I felt sheltered in the warmth of Paris, and at the same time
directly connected to the entire planet. Just to peek at those addresses was a
thrill, reminding me of a visit once with Olga to Orly airport on a Sunday to
watch the planes take off and land, and to listen to the P.A. system announc-
ing departures to distant cities. The one that gave me goose bumps was the
boarding call for the Air France flight to New York, expressed in an incredibly melodious woman's voice, first in French then English: "*Air France vol...à
destination de New York. Embarquement immédiat porte numéro...*"

That particular day in Madame Perret's kitchen, I felt pressed to respond
to her imperious invitation, and agreed that architecture was the most fascinating of all the professions. I wasn't saying that just to please her. I liked
nothing better than to stroll in the streets of Paris and look at buildings and
monuments, especially after being prepared by her energetic, learned orienta-
tions. But I also felt compelled to admit that I was hopelessly deficient in art
and drawing.

"It's-not-the-end-of-the-world-you-know-so-don't-quit-before-you-
try," she rattled off in a single burst, like a machine gun volley. "But if you
prefer, since French seems to be your favorite subject at school, and since you
say you lack aptitude in the visual arts, perhaps you could draw with words
and become a writer, like our friend Balzac next door." And, to emphasize her
point, she pulled me to the edge of the terrace to show me the house of this
illustrious 19th Century neighbor, tucked away in the garden at the foot of
our building and preserved as a museum—a quaint reminder that the Passy
neighborhood was then just a village on a hill overlooking the Seine.

The Church of Notre-Dame du Raincy harbored an aesthetic secret, I was
sure of that, but what did it consist of? If I had some reticence regarding the
style of 51 Rue Raynouard, the Church left me even more perplexed. To discover its beauty, one had to be initiated, but I didn't dare question Madame

Perret, for fear of offending her or appearing stupid. Why and how was this not particularly beautiful tower so admirable in her eyes? I knew she'd have an answer, but I didn't know how to pose the question. I also waited for an opportunity to ask her what she found so great in artists like Picasso, whom she raved about and seemed to know personally, what with his portraits of one-eyed people with multiple noses. She had already enlightened me about such things as French landscaping, after I described to her an experience of mine in the Tuileries gardens:

I was strolling along the gravel walkways between the Carrousel Arch and the Impressionist museum, with a tennis ball in my pocket. A lawn beckoned. No one in sight. Disregarding the sign that forbade stepping on the grass, I started to kick the ball around on the green patch. A boy my age appeared from nowhere and took position across the lawn, without a word, in the silent fraternity of soccer. No wind, perfect conditions, very few people ambling on the gravel paths or sitting on the benches. Our handkerchiefs and jackets formed improvised goal posts, and we practiced shooting penalty kicks back and forth. A few minutes later, a shrill whistle sounded. A park warden appeared, out of breath. He pointed to the lengthy list of rules in fine print posted on a panel. The sanction for our violation: immediate expulsion from the public garden. "Out of here! Disappear! I don't want to ever see you again, or you'll have to deal with me!" the guard yelled.

I recounted this experience to Madame Perret, in order to denounce the absurdity of planting a lawn, and then forbidding access to it.

"No, no, you don't understand," she replied with her usual vehemence. "This rectangle of grass is not placed there so that you can roll on it, or damage it by kicking a ball around, or for the dogs of the neighborhood to poop all over it (she preferred cats but owned no animals). The grass, young man, is there for the satisfaction of the mind, for the contrast with the gravel of the walkways, for the contrast between the green vegetal substance and its white mineral counterpart. Do you understand that? It's an aesthetic pleasure, an intellectual pleasure. You should develop your sensitivity to the beauty of geometric forms applied to nature, by visiting the gardens of the Palais-Royal for instance, or Versailles. This style embodies French cartesianism, it's very specific to our country. The English have a completely different tradition in garden design and other things. They're allergic to reason. They haven't even accepted the metric system, they still measure in thumbs and feet. They have a sentimental attachment to quaintness, which can be charming, but also immature. The paradox is that they're way behind us in some respects, and way ahead in others, for example civility; they have the best table manners and the worst food."

I managed to grasp some of the intriguing notions Madame Perret heaped on me, but others just flew over my head. From my standpoint that was all right too. It would have made me dizzy to delve into the ramifications of everything that came out of her mind. She was erudite, but not pedantic. I loved to hear her carry on. Her comments were never boring. She obviously wasn't accustomed to speaking to young people, but at the same time I felt honored by the lack of condescension on her part. She didn't talk down to me, she considered me worth the effort of an explanation, which often turned out to be a full-fledged lecture, and it was also incumbent on me to try to reach up to her level. She was nurturing my cultural pole. The rest mattered less to her.

At 51, Rue Raynouard, the Perrets have reserved for themselves the entire top two floors of the building, with a penthouse surrounded by an open terrace. The kitchen isn't big, but the rest of the apartment is vast enough for me to not yet have encountered Monsieur Perret, despite my frequent visits to Olga's. The glass elevator outside the building is designed so that one can see from it Balzac's garden below, and then from the higher floors a panorama centered on the Seine and the Eiffel Tower. Everybody is authorized to go up in the elevator, but the domestics employed on each floor are supposed to take the service stairs to go down. They sometimes cheat, Olga and I too, not because we're lazy, but because it's so much fun to ride the elevator. When I'm sent out on an errand for this or that, I try to forget part of the order on purpose so I'll have an excuse for yet another ride. Monsieur Perret had a great idea putting the elevator outside instead of enclosing it in a dingy interior shaft, and I hope his design catches on, but so far I haven't seen it in any other building. I could then wander around Paris, and go up and down the elevators, in addition to, like now, randomly exploring the inner courtyards that look interesting.

The entry hall of 51 Rue Raynouard, enclosed in a black metal grill with a small statue of winged cherubs above the portal, resembles an Egyptian temple or an austere palace in Sparta. The windows of the domestics' rooms, including Olga's, open up on Balzac's garden on the hill, and are set below street level on the steep incline. The maids aren't happy about that. They would prefer to be housed like they used to be in the more traditional build-ings, in rooms on the highest floor with a view of the rooftops and the sound of raindrops overhead.

So, today, in this pre-Christmas season, I'm seated at the table in Olga's kitchen with three piles of comic books in front of me. To my left, the thick-est stack, the Nickeled Feet trio, then in decreasing order Buffalo Bill and Red Rider.

Suddenly, Madame Perret bursts in, brandishing her magnificent Parker fountain pen, uncapped. I gape at it with envy, me and my scratchy Visor Pen bought at the Prisunic discount store. She hones in on my magazines:

"Milan, reading that stuff again! You shouldn't waste your time with this trash. Why don't you instead go visit Balzac's house next door, and then read his books, for instance *Le Père Goriot*. Or have you read it already?"

I remain silent. I don't want to lie by saying yes, and I don't have the courage to say no. She points the now menacing beak of her pen toward my comics, as if she was about to spray them with venomous ink, like a cobra.

"Young man, I don't understand how, next to the house of one of our most illustrious writers, you can wallow in such inanities. That stuff you're reading is totally worthless, if not harmful. It doesn't teach you anything. Olga, you shouldn't buy junk like this for your brother. If you want to spoil him, give him the classics, I'll be glad to suggest some titles, or take him to the Théâtre National Populaire at the end of our street, or to chamber music concerts at Salle Gaveau. And you, my girl, although your French is improving, for the next step it's imperative that you go to night school. All right, enough said, I'll let you young people be, I'm going to finish my *correspondance*."

As soon as Madame Perret leaves, Olga shuts the kitchen door and takes a deep breath. I sense that her heart weighs heavy, and I no longer even notice her Slovak accent or broken French: "You know, Milanko, Madame Perret is very nice, she never rings me in my room, at 8:00 p.m. my duties are finished, it's over for the day. I can count on my afternoons being free and I have Satur-days off after I put away the lunch dishes. So, compared to my girlfriends in the building, I can't complain. I'm lucky, she respects my free time, but still, she gets on my nerves. Before, she constantly corrected my French, and now she wants me to attend night school, but I wonder if she doesn't say that without think-ing. She would have to prepare dinner herself instead of me, and she's never

offered to do that, except on Saturdays. She watches me for Maman and she
fills up her head with her "culture" stuff every time she sees her. It's plain to see,
Maman would approve of us going to the theatre or to classical music concerts,
but not to the movies. So where does she get these ideas? From Madame Perret
of course. Me, I like to go to the movies, but Maman, she sees red as soon as
she hears the word '*cinema*,' or '*Vél d'Hiv*' for indoor sports events, or worse yet
'*Salle Wagram*' for the Saturday night dances. If you go with me to the *Vél d'Hiv*,
tell her we went to a concert, so we have peace."

"Yes, I know..."

"We're getting along worse and worse, me and Maman. Every time we
see each other, we have an argument. She doesn't understand that I'm fed up
with being a live-in housekeeper. Ever since I turned fifteen, I've been doing
this kind of work, in different homes. For a couple of months between when
she left the Lavrils and started at the Kapferers, she even had me work with
her at the Lévys in Boulogne, and that was a nightmare. Not with the Lévys,
with her. Madame Perret is by far my best boss yet, but I'm fed up. Maman, it
doesn't bother her, she loves her job as a cook and her live-in situation. And she
is relieved that we're all set up, Evička in Slovakia with relatives, you at boarding school, and me at Madame Perret's, who reports to her on my whereabouts,
I'm sure. But me, I want to be independent, to have my own room, to live elsewhere than in my employer's building. How I would love to be free! **I HAVE TO
LEAVE MADAME PERRET!** A girlfriend of mine works in the subway as a ticket
puncher. Maybe she could get me a job there. My work would be so pleasant!
I would see all kinds of people passing in front of me all day. The only hard
part would be to hold them back behind the door when the train arrives in the
station, even if they grumble. And besides, I wouldn't always be busy. There
would be lots of free time. I could read *Nous Deux* or other photo-romances.
The métro ticket punchers always have a magazine open on their lap. I would
find a furnished room in a lively district, around the Gare du Nord like Maman's friend Thérèse, or near the Bastille. I would not have to report to anyone.
I could go to the movies or to the Salle Wagram dances whenever I wanted
to. I would have an entire day free each week. I would take you more often to
basketball games or indoor bike races at the *Vél d'Hiv*. I know you like that."

That's an understatement. I love to go with Olga to the *Vél d'Hiv*, just across
the Seine from Rue Raynouard, at the place where the green and red elevated subway trains are swallowed up into the city after crossing Bir-Hakeim

bridge. I'm up-to-date on everything that's happening in sports, so I comment on the action; she attends as a casual onlooker, more for me than for herself I'm sure. The electric atmosphere of the smoke-filled velodrome is intoxicating. When we walk along the hallways to stretch our legs at half-times, Olga says to the guys eyeing her: "Please excuse me, I am with mine little brother." Proud of my importance, I withstand their spiteful glares. I wish I could protect her that way at the Salle Wagram dance hall. It's reputed to be the place in Paris where rich boys go to pick up servant girls for fun. I don't like to hear some of the older students at the lycée brag about their weekend adventures at Salle Wagram.

I had no idea Olga was so unhappy, even though I sensed things were not going well between her and Maman, who constantly reproaches her for not saving money: "You never put nothing on your savings account." Olga's retort: "I not make enough money to save."

I hold Olga's hands and try to console her, regretting that I can't do anything tangible to help her, but I promise her that someday I'll be rich and I'll pay her rent. She smiles bravely through her tears.

She has hardly recovered from her emotional outpouring when her employer reappears in the kitchen. Madame Perret's shrug betrays her disappointment in seeing the comic books still spread out on the table. With a resigned air, she says:

"Milan, Monsieur Perret would like to see you in his studio. Please excuse his attire, he is taking advantage of the privilege of working at home."

At long last, I'll finally meet the eminent architect about whom I've heard so much.

A frail elderly man receives me in the spacious loft with its panoramic vista extending over the Seine all the way to the Citroën automobile factory on the right, and to the Eiffel Tower on the left, with Swan Island and a scaled down replica of the Statue of Liberty in the middle. He is wearing striped pajamas, house slippers, and a robe, yet he looks very dignified. With his white beard, he reminds me of a scientist of the past century, Pasteur maybe, except that instead of a lab with vials and beakers, he works among scale models, sketches, plans that are furled, unfurled, spread out all over the studio on flat surfaces or diagonal drawing tables. I'm overwhelmed by the notion that someone can actually produce and understand such a maze of materials. He extends his hand:

"Glad to meet you, young man. I've heard a lot about you from Madame Perret. She told me you're a scholarship student at the lycée of Saint-Germain-en-Laye. Congratulations, we're proud of you, and of the rural schoolteacher who educated you. Primary school is without question the most important institution in our republic. It's what allows children like you to rise. How unfortunate that your sister did not enjoy the same conditions. Having her leave her homeland of Slovakia at thirteen was probably a bad idea. Madame Perret and I are worried about her. Anyway, I wanted to meet you and give you a small souvenir."

He sits down at the main table, opens a drawer, pulls out a black compass case worn at the edges:

"It's my first drawing set. I've had it ever since I began my own lycée studies, a long, long time ago. I want to offer it to you for good luck now at school and also later in life."

"Oh, thank you very much, Monsieur."

I have a lump in my throat. I'm at the same time honored by his present, and shaken by what I've just heard him say about Olga. She's disadvantaged, yet so generous! And although I'm touched by Monsieur Perret's gift, I feel I don't really deserve it. Except perhaps for geometry class, the compass set will have for me only a sentimental value. Others could probably make better use of it. I totally lack visual imagination. If I'm asked to draw a house, I can only come up with a basic rendition of the one in which I grew up in the village, with three holes for the windows, one for the door, and two for the attic. Regarding math, I think I would be fine, I'm sure I could learn to build walls that don't collapse, but I would have to be told where to put them. It was like that too when we had music theory at the lycée. I understood nothing of it, beyond "do, ré, mi, fa, sol, la, si, do." Absolutely nothing! I was born that way, I guess, with compartments missing in my brain. Good thing Madame Mercier overlooked our shortcomings in her school.

Among the profusion of plans and drawings in the studio, my gaze stops on an open file on the table: "Auguste Perret: Plans for rebuilding the city of Le Havre." Then, my attention shifts to the sweeping view on the opposite bank of the Seine. Monsieur Perret follows my glance and steps up to the glass wall to comment:

"Impressive, isn't it, this 'rumbling city' out there. I think that's how Baudelaire described it. You know, Paris is a prodigiously alive metropolis.

It's in constant evolution, sometimes very fast, like under Haussmann during the last century. Twenty years from now, the bank of the Seine across from us won't be recognizable. Except for a few untouchable spots, the entire 15th District should be rebuilt. The two big questions for Paris in the future are the role of the automobile, and improved housing. Regarding that, Corbu is right: inner courtyards are doomed, things need to be aired out, the sun must penetrate into dwellings, we have to improve hygiene. We're really behind compared to the Scandinavians in this regard, but we can catch up, there's so much to do and I have so little time, this will be for other architects, other urban planners."

"And will the 16th District be transformed too?"

"Much less, I'm sure. It's a very bourgeois district, solidly built. But it depends where. For instance, here, just to our right, you can see the great worksite for the Maison de la Radio. But why do you ask?"

"Because next to the Kapferers' mansion on Avenue Henri-Martin, across from the 16th District town hall, there's a new ten story apartment building going up."

"Yes, I see where that is. I know Avenue Henri-Martin very well. With its equestrian lane running along the middle and its four parallel rows of chestnut trees, it's one of the most beautiful green swaths in Paris. The three mansions that remain, next to the intersection with Rue de la Pompe, are sure to be sought after by real estate developers for luxury apartment buildings. Are your mother's employers old?"

"Yes, pretty old."

"Then I fear their mansion will disappear with them. Are you attached to that house?"

"Yes, Monsieur, a lot. My mother too. But why would such a beautiful house be demolished?"

"Because the big mansions no longer suit the needs of the heirs, who want to live individually, that's understandable. If we had time, I would discuss with you a question which deep down gnaws at us architects: 'Don't we risk burdening future generations with what we leave behind?' For instance, right now people are seeking a certain level of comfort in housing, I myself advocate that, but we have to be careful to not be completely mesmerized by this aspect. Anyway, you're young, you can think about that later. I'll let you run, I have to get back to work. Courage, and good luck in your studies. Please keep Madame Perret informed."

I leave our encounter stunned, moved, conscious of having met an intellectual giant, a thinker such as those one finds in history books or on the frontispice of the Panthéon. And with a fitting first name: Auguste!

Return to the lycée, Sunday night, Christmas vacation over already. Crushing sadness between departure at Saint-Lazare rail station and arrival in the dorm, where only the jokes and carryings-on of friends allow me to forget the heartache that assails me whenever I leave Paris. What luck, what joy to know a city where the rumble of the Métro under the sidewalk, and its smell coming up through the grates, make me unexplainably happy, but what misery to be severed from it. I'm not the only one who feels that way. Suffice to hear the multitude of love songs dedicated to the city. I carry everywhere in my head Mouloudji's nostalgic refrain *"Le long des rues de Paris, mon Paris..."*

After crossing the darkened courtyard of the lycée, I get over my blues by running up the stairs leading to the brightly lit dormitory. Like each returnee, I'm greeted by good-natured jostling, which a bit later, when I hit my teens, will include the recurrent taunt about "another week-end, and still a cherry." I'm pushed around, slapped on the back, my school bag is wrested from me.

"Eh, guys, look, Kovaco brought back his box of goodies. Grab some, help yourselves, yummi yummi caramel, yummi yummi cookies."

I let the vultures pounce on my weekly supply of sweets made by Maman. Although I wish I could afford store-bought packaged stuff, my classmates prefer homemade candy and pastries, and they tell me I'm lucky to have a housekeeper who spoils me like that.

My box is returned empty. Vuillemin, champion harasser, continues to rummage through my bag. He ferrets out Monsieur Perret's compass case:

"What's this old piece of junk?"

"Don't mess with it, Vuillemin. Give it back to me, don't touch it."

"Where did you dig it up? At the flea market?"

"No. Don't touch it I said!"

"Okay, Okay, don't get mad. Anyway, it's all beat up, it's just an old piece of junk. Look, the velvet lining inside is all worn out."

At this point, Duvignaud, medical student and the most sadistic of all the preceptors at the lycée, stops by us and rubs his beard joyfully.

"Well, well, I was looking for two people, so I guess it will be you, Vuillemin and Kovaco. You might as well make peace now."

"We weren't arguing," protests Vuillemin.

"Two people what?" I ask in turn.

"You'll soon understand," says Duvignaud, pulling his whistle from his pocket. "Fall in! Formation! Everybody in front of me this minute."

The fifty or so boarders who have returned to the dorm immediately obey his order. Some rush out of the washroom, toothbrush in hand, others have already put on their pyjamas.

"In a half hour, I'm turning off the lights," Duvignaud trumpets, "and after that I don't want to hear a sound, I have to study for an important exam. If there is any commotion, or if anybody gets rolled out of bed, Vuillemin and Kovacovic will be held in detention next Sunday. Is that clear? You can settle this among yourselves."

Some choice swear words are muttered here and there, but Duvignaud remains steadfast.

11:00 p.m. Complete silence in the dorm except for a few sporadic snores and incoherent fragments of dreams blabbered aloud. Until now alert in bed, I'm slowly sinking to sleep, Monsieur Perret's compass safely tucked under my bolster.

Suddenly the beam of a flashlight startles me, followed by a whisper.

"Kovaco, you're sleeping?"

"No, who is it?"

"It's me, Vuillemin. Take a look!" And his flashlight illuminates a carton of Lucky Strikes that he places on my bunk. "You interested in these?"

Although I'm at first hesitant, I make a snap decision: I haven't smoked much yet, but there are enough cigarettes in Vuillemin's carton for me to get a lot of practice and learn to inhale; it's a fantastic opportunity, so I might as well see what he has in mind.

"Euh, well, yes, I'm interested, why?"

"Okay, then," says Vuillemin, "I'll trade you this carton of American cigarettes for your old beat up compass set. Okay? You know, Lucky Streeks are very expensive at the tobacconist's."

"Yeah, but yours are smuggled, I can tell, I've already seen cigarettes like that without the blue SEITA seal. They've probably been transferred at sea because they're warped and stained by water, you bought them cheap somewhere, but wait, let's see, all right, okay. Yes, okay, I'll trade."

And that's how I began to smoke more assuredly, and how I lost, in such a foolish and shameful way, an object that had a unique sentimental value.

As for Vuillemin, he was soon afterwards expelled from the lycée, for "repeated violations to the institution's discipline code." The authorities showed no patience for chronic recidivists. He vanished with my compass, and was probably placed by his parents in some private boarding school.

But how trivial this is, compared to what befell Olga. A few weeks after my Christmastime visit with her, she left Madame Perret. I was at Maman's when the telegram arrived: "Olga gone. Call me right away. Madame Perret."

We rushed to the concierge's quarters, where we could use the telephone. I listened on the external earset. At the other end of the line, Madame Perret, shaken, could barely talk: "She told me she wanted to live her life. I hope she didn't leave because of me. I tried to understand her. She was such a nice girl. She left no address, nothing."

We then started to periodically receive letters from Olga, in French. They had the same wording as the letters that Pépère, who was in charge of writing in Saint-Aquilin, required Mémère's boarders to regularly send to their mothers in Paris. He'd bring out a sheet of paper, an envelope, the wooden penholder, the bottle of purple ink, and he'd sit us down at the kitchen table for the dreaded task on the fifteenth of each month: "Now write!"

Olga and I were uninspired and faced a complete blank, so we resorted to a standard formula taught by Pépère. And taught well, because we all reproduced it, even his eldest son Pierre, who sent him the same terse message each month along with the small money order, and whom we never saw during my ten years in Saint-Aquilin.

Olga's letters were mailed from Paris, with no return address:

"Dear Mama and Milanko,

I take my pen, my best pen, to send you a few words and give you news from me that are good for the time being.

Otherwise, nothing special to tell you for today.

Je vous embrasse bien affectueusement,

Your daughter and sister,

Olga"

One day, about six months later, at the outdoor market on Rue de l'Annonciation, Pavel Harmady hailed Maman and me to come talk to him behind his salad stand.

"Olinka been here yesterday," he said. "She seem okay. She little bit pale, but she always been like that, pale complexion with brown hair is part her charm. She did not want to leave address. She come to borrow money so she can go to dentist. I think maybe she need tooth pulled."

"How mach money?" asked Maman.

"That's business only for her and me," replied Pavel.

"Listen, you tell me how mach. Tomorrow, I give money back to you, and when you see her next time, you tell her she owe you nothing."

Following her disappearance, I saw Olga only once, two years later, shortly before Maman and I left for America. She had learned of our emigration plans, probably from Pavel, and she had phoned me at the Kapferers' concierge to tell me where I could find her.

I was shocked to discover that she lived directly on the ground, yes on the ground, on compacted clay, in a hovel that formed with several other shanties the beginnings of a "*bidonville*" in the Vincennes Woods on the eastern edge of Paris.

I had known poverty before in Saint-Aquilin, but it was a rich kind of poverty, and there at least the mud stopped at the door. Here I discovered absolute destitution, not even a stone floor or a slab, nothing to isolate yourself from the damp earth swelling underfoot. And yet Olga had covered the rickety table in her lean-to with a spiffy oilcloth, and the rabbit stew she was cooking on a wood stove smelled every bit as wonderful as if we had been in the Perrets' kitchen. But what abject misery! How could anyone find themselves in such a predicament? How could this have happened to her?

We didn't get a chance to talk as much we needed and wanted to, she and I. The "neighbors" joined us. They were eager to meet this brother of hers about whom they had apparently heard a lot. And they wanted to celebrate the occasion. Someone scurried around the compound to gather enough drinking glasses, and then, to loud cheers, popped open a bottle of sparkling wine that had been kept cold in a nearby puddle. Another person sliced a salami to munch on while the stew simmered. Then someone appeared out of the woods, to more cheers, with an armful of baguettes. The bread was passed around, and everyone tore off a piece, dipping it in the kettle for an appetizer.

After the bubbly, we moved on to the glow of red wine, except Olga, who was allergic to alcohol like Maman and Mémère. A festive atmosphere took over. There weren't enough chairs to sit on, and the ground was too damp, so we stood, or plopped down on the fallen tree trunks ringing the clearing. There was no outhouse, just the woods.

I was touched by the warm welcome extended by Olga's new friends, a family really, and by the solidarity evident in their little community; but they seemed to be inhabitants of another planet, too bizarre to fathom, and they probably held the same view of me, a visitor from the ritzy Sixteenth.

When I said goodbye to Olga that day, for what I thought would be the last time (I couldn't imagine ever returning from the faraway New World), she begged me not to reveal her situation to Maman. I promised I wouldn't, and kept my word. But her eyes seemed to implore "Don't abandon me here."

Cruel life, miserable life that destroys beings so dear, so kind, so brave as Olga.

Chapter 11

64 Avenue Henri-Martin

"One of the images that has come to me is a bouillon your mother
made for us perhaps eight or nine years ago. Clear and beautiful,
with a few small, airy dumplings floating in it, and a little bit
of chopped parsley on the surface. It was perhaps the
most elegant thing I have ever eaten."

— *Judith Wahl Kachinske*

The entire Kapferer family, a dozen persons in all when everyone was present, gathered regularly for the main meal of the day, lunch, served at 12:30 sharp. In addition to Monsieur and Madame Kapferer, the resident household was comprised of their two divorced daughters, Madame Legrand and Madame Dudock, who each occupied a suite of her own in the mansion, and who each had a daughter, respectively Chantal, age eight when I moved there as a ten-year-old, and Sandra, four. Each girl also had her own live-in British nanny, and was thus raised bilingual. The nannies, who rotated annually, ate their meals in the dining room with the family.

Other core members of the clan often present at lunch included Madame Legrand's older children Alain and Francine, who lived elsewhere in the 16th District with their father. And finally the Kapferers' third daughter, Madame Martine, domiciled with her husband Daniel Wildenstein and sons Alec and Guy in their château near Paris during spring and summer, and in New York's Hotel Pierre fall and winter.

Everyone had to signal their lunch intentions to Madame Kapferer the evening before, or in the morning prior to eight o'clock, when Maman met with her to discuss the day's menu and the number of people to expect. Whims and spontaneity were proscribed, as either alien to the highly structured *haute bourgeoisie* lifestyle, or out of consideration for the domestic staff—a respectful attitude instilled by Madame Kapferer to her whole family.

Everyone adhered to the inflexible schedule, *noblesse oblige*. These well-born people applied diligently King Louis XIV's precept that "Punctuality is the Courtesy of the Mighty." Only Alain, son of Madame Legrand, had the gumption to occasionally deviate from these rigorous constraints, and to come down to the kitchen to seek special treatment from Maman, in the rare instances he happened to be late:

"Madame Eva, please forgive me, I'm sorry, but today I had an exam at school for which I had to stay longer. Would there by any chance be anything left to eat, if that would not be too much trouble?"

"But of course, Mussieu Alain, that not be problem. Wait upstairs in dining room pantry, and I send something for you in dumbwaiter."

And she improvised a light meal that he delighted in before running back down to the kitchen to thank her. His gratitude was her best reward. In addition to Madame Kapferer, whom she held in reverence, and Madame Martine, who kept me well-clothed, Alain was a favorite of Maman's in the family. She liked his politeness and good manners.

Would she have considered special requests from tardies other than Alain? Her capacities to pass judgment on such importunities remained untested: the mansion's occupants either respected the schedule, or else settled for whatever crumbs they might find in the dining room pantry. All the foodstuff was stored in the kitchen, a place that remained de facto off-limits to everyone but the cook.

I doubt anyone else in the household would have known what to do in a kitchen anyway. For people accustomed since infancy to being served, even the simplest form of cooking is a daunting task. Madame Kapferer herself rarely ventured into Maman's domain, and if so only to convey a message in person, rather than through the intercom.

The evening meal, simple and light, took place at 7:30 p.m. It was a smaller gathering than lunch. Madame Martine had gone home, Francine and Alain were back at their father's, and Madame Legrand and Madame Dudock dined out nearly every evening. However, the Kapferers were often joined by Madame's sister and her husband, the Machils, who lived in a quaint ivy-covered brick cottage in back of the garden. The atmosphere at table among the in-laws always remained warm and familial, although the Kapferers were devoted readers of the center-right newspaper *Le Figaro*, and the Machils of the center-left *Le Monde*.

Breakfast was the responsibility of the chambermaid Marie. She served tea, coffee, or hot chocolate to the residents in their respective suites, along with fresh bread and croissants.

Madame Kapferer, then in her late sixties or so, managed the household alone. With remarkable calm and efficiency, she accomplished this demanding task from the small mahogany desk in her boudoir. She relied on the concierge, Mr. Allais, for the technical oversight of the workmen who always seemed to be servicing something or other in the mansion (the "kilometers" of pipes leading to radiators from the monstrous oil furnace on the ground floor were a sight to behold) but she handled the scheduling and accounting herself. And she personally directed her live-in household staff, which consisted of, in addition to the nannies:

The concierges, Monsieur and Madame Allais. They had their own kitchen and apartment on the ground floor, and were in charge of gardening, window washing, carpet vacuuming, and brass and silverware polishing. They also supplied the household with mineral water from the artesian well in nearby Square Lamartine, and thrice daily brought in fresh bread from the corner boulangerie. These tasks in addition to the remote control of the front gate, for which the household members used a secret code—three short rings, two long.

The chambermaid Marie, long in the service of the Kapferers. She served the meals and tended to the needs and requests of the adults, most notably Madame Legrand with her frequent changes of clothes.

And in the kitchen, Maman, referred to by the Kapferer grandchildren as "Madame Eva," because of her enhanced respectability as a middle-aged widow with children.

Familiarity did not come easily to Maman. She remained on a formal "*vous*" basis with Marie, as well as with Thérèse, the cleaning woman/laundress who came in daily and was the only member of the domestic staff not housed on the premises. Maman stayed on a formal basis with her friends too. That left only me, raised in a French environment, and her siblings in her far away native country, to communicate with her in the informal "*tu*."

Actually, at the time she was hired by the Kapferers in 1950, at 45, Maman was apprehensive about the alleged snobbism of Avenue Henri-Martin, where, she heard, employers might not even accept the "*vous*" level of formality, considered too direct. Fortunately, that was not the case with the Kapferers.

Maman was already struggling enough with the basic difficulties of the French language; she would have been unable to adapt to further grammatical contortions. A simple question, with an already impossible verb, such as "For today's dessert, Madame, would you prefer (*préféreriez-vous*) an apricot tart, a baba au rhum, or floating islands with caramel?" would have posed insurmountable difficulties in the still more formal third person: "For dessert today, would Madame prefer...." (*Madame préférerait-elle*).

In the beginning, to help Maman better understand her directives, Madame gave her a big book, the 1936 edition of the standard reference manual for upper class households, *L'Art Culinaire Moderne*, by Henri-Paul Pellaprat. She suggested they use this tome as a starting point for the choice and discussion of menus. However, Maman preferred to rely solely on instinct. Her talent for the culinary arts had been discovered, nurtured, and developed by Madame Lavril—her previous employer of twenty years. She had not learned her craft from books.

Madame Kapferer quickly realized she could give her new cook carte blanche, and they pushed aside the hefty *L'Art Culinaire Moderne* bible, but not before Maman had a chance to glance at the preface and notice a sentence that flattered her, because she considered herself primarily a baker: "Henri-Paul Pellaprat, born in Paris in 1869, began his career with a three-year apprenticeship as a baker, following the precept of our master Auguste Escoffier who maintained that a cook must first be trained as a baker." In her mind, this settled once and for all the thorny question of ranking between those related disciplines.

Maman also absorbed at the Lavrils, and further refined at the Kapferers, the incomparable French "art of living." The unfolding of meals in several courses, according to a long-tested tradition, a civilization really, conferred a cosmopolitan aura to some of her most regional, ethnic, even folksy preparations. Thus, for dessert, her poppy-seed "*kolačky*", or her "*makovniky*" with *fromage blanc*, were metamorphosed into "Madame Eva's Slovakian pastries," eliciting murmurs of delectation among these most sophisticated guests on the planet, suddenly infatuated with Central European peasant simplicity. It was like that too with Maman's mashed potatoes, that people raved about; or her soups (the one with pungent dried mushrooms sent by our relatives in Slovakia; or the one with potatoes, string beans, a little cream, a little vinegar—perfect!); or her indescribably savory *pot-au-feu*, which she never learned to pronounce correctly—it came out as *pot-au-fou* (crazy pot). She had the proverbial "magic touch."

The same with flowers. As soon as the delivery boy from Primevère, the celebrated florist on Rue de la Pompe, dropped off his weekly consignment of spectacular bouquets and sprays, Maman rearranged them, recreated them, in her manner, according to her taste. In those superb but impersonal floral arrangements put together by professionals, she imprinted her own mark, the naive gaiety of Slovakian folk costumes, the color and simplicity of the poppy fields of her native landscape.

Madame, amused and delighted, allowed her employee to do as she pleased. She perhaps had in mind this passage from their 1936 *Pellaprat* concerning preparations for formal dinners?

"In former times, the table was loaded with large silver pieces and pedestals, all very beautiful but totally useless accessories. Today, flowers constitute the most graceful table decoration. Sometimes, the lady of the house herself decorates the table, with the artistic taste that characterizes her. However, she most often leaves that task to the florist, more accustomed to this long and painstaking work, which furthermore coincides precisely with Madame's wardrobe and make-up preparations...All conceptions are permitted; however, one must not lose sight of the fact that guests can be indisposed by flowers that are too fragrant in a very warm room."

Monsieur usually left home about ten o'clock in the morning, with a chauffeur who came to fetch him at the gate. In back of the garden stood an empty glass-roofed garage big enough to hold a dozen vehicles, plus a mechanic's pit and a hoist. But no one in the household had a car! I made good use of this vacant court-sized indoor space to tirelessly whack a tennis ball against the wall.

Monsieur always returned by 12:30 for lunch. In these morning outings, said the staff, he went to the stock market, where he could watch over his investments.

Saturday evenings, he received guests for poker in the main reception room decorated with paintings by great masters, some perhaps selected from the collections of their Wildenstein in-laws. At these gatherings filled with cigar smoke, pastries prepared by Maman were served.

Otherwise, Monsieur's presence remained muted (he, Mr. Allais, and myself were the only males residing in the household). Above all, he liked to tinker. In the salon, on the table on which he spread out a newspaper, he patiently took apart small mechanical objects such as light switches, or door locks, which he repaired while Madame read *Le Figaro* in her armchair, magnifying glass in hand, her big black and white cat Minet purring on her lap. I often found the Kapferers thus installed on Sunday evenings, when Maman prompted me to go bid them goodbye before I returned to boarding school. To my "I've come to say *au revoir, M'sieur Dame,*" they would look up from their activities, extend a hand, and reply in unison: "Have a good week at school, Milan. See you next Saturday."

Monsieur remained a mysterious figure to me. The domestics rarely talked about him, but they giddily rejoiced whenever, on Mondays, chauffeurs with a contrite expression delivered thick envelopes on behalf of their employers unlucky at poker the previous Saturday. I rarely ran into him in the mansion, except for the brief encounter of our Sunday handshake. A particular image of him remains, however, etched in my memory:

One day, when I had gone up to the dining room pantry to retrieve the cheese tray for our lunch in the kitchen downstairs, I caught sight of the patriarch, at the head of the table, having coffee, his chair slightly pushed back, his napkin already replaced into its ring. He appeared visibly satisfied with his meal and his chirping den of females, and seemed to have only one care in the world at that moment: where to dispose of the ash building up at the tip of his cigar. "Just reach for the bell and have Marie bring you the big crystal ashtray," I thought. His responsibilities, if any, remained distant from the household, in which he did not exist, except as the head of the dining room table, or as the decider in matters of utmost importance that were in his purview. For instance, my eventual "placement" after the end of my studies.

I almost forgot one important function fulfilled by Monsieur in the running of the household: the selection of wines, brought in by the delivery boy from the *Chez Nicolas* store, whose job seemed so pleasant to me: pedal around our neighborhood on a three-wheeled bicycle cart loaded with wine bottles! I couldn't understand why this kind of employment was considered disgraceful in my proletarian milieu. How many times had I heard Thérèse relate the admonition she gave to her son every time she went to visit him at his caretaker's in the country: "Do well at school, *mon chéri*, otherwise when you turn 14 you'll end up being a street sweeper or a delivery boy."

By his first name, and by his carefree attitude, Monsieur reminded me of Pépère, my childhood mentor. The two Marcels. How I have always dreamt of their nonchalance! On his cuff links, Monsieur even bore the same initials as mine, M.K.

In their highly structured lives, the elder Kapferers observed two other traditions. Each year they spent the month of February at the Carlton Hotel in Cannes on the French Riviera, and the month of August at the Majestic Hotel in Evian, near the Swiss border on Lake Geneva.

Under Madame's magnanimous guidance, the household navigated smoothly through the days, the months, the seasons, like a ship piloted by a calm and confident captain. I adored her and the warm atmosphere she created in her home. An all-encompassing benevolence radiated from her being. She was a secular Jewish saint who became my new Mémère, different and more distant than the first, to be sure, but I too had evolved, from a peasant child to a Parisian youth.

At the Kapferers Maman became an ardent judeophile. She lost any trace of the ingrained anti-Semitism so prevalent in the lower classes, especially in Slavic countries. "I never meet Kristians so kind like this Jews," she often declared.

The only signs of Judaism in the household were an unused menorah on the dining room buffet, and the fact that Madame, in speaking with the staff in an unconsciously self-censored way, referred to her daughters as Madame Legrand, Madame Dudock, and Madame Martine—as if the latter's otherwise distinguished family name, Wildenstein, was too "explosive" to pronounce to gentiles in the still skittish post-Holocaust European context. (More recently, in 1994, an older French Jewish friend of mine, unaware that in America Hebrew first names had lost any religious connotation, exclaimed upon learning that my newborn son was being named Aaron: "You can't do that to him, especially with a double "A"!)

Speaking of first names, I thought for the longest time I had forgotten Madame's, and was greatly troubled by this lapse of memory, until I realized I had never heard nor seen it, including on various documents certifying Maman's employment. They bore only Monsieur's name. Madame of course filled them out on his behalf—household management being her purview— and simply signed "Kapferer." His profession, as listed on those documents: *Employeur de gens de maison* (Employer of domestic help).

Maman began her workday at 8:00, when she tidied up Madame's bedroom—her only other household task besides the kitchen. She also used that time to discuss with her the lunch and dinner menus. For the food purchases, she received a weekly sum of cash on which she reported every Monday with a precise tally in her ledger book. And during the elder Kapferers' month away in February and August, she was empowered—with considerable funds that she kept in a shoebox—to make all the decisions regarding meals for the staff and the remaining family members.

Right from the start with Pellaprat's *L'Art Culinaire Moderne*, Madame sensed that she could have full confidence in Maman for all matters, whether financial or culinary. She only needed to express a wish or a suggestion now and then, and rely on her employee for the rest. The only certainty was that following French tradition, there would be fish on Fridays, and even then, the choice was left up to Maman, who was eager to vary the kinds (trout, sole, hake, merlan, turbot, salmon) and the preparations (in sauce, au gratin, poached, baked, pan fried).

Maman sought to avoid boredom and routine in meals. She deliberately maintained an element of surprise in order to tempt the guests. And their most common reaction at serving time, "Yum! This is mouth-watering," confirmed her success.

For lunch, she prepared an appetizer, followed by a main dish of meat or fish with vegetables, and dessert, often a pastry. Salad and cheese tray, needing no cooking, completed the noon meal.

For dinner, she usually served a soup and a main dish, consisting most often of pasta in white sauces—Madame adored gnocchis, and Maman, for whatever reason, frowned on red sauces, although baked tomatoes with various stuffings were a lunch appetizer she liked to make. Salad, cheese tray, and fruit basket or yogurt completed dinner. Her cooking had an eminently wholesome, fresh, varied, balanced, flavorful character.

Maman valued having the material resources that allowed her talent to flourish, in addition to an enlightened and receptive audience. And Madame was only too happy to liberate herself from the unrelenting constraint of culinary choices ("What are we going to eat today?"). By taking over those prerogatives, Maman was breaking down an open door.

In the daily schedule, once Madame's bedroom was tidied up, Maman grabbed two oilcloth shopping bags and headed out to the foodshops.

At the butcher's, on Rue de la Pompe, where a crowd always overflowed onto the sidewalk, she didn't wait in line like the other customers. Sure of her authority, she remained near the curb, put down her bags, and pretended to look at the meat displays. Soon, the owner himself, sliding like a portly figure skater on the tile floor sprinkled with sawdust, scurried outside to guide her in and bypass the queue: "Good morning, Madame, follow me, follow me please." It was their usual routine to avoid the grumblings of the less important clients.

Live-in domestics are in many ways similar to children. Instead of "My father is stronger than yours" they think in terms of "My master is richer than yours." Contemptuous of the lowly nobodies around them, they bask vicariously in the prestige of their employers. Maman stood above the lot on the shoulders of the Kapferers, who owned the largest and best located of only three mansions remaining on celebrated Avenue Henri-Martin, now lined with luxurious apartment buildings.

While escorting Maman to a quieter spot at the back of the store, the butcher would ask her about the results of the previous day's purchases:

"So, Madame, those filet mignons yesterday, tender weren't they? I bet they melted in the mouth. Come on, admit it."

"Yes, they be okay" she answered, ever so careful not to reveal too much enthusiasm, lest he get the upper hand.

A strange mixture of antagonism and complicity prevailed between Maman and her butcher. She annoyed him, that's for sure, but he respected her competence, and couldn't dismiss the monetary worth of her purchases. She, on the other hand, liked the special treatment he granted her.

Maman exhibited an instinctual wariness about commerce, derived from her peasant background: "Shopkeepers all thieves. Small shopkeepers small thieves. Big shopkeepers big thieves." That's why she refused to consider pre-cut meat. Not for her, this merchandise destined for a gullible public. She wanted customized cuts, done before her eyes, from slabs stashed away in the refrigerated room for demanding patrons. She could thus determine the exact thickness of the cuts, and insist on the removal of fat before weighing. The butcher good-naturedly lent himself to her orders, became a mere handler of knives carrying out her wishes: "You want it sliced like this, Madame? Or like this? Is this all right for you?"

Each day's transaction ended with a gift. The butcher would unhook the enormous cow's lung hanging from a chain on the back wall, and with his sharpest blade, biting his lips with the concentration of a surgeon, he'd tear a perfect slice out of this mass of limp flesh: "Eh, Madame, let's not forget lunch for Minet. Have a good day and see you tomorrow."

In the creamery shop, across the street from the butcher's, Maman didn't jump the queue. There, she waited in line, like everyone else. I felt more comfortable accompanying her to buy eggs-butter-and-cheese than meat.

When it was her turn to be served, though, her persnickety attitude surfaced again: "This Camembert too runny. You not have others?"

With an expert thumb, she squeezed the new cheese brought to her, raised it up to her nostrils, asked for still another so she could compare to her full satisfaction. She then went on to the next order:

"Please cut me kilo butter. No, no, not from this block, from one next to it."

She examined eggs one at a time under the ceiling light, as if she was looking for something suspicious under their opaque shell, and invariably asked:

"Is fresh these eggs?"

"Yes, Madame, absolutely. Guaranteed laid at the farm yesterday. Are they for soft-boiling?"

"No, is for pastry dough, but I want best eggs. If I send mine son to do shopping for me, you serve him like me, you understand?"

Once, the girl in charge of the egg section reacted to Maman's gruffness with an irritated look. I overheard her mumble to a co-worker:

"It's the Kapferers' cook, from Avenue Henri-Martin. You can't believe what a pain in the ass she is."

I pretended not to hear, and Maman remained oblivious to the whole thing, but the owner cast a murderous glance at the girl from her elevated cashier's booth in the middle of the store. Undoubtedly Maman's abrasive manner was due in part to her awkward language skills in French. She didn't know how to get her point across in a nuanced, diplomatic way.

Maman had determined that I was qualified to do the shopping too, except at the butcher's, which I preferred to avoid anyway. The subtle distinctions between the various cuts of meat eluded me; they all looked pretty much the same.

My help saved her time, and it also enticed her to shop at the more distant open-air market on Rue de l'Annonciation, where fruits and vegetables were considerably cheaper than close by in the exclusive Rue de la Pompe shops. Her purveyors at the market knew me too, and were supposed to serve me with the same care and attention they granted her. If they didn't, watch out, they'd hear about it the next day! She was intolerant. She demanded the best quality and didn't hesitate to return the merchandise and make a scene if she felt cheated. Once, her complaint backfired:

I had gone shopping at the Rue de l'Annonciation market, and after returning to Avenue Henri-Martin, I was helping her in the kitchen. When she walked past the table where I was busy grating carrots, she took a pinch, tasted it, and spat it out in disgust:

"*Bo Dié! Saloperie!*" she yelled (God damn it! Garbage!)

"What? What's the matter?" I asked, puzzled.

"They not good. They bitter. I not can serve that."

I sampled the carrots. She was right, I had encountered better ones in the past, but what the hell, with a little sugar and some lemon juice or vinaigrette, the taste could be made acceptable.

"Tomorrow, you return them where you buy them," she said. "Right now, you run to Rue de la Pompe to buy new carrots. Go kvik!"

While sprinting full blast the distance of two blocks to get these new carrots, my heels grazing the small of my back with each stride, I resolved to throw the old ones into a sewer grate, if Maman insisted that I return them the next day. I would then buy a new bunch out of my own money and thus avoid a double confrontation—with her if I refused, with the seller if I accepted.

The following day, to my great relief, she decided to return the carrots herself, so she could personally express her displeasure.

The merchant was apologizing profusely, when his wife, who up until then had been listening from the back of the shop with her arms crossed and an impatient look on her face, stepped in front and interposed herself between him and this upset customer. She was glaring at Maman, but actually talking to her husband, who now stood behind her:

"Listen, Jacques, I'm fed up with these foreigners. Not only do they take our bread away from our mouths, but on top of that they complain. If she doesn't like our French carrots, she can go back to her country, that hag. It's simple, from now on I don't want to see her face, we don't sell her anything. You hear me, Jacques?"

Rough as it was, the shopkeeper's reaction wasn't as vulgar as that of the fish woman a few weeks earlier, to whom Maman had posed her standard, annoying "Is fresh?" question about all the food she bought. Holding up by its tailfin a beautiful sole she had picked up from the glistening bed of ice and seaweed, Maman asked:

"Is fresh this fish?"

The enormous woman towering above us on the platform reached under her apron and, with her hand on her crotch, replied:

"What about my balls, lady, are *they* fresh?"

In the comedy of shopping, sanctions such as those of the carrot seller were without consequence. Despite our genuine desire to remain loyal, we had choices galore among the vendors. From opposite sidewalks, they vied in fierce competition.

On Rue de l'Annonciation, we never failed to say hello to Pavel Harmady, and to buy green salad from him, Belgian endives in winter. And ever since Olga's "disappearance," we also often ran into her former employer, the learned Madame Perret, with whom conversation was never banal.

One day, I mentioned to her my attachment to the *Vél d'Hiv* indoor sports arena across the Seine from her residence, and how much I missed going there with Olga for basketball games and the six-day bicycle races.

"Yes, but you know, it's a bad place," she replied. "If I were you, I wouldn't go there."

"Why?"

"Why? Haven't you heard about the roundup there in 1942? Surely one of the darkest moments in our history, comparable to Saint-Barthelemew's day in the sixteeenth century. A dishonor for France. It's the place where several thousand Jews of the Paris region were herded, before being packed into boxcars and transported East to the extermination camps. Can you imagine the horror?

"Oh, I'm sorry, I didn't know. It's terrible, what the Nazis did."

"Worse, the people responsible for that shameful event were French."

Maman took the trouble to lug those heavy bags all the way from Rue de l'Annonciation, not to save money for Madame (it would have been a ridiculous excess of zeal), but to earn a supplement for herself. On her ledger, she wrote down the prices prevailing in the expensive shops where she was expected to go, just around the corner from home. That was the official rate she inscribed in her tally. Madame accepted it without hesitation, all the while being aware of Maman's stratagem, I'm sure.

The essential aspect in this ploy, limited to fruit and vegetables, had to do with bookkeeping. Maman was very careful about that. Accurate tallies gave her the feeling she wasn't cheating. Her scheme could not tolerate errors or disorganization, which would inevitably cast suspicion of dishonesty. The prices listed were authentic. Madame could verify them herself if she wished when she walked down Rue de la Pompe, with her stiff gait, to join her lady friends for afternoon tea at the Marquise de Sévigné salon.

There seemed to be an unspoken pact between her and Maman, with nothing asked, nothing hidden, nothing revealed. She knew that her cook bought things elsewhere and manipulated figures, but for merchandise of equal quality, she probably considered the extra effort deserving of self-granted rewards.

And God knows, the effort was huge! Shopping bags on wheels, that immeasurable improvement in quality of life, hadn't yet been invented. Our arms nearly fell off under the weight of our purchases. I walked like a beast of burden, eyes looking straight ahead, shoulders stooped, setting the bags down on the sidewalk for a pause at every street corner. Between the ages of 45 and 51 for Maman, and for me 10 and 14, this itinerary constituted our daily way of the cross.

When she returned to her kitchen, Maman treated herself to a strong cup of coffee, took out a clean apron, and started preparing lunch. The tension level then cranked up immediately. Her work demanded complete concentration. She had at her disposal a cast iron stove with eight gas burners, two ovens, and a bain-marie, plus, if needed, a butane stove with four burners and a third oven in the kitchen-size pantry, from where she sent trays on the dumbwaiter to the dining room above.

Once things were started, she juggled the pots and pans, watched over the cooking with one eye, and with the other kept track of the fateful 12:30 deadline on the wall clock. From time to time, she dashed to the pantry for something or other, and in each instance ranted about the absurd counter separating this room from the kitchen. She tasted the sauces, added salt here, spice or pepper there, flattened thick mounds of flour-covered dough into thin almost transparent strips under her energetic pastry roll, which she ordered me to clean up for her "Hurry, hurry, we not have time!"

She appreciated my help when I was home from school, but I felt that my mere presence hindered her concentration. Madame had offered to hire a regular teenage assistant, to peel vegetables and do sundry other tasks, and to wash the pots and pans and utensils that Maman used with abandon, like all good cooks. What was needed was a *garçon ou fille de cuisine* (a kitchen boy or girl), certainly not an apprentice, in other words someone who would be extremely quick, silent, and efficient. Luckily, a rare individual fitting those qualifications was found in Solange, a seventeen-year-old girl who got on very well with Maman. But Solange didn't last long. She fell in love with a young man, whom she introduced to the Henri-Martin staff to get their approval. He passed the test handily, especially with Thérèse who gushed: "My God, girl, you and him are like two lovebirds, don't hesitate, go ahead, marry him. This is a golden man. He is handsome, he doesn't beat you, he smokes less than a pack a day, he doesn't drink outside of meals, and best of all he has a steady job as a mailman. What more could you want! You are so fortunate!" Solange heeded this heartfelt advice shared by everyone. She was missed but not replaced.

At work in her kitchen, Maman reminded me of an Italian film director I had observed shooting a scene on location on the Trocadéro esplanade facing the Eiffel Tower, a few blocks from home. I had just come out of my favorite haunt there, the Museum of Man, with its fascinating anthropological displays, especially the Jivaro shrunken heads from Amazonia. The Italian director acted like a tyrant, gesticulating and yelling at everybody on the set, without restraint. He comported himself like an angry Jivaro warrior. Later, though, the crew took a break at the café on the plaza, and there, suddenly transformed, he showered everyone with guilt-laden cordiality: *Prego! Prego!* He offered cigarettes all around, lit them, kissed the ladies' hands, pulled chairs out for them, patted the men on the back, tried by every means to expiate for his behavior that had been so impulsive and odious only a few minutes before. And, surprisingly, everyone seemed to forgive him.

Maman's attitude in her kitchen resembled that of the director. She didn't tolerate interruptions, couldn't accept having her attention broken. Even a simple "*Bonjour*" irritated her. She relaxed only when the upstairs lunch was finished, and we could proceed with the staff meal at the kitchen table. There, she made amends for her morning rudeness by spoiling us.

Once, poor Thérèse suffered a particularly harsh rebuff. Around eleven o'clock, when Maman was flying from one pot to another, she entered the kitchen and said casually, as she lit up a cigarette:

"Eva, I'm taking a little break from the laundry to shoot the breeze with you. How's it going this morning? Things moving forward okay?"

Maman exploded: "Thérèse, you going make me burn someting!"

In fact, at that very moment, she singed her forearm on a pan. Yelling *"Merrda, merrda, merrda,"* she pushed Thérèse back into her steam-filled laundry room, and slammed the kitchen door shut.

Usually, she contained her impatience better, and merely acted unpleasant. Later that day, she made up with Thérèse, who never again disturbed her in the morning, and the two of them ended up becoming excellent friends. They had in common the experience of raising their sons "out in the country" in a foster home, although Thérèse suffered greater stigma. She was an unwed mother, not a widow.

Many years later, I gained some understanding of Maman's impatience, when, on occasion, I was faced with the same predicament as she in her kitchen, in my case at the office photocopy machine. Having gone there to do complicated cut and paste procedures requiring my undivided attention, I had to put up with people who wanted to gab while waiting for their turn at the copier.

At exactly 12:30, Maman sent the appetizer tray on the dumbwaiter to the dining room pantry, where the chambermaid Marie stood ready to begin serving. She then sighed with relief at yet another victory against the clock and the morning's inevitable bunch of aggravations. And right after that, she responded to Minet's insistent meows. He was accustomed to demand his piece of lungmeat at the first rumble of the dumbwaiter.

Maman didn't have the same rapport with Marie as with Thérèse, but she valued her live-in co-worker's serious attitude and discreetness ("She not chatterbox, that one"). Only two incidents occurred between them. Madame successfully defused both.

Shortly after her arrival in the Kapferer household, Maman discovered that—sacrilege!—Marie served hot dishes on plates that had not been warmed. How to make her understand that this practice was unacceptable? In the adjustments to her new job, she was reluctant to criticize Marie.

Madame felt that something was wrong when Maman, to avoid a head-on confrontation with Marie, proposed to her employer that she would warm the plates in the kitchen and send them up on the dumbwaiter at mealtime.

"That's too complicated, Eva," Madame replied. "With all this handling, there would be an increased risk of breakage, and you have enough work already without worrying about warming up the plates. But since you seem to absolutely want that, I will speak to Marie, and tell her to warm them up in the dining room pantry's oven, as if the idea came from me."

In the second incident, regarding a problem about maître d's, Marie greatly upset Maman by quoting from the *Pellaprat* book.

For formal receptions, not frequent at the Kapferers who had now retreated into an almost exclusively familial life, Madame hired two extra maître d's to help serve, as was customary in upper class households in those circumstances. Tradition had it that at the end of the evening, the extras were responsible for washing and drying the crystalware, with a perfectionist zeal and a pile of lintless dish towels. A particular duo of maîtres d's had established itself as regulars for these receptions. When things wound down and it was time to clean up, they were reluctant to plunge their hands in dishwater and risk soiling their tuxedos. So they pressured Marie, who was wearing a comparable uniform, white apron on black dress and white headband in her grayish hair, to help them, under the pretext of a flurry of work and the late hour. Of course, she ended up washing the glasses, while these gentlemen reserved for themselves the drying operation and the careful examination of the results against the light of the chandelier. She then complained to us, holding up her hands shriveled from the dishwater.

Marie had had enough of that. One day, she brought her annotated *Pellaprat* to the kitchen and showed Maman a relevant paragraph, to elicit her support and convince her of the validity of her complaint:

"The maître d's clear the dining room of all the glassware; they then wash it, dry it, and put it away under the direction of the head domestic in the household, butler or chamber maid."

However, from this explicit and clear excerpt, with which Marie decided to confront the maître d's by underlining "*wash*" without involving Madame in the controversy, Maman retained only the last sentence. What? Marie the chambermaid, head domestic in the household? On what grounds? Was the cook just another servant, like the rest of the personnel, or was she a different category of employee, with special skills? Maman had received no formal training, but she felt that at the Kapferers she performed the duties of a full-time cook, not those of a maid or housekeeper.

In the formal receptions, this difference was recognized by the guests themselves: they gave tips only to the personnel who waited on them. Maman occasionally donned the black and white uniform to earn a little supplement and also have a direct look at how her *canapés* and *petits fours* were received in the salon, but usually she preferred to stay in her kitchen rather than serve upstairs. The preparations for these evening events were less demanding than for the all-important daily lunch, and the atmosphere less stressful, thus she was not at all displeased if guests came down to congratulate her, which sometimes occured; but there no one ever slipped a banknote in her apron pocket, for fear perhaps of offending her. In her kitchen she was not perceived as a servant, but as a skilled practitioner.

Finally, after stewing over this, Maman asked her employer to clarify the situation: "Madame, is Marie mine boss?"

"Of course not, Eva! Where did you get that idea? Do you have trouble getting along with her?"

"No, no, but she show to me in book where they say that butler or chambermaid is main domestic in house."

"Yes, but that has nothing to do with you. For any problem pertaining to the kitchen, be sure to deal with me directly. If this hierarchy exists in some houses, but not in mine, it's only because the chambermaid is in more direct contact with her *patronne*. Really, that's all there's to it, believe me."

Madame showed great tact in resolving the complications that inevitably occurred in running the household. And she always radiated an all-encompassing kindness and empathy, an attitude no doubt born from deep suffering (several members of her family had vanished in extermination camps during the war).

Around 1:30, after having served dessert and coffee in the dining room, Marie came down to the kitchen to join Maman, Thérèse, and me for the staff lunch, carbon copy of the meal just finished upstairs. In view of the late hour and the tantalizing smells, we were all famished, especially Thérèse. She had already set the table, opened a bottle of wine, and filled a carafe with the water brought in from the Artesian well. She had also ground some coffee, shaken a fresh head of lettuce, sliced a baguette, and retrieved from the upstairs pantry the cheese tray laden with its usual complement of Camembert, Roquefort, Chèvre, and Gruyère. She had unfurled her napkin from its ring, rolled up her sleeves to be more comfortable, and she waited expectantly, elbows on the table. As soon as Marie arrived, we ate with an appetite heightened by the release from the morning's tensions.

With her gusto of former Parisian street urchin, Thérèse heaped praise on Maman, and teased her about her teetotalism: "Oh, Eva, fabulous, your leg of lamb. Marie, a little more wine? We have to drink to the cook, you know, since she doesn't touch that stuff herself! Come on Eva, take some more beans, they're scrumptious. One of these days we're gonna have to get you to drink some red too. Aren't you tired of sipping only water with your meals? You're gonna wind up with frogs in your belly."

A cup of coffee and a Gauloise cigarette closed off the meal for Thérèse. She ate, drank, smoked, talked ravenously. I loved her exuberance. And yet she endured a hard life, what with her chronic backache after leaning over the tub in the laundry room, and her daily subway ride through sixteen stations, at rush hour, standing the whole time, with a connection at Strasbourg-Saint-Denis where she felt crushed by the crowd; and from the financial standpoint, the board and lodging she paid to her son's caretaker, and the rent for her own room, under the roof, in a sixth-floor walkup. Lunch at the Kapferers was for her a rare moment of respite, if not joy.

Thérèse liked to talk, but Marie and Maman were not the best conversation partners. She tried to get the ball rolling for gossip and such by describing incidents she encountered in the subway or in her lively neighborhood, next to North railroad station, where tides of harried commuters from the Paris suburbs butted up against the more relaxed travelers to London, Brussels, and Amsterdam. Marie stayed pretty much mum. This unnerved Thérèse, who hoped to glean at least some tidbits about the mysterious life of glamorous Madame Legrand, Marie's primary charge in the household. But Marie, forever indebted to the Kapferers for having rescued her from an orphanage during adolescence, and for having kept her in their home for now four decades, would have preferred to die rather than divulge any secrets, such as Madame Legrand's destinations when she left the mansion in evening gowns, with liveried chauffeurs picking her up at the front gate in Rolls Royces or other fancy cars.

Maman didn't have much to say either, but unlike Marie, her life had been so eventful and unusual that she could abstain from participating in these discussions by simply declaring in a detached, knowing tone "Every family have story." She did however go outside her personal circumstances with a tale that gave Thérèse and Marie goose bumps each time she repeated it, at the urging of Thérèse, who acted in these requests like a child pleading "Come on, pleeaase, scare us again."

Maman basked in the aura she derived from telling this story, which had taken place, she said, in a village near hers in her native Slovakia—a region perceived from the vantage point of Parisian worldliness as a quaint, benign, remote, archaic place sheltered from the violence and corruption of modern urban life. But even the lifelong megalopolis dweller Thérèse recognized that Maman's tale surpassed any she had heard before.

The jist of the story, delivered with a sense of timing and suspense that compensated for Maman's awkward French, went like this: The village's richest landowner, a widower, had married a woman twenty years younger than he. One day, he came home to the farmstead earlier than usual and found his wife in amorous embrace with his son in the hayloft. In a fit of rage, he set the hayloft on fire and incinerated them both alive. Then he hung himself from the branch of a nearby tree. The charred remains of his wife and son, found in each other's arms, explained what had happened.

Thérèse and Marie never tired of hearing this story, nor Maman of telling it. She knew it couldn't be topped, and she relished seeing their reaction, Thérèse gasping "My God!", Marie covering her eyes as if to dispel the frightful sight, both women emotionally drained by the familiar yet each time horrifying tale, and both thankful in contrast for their quiet, uneventful lives—only recently so for Thérèse, who clearly had an "interesting past."

Then one day, Thérèse could contain herself no longer. After hearing Maman's account once more, she turned to Marie and angrily blurted out: "You know, Marie, it's just not fair. You enjoy listening to our stories, but you, you never tell us any!"

After lunch, Maman was free until dinner, as well as Saturday evenings when Marie served cold cuts prior to Monsieur's poker games. In her leisure time she liked to leave the mansion and "clear her head" rather than rest in her room on the fourth floor, whose window looked out on the clock tower across the avenue, above the canopy of chestnuts trees.

Three destinations beckoned to her regularly: the fabric stores on Rue de Steinkerque at the foot of Montmartre hill; her seamstress in the nearby suburb of Boulogne; her dentist, at métro station Réaumur-Sébastopol. Between the dentist and her seamstress, she could expect at least two appointments weekly. Adding to this the sending of "care packages" to Slovakia, and all her salary was eaten up. The supplement gained from the fruit and vegetable purchases came in handy.

The visits to the dentist seemed a costly struggle lost in advance. Maman was not in acute pain, but her teeth needed to be shored up, reinforced, replaced by bridges and crowns that had to endlessly be installed, modified, repaired. Could she have confidence in this doctor, or had she thrown herself into the claws of a swindler who would take all her hard-earned money? Would there ever be light at the end of the tunnel? What outcome could she hope for? To one day have all her teeth pulled out and look like Mémère? At least in the city she could have dentures made, but this extreme solution would be so humiliating! Distraught, she preferred not to think about that eventuality. She didn't understand the damnation that had befallen her, she developed a complex about it, often spoke with her hand in front of her mouth, hesitated to smile. And since she couldn't afford gold, she was outfitted with chrome-plated teeth. In contrast to her deteriorating dental condition, she had a radiant kind of beauty, with clear, piercing grey eyes, a curved forehead, smooth, glowing skin, and waist-long black hair streaked with gray that she combed each morning into braids wrapped around her head, never varying from this style until her stroke at 70, when she reluctantly had to shear her tresses.

On Rue de Steinkerque, she bought fabric for her clothes, which were then custom-made to her specifications by her seamstress and confidant. She couldn't find anything to her size or liking in ready-wear stores, which were more expensive than the seamstress anyway. But above all, she bought fabric for my sister Eva and our family in communist Slovakia, to alleviate the shortages they lived under.

Maman packed those fabrics in cardboard boxes that she tied with string. Then, as if she sought to give me an opportunity to participate in the effort, she asked me to write the address on the packages and take them to the post office. In the sharing of roles in our tiny family enclave, I was in charge of administrative matters, as often occurred in France with the children of foreign workers. Occasionally, while waiting in line at the post office, I was approached by sheepish adults who asked me to decipher or fill out forms for them. I must have had inscribed all over my brow that I was a "public writer," a now vanished occupation that probably continues to be needed.

Those were Maman's afternoons, without omitting the labyrinthine bureaucratic procedures in various Paris locations, veritable tests of patience and endurance, for which she also elicited my assistance: Prefecture of Police, near Notre-Dame Cathedral, for her residency permit, her work permit, and her repeatedly required and repeatedly blank police record; my French passport, which she thought I should have, just in case (of what? Maybe to spare me the difficulties encountered by foreigners), and which I obtained at age ten, after gaining official citizenship; the social security office, in the

Fifteenth District, for her paltry single-wage-earner allocation; the Czecho-slovak Consular office, Rue Bonaparte on the Left Bank, for a series of arcane documents from her native country that had to be translated; the Office of Refugees and Stateless Persons, near the Arch of Triumph, for her "travel document" in lieu of a national passport; and finally, a red tape undertaking of epic proportions, in terms of challenge and consequence, at the U.S. Consulate on Place de la Concorde, for our immigration visas to America.

Là tout n'est qu'ordre et beauté
Luxe, calme, et volupté.

— Baudelaire

My stays in the Kapferers' mansion provided a wonderful respite from the prison-like confinement of boarding school. Though the spartan atmosphere of the lycée was somewhat mitigated by friendship and solidarity, it lacked any feminine presence except for three or four teachers and a similar number of women who toiled over the dishwashing sinks in the deafening clatter of the dining hall. In comparison, 64 Avenue Henri-Martin seemed a haven of *ordre et beauté / Luxe, calme, et volupté*, especially Madame Legrand's suite, which looked like the den of a siren. With these extreme contrasts, and with the awakening of my senses, it was inevitable that I would be attracted to Madame Legrand.

The social life of this divorced Kapferer daughter took place exclusively outside the home. Her suite, faithful replica of her temperament and originality, served as a personal refuge. An aura of mystery surrounded her. The chambermaid Marie was the only person who could have provided any details about her life, but Marie, the very model of a discreet servant, was intent on protecting the privacy of her masters. It is often the opposite among live-in domestics, who vicariously escape from their dull and solitary existence by engaging in savory gossip about the adventures or misfortunes of their employers. Not Marie.

Madame Legrand was the embodiment of glamour. She heightened her natural beauty with makeup fit for an Egyptian queen. She wore alluring hairdos, bewitching perfumes, sumptuous clothes, dazzling jewelry, always in the best taste, with an innate sense of style. No frumpiness, ever, even in the most unguarded moments. And no apparent effort to achieve that spellbinding appearance.

Outside of my Sunday evening goodbyes to Monsieur and Madame Kapferer in their salon, I seldom ventured into the masters' wing. Madame Kapferer was the only person who circulated randomly throughout the mansion. Every one else tended to stay "home" within their respective suites or work places. My zone of activity was vertical rather than lateral, from top to bottom off the service stairwell. But on the fourth floor, this distinction between the various spheres wasn't as clear. The door separating the two wings stayed open most of the time, to give Chantal free access to her mother. And Madame Legrand too had to enter the service area on our floor to visit her daughter's room.

I first was attracted to Madame Legrand's lair by the nose, like a cat discovering a batch of catnip. Intoxicating yet subdued scents, which reminded me of a luxurious perfume shop on nearby Avenue Victor-Hugo, radiated from her place and fanned my curiosity. I couldn't remain indifferent to this spell, contrasting as it did with the lycée's cold dorm, where drafts were deliberately fostered to neutralize stale air or unpleasant odors.

The doors leading to Madame Legrand's suite were padded, the windows framed with drapes that matched the walls covered in beige silk. Transparent curtains filtered the exterior light. An armchair and sofa surrounded a low glass table always decorated with a magnificent bouquet. Potted palms in the corners of the salon created the ambiance of an oasis, or rather, in my thoughts, a harem.

Several times I had been unable to resist temptation. Taking advantage of Madame Legrand's absence, and having made sure I would not be seen by any of the other residents, I entered her place through the always open door of her salon. I took off my shoes before stepping on the thick carpet, beige like the rest, which created an exquisite sensation of softened reality. As if I were visiting a temple or a holy place, I had prior to that even put on clean socks. Despite these respectful precautions, I was tormented by an opposite desire: to desecrate the shrine, to jump on the armchair, to walk on the sofas, but I resisted this urge. And I imposed on myself another limit in sacrilege: already troubled by my transgressions in the salon, I didn't dare enter the bedroom.

My secret infatuation with Madame Legrand began one evening when I saw her descend the stairs of the mansion in a pale yellow evening gown, shoulders bare, diamonds shimmering on her neck. A chauffeur was waiting for her at the gate.

Her daytime attire departed markedly from the formal evening look. That she was able to remain elegant in any garb attests to her stylishness.

In the mornings around nine, suited up in her equestrian outfit, her knee-high boots freshly shined by Marie, riding crop under her arm, cap pulled down on her forehead, she headed out to the not too distant stables with a purposeful air. I would then see her, surrounded by a group of riders, trot down the equestrian lane in the middle of Avenue Henri-Martin between the Boulogne woods and the Trocadéro esplanade overlooking the Eiffel Tower.

In the afternoon, on days when she continued with sporting activities, it was either tennis, for which she wore a girlish outfit, all white, with short skirt and ankle-high socks; or golf, with traditional tweedy garb and cap à la Sherlock Holmes. She wore regular city clothes, always chic, mainly for late afternoon shopping.

Between her diverse changes of wardrobe, Madame Legrand basked in lengthy ablutions and walked around her suite in a white terry cloth bathrobe, with a towel wrapped around her head like a turban. I often saw her thus attired from the hallway on her floor. So far, innocuous stuff...

Then one day, everything toppled. Wearing her robe, she opened the bathroom door to let the cloud of steam escape. I could see her through the mist. She then put her foot up on the edge of the bidet to massage her ankle with one of the numerous lotions lined up under the mirror illuminated by a row of lightbulbs, like in a dressing room at the opera. The inside of her thigh suddenly showed through the opening of the bathrobe, taking my breath away. In my imagination, my eyes then went up Madame Legrand's body, her bathrobe continued to open, revealing her breasts, while my blood beat more and more violently against my temples. To finish my movie, our faces came closer, and she offered me her lips. The script unfolded in this seemingly reverse way because, in order to complete my "*éducation sentimentale*" begun in a sordid hotel on Rue de Provence, I still needed to conquer a woman, which meant to kiss her on the lips.

How to fulfill this fantasy and move to action with Madame Legrand? This dilemma, like so many in life, resolved itself without requiring a solution: I soon thereafter left for America.

Did Madame Legrand have any inkling that this shy and awkward adolescent entertained lustful thoughts about her when their paths crossed in the hallway? At our last encounter, the day of my final departure from her home, all reserve broke down between us and we...exchanged a handshake. "Bon voyage and good luck, young man" were her parting words as I turned to face my new life on a far-away continent.

The Kapferer mansion at 64 Avenue Henri-Martin.

Part IV

U.S.A., A Jagged Journey

Mr. Spanek on his way to work through Paris's Boulogne Woods (photo courtesy George Spanek).

Chapter 12

Americas

> "America doesn't exist. I know, I've been there."
>
> — *Alain Resnais, Mon Oncle d'Amérique*

*I*n the same way that an only child is by necessity impelled to form strong friendships, my scant family unit bonded in Paris with an adopted set of relatives, the Spaneks. I ended up living in the home of these serial immigrants from Czechoslovakia, my new foster parents really, for more than three years, in Chicago and San Francisco. The Spaneks had a huge impact on my upbringing and destiny: Maman would have never imagined moving to America if it hadn't been at their urging.

Their Old World Occupations

In the postwar Paris of 1944 – 1952, Anna Spanek reigned over the Rue de Passy section of the wealthy 16th District. A self-employed culinary artist, she was regularly called upon to prepare formal dinners in households that lacked an expert live-in cook among the domestic staff.

"Madame Spanek," as she was called by her employers (and by me too), would thus parachute into a kitchen, where the supplies she had selected earlier that day at the food shops on Rue de l'Annonciation awaited her, and she proceeded to do her magic with the assistance of the resident staff, leaving in her wake heaps of pots and pans to be cleaned up later, like a surgeon or an airline pilot abandoning the premises when their work is done. "Good cooking take time and lots utensils," she reminded her helpers, as if to excuse herself. To relax afterwards, she liked to go to the late movie at nearby Royal Passy cinema with her husband Jiří, but not before first stopping home with the choicest morsels, which she had set aside for him and their two sons George and Denis. Anna considered this ploy a legitimate prerogative, equivalent to a bus driver's expectation of a free meal at a restaurant when he brings in a load of tourists.

This resourcefulness on her part, added to the high demand for her husband's house calls to repair radios and record players in the evening (during the day he worked as a technician, quasi-engineer, in a plant manufacturing those same sets), enabled the Spaneks to live, despite their relatively modest official income, in a spacious second floor apartment located in the heart of the Passy district, at 3 Rue Guichard, with large French windows opening up in front on the narrow, lively street, and in back on an inner courtyard paved with cobblestones. Fabulous lodgings, with everything and anything one could ever want within easy walking distance, including the open spaces of the Ranelagh gardens and Boulogne woods.

Prior to taking occupancy of these premises, the Spaneks lived in a cramped unit on the fifth floor of the same building. Although the large apartment on the second floor was vacant, it had been sealed off by the Nazi authorities then ruling over Paris. In 1943 the popular French singer Maurice Chevalier undertook a performing tour of Germany, purportedly (collaborationist allegations clouded his trip) under the condition that a number of French prisoners of war would be freed. One of the released captives—an officer, single and without dependents—was allotted the cordoned off apartment at 3, Rue Guichard. But he felt ill at ease with so much space, and mentioned this to the concierge, who suggested a trade with the Spanek family hemmed in on the fifth floor. The owner of the building approved, and the switch took place. However the Spaneks' lease of this beautiful apartment sparked jealousies and resentments that would haunt them later. In socially stratified, housing-short Paris, envious people felt that this upstart immigrant family was overstepping class boundaries.

Anna's husband Jiří had left Czechoslovakia in 1924 at twenty-one to find work in France following an apprenticeship as an electrician in his native country. He had received only limited formal schooling, but he was extremely bright and interested in intellectual pursuits, especially literature and politics. He possessed the voracious appetite for knowledge that is typical of self-educated people, though uncharacteristically he was neither a communist sympathizer nor a labor activist. With the proper set of credentials, he could have become a philosopher or a statesman. Above all, he strove to serve his homeland from abroad. He felt its name should be spelled with a hyphen, Czecho-Slovakia, in order to at least symbolically recognize ethnic equality and thus defuse the tensions that later, in 1993, led to outright separation through the so-called "Velvet Divorce."

Adept at sports, Jiří gravitated in his free time to the Paris branch of the Sokol, a gymnastics organization founded in Prague, and whose numerous chapters worldwide served as community centers for the Czechoslovak emigrant and refugee diaspora. He fervently espoused the "sound mind in a sound body" principles of the Sokol movement, and the implicit social democratic center-left political stance of its founders, who vehemently opposed emerging fascist and communist totalitarian ideologies.

At the Paris Sokol Hall, where he volunteered as an instructor on the parallel bars and other apparatus, and also edited the organization's bulletin, Jiří met his future wife Anna, then eighteen and employed as a live-in maid for a rich Parisian family. Her parents had not opposed her desire to seek her fortunes abroad, first in Germany at fifteen, and then France. They were lower-level civil servants who, much like lighthouse keepers, tended a railroad crossing in rural Bohemia, lowering and raising the gates with a hand crank when the trains passed by. Through observation and experience in her sophisticated new Parisian milieu, their daughter soon became, like Maman, an accomplished practitioner of "*la cuisine bourgeoise*" (classic French cuisine).

Jiří and Anna married in 1926, their first son George was born in 1931, and Denis surprised everyone with his arrival fifteen years later, in the 1946 baby boom celebrating the end of World War II. Anna brought to the marriage an extraordinary sense of initiative and resourcefulness, and Jiří contributed a much different but likewise remarkable set of qualities. Both were of a bold, enterprising nature, as evidenced by their early decision to set out into the wider world from their small native country, yet their temperaments and attitudes contrasted sharply. Her tendency to always push on the accelerator (an inappropriate image for, surprisingly, this emancipated woman never learned to drive) was tempered by his contrary inclination to step on the brakes and examine things, before throwing caution to the winds and taking huge leaps too. A lifelong couple, they embodied the complementarity of opposites.

In keeping with her adventuresome nature, Anna traveled to America in 1937 for a period of six months, as a cook accompanying an eminent Paris surgeon and his wife on a professional journey to New York City, Chicago, and Houston. In those days, travel by ship involved extended stays, and the wealthy liked to take along trusted domestics and mounds of luggage. This particular couple was apprehensive about the food in "White Bread" America, a nation then untouched by the cosmopolitan influences and culinary fastidiousness of the late twentieth century. So they hired Anna to join them for the voyage and thereby solve the anticipated problem. Given her temperament, she could not refuse such a unique opportunity, despite the separation from her husband and six-year-old George.

In Texas and Chicago, Anna established contact with the local Czech communities, and upon returning to Paris she tried to convince her husband that, with war looming on the horizon in Europe, they should immediately emigrate to the New World. At first reticent in his customary manner, he nonetheless agreed. Although he loved France, he had been deeply wounded by the occasional insult of "*sale étranger*" ("dirty foreigner") thrown at him by boorish, uneducated French people, because of his accent. Interestingly, this kind of xenophobia prevailed only among the lower class ("Those damn foreigners taking our bread away!") In the Passy district where he lived, Slavic émigrés on the contrary enjoyed a mythic aura of soulfulness ("*l'âme slave*"), derived from their alleged emotionality ("Those people love to weep at the sound of violins"). They were also admired for their reputed talent at languages, and Prague vied with Venice as one of the favorite destinations of French esthetes.

In 1937 – 38, for whatever protectionist reasons, the U.S. limited its immigration quotas, so the Spaneks' visa was denied. They settled back into French life for more than another decade, before a new attempt to leave for America, successful this time.

What prompted the Spaneks' second decision to emigrate seems paradoxical, considering the pleasant life they led in Paris. The seed was planted through the connections Anna established with the Czech-American community during her 1937 trip. In 1946, at the height of post-war euphoria, the Weber travel agency in Chicago, specializing in once-in-a-lifetime visits "home" by Czechoslovak immigrants in America, contacted her to see whether there was anything she could do to expedite a frustrating red tape procedure: after arriving by ship at Le Havre, Weber passengers, numbering about a hundred each month, had to wait several days in Paris to obtain visas to cross the French-occupied section of Germany on their way to Prague. Cut through a bureaucratic process? The agency had asked the right person.

For her services, Anna received a fee deposited in her name at the Skala bank in Chicago's Czechoslovak neighborhood of Cicero. In addition, each traveler paid her a gratuity in cash, and the hotel where she housed them overnight, a commission. Her entrepeneurship nicely "put some butter on the spinach" for her family.

But in 1948, a new catastrophe occurred. The Spaneks' native country of Czechoslovakia fell under communist domination, its borders were clamped shut, travel came to a standstill, Europe was divided in half by an impenetrable iron curtain, plunging the continent into a "cold war" that would last forty years. Furthermore, in the late 1940s the Communist Party gained considerable strength within France too. "**U.S. Go Home**" and hammer and sickle graffiti appeared everywhere. The leftist attraction even filtered down to the previously apolitical or primarily social democratic Paris Sokol. The Spaneks' apartment, in the abhorred bourgeois Sixteenth District, became a "problem" for some of the "comrades" who accused their Sokol "brother" of being a class traitor.

After seeing the downfall of his homeland and the hostile attitude developing against him in the Czechoslovak community in Paris, Mr. Spanek, who had aggressively fought Marxism throughout his adult life in his journalistic writings and his actions, began again to think about emigrating to America. Xenophobia was no longer a factor of estrangement for him in France. He had been decorated after the war by the French government for his Resistance activities, and he could use that distinction to deflect any affronts. This time, unlike previously, the decision to emigrate came from him rather than from his wife, for no tangible reason except an exaggerated political apprehension, a mistaken foreboding of things to come. He was so traumatized by the collapse of his native country into totalitarianism, that he overreacted. The family prepared to leave for Chicago, where Anna's small bank account from the Weber travel agency would help them start a new life. George went first in 1950, at 19. His parents followed with Denis two years later.

In America, Mr. Spanek grew more cantankerous in his political views. Without relinquishing his concern for social justice, he became increasingly attracted to concepts of personal responsibility and individual freedom. After his naturalization he remained a faithful Democrat and voted for Kennedy in the 1960 election, while Mrs. Spanek opted for Nixon. When I asked him why he was so allergic to communism, whose egalitarian principles we both found appealing, he said he considered it a flawed utopian doctrine—because, since humans are imperfect beings, the discrepancy between theory and practice inevitably results in corruption or oppression. He was a reformist who preferred solidarity to collectivism and found revolutionaries at best naïve, at worst dangerous.

My family first met the Spaneks during the war, in 1943, when George—then twelve years old—was sent on bicycle by his parents fifty-five miles from famished Paris to the Lavril dairy at Moulin-Sagout, where my mother and father worked. Mrs. Spanek had heard through the Czechoslovak grapevine that abundant food was available there, particularly Camembert cheese of the renowned Lavril brand. George viewed those monthly smuggling trips (fraught with suspicions of black marketing, in his case unwarranted) as a burdensome activity taking him away from his friends who meanwhile, their schooling disrupted, were running unsupervised in German-occupied Paris. But his stomach enjoined him to comply with his parents' wishes. His father was himself involved in illegal activities, installing at night, on rooftops, antennas of his own design to circumvent the Nazis' scrambling of radio broadcasts from London.

Following my father's death, and continuing in the post-war period, the Spaneks remained close to us. Since she had inside knowledge of the working conditions and hiring opportunities for domestics throughout the 16th District, Anna found live-in employment for Maman as a cook at the Kapferers, and for Olga as a housekeeper at the Perrets. A good-natured rivalry inevitably developed between her and Maman. They ended up concluding a tacit pact. On the rare occasions they worked together, Anna took care of the meal, and Maman the dessert.

They both had high standards and strong convictions. For instance, my first meal in a restaurant occurred during our crossing of the Atlantic aboard the "Liberté", when I was almost fourteen years old. Until then, for Maman and me, the notion of "restaurant" didn't exist. It was a place meant only "for people not like us," out of our realm financially. But a second taboo, just as powerful, kept us away from restaurants: it was unthinkable to pay such a high price for a meal, since no performance passed muster with Maman's expectations. Her hyper-critical attitude was shared by Madame Spanek. They were aware of the stress and concentration involved in meal preparation (talking was prohibited in Maman's kitchen), and they refused to understand how a chef could possibly cope with the added complexity of allowing guests to have whims and choices, without undermining quality. If Madame Spanek and/or Maman had run a restaurant in Paris, it would have had a single menu and set hours, just like the households in which they worked. But I venture to say that similarly as in those places, the guests would have been pleased with the results.

For train trips, we took along our provisions in a bag. I was ashamed of the chicken legs, the hard boiled eggs, the salt shaker, the baguette, the Camembert, the grapes that we unwrapped in front of the other passengers, on our laps protected by a sheet of glazed paper. My unattainable dream of luxury, spontaneity, and freedom: to lean from the train window at a railroad station and buy a sandwich from a vendor hawking his stuff on the platform.

It is said it takes a village to raise a child. I would include in that village a mentor, someone who in addition to a parent, inspires a child with a particular way-of-being. Fatherless, I was fortunate to encounter two such role models: Pépère, who inculcated to me his lackadaisical peasant's attitude; and Mr. Spanek, who provided a completely opposite model, one of determination and efficiency. Whereas with Pépère I was able to spend entire days on our front stoop watching cars drive by, with Mr. Spanek I felt compelled to purposeful action. Consequently, although my favorite activity remains *farniente* (literally, to do nothing), I have on occasion plunged into projects with manic resolve, forsaking even normal life and sleep in the process.

My only reproach concerning Mr. Spanek was his impatience. He was prone to well-intentioned hectoring in his Czech-accented French: "*Ti dvois*, " "You must." These "musts" could be very concrete: "You must wear a cap," he hounded me in winter, whereas I liked the feeling of wet hair frozen on my head. Or: "No matter what, you must save some money!" an edict he expressed with the same contempt for thriftless people as for smokers or alcoholics. On that score I have chronically failed, modeling my attitude on improvident, carefree Pépère.

Sometimes Mr. Spanek's admonitions were very abstract: "*Ti dvois percer!*" "You must rise!" He told me he had not understood my father's lack of ambition despite the opportunities offered to him by his employer Mr. Lavril at the Moulin-Sagout dairy. Madame Mercier, on the other hand, criticized the same Mr. Lavril for failing to promote my father to foreman despite his leadership qualities. Which of those opposite perceptions was accurate? This quandary remains one of my most vivid experiences of miscommunication, misunderstandings, or contradictory viewpoints about the same reality.

Mr. Spanek advocated, like the sixteenth-century essayist Montaigne, that a man should have a room of his own free from the turbulence of children and domestic matters, a place where he could read, write, think, leave his papers undisturbed. Also, anticipating on the feminist revolution, he opined in an untranslatable pun: "*Il faut que les femmes travaillent, sinon elles travaillent du chapeau*" ("Women must work, otherwise they go nuts"). He meant of course work outside the home.

At 5:00 a.m. each day, he prepared coffee, and devoted the next two hours to his worldwide correspondence in the Czech language. The letters he received were lined up on his desk, and he answered them within two weeks at most. Writing flowed effortlessly from his pen or typewriter, which he hammered at a rapid pace using only two fingers. His diligence has fostered unending admiration in me, and shame for having lost contact with a number of treasured friends and former students, because of unfathomable procrastination on my part.

I was impressed too by his local anchoring wherever he lived. In Paris he read *Le Monde*, in Chicago *The Tribune*, and in San Francisco *The Chronicle*. Of the three he preferred *Le Monde*, because it was an afternoon newspaper, and as such didn't interfere with morning concentration, which requires holding the world at bay, including the still sleeping family. "Leave the outside world for the evening," he said, and practiced what he preached by way of the numerous meetings he attended, Sokol, Czechoslovak National Council in Exile, etc. Between his house calls for radio and TV repairs, plus those meetings, he spent most evenings away from home. Dinnertime though, at 5 p.m. in the Spanek household in America, was sacred, and that's when meaningful connection took place. Although I admired his way of living— his activities seemed intertwined into an organic and complete whole—I wasn't sure it suited me.

Mr. Spanek sought to orient me, without being too prescriptive or pushing me too much. When I think back to how I behaved when I lived at his home in Chicago, with a volatile mix of docility and adolescent rebelliousness (for instance smoking and getting tattoos at age 14, a sure sign of deviance in the 1950s), I can only pay homage to the way he handled our complicated semi-familial relationship. I think he felt invested with a sort of paternal responsibility for the upbringing of the child of a deceased *compatriot*—a recurrent, revealing word in his journalistic writing. He was glad to see that I liked to read, and he therefore assumed I was predisposed to the academic studies of which he had been deprived, but he tried to redress my tendency to inertia, which worried him.

This aspect of my personality had glaringly revealed itself in an incident that took place when I was eight years old and vacationing with the Spaneks in Pornic, on the Atlantic Coast of France:

At the end of a family dinner, Madame Spanek had served for dessert an assortment of *kolačky*, the small Czechoslovakian pastries filled with poppy seed or fruit jelly. Since I was already full, but didn't want to displease her, I discreetly wrapped the offering in my handkerchief and stuffed it in my back pocket, with the intention of getting rid of it at the first opportunity. But the cookie flattened when I sat on it, and I completely forgot its existence. It became an integral part of my clothing.

A few days later, Mr. Spanek's horrible discovery, in front of guests, the Gelet family, for whose daughter Martine, eight like me, I had a secret crush:

"Milan, what is stain on your back pocket?"

"Stain? I don't know."

"Yes, look, purple color is bleeding through cloth." And already he was pulling out of my pocket the handkerchief sticky with plum marmalade.

I was mortified, my embarrassment multiplied by all those eyes looking at me, especially Martine's. Her parents stepped forward to console me. They had a car, and they promised to let me ride with them back to Paris, and even let me sit in front so I could share the driver's view.

Mr. Spanek could not conceive that anyone might be so neglectful or slovenly as to shove a pastry into one's back pocket, and be so absent-minded as to leave it there. Incomprehensible! He didn't realize that excessive politeness and groundless shame were what had caused me to hide the damn cookie there in the first place.

My inertia originated under Pépère's influence. In addition to watching cars drive by, he sat a lot, especially on the collapsed wall behind our garden. He observed the world with an inexhaustible serenity, despite his afflictions. In his nonchalance, he seemed to embody wisdom. His favorite saying: "It's not worth getting riled up about anything, not even the weather. It too will pass."

My unanswered mail, neglected repairs, ignored maintenance, everything that is pending or delayed, I owe to Pépère. But I am also dogged by Mr.

Spanek's efficiency. I am thus made up of two contradictory influences, with Pépère's holding sway.

To conclude this overview of Parisian occupations, after the Spaneks' and Maman's there remains mine: scholarship student. *Boursier d'État*, simultaneously ward of the State and chosen child of the Republic, I was earning my living since age ten from my school work at the lycée, without conscious effort, but with an acute awareness of my good fortune and my obligations.

Of Emigration

Condemnation to exile, even to a hospitable place, is one of the cruelest forms of punishment devised by man. Witness, for example, two of the great banishments of history: Victor Hugo on the Anglo-Norman isle of Guernsey, Solzhenitzin in Vermont. That said, unless one is a refugee fleeing famine, natural calamity, or unbearable persecution, why choose to emigrate of one's own free will, indeed with enthusiasm and determination, as have done and continue to do millions of people?

Perhaps to quench an immoderate taste for adventure? Or to reinvent oneself by escaping from the confines of family and habitual surroundings? Or for purely economic reasons, legally or not, from South to North or East to West, in the hope of attaining a better standard of living, especially if there is nothing much to lose in the country of origin?

Occasionally, people emigrate for a specific reason. That was the case for a friend of mine's great grandfather Viliam, eldest of thirteen children, who left his native Estonia for America to track down and kill his father, who had deserted the family. He never found him.

These diverse motivations no doubt occur in various combinations. Most often perhaps, people emigrate without really knowing why, to appease an undefined restlessness, curiosity, or dissatisfaction. Maman and I probably fall in that category, exacerbated by the dire housing shortage in Paris during the postwar decade.

In the collective imagination of the world, America-the-land-of-opportunity (and to a lesser extent its northern neighbor Canada) remains the quintessential destination of choice for voluntary exiles, whether emigrants or refugees. This American attraction is true also for two other kinds of emigration: "brain drain," with greater allegiance to profession than to homeland; and capital flight, wealthy émigrés fleeing from revolution or social change. And if the itinerary sometimes leads to alternate places, such as Australia, Western Europe, or South Africa (the latter for Whites lacking social conscience in the time of apartheid), those are often considered second choices compared to the mythic U.S.A. For instance, in the mid 1990s, the French were deeply insulted when a group of Bosnian refugees, who had been housed in a refurbished *château* in central France, slipped away during the night to *walk* to faraway Paris so they could apply for immigration papers at the American embassy. As if to prove this magnetic centrality of the U.S., Americans who choose to live abroad are considered expatriates, not emigrants.

Yet another category of immigrants come to the U.S. because of marriage to American travelers, military personnel, or business people temporarily stationed abroad. They step into ready-made lives they may or may not appreciate. Independently of the reason why they have resettled, all immigrants are confronted with the recurrent, naive, well-meaning, but brutal question from Americans: "How do you like it here?"

In theory then, immigrants throw themselves into adventure with a conquering attitude. High on adrenalin, some of them advance very fast in their adopted country, and generate resentment or envy among their already settled predecessors who, after having helped the newcomers (ethnic support networks are usually in place)—and after having recommended initial patience, parsimony, and levelheadedness—see those upstarts disregard their advice and leapfrog over them. The craving for success of the recently-arrived people, their fresh view of things, their dynamism, their ignorance of obstacles, have given them powerful wings and large appetites. They embody the American dream.

However, many if not most immigrants burn up their entire capital of initiative, resourcefulness, and energy in the very act of expatriation. As soon as they settle down, traumatized by this wrenching experience, they hunger for security, relinquish risk taking, withdraw from the fray. The fate of immigrants is thus sealed quickly. A few months after their arrival, a pattern has emerged, the die is cast determining success or stagnation, or, as was the case for the Spaneks, Maman, and me, downfalls of varying durations, some of them permanent. "Success" is then hoped for the next generation.

Among the unfortunate immigrants who experience retrogression, very few accept—because of wounded pride—to recognize their mistake and return to their country of origin. Such an admission of defeat would be devastating from a psychological standpoint, and, prior to the democratization of air travel starting in the 1960s, unthinkable for financial or logistical reasons. Until then, emigration such as ours or the Spaneks' was a one-way voyage, with at best a single visit "home" during the remainder of a lifetime.

Failure in America—the land of opportunity, free enterprise, and corollary "duty to succeed"—was and continues to be perceived as a dishonoring humiliation. It is kept hidden at all cost, through lies, omissions, distortions, which compound the problem by misleading others who then take up the same path. Where can one succeed, if not in America? Those who have the courage to tell the truth and admit their demise to their friends and relatives back home endure mortifying sarcasm: "You didn't need to go through all that upheaval to end up with a job working the midnight shift on a factory assembly line!"

A bleak factory fate was precisely what nineteen-year-old George Spanek experienced in 1950, when he emigrated from Paris to Chicago with the dream of playing professional hockey, perhaps even with the Blackhawks. He, and a Czech refugee friend and hockey star named Bohdan Vonka, were accustomed to play in the Central European style valuing technique and finesse. They were taken aback by the violence of American hockey, which required a willingness to have one's teeth knocked out. That was too high a price to pay for those two good-looking guys. Vonka, who had received formal training as a waiter in the Czech resort of Karlovy Vary, traded his skates for a tuxedo and ended up as a suave maître d' in an exclusive French restaurant in Manhattan. George stayed in Chicago.

From the Thor washing machine factory floor, where he polished metal on the graveyard shift for $72 per week, George reported back to his friends and parents in France that everything in America was great. What else could he say? He didn't want to burden them with a tale of woe, and he was too ashamed or embarrassed to reveal his true feelings, especially after all the hoopla of departure.

During the postwar period, when Europe lagged far behind America economically, it was easy to masquerade or misrepresent things. Thus George flaunted that he owned a car, and even sent pictures of himself proud at the wheel, but he omitted to say that in the U.S. an automobile was a banal necessity, not a luxury. He bragged that with only two weeks' salary he could buy a TV showing three different channels! He gloated that he lived in his own apartment, with a bathroom no less, an unattainable aspiration in Paris for young people and others like Maman and me, but he failed to mention that his lodgings were located in a basement, a horrifying situation by French standards. And he wrote that food, which took the largest chunk of a family's budget in Europe, was extraordinarily cheap in easy-living America, but he forgot that his mother had found ingenious ways to mitigate this central problem of Parisian life. In reality, he was depressed and imprisoned in a Czech ethnic ghetto, where he did not even learn English.

George saved himself by enlisting in the U.S. Air Force, which sent him to...Panama, in the midst of the Korean War. But his move to America started a Paris-to-Chicago chain reaction which continued on to the West Coast after he returned from military service and "emigrated" again, this time internally, to San Francisco. Although he was eleven years older than me, I am amazed at the number of parallels in our itineraries. He was the scout leading the way to new territories, the locomotive that everybody followed. His parents moved from Paris to Chicago with six-year-old Denis in 1952, and sent back chimerical reports as well, prompting Maman and me to follow suit in 1956. Fortunately, the transatlantic migration ended with us, although we too painted our dismal scene to others with a rosy glow. I say "fortunately" because after all people live everywhere, and it's perhaps often best if they stay put wherever they are.

I have no explanation for our exodus from Paris, except ignorance, crass ignorance, and self-deception, the Spaneks', our own, mirages, false myths, the temper of the times. When she was pressed for a motive, Maman used a delusional cliché: "For future of mine son." She probably believed it, unaware as she was of the academic and social implications of my scholarship at the lycée, beyond the free room and board it provided.

Sometimes, I wonder whether a latent desire to live in lodgings of our own might have been a factor for me. I don't think it was for Maman. She was so accustomed to *logé nourri* live-in employment that she feared the responsibility of having her own place. Like kibbutz workers or uniform wearers, she found freedom in limited choices and responsibilities. Years later, when I showed her a large house belonging to a friend of mine, she expressed sympathy for whoever had to wash all those windows, and pity for the owners when I told her there were no domestics in that household.

George, his parents, Maman, and I could have returned to Paris and resumed our French lives. For all the reasons mentioned above, we didn't.

Madame Kapferer had expressly told Maman that she could have her job back if things didn't work out for us in America, but Maman was too proud and too stubborn to take her up on the offer. Besides, she had used up all her savings for our westbound voyage across the Atlantic.

We had received two dire warnings before our departure, and discounted both. The first took place at the crowded Rue de l'Annonciation sidewalk market where, upon hearing of our emigration plans, the straightforward Madame Perret publicly reprimanded my mother: "Madame Eva, you are demented, and so ungrateful! In France, the State takes care of your son. You will never find that in America. And what about your daughters?"

The other occurred at the American Express office near the Paris Opera, where we had gone to exchange our francs into dollars in preparation for the journey. The employee who handled the transaction turned out to be a man also of Czech origin, a 1948 D. P., Displaced Person. He pleaded with Maman: "Madame, don't go to America! You're making a tragic mistake. I've been there myself. I couldn't adapt. It was too hard. And there aren't any people in the streets. Madame, please, think a little: you're over fifty, you can't speak the language, you can't drive a car, and on top of that you're taking along a child at the critical age of thirteen. Don't go!" He concluded his harangue with a sweeping pronouncement: "America is fine only if you're desperate, if you don't get sick, and if you have a trade, like plumber or carpenter. Me, I was a teacher of Latin and Greek in Prague, and I also knew German, French, and English, so I thought I would do well. But I couldn't find a decent job even with those qualifications. I don't mean to be disrespectful, Madame, but your fancy cooking may be as unappreciated there as my Latin and Greek, and you'll probably end up being a charwoman."

His vehemence startled us, but didn't change our resolve. When we left the American Express office, Maman rejected his diatribe: "I not believe him. He wrong, most difficult age with children not thirteen, most difficult age seventeen." She was alluding of course to her experience with Olga.

George and I no longer regret having emigrated to the U.S. We have come full circle and now greatly appreciate our American lives, but at the time, leaving France made no sense. All of us lost so much! Our parents underestimated the limitations of age and language, and never regained their Parisian status. To make things worse, we left France at precisely the wrong moment, on the eve of a unique, astonishing window of economic opportunity and social transformation (The "Thirty Glorious Years," with middle-class aspirations for all). Some classmates of mine from Madame Mercier's one-room schoolhouse, who had finished their formal education at the legal age of fourteen, went on to become high level business executives. Maybe that's why, despite all the good things that have ultimately happened to me in America, I continue to view myself as an *emigrant* rather than an *immigrant*. So does George. Denis left at too young an age, six, to form divided attachments. His bonds to Paris are more intellectual than emotional. I don't think the city evokes for him the nostalgic "paradise lost" image that it does for his brother and me.

Maman's decision to leave France for America was an act of sabotage or self-destruction, to which I collaborated fully. The idea came from her, following the encouragement of the Spaneks, but I could have voiced a veto. Why I didn't is still unclear to me. I can only surmise that I wanted to avoid disappointing her, that I shared her sense of adventure, and that I was probably eager to live in lodgings we could call our own—an unattainable goal in Paris.

People were also hesitant to remind Maman of another glaring oversight: the two daughters she was leaving behind—Olga, at twenty-three, estranged in Paris, and Eva, twenty, raised by relatives since infancy on the other side of the iron curtain in Slovakia. At fifty, Maman abandoned a fabulous job in a fascinating city, and I, about to turn fourteen, discarded the dual support of the French Republic and the Kapferer-Wildenstein family. All of that thrown overboard to the seagulls following us in the wake of the storm-tossed "Liberté" across the Atlantic.

Their New World Destinies

When we arrived in Chicago in April 1956, Maman worked on an assembly line in a canning factory for several months, and I started eighth grade while we lived at the Spaneks'. She then took up the live-in domestic job stipulated by her immigration sponsor, in the suburban town of Elmhurst. Her employer, Mrs. Levinson, was a recently divorced woman who owned and ran a local department store. Mrs. Levinson knew enough French to communicate with Maman, often by phone because her work kept her late at the office much of the time. Her daughter Nancy was away at college, and her son Ricky, then going through an uncooperative pre-teen period, became my mother's real boss. To everyone's astonishment, the pair got along famously.

Maman indulged him, catered to his whims, fulfilled through their relationship the maternal instincts that circumstance had caused her to forgo with
her own children. And he in turn abandoned his oppositional ways, although
they sometimes reemerged with his mother.

European household workers were highly valued at the time. They were
considered more reliable than Americans—who, except for Blacks, shied
away from domestic work, perceived as demeaning. Maman carried out in her
usual conscientious way her new housekeeping duties, ceaselessly glorified in
television advertising: cleaning, dusting, doing laundry, washing dishes, waxing floors. She ironed clothes with a perfectionist's zeal, vacuumed the thick
wall-to-wall carpets without leaving streaks against the grain, polished the
windows to a bright shine. Her culinary talents, however, went largely unused. Although Mrs. Levinson was a cultured woman with discerning tastes,
she was too busy to involve herself closely with domestic matters or adhere
to any sort of predictable schedule.

Maman made some attempts to expand Ricky's food choices. "What's
THAT, Eva?" he asked with a skeptical look, but then delight, when during
one of my visits she served us succulent lamb chops sprinkled with freshly
ground parsley. But mostly she prepared the simple meals he requested—
hot dogs, hamburgers, bologna sandwiches with bright yellow mustard, or
Velveeta cheese on Wonder Bread with Miracle Whip, washed down with
prodigious quantities of milk, and served on a folding tray in front of the
TV. Despite the language barrier, she and Ricky communicated very well.
He raved to his mother that Eva was the most wonderful housekeeper they
had ever known. For dessert he helped himself to heaps of ice cream, stored
in rectangular boxes in the freezer. Why bother with complicated pastries
since this was good enough, Maman thought. And so plentiful! In France, ice
cream was a seasonal treat, purchased in the summer from outside vendors,
who doled it out in two or three puny scoops barely larger than marbles. And
while initially Maman missed the daily banter with the butcher and the other
shopkeepers she had patronized in Paris, she soon came to appreciate the
comfort and convenience of once-weekly forays to the supermarket aboard
Mrs. Levinson's air-conditioned Cadillac.

Not challenged from the culinary standpoint, Maman fell back upon
facility and marveled at stunning discoveries, such as Jello in diverse colors,
Philadelphia cream cheese, Wonder Bread (more compatible with her ever
more fragile teeth than Parisian baguettes, and so white it *had* to be good),

Skippy peanut butter, so practical for sandwiches with grape jelly when Ricky wanted a change from bologna or Velveeta. She got used to eggs that broke at the slightest touch, to hard tasteless tomatoes, to rough and bitter sticks of cellulose passing for carrots. Her former picayune standards fell by the wayside, and resurfaced only on special occasions.

I stayed at the Spaneks in Chicago for two years, until Maman set up her own household by marrying a man to whom she was introduced by a former grade-school classmate of hers, Mrs. Royko. She had literally bumped into this childhood friend on the sidewalk in Cicero. Despite the passing of more than four decades, the two women instantly recognized each other.

Maman's new husband, Bohumil, was a Czech immigrant from the 1920s, at 59 six years older than she. He was a childless previously divorced widower, and a welder by trade. That became the first time in my life I experienced living "at home," albeit with a stepfather who wouldn't teach me how to drive—no problem, like everything else I learned that by myself too, by "borrowing" his car from the parking lot while he was at work.

I greatly welcomed Maman's marriage. It relieved me of the overwhelming burden of being her sole anchor in this new land whose language she didn't speak. She continued to clean houses, until her stroke at 70. Ever since childhood, she had known only toil, except for her "six wonderful years" (her words) in Paris at the Kapferers, where her activities didn't feel like labor to her, but simply active participation in the life of a large extended family, with genuine empathy for Madame Kapferer's responsibilities in managing the household.

In America, Mr. Spanek experienced regression too. As a blue-collar worker at the Zenith television factory in Chicago, he inspected the TV sets at the end of the unrelenting speeded-up assembly line. He either rejected or approved them by affixing a tag that bore his number, not even his name. He felt dehumanized by the mind-numbing, repetitive nature of his job, but he bravely endured, never missing a day: "Milan, don't ever work like me on an assembly line in a factory, it's slavery!" he admonished me every evening upon returning home from the Zenith plant. As if to enable me to avoid that fate, the first thing he did when I arrived in Chicago was to take me to the public library and let me loose among all the books and magazines, which, incredibly, you could take home if you wanted. I had never been to a library before! I didn't even know whether they existed in France. My presumably "elite" boarding school didn't have one. Notwithstanding my general disappointment with the "New

World," French-American comparisons became fraught with huge paradoxes and contradictions, some of them highlighting severe gaps in my background.

Mr. Spanek continued to supplement his income by doing television home repairs in the evening at a time when electronics required permanent retraining, with the artisanal concept of "repair" evolving towards one of "parts replacement." He was at once mystified and exhilarated by technological progress. He marveled at the enormous improvements it brought to daily life, starting with the replacement of the coal furnace in his basement with a clean gas unit controlled by thermostat. "New" was the buzzword then prevailing in America, the pathbreaking country for modernization. He was frustrated later to see that buzzword change to "No": "No nuclear energy. No supersonic transport. No this, no that, no everything. No, no, no!" Even more than previously in Paris, he fell back on Czech associative life as his main source of fulfillment, besides his family. He faithfully drove Denis to his weekly accordion lessons, and at Maman's request, he even took me to a Slovak protestant church on several consecutive Sundays, until I lost interest.

To justify his immigration in his own eyes, he began to vaunt the positive aspects of American life, and to denigrate France. This phenomenon of self-protection is well known among unsuccessful immigrants, who leap into flights of bad faith as a last-ditch effort to contain their disappointment, so much so that their attitude borders on incoherence. Indeed, his passionate enrollment, at the same time, in an organization of French war veterans in Chicago, revealed his emotional disarray.

One day, to emphasize a point, he stated that America was leading the way not only in the technological realm, but also in human relations, by making credit easily available to all.

"How so?" I asked, puzzled.

"Because in France," he replied, "you have to save for something before you can buy it. And if you want to borrow money, you can only get it from your friends, not from banks, and believe me, it's not good to mix friendship and finances."

In what country other than the United States, he asked, can workers go to their jobs driving their own cars, as he himself did at the wheel of his Nash. He also found the American workers more intelligent than their French counterparts embittered by the sacrosanct class struggle. He quoted the reaction of the already well-motorized American worker, at the sight of the boss's Cadillac: "I'll work hard, and some day, I'll have a car just like his."

The reaction of the French worker in a similar situation: "Some day, that bastard will walk, just like me."

He also ridiculed the archaic French telephone system, compared to its modern, reliable American counterpart. He vilified the grime and soot of timeworn Parisian buildings, the leaky smell of "gaz on all floors," the leprous walls, the dank courtyards. In Paris he knew people who, for hygiene, had only a faucet above the kitchen sink, and no bathroom or toilet within their lodgings. Unthinkable in America, he said.

I tried to temper his rants by reminding him that, paradoxically, the run-down overcrowded districts of Paris inspired an outpouring of songs and poetry, odes to the beloved city.

"Don't romanticize dinginess" was his retort.

I myself was shattered by emigration, and prone to the same overstatements, but in reverse. I disagreed with him on just about everything and stood my ground, while at the same time trying not to push provocation too far. We argued like two wounded fighters sparring with muffled blows. In response to his admonition that I should learn to speak Czech better, I let fly "Czech is a dead language, just like Latin," and immediately regretted my hurtful words.

I pointed out to him that in almost every house or apartment building in Chicago, basements were occupied. I was shocked to see people live like that, underground, like moles, in the damp earth, unthinkable in France, where in the village people still felt compelled to air out their bedding on windowsills each morning. Touché!

I was also appalled by the transformation of American rivers into sewers, whereas one could swim and even catch fish in the Seine in Paris. On this point, Mr. Spanek could not contradict me. One day, returning from a visit downtown, we walked across the bridge spanning the Chicago River and paused to look at the water. Horror! Under our eyes flowed an uninterrupted stream of feces and waterlogged condoms. Embarrassed, he yanked me away from the railing. Touché!

"Be careful, Milan, you have tendency to look for the bad side of America, and find it. Why don't you try instead to look at the good side, it exists too, you know."

"Yeah, where?"

Back then I saw Chicago only as an immense expanse of straight, uninviting, semi-deserted perpendicular streets not meant for ambling, more like roads really, where brick bungalows with pocket-size lawns differed from each other only by the number inscribed above their front door (1817 for the Spaneks, on South 57th Court). Good luck trying to find your house if you were ever so slightly inebriated! Chicago, mythic capital of work life, where immigrants could always find employment in some warehouse or factory. Strictly utilitarian city: no fantasy, no surprises, no landmarks, save for intersections, identical to all others: Kedzie and 12th; Kedzie and 22nd; Kedzie and 26th. Four-lane 48th Street, also known as Pulaski Road, and referred to as the "widest boulevard in the world," what with Czechoslovakia, with its Bohunk a.k.a. Honky population on one side of the street, and Africa on the other. Chicago, an abyss for the soul and the spirit. The contrast with Paris, lively city conducive to random strolling in numerous districts with varied personalities, sickened me. I suppose that what I missed, in an immature way, was the teeming street life and sense of history permeating Paris. I had never been inside the Louvre or Notre Dame but I liked to walk past those monuments and know they existed.

I was too unhappy at the time to detect Chicago's compelling attributes (since then recognized in official sisterhood with Paris, New York being viewed from the French capital as a mesmerizing rival city). I reached the point of closing my eyes to the spectacular row of skyscrapers facing Lake Michigan, so fake did it appear compared to the reality of what lay behind for straight, flat, endless miles. This facade on the world, built of glass, concrete, and steel had no more substance that a plaster prop in a Hollywood movie. Several shanties had sprouted up on the edge of Paris, but they were on a small scale compared to the devastation one saw from the windows of the "El" train on the way to Chicago's downtown, and at least people in France were morally troubled by the existence of their *bidonvilles*.

"Listen," Mr. Spanek would say in our debates, "I'll tell you a field in which the Americans are unbeatable: the quality of their manufactured products, their machine tools, their technical and scientific progress. Compared to that, the Europeans are way behind. The Germans haven't yet fully recovered from the war, the French are unreliable, look at their Renaults, and the Japanese are going in the wrong direction by producing only cheap junk. Quality is what counts today."

My response: "I thought that quality in America was worsening. Everybody says that things were built better before." Another paradox occurred to me later: Why was it that in superior America, the label "imported" meant "better," or at least more expensive?

Regarding the past, how many times had I heard Pépère say "It was better before." And in fact, from his standpoint, he was right. For him, who had lived in the closed, immutable world of a peasant in wooden clogs, the only change he could observe was his own decline.

But Mr. Spanek, steeped in the technical realm, lived the opposite situation: in his eyes, everything was becoming incomparably better, and would continue to do so. "No, no, you're mistaken," he said in one of our jousts, "quality has improved a lot. Take automobile tires. Nowadays, a flat is a rarity. Before, it was common. Or take a wash machine, a Maytag like ours. Indestructible! It will still run after I die."

The transistor revolution was another example; it marked the end of radios with vacuum tubes that were slow to warm up, and petered out at any moment. He didn't deplore their disappearance; their time had passed, they had ensured a nice supplement to his income for many years. He loved progress, and he respected machines, treated them kindly, like sentient beasts of burden. He gave his car ample time to warm up on cold winter mornings, and was appalled by the abuse Americans inflicted on their faithful mechanical servants, for instance throwing gym shoes into a wash machine.

That year, the Russians launched their Sputnik and caught America, the powerful giant, sleeping on its laurels.

Shortly after the ill-timed purchase of the Maytag washing machine—an important milestone in American family life—Mrs. Spanek, *"Cordon Bleu"* culinary artist in Paris, was hired as a cook in the cafeteria of a competing appliance factory, Hotpoint, where she could have obtained a discount. She worked the midnight to 8:30 shift. As a safety measure, since she didn't drive, her employer provided her with taxi transportation to her not too distant workplace. She walked home in the morning, her husband already gone to the Zenith factory.

She adjusted to the industrial food production that was expected of her: make jello, slice heads of cabbage for cole slaw, prepare large quantities of rudimentary dishes. Like her husband, she had self-defense reactions. She divested herself of her gastronomic talents and expectations (fortunately, as with Maman, they resurfaced at home), she stopped being upset that people drank coffee as a beverage with their twenty-minute meals. She continued to be troubled, though, by the unappetizing way chickens were delivered to her kitchen, dripping wet or semi-frozen in plastic bags.

Always alert at work in her cafeteria despite the fatigue of night hours, Anna took advantage of her long periods of solitude, to cogitate. And one morning, *Eureka!*, she proudly announced upon returning home earlier than usual from Hotpoint, in a state of feverish excitement, that she had invented a new concept for roasting chickens, vertically. She wanted to share the news with her husband before he left for the Zenith factory, and prevail on him to build a prototype as soon as possible. She had in mind a simple implement in the shape of an Eiffel Tower made of stainless steel wire, which she named the "Spanek Vertical Roaster." The chicken would be impaled on it, and thus roasted in a more efficient and uniform way, from the inside as well as the outside, with the juices cauterized in the meat, and fat draining to the bottom. It was without question a fabulous idea, ahead of its time. By its very principle, the Spanek Vertical Roaster prefigured the emerging concern for healthful cooking and the banishment of grease. Its simplicity represented a perfect melding of form and function.

Her dreams and her imaginings sustained Mrs. Spanek during her tedious nights at work. Unfortunately, she didn't know how to market her invention, except to her friends, to whom she offered the vertical roasters as gifts. She was intimidated by expansion beyond her familiar Czechoslovak circle. She suffered cruelly from the obstacles, incomprehension, and mockery she encountered; and she discovered the bitter definition of heaven and hell in the entrepeneurial culture of America: "Heaven is having a brilliant idea. Hell is implementing it."

When the Spaneks moved from Chicago to San Francisco two years after their son George, they left hundreds of unsold vertical roasters stacked in my parents' attic. And when my parents later undertook the same westward migration, they received her permission to discard those cumbersome objects in the city dump.

Sadly, Mrs. Spanek passed away in 1973, from cancer, at the age of sixty-five. To honor her memory, her son Denis, a successful twenty-seven year old real estate broker in San Francisco, decided to apply his marketing talents to her invention. He enjoyed tremendous success following breakthrough appearances on late night television infomercials for insomniacs, where he can be seen in a chef's apron, accompanied by Hollywood celebrities, preparing chickens so tender that he cuts them with a ...carrot! The concept has reached not only a large popular audience (so far, several million roasters have been sold), but also a number of the world's greatest chefs ministering to heads of state, at Buckingham Palace in England, and at the Élysée and Matignon Palaces in France. Anna Spanek's name is even featured on the menu of London's five-star Connaught Hotel.

After his painful start as a metal polisher at the Thor factory in Chicago, followed by other employment in the airlines and real estate, George also enjoyed a highly successful career as U.S. sales director based in San Francisco for the wine importing firm Bercut-Vandervoort. For his untiring promotion of the French "art of living" in America—with extensive business travel throughout the nation, including more than eighty round-trips to Hawaii—he was awarded the "*Médaille du Mérite Agricole*" by the French government. Following retirement, he became a self-employed international trade facilitator.

At least once a year during their career, the two brothers traveled from California to the Regina Hotel in Passy to conduct business and reconnect with their roots, each spot of their native Parisian district bringing back vivid memories, especially for George. "The maid's room up there under the roof of that building is where he was conceived," his father once told me from a bench in the Ranelagh garden.

The Spanek sons succeeded where their parents had failed. It is tragic that Mrs. Spanek did not live to see the success of her invention, and that Mr. Spanek, who died in 1987 at 84, did not witness the fall of communism, against which he had fought so long. On the other hand he would have deplored the split between the Czech and Slovak Republics in 1993.

Among this list of personal destinies, America remains for me a land of marred success. From a promising outlook at the lycée and potential future with the Kapferer-Wildenstein family, I became a metal polisher, like George a decade earlier. It was a dreadful occupation requiring a high school diploma, and therefore, ironically, closed to my more fortunate American friends, who were spared that experience by having dropped out of school at sixteen.

If, after many detours, I finally overcame this downfall to become a tenured faculty member at a university—from my perspective an enviable outcome—I must recognize that I owe my American upward mobility solely to the Vietnam war. The fact that my salvation derived from such a cataclysm precludes any gloating or self-satisfaction on my part.

Chapter 13

School Daze

"Schooling: Free and mandatory _____." (Fill in the blank)

— *Gébé*

I started school in Chicago in April 1956, a few days before my four-teenth birthday, and was placed in eighth grade, along normal age lines, without any special arrangements or concessions for my scant abilities in the English language. Sink or swim. At least I would no longer be the young-est in the class. I was naive or unconscious enough to start my new life in America with unbounded confidence and eagerness, despite some initial dis-appointments with lack of street life compared to Paris, except for the down-town Loop during business hours.

A month earlier, Maman and I had crossed the Atlantic aboard the "Lib-erté." The journey had been an unmitigated ordeal. We had endured a long and violent winter storm, one of the worst ever according to the crew, even for March, when gale-force icy winds commonly wreak havoc upon the Northern seas. A bad omen. At the end of our harrowing seven-day voyage, a breathtaking, eerie, silent apparition: New York City, its streets buried in snow, its skyscrapers shrouded like ghosts against the grey morning sky.

In the confusion of arrival, I wound up on the wrong side of the ship to get a view of the Statue of Liberty welcoming us to the New World. I had often admired the scale model of the famous lady in Paris, on the island in the middle of the Seine below the Perrets' penthouse, and looked forward to seeing the real thing. But by the time we disembarked in Manhattan, I no longer cared about missed opportunities. My stomach could finally settle, and my sea legs readjust to stable ground.

We stayed for two weeks in Queens at the home of my paternal aunt Katherine and her husband Pavel, who had emigrated from our family's Slovakian native village to America instead of France at the same time as my parents. It was good to hear them speak Slovak, as if we were back in the warm cocoon of Bzince.

Uncle Pavel, a house painter, liked to relax every day with a cigarette and a shot of whisky after he returned home from work and plopped down in his reclining chair to watch the evening news on the television set. He even turned off the ringer on the phone so he would not be interrupted during the broadcast. He invited me to put my feet up too, on my aunt's ottoman, and to join him in this daily ritual, thus signaling that in his eyes I had become a man who no longer needed to hide from his mother the fact that he smoked. When a particularly disturbing segment appeared on the newscast he reached down for the bottle and poured us a second shot of Jim Beam, and no more. My moderate consumption of whisky seemed to pose no problem for Maman and Aunt Katherine, but they grumbled from the kitchen that he should not be fostering in me the foul-smelling habit of smoking. To cut short their nagging, he threatened he would also teach me to drive, even though I was too young to get a permit.

I admired Uncle Pavel's boldness and serenity. He parked his Chevrolet each evening in the attached garage, with a sure eye and only a few inches of clearance on each side, while complaining that cars were getting wider with each new model, and what would he do three years hence when he traded-in his '56 for another Chevy? Although he and Aunt Katherine had a cozy home, the sleepy bungalows of Queens didn't quite correspond to my electric image of America, embodied in my imagination by Manhattan, where we went sightseeing only once during our stay, after the snow had melted.

Following our two weeks in New York, Maman and I pushed on by rail to Chicago. I took advantage of the long train ride to sample openly, under her resigned glare, different brands of American cigarettes, savoring their freshness compared to the water-stained contraband Pall Malls and Lucky Strikes we used to smoke in the lycée.

During the journey, somewhere in Ohio, I got thirsty from the delicious salami sandwiches my aunt had packed for us, so I walked over to the dining car and ordered a beer. However, it became clear from the bartender's animated response that my schoolbook English must have been incomprehensible to him, so I retreated back to our wagon, puzzled, thirst unquenched.

As the train edged into Chicago's Union Station, I gaped at the monumental height and unity of the Michigan Avenue lakefront, comparable to the Manhattan skyline. We had at last reached our final destination. Our new lives could begin.

The Spaneks greeted us on arrival and took us to their home in Cicero, fifty-seven blocks West of downtown, where they generously offered to put us up as long as needed. For Maman this would turn out to be three months, and for me two years. But the ride there on the "El" proved anticlimactic. After the initial excitement of the spectacular lakefront, the magnitude of the slums and the dispiriting sameness of much of the rest of the city left me perplexed. And why did so many people live in basement apartments, even in the better parts of town? The warnings of the Czech employee from the Paris American Express office rang through my mind.

The first day at school, I wanted above all to make a good impression on my classmates, particularly girls, who had been missing from my all-male lycée. Would I know how to act in front of them? In addition to the new language and culture, many adjustments awaited me. But amazingly when I look back, I experienced feelings of curiosity and anticipation, rather than anxiety or apprehension. After the radical transition from my peasant village to boarding school when I was ten, I felt I could take anything else in stride.

I made careful preparations for that first day of American schooling, but had no idea what to expect. I tried several clothing combinations, hesitated for a striped suit with tie ("dressed to kill, Kovaco," I could hear my friends murmur admiringly back in Paris), but at the last moment opted instead for a white shirt with open collar and a silk scarf, cotton slacks, and brown suede shoes. Sartorial carbon copy of Alec Wildenstein, whose clothes I was wearing, I looked like a billionaire's son just off the family yacht. I was tempted also by a more "hoodlumish" look, with a leather jacket, but I presently couldn't afford one. It would have to wait 'til later.

In a school supplies store that seemed bare compared to my favorite haunt in Paris—the Gibert Jeune emporium in the Latin Quarter—I made a pleasant discovery: the American notebooks with their unobtrusive horizontal lines, which I preferred to their French counterparts, divided up in little squares. Better yet, I would have liked no lines at all, total freedom, but such notebooks apparently didn't exist.

I would now also be able to "officially" use the beautiful Parker fountain pen that Madame Perret had offered me just before we left Paris as a good-luck charm, with her last objections: "What a mistake to go like that to adventure and leave everything behind. Your mother is crazy, completely crazy. I've never met anyone so stubborn. I tried to change her mind, but she wouldn't listen."

Ah, Madame Perret, she didn't mince her words. I was touched by her gift, especially after my unforgivable loss of her husband's compass set, which I had so shamelessly exchanged for cigarettes.

When I arrived at Burnham K-8 Elementary School, carrying my faithful leather bag nicely worn by four years of daily use, I headed for the principal's office, where I had been told to report. In the play yard, conversations stopped, kids pointed at me, without hostility, but with a bothersome curiosity. I wanted to be noticed "Look, a new kid, let's get to know him" yet at the same time I was embarrassed by the attention and wished I could slink by incognito.

A slightly mocking gesture of choking around the neck made me understand an immediate problem: "...*the scarf, take off your scarf, you jerk, nobody else is wearing one, look around, they're all casual, no jeans though, who knows, maybe it's forbidden, damn, you made a mistake, they don't dress up for school, good thing you didn't come wearing a suit and tie, you'd have looked totally ridiculous.*

Hop, the scarf in the school bag, now it's better, I won't be noticed. But no, they keep staring at me, do they want my picture or what? I don't think it's my brown suede shoes, it's not my hair either, there's lots of redheads in America, well let's say more than in France.

THE SCHOOLBAG, *yes, that's it, it's my schoolbag they're staring at, I can't believe it, nobody else has one. They're walking around empty handed, completely nonchalant, with no school stuff. The few who have books carry them in their arms or dangling at the end of a strap. It's nuts. What do they do when it rains? What should I do? I can't imagine being without my bag.*"

The principal walked me over to the classroom to which I was assigned. I was greeted warmly by the teacher, kind gray-haired Mrs. Stewart. She introduced me to her students by Americanizing my first name, as often occurred to foreigners, Stefan becoming Steve, Bohumil Bob, and Jaromír Jerome.

"Class, this is Milton, he comes from Europe and he doesn't speak English very well, but like all new immigrants, he is happy to finally be living in the land of the free and he'll soon learn our language, won't you Milton?"

I understood pretty well everything she was saying, including that because of my last name, she was mistaking me for a refugee from communism, a D.P., displaced person, of which there were many in our predominantly Czechoslovak neighborhood. I nodded in agreement and found her use of my first name pleasant. Was it the equivalent of the familiar form of address in French, "*tu*"? At the lycée, teachers used only our last names, and, except for the general overseer Mr. Blau, addressed us with the formal "vous," as if they considered us young adults who some day would become important: "Kovacovic, *allez au tableau* go to the blackboard, and write out your translation of today's assignment in Virgil."

"We want Milton to feel welcomed at Burnham School," Mrs. Stewart said, her words accompanied by a sweeping gesture to indicate that those good wishes were being extended to me by the whole class. "I would like somebody to volunteer to orient him during the next few days."

A wall of hands shot up. I hoped Mrs. Stewart would choose one of the girls, but instead she picked a boy, Steve, who turned out to be very helpful and likable. He showed me around and answered whatever questions I was able to formulate. He patiently explained a number of arcane things, including the complicated rules of baseball, and the dress code, which forbade not only the wearing of jeans, as I suspected, but also the positioning of one's belt buckle on the side instead of in the middle, as a gesture of defiance. Most importantly, he introduced me to the smokers' corner, a gathering place behind some bushes at the far end of the playground.

Predictably, American cigarettes were banal and commonplace there. They didn't have the same cachet as in France, where they contrasted with the cheaper Gitanes, Gauloises, or Caporals made of dark-brown tobacco. As I passed my Camels around to break the ice, approving glances informed me I had chosen a good brand.

Things were moving along nicely, until Steve took me aside at the end of that first day to let me know gently but firmly that I had to get rid of my schoolbag, or else he would no longer be able to show me around or be my friend. I complied.

What also surprised me when I desperately sought to observe the local customs and adapt to them, was the singularity of my fountain pen. I was the only student who had one. And yet the world-famous Parker pens, so prized in my French lycée, and so inaccessible for me until Madame Perret's gift, were manufactured right near Chicago, in Janesville, Wisconsin, where I would gladly have gone on pilgrimage. In American schools, apparently, this fetish of French lycée life was unknown. The same applied to jazz music. Nobody I met had ever heard of Miles Davis.

At the lycée, among the boarders from the colonies, one of the Vietnamese, Pham-Nhu-Hiêp, whose name lent itself to teasing (*"femme nue"* = "naked woman"), was admired for his beautiful handwriting, almost calligraphic. He had three Parkers, like a collection of pipes, one with blue ink in his coat pocket, the other two with red and green ink in a soft-leather pouch. And here at Burnham School, not only did no one have a fountain pen, but I hardly saw any ball points either. My classmates wrote with ...pencils! I couldn't believe it, I hadn't written with one since first grade.

A pencil sharpener was installed on the wall of each classroom, and students waited in line to sharpen their instruments. What? Was all the work done in class eraseable, provisional, did the students write only drafts?

Worse, I discovered during the following days that no writing took place at all, at least no writing of complete sentences. My carefully chosen notebooks turned out to be useless. Whereas I had anticipated the pleasure of pushing my Parker around on a page, nothing. We were handed mimeographed sheets printed in smudged blue ink, on which we were supposed to circle True or False, or choose alternatives A, B, C, or D on multiple-choice questions. Mrs. Stewart then graded our papers by placing over them a cardboard template with holes in it. I couldn't understand the meaning or the objectives of this system, which seemed at once simplistic and complicated, mysterious and restrictive. I was used to open-ended commentaries on particular questions. They required a minimum of form and content and also offered, as a last resort, the possibility of getting around knowledge gaps with a little bit of clever b.s.

The more I analyzed the multiple-choice questions, the more I was dumbfounded: *"Is a question that can be answered 'true' or 'false' worthy of being asked? And what are they trying to ascertain through a factual question whose answer seems obvious? Evidently, there must be a ruse somewhere. And how does one express one's own ideas?"*

Thus, for instance, for a question on the history test "In what year did Christopher Columbus discover America? A. 1776 B. 1492 C.1066 D. 1592," the answer seemed so obvious that I suspected a subtle trap either in the framing of the question, or in the various answers offered. The ambiguity between B and D seemed gratuitous, one of those two alternatives being manifestly the correct one. Why not simply ask the question, without suggesting possible answers (in real life, isn't that the way questions are posed?). And what about the debate concerning the legitimacy of the word "discovery"?

I figured out the system fairly soon and adapted to it. There were no traps, tricks, or ambiguities. Don't think or agonize, just react quickly and move on to the next question.

A third kind of test, which required an even more tortuous mental process, entailed filling blanks in sentences with missing words, or missing numbers in arithmetic operations (in France, I had already been studying geometry and trigonometry). Always these mechanical gestures: jot down a check mark, circle "True" or "False," choose from several alternatives, fill-in a blank, without any opportunity to go through a complete process of reasoning.

Spelling was also tested through single words, plucked out of nowhere, instead of dictations involving longer texts. That too seemed to make no sense.

Though I was fairly confident about my comprehension of English, I felt frustrated about my awkwardness in speaking. An unmistakable sign underscored my shortcomings: I was often asked to repeat what I said.

"Say What?" was a frequent reaction from my interlocutors, after I said things that probably sounded like "I liked it also ze Lucky Streek when I been in Paree." And whenever I didn't fully understand something, I pretended I did. The differences in vocabulary and pronunciation between the British English I had learned at the lycée, and the American English at Burnham School were only a small factor in my problems. I was astonished by the discrepancy between my expectations (this will be easy) and reality (language is resisting me). Still, in my blissful state of unconsciousness or denial, I remained somewhat impervious to those difficulties and didn't unduly suffer from them.

Paradoxically, Burnham School had a library, refuge not only unimaginable, but unimagined in my "brilliant" lycée, where such a library would have been valued, especially by the boarders cooped up in the evening in a bare and bleak study hall. The library was an example of the prodigious post-war wealth of America, envied by Europeans.

But this bounty of books, magazines, and encyclopedias was reaching me at the wrong time. I was beginning to lose interest in school. Finally, to complete my lobotomy, at the end of the school year, Mrs. Stewart divested me of my personality: "Milton, in America, you can't sign your name in the fanciful way you do, with a big "K" and the rest illegible. You must simply *write* your first and last name, normally and legibly, like everyone else. It's simply a matter of courtesy."

What I didn't know was that there existed, especially in the Northern suburbs of Chicago, for instance Winnetka, schools that were vastly superior to my Parisian lycée, if only for having a library and a rich array of extracurricular activities. However these schools were beyond my reach. A couple of years later, I got a whiff of this fabulous "other world" in American education, when I played in a varsity soccer game against New Trier, a public prep school that furthermore humiliated us in sports too.

Maman was unaware of my scholastic downfall; she deplored only my sartorial decline. In Paris, she had been proud of her son's distinguished demeanor and appearance. I rarely left the Kapferer mansion without wearing a tie. Now, open collar, casual attire, "You look like a vagabond" she lamented.

Too bad, too bad for her, too bad for me, I now had more urgent problems to solve. Anyway, with emigration, my supply of expensive clothes had vanished.

Those two months of eighth grade went by quickly. Following summer vacation, I enrolled at Morton, the first of three high schools I wound up attending. My big shock in ninth grade was the swimming class in boys' P.E. (another incredible American luxury), with everyone lined up and jumping in and out of the pool *stark naked*, like in a nudist colony. In addition to a loss of privacy I hadn't experienced before, the sudden realization of another glaring, puzzling difference: Were my classmates all Jewish?

Chapter 14

Narrow Escape

"The four boys parted ways. Without realizing it, according to fate
and circumstance, each of them would go on to fulfill his destiny,
scandalize his kin, and gravitate toward glory or dishonor."

— *Baudelaire, "Vocations"*

After we arrived in Chicago, Maman didn't know much about my
whereabouts or my doings:

"Where you go?"
"Out."
"Where?"
"Nowhere."
"Who you go with?
"Nobody."
"And what you do?"
"Nothing."

My anwers were true. I rarely had any specific destination or activity in mind,
beyond just going out, to the street corner where you could always find some
people hanging out, or to the ice cream parlor with its pinball machine, to see
what—if anything—was happening. Most of the time, nothing...

Prone to pass judgment and blame others, Maman feared that I might be
led astray by "bad associations." She was ill at ease in her maternal role except
for domestic tasks, which she accomplished with great care and devotion.
She did however know that the teenage years can be the most perilous in the
relationship between children and their parents, as she had experienced in
Paris with Olga. She attributed my sister's disastrous quest for independence

to the negative influence of her friends, her "bad associations" (which in fact wasn't the case at all—Olga merely aspired to have a room of her own some-where in Paris, and emulate a girlfriend of hers by becoming a ticket puncher in the subway).

For Maman, the very word "friends" had acquired an alarming connota-tion. Friends and "cinama," a form of entertainment she deemed corrupting, were in her eyes the minefields of adolescence, even though she knew noth-ing about the company Olga or I kept, nor for that matter about movies—to the best of my knowledge, she had never been to one.

Since I didn't have a true "home" where I might invite friends—who wouldn't have come anyway, allergic as they were to confinement and paren-tal supervision—and since I didn't want to unduly impose on the hospitality of the Spaneks where I boarded, I spent a lot of time just hanging out, espe-cially after school in the afternoon.

I usually saw Maman on Sundays, when she visited from her live-in job in Elmhurst and grilled me about my doings. She was not totally wrong in her apprehensions about the people I associated with, and I was far from ir-reproachable myself. If given the opportunity, I might well have engaged in activities that were bandied about on the streets, for instance shoplifting, car theft, or underage drinking. Smoking didn't count, it was normal.

Fortunately, my after-school idleness soon ended. I responded to a "Help wanted—Inquire within" sign displayed in the window of the 22nd Street Li-noleum and Dinette Store, which I walked by regularly. I was hired to work two hours after school each afternoon and all day Saturdays.

Thank you, thank you Harry and Art Rosenberg, owners of the store, for rescuing me from the streets of Cicero. The traditional employment oppor-tunity for teenagers—pinball spotter in a bowling alley—was disappearing, replaced by automation, and there wasn't much else available.

Set in their ways and nearing retirement, the Rosenberg brothers squabbled constantly for the most trivial reasons, sometimes even in front of custom-ers. I tried to stay apart from their bickering, but they often asked me, their fifteen-year-old helper, to take sides in their disputes.

Without realizing it, Harry and Art rivaled the best comedy duos, Laurel and Hardy, or Abbot and Costello. Furthermore, they both resembled Curly of the Three Stooges, bald pate on top, tousled hair sticking out on the sides. Arguing, arguing, always arguing. Their "efficiency" had measurably increased of late, though, after they finally decided to hook their reading half-glasses on a string around their neck. Prior to that, they spent a good part of their days rummaging around the store for their "damn glasses," and enlisting each other's and my help for the searches. Like clowns, they looked funny yet had a sad air about them; the rare times they forced a smile, it came out as a grimace. In their bickering, Harry's arguments bordered on absurdity, and Art's on senility, so I tried to balance my verdicts by siding sometimes with one, sometimes the other.

They paid me the going wage for teen-agers, on the up and up, by check, not cash like some employers. Harry was in charge of the paperwork: "One day you'll need social security, Kid, you can thank FDR for that program, he was a great man, and believe me that day will come faster than you think, look at me and Art, we're there already and it seems like only yesterday we were your age."

The paychecks were the only indication my employers actually knew my name. Otherwise, they addressed me as "Kid," or "Hey Kid" and referred to me in their conversations as "the kid." During my entire time in their employ, they also not once referred to my accent or my foreignness. I liked that.

Both married but without children, Harry and Art were tormented by the question of their succession. Who would inherit the store they had built up through the years? They often mused aloud about how wonderful it would be if their nephew Abe could take over the business. They spoiled him out-rageously, talked about him all the time, Abe this, Abe that, yet not once did he visit his uncles in the store during the year I worked there, although it was clear that the Rosenberg clan, living for the most part in the Chicago area, gathered regularly for holidays and family celebrations.

Abe was studying at the university. Deep down, Harry and Art feared that their nephew would not be interested in their offer. So they postponed asking him the fateful question. Harry, disappointed yet at the same time admiring of Abe, lamented: "La di da, once young people think they can become a doctor or a lawyer, or God forbid a professor, they look down their noses at business."

"Harry, why do you denigrate professors?" Art asked his brother.

" 'Cause they can't be that smart. All them studies, for so little money."

In 1957 – 58, the year I worked for the Rosenbergs, linoleum sales continued to move at a slow, regular pace, but the formica kitchen tables and matching tubular chairs with padded seats and backs covered in smooth plastic were starting to fall out of fashion. Like the two brothers, who were stiff at the joints and slightly hunched, the dinette section was beginning to show its age.

Leaning back against the remnants of linoleum rolls lined upright along the wall, or pensively seated at one of the dinette sets in the middle of the store, Harry and Art spent their days racking their brains about how to increase sales. All the while, their eyes were riveted on the sidewalk out front where people walked by without even glancing at our sun-drenched display window encumbered with a jumble of tables and chairs and linoleum samples that I dusted off each week without succeeding to revive their fading colors.

The Rosenberg brothers cogitated endlessly, but succumbed to inertia and never moved to action, including getting around to asking Abe whether or not he would like to take over the store.

"How the heck could we draw more customers? What new merchandise should we consider? Should we modernize? Would it be worth going through a lot of trouble so close to retirement? And what about Abe?"

In their mullings and their speculations, the brothers sometimes talked like visionaries, other times like hopelessly blind people. Harry maintained that because of changes in society, with extended families giving way to the nuclear kind, dining room tables had become useless, except for piling up incoming mail and newspapers. However he believed that dinette sets in the kitchen had a future, because the kitchen was where neighborhood housewives sat down for midmorning coffee klatches.

Art countered that women were entering the workforce in increasing numbers, either because they were bored at home or because their households needed more money, and that soon these coffee klatches would be a thing of the past. "And besides," he added, "TV trays and TV dinners are also replacing sitting at a dinette table at supper time." He even predicted that the kitchen of the future would not be equipped with a table and chairs, but with a counter and bar stools, because everybody would eat on the run and always be in a hurry, like the people walking past our display window.

"There you go again with your negativity," Harry the optimist responded, "Don't tell me families aren't always gonna want to sit down and have a leisurely meal at the kitchen table, which everybody knows is the favorite place in the house."

"Nothing is permanent except change," Art opined philosophically, whereas the store in fact seemed to symbolize a desperate attempt to freeze things in a permanent state and stop the unrelenting march of time.

As soon as a customer entered the premises, the brothers interrupted their debates and scurried to the front door. The challenge, for the effective salesmen they fancied themselves to be, was to not allow the client to leave without making a purchase. It would have been a blemish on Harry's dignity especially. He wanted to measure himself one on one with the person, and he therefore signaled with discreet but firm gestures for his clingy partner to scram whenever such opportunities arose, lest the encounter be sabotaged by one of Art's nonsensical comments.

One day, Art seemed particularly glum, as often occurred to him, for no apparent reason. Harry reproached him for these fits of moroseness, which he feared might discourage customers. This time, Harry could not refrain from reprimanding his brother more sternly than usual:

"If I was a customer, Art, and if I saw the face you're making, I wouldn't buy anything in here, I guarantee you that."

"My face? And what about yours, Harry? Have you had a good look at yourself in the mirror lately? How do you know it's not you who's scaring them away?"

Art's remark started another squabble. I enjoyed their feuds, because during those flare-ups I could twiddle my thumbs, both brothers forgetting I was there to do some work.

This time, following Art's suggestion, Harry rushed into the back room to check his face on the yellowed wall mirror topped by a dog-eared calendar from the 1940's featuring a pin-up girl in a tight-fitting sweater. He returned immediately with a triumphant air:

"Well, Art, I looked at myself, I still have the same face, the face of one of the best retailers in Chicagoland, don't forget that, don't forget it I say, because if it wasn't for my talent as a salesman, we would have gone belly up a long time ago. May our poor father rest in peace."

"Yes," replied Art, " but you'd sell more if you got rid of..."

Art sometimes got confused and uttered preposterous accusations. His paranoia was unpredictable. I tensed up at such times, expecting I too might be blamed for something or other. But it was Harry who felt directly targeted. He interrupted his brother with a gibe:

"Of what? If I got rid of what? Or of whom? Well, go ahead, big shot, I'm listening. Go ahead, I dare you...Because, I'm telling you, I have some ideas about that too."

The exchange of arrows was becoming unbearable. Who was going to perish first?

"If you got rid of...of...your bow tie!" blurted Art.

"Well, that's a good one!" exclaimed Harry. "My bow tie! I've been wearing bow ties for years, and it never seemed to bother you before. Why now, suddenly? Explain!"

Although they were both cantankerous, neither brother was capable of meanness.

"It has to do with the fact that customers don't like it because it looks old-fashioned, like the dinette sets," said Art, who must have been mulling over this vengeful analogy for a long time. His grumbles were sometimes based on flashes of lucidity.

"Well, Art, I hate to tell you, but you're wrong. I sell better with a bow tie, because it makes me look distinguished," Harry replied. Then, challenging his brother, but pointing at me: "Tell you what, let's ask the kid what he thinks, he's young, he'll give us a modern point of view on the question."

"Yes, Kid, what do you think about that?" stammered Art, begging for my complicity, and looking like a beaten dog.

I decided to play my all, and lost even my discomfort with the American easy use of first names for older people, including bosses.

"Art, you and Harry are both right and both wrong." (I really thought that, as in most of their disputes). "Are Sears stores modern?" (I used for my demonstration a hallowed name in the retail business—Sears had the reputation of providing the most desirable but hard-to-get jobs in America, with good wages, a profit-sharing plan, transfer opportunities, and lifetime job security).

Harry answered for his brother: "Yes, of course they're modern, and because of that they wipe us out. We can't compete. Large chain stores like Sears are going to swallow us up, us small businessmen."

Then he felt compelled to explain why he thought this would occur: "Sears caters to the entire range of customers. They stock every item in three categories, good, better, and best. We can't compete with that."

Art saw an opening there for a contrary statement: "That shtrategy (he shlurred his s's) doesn't make sense to me. How could you be happy buying something that you know isn't the best?"

"You can," Harry retorted, "and I'll prove it to you. If you want a car, you can buy a Chevy, an Olds, or a Caddy, good, better, or best. Well, mister, let me tell you, I'm perfectly happy with my Olds, I don't need a Caddy, and Chevies are pretty good too. So there."

At this point I jumped back in with my demonstration: "OK, Art, Sears is very proud of its after-sale service, right? And how are its repairmen dressed?"

A frown, and a twitch in the furrow separating his wrinkled brow from his smooth and shiny pate, signaled that Art had smelled a trap... and thrown himself into it. I was embarrassed to put him on the spot like this, but too happy with my mediator's scheme to let it go.

"They wear a bow tie," Art said in a tired voice. And after a long silence, he reared up with a desperate last burst "It's part of their uniform!"

Art's remark plunged us into an impasse. But after another pause, he himself proposed a solution that would reconcile all points of view:

"Tell you what, you all, starting tomorrow I'll wear a bow tie too. That way, me and Harry will look a little bit like we're wearing uniforms. It'll make us look more businesslike, it should please the customers."

Harry sighed with relief, and to celebrate the happy end of this ump-teenth family quarrel, he closed the store, left a note "Back Soon—Please Wait" on the door, and invited his brother and me to Ann K's ice cream par-lor across the street for one of her scrumptious banana splits.

"But what about the customers?" Art protested, stopping abruptly in the middle of the street, ready to head back, his stomach knotting up.

Harry had the last word: "Enough of that, Art, enough. To hell with the customers. Do like me, relax, forget about them, at least for a few minutes."

I found it astonishing that the Rosenberg brothers managed to remain sol-vent after so many years of ineptitude. The store was a mess. Absent-minded and easily distracted, Art often made mistakes in labeling. He would also frequently lose, misplace, or mix up invoices and delivery slips. In the delivery van in which I accompanied him, getting to the correct addresses made us lose untold amounts of time. He was concerned for my well-being when we had to maneuver rolls of linoleum or dinette sets up steep staircases, "Care-ful so you don't hurt yourself, kid, don't worry if you scratch the walls or the merchandise," whereas it was he who huffed and puffed throughout these endeavors, too demanding for someone of his age and condition. He further-more tended to drool when out of breath.

Sometimes, his kindness was counterproductive: when cutting linoleum that his brother had sold, he would, if in a good mood, add a few inches to the piece, as a well-intentioned "extra gift"; the customer would then call to complain about the wrong measurements. Did Art suffer chronic pain from some secret ailment, and did he become immoderately indulgent during periods of relief, as if to celebrate the moment?

One couldn't help but wonder by what miracle the store survived. Yet Harry looked prosperous enough. In addition to his extensive set of bow ties and dapper though old-fashioned clothes, he owned a beautiful two-tone 1954 Oldsmobile hardtop. He knew I lusted after the car ever since—thrilled by the ride back with him on the expressway after some errands downtown—I offered to wax his beautiful machine on my own time. I wanted to rub the aquamarine and beige finish so smooth and shiny that the polishing mitt would slide down the entire length of the hood like a feather. "OK with me, kid, if it floats your boat," Harry said, "but I want you to do it on company time. I'll send Art out to get you some Turtle Wax."

After that, to signal my lunch break each Saturday, Harry would lob me his car keys from across the store, in a disinterested way, like a piece of challah bread. "Here kid, catch'em, but don't turn on the ignition. You gotta be sixteen to drive."

He allowed me to sit in the car and listen to the radio while I ate my sandwich behind the wheel. The chrome hood ornament and the "Rocket 88" inscription promised a repeat of the strong sensations I experienced in the earlier ride downtown. There were only two minor things that bothered me about his dream machine: The seats were wrapped in clear plastic covers embossed with small bumps and grooves, to minimize their stickiness in hot weather and at the same time protect the original naugahyde upholstery. And I wished the exhaust system had been modified with glasspack mufflers producing a throaty, rumbling sound, instead of the silky "whoosh" I heard when Harry hit the passing gear on the expressway to show me what his "Oldsmobubble," as he called it, could do. Apparently, he earned a decent enough living, even after splitting the profits with his brother.

When I wasn't sweeping the store, cleaning the front window, or in the van delivering merchandise with Art, I spent my time cutting up cardboard boxes and throwing them in the incinerator in the building's basement. This dingy place reportedly served at night as a hideout for lovers seeking privacy, which was difficult to find in the neighborhood. All one had to do was go down the steps with a flashlight, and latch the door from inside. Not very romantic, but I wouldn't have minded to try something like that myself, if I had a girlfriend. Some of my buddies said that Rosemary Montanaro, an Italian girl with jet-black hair and burning eyes, had a crush on me, but I didn't quite know how to approach her.

My experience at the 22nd Street Linoleum and Dinette store taught me an important lesson, better than the career orientation tests we took at school: I didn't understand the wheeling and dealing of commerce. I wasn't suited for the stress it entailed, often without results or at the mercy of imponderables beyond one's control, like duck hunting from a blind. But as a bystander, whether at the Dinette store or earlier at the Paris food markets, I also saw shops as a sort of theater, and as such one the most enjoyable of all public places.

While I had heard that in earning a living, business was the only way to make real money, the Rosenbergs helped me discover early on that by temperament and personality I was more suited for the wage-earner life, with a modest but regular paycheck at the end of each week. No great ambition, content to remain a subordinate. *Logé nourri*, room-and-board, my core mentality.

My ideal would have probably been to aim for a profession like Harry and Art's nephew Abe, but this goal, requiring long studies and credentials, was out of reach for me in America. I had forfeited any such aspirations by leaving France.

At the linoleum and dinette store, I navigated as best I could between the often contradictory orders of my two bosses, all the while enjoying my stay in the lunatic asylum, in a climate of genuine, unspoken affection absent from most workplaces, as I have since discovered. And therein lies the principal value of my experience with the Rosenberg brothers. It helped me be patient and tolerant, and appreciate simply good, honest people, with all their idiosyncracies, which often create their charm and enrich the world around them. Shopping or working at the quirky, archaic 22nd Street store was certainly more fun and more interesting than the same activities in the modern, efficient, but depersonalized, nondescript atmosphere of Sears, a retail establishment that furthermore has radically declined since its former glory days. And each year, I look fondly at my new social security earnings report. The first entry in that chronological listing, 1957, never fails to transport me back to the Rosenberg brothers.

I hated to leave their employ, but had to do so when my mother remarried and we moved further west in the suburbs to Downers Grove, to a modest house facing the boonies, where, unfortunately, I experienced somewhat of a relapse of my pre-Rosenberg attitude and behavior.

Chapter 15

Hobo Junction

*M*idnight, Hobo Junction—a trampled patch of land nestled against the embankment of the Chicago-Pacific Coast rail line, at the edge of a corn field. The silvery tracks gleam in the moonlight all the way to the western horizon.

Hobo Junction, a gathering place at the end of a path hacked through tall grasses by the repeated passage of cars. Remnant of the vast ancestral prairie of the Illinois tribe, now encroached upon by agriculture and subdivisions on the outskirts of Chicago, and dubbed "Hobo Junction" since the Depression of the 1930s.

During those years, the freight trains slowed to a crawl as they approached a switch, and hoboes took this opportunity to jump on or off the wagons. The tracks served as the highway between Mid-America and the West Coast for a multitude of jobless men drifting around the country. Hobo Junction was a well-known meeting place. At night, a fire glowed there permanently. Gathered around the embers, the vagabonds cooked their food and traded stories of their travels.

Trains no longer slow down at Hobo Junction, rail traffic has decreased, the switch has been removed. And aimless young people have replaced the unemployed nomads of the 1930s. Instead of a fire pit, flashing headlights now beckon "Come on over, we're here." Wandering has become motorized. In the America of 1960, nearly everyone has a car—clunker, hot rod, or just plain wheels.

The group hanging out at Hobo Junction is made up of dropouts who have quit school at sixteen and now more or less laze around, a lost generation of sorts. In addition to being a gathering spot, the place can also serve as a refuge of last resort.

For Phil, for instance, thrown out of the house by his parents, and residing at Hobo Junction for the past two months in a long-abandoned Cadillac resting on its axles, wheels and tires gone, much of the rest cannibalized. He lives off mooching, and every week or two, someone volunteers to drive him to Lake Michigan or the Lemont quarries so he can soap himself up from head to toe. We've nicknamed him "The Park Warden," but his downfall isn't that funny.

It's the end of June, not even full summer yet, and already a humid heat sticks to the skin. If we don't soon get a thunderstorm, it'll be another night of going home to sleep naked, boozed up, in sheets drenched with sweat, after the usual spinning of the room when the head hits the pillow, three, four turns and...lights out.

The mosquitoes have spotted us. Within a few days the spray trucks will have taken care of this plague. Meanwhile, the pesky beasts harass all living things.

Quarts of Bullfrog beer are being passed around, the last ones of the evening. When the bottles are empty, we wait for a freight train to go by, so we can throw them against the thumping wheels or the rusted sides of the wagons. In the group, there are a few baseball players who already show the beginnings of beer bellies. Cut off from school sports, they'll resume their favorite pastime when, at twenty-one, they can participate in teams sponsored by the local taverns. Meanwhile, to stay in shape, they throw bottles against the trains, and chew the traditional cud, with cheeks puffed and spit ready. Bizarre custom, this tobacco chewing linked to baseball. In France, I associated it only with rural old people like Pépère.

Out of awe and respect, we don't mess with the California Zephyr, the aluminum passenger train piercing the night at full speed like an illuminated arrow. When it disappears on the flat horizon, its rear light leaves us pensive. One day we too will cross the continent all the way to the West Coast. We'll head out to one of the two destinations that make us dream: Los Angeles, for most people, on Highway 66; San Francisco for others, via Highway 40. It should soon be a breeze to drive to those places, when the Interstate Highway System is completed. As of now, the Chicago-L.A. speed record is held by Larry Waldham in his souped-up '58 Chevy. He is able to pass whole clumps of cars and trucks in one swoop when he downshifts into third gear. The toughest part of the journey is the Ozarks, he says, because of all the hills and curves.

Tonight about half a dozen cars are still at Hobo Junction, parked in a circle, conclave of chrome and paint shining under the moon. A little further from the huddle, Phil's "house" looks as if it has exploded from within, trunk and doors wide open to let some air pass through. Only the hood is closed.

People are leaning back against the cars, or sitting on the fenders, legs dangling, heels tapping the tires. Cigarettes glow in the dark. Fragments of conversation can be heard, barely above whispers. Some couples are making out in cars, nothing requiring privacy. All the radios are tuned softly to the same top 40s station.

What a difference from the city! Here, we can be free, we don't bother anybody, and nobody bothers us. The police close their eyes on the comings and goings in this zone, a safety valve removed from the rest of society.

If nothing happens within the next hour, everyone will go home, and it'll be another night killed. "I'm smashed, I can't walk, but I can drive, who wants to ride with me?" says one of the stragglers, tugged between the shame of admitting he's drunk, and the fun of scaring his passengers. "And who can give me a buck for gas, I'm broke." Gas, beer, cigs, we all chip in for the basic necessities.

Always this recurrent need tormenting us: To show up at Hobo Junction, to see what's going on, to not miss anything. Most of the time, nothing happens. We drink, we smoke, we talk, we wait. Wait for what? Wait for something to happen.

Wait for some headlights to flash, a hundred yards away, at the entrance to the path, so we can respond like ships in the night, "We're here, we're here, come on over," and wonder who it'll be this time. Chicks maybe? Renewed hope. Inexhaustible, devouring expectation.

The imperative: to wind up with a girl by evening's end. But not at the beginning, so as not to miss out on anything...

Couples who go steady tend to withdraw from circulation. They become openly domesticated, couch potatoes, young old people. They stay home with their folks to watch TV, or play cards with the family, or in some cases even shack up in the parents' house without being married. In moments of candor, they admit they're bored. Their quiet existence frightens me, but I sometimes envy them.

Still, I don't feel ready to close myself up in that kind of life. Above all, I can't imagine the pain of an eventual breakup. Better nothing than everything, at least for the time being. That's why I like the free-spirited girls, like Jackie. She is mine without belonging to me, and vice versa. I've never thought of "dating" a girl, neither Jackie nor any other. Lack of manners? Boorish behavior? Fear of rejection? The only "relationship" I know is to meet more or less spontaneously at Hobo Junction, and then go park on the edge of some corn field. Consequently, I end up with a certain kind of girl. Or, more often, none.

I know my attitude isn't considered "normal" outside the world of Hobo Junction, but this world is all I have. I don't know any other. We're an anti-social bunch, and although I still aim to finish high school, I have nothing to do with that scene or its extracurricular activities, don't go to dances or organized celebrations, don't ring the doorbell at girls' houses—we just blow the horn from the street, without meeting the parents, who don't seem to care anyway.

The guys who end up at Hobo Junction can be identified early. Starting at thirteen or so, they hitchhike to school. A few yards from the bus stop, they stick out their thumb to catch a ride from passing cars. That's their way of showing contempt for the system and the goody-two-shoes waiting for the regular mode of transportation.

Although we don't deal with girls' parents, we occasionally do pass through friends' houses. My buddy Jim's father, overhearing one day his son and me talk about Hobo Junction, scolded us without hiding his irritation: "I can't stand seeing you boys waste your time like that, and believe me, time is the most precious thing in the world!"

He was about fifty years old. The lazyness, the inertia, the sleeping-in, the memory lapses of his son scandalized him—entire sections of his life drowned in beer! "You hang out, you hang out 'til late, you only think about sex, booze, and cars; you chase easy girls, it don't lead nowhere. If I was you boys, I'd go to church, that's where you meet nice girls, that's where I met your mom, Jimmy."

We appreciated the concern he expressed that day, but didn't agree with his judgment dripping with Baptist religiosity. He had only two goals for us: get a job and get married. That was his message. "Otherwise great perils await you." He sounded like a preacher when he said that, with his Southern accent. And he repeated a proverb he had heard somewhere: "Work'll protect you from three evils: boredom, vice, and need."

I didn't dare disagree, but Jim allowed himself some sarcasm: "Vice maybe, Daddy, but for the rest you're wrong. Show me a job that pays enough and ain't borin'."

Jim's father feared the example set by his brother Nate. Tall, bony like a jackal, and with a protruding Adam's apple, Uncle Nate had become a sort of outlaw with no stable domicile and no visible income. Yet he always seemed to have plenty of cash, which he carried in a silver money clip decorated with a turquoise stone. This prodigal uncle knocked about the Southern states from Arizona to Florida. He came up from time to time to Chicago—dapper in suit, tie, hat, and polished shoes—at the wheel of his slinky black and white DeSoto two-door hardtop with air conditioning.

An aura of mystery and awe surrounded Nate, derived in part from the story of his visit to Riverview amusement park, where he had once taken Jim and a couple of his buddies on an outing. There, the younguns (as he called his nephew and his friends) were transfixed with panic, then admiration, when they saw Nate pull out a small but nasty-looking Beretta to chase off a big brute who had ridiculed him when he stuck his long nose into a ball of cotton candy. According to the account, Uncle Nate, who claimed he hated violence, didn't even raise his voice: "If you don't get out of my sight, fat ass, I'm gonna plug you between the eyes. One, two..." The hulk disappeared before the count of three.

Uncle Nate also had quite a reputation as a poker player. That's probably where he made his money.

With a wife at home, Jim's father thought, Nate would have found a steady job, raised a family, attended church, in short settled down. "If you guys meet an interesting girl, serious, pretty, well brought up, court her and ask for her hand before anybody else does; pray to God that she accepts, then marry her, read the Bible together, and love will follow even if it ain't already completely there. The young people of today have it all backwards. They marry because they have a crush on someone and a year later there's nothing left, their relationship had no substance, they divorce. Look at the stastistics, it's a disaster. I fear for you guys."

Jim's father was perhaps right, especially about us wasting time. I was aware of that too, but I had been for now more than a year trying to juggle three things simultaneously: finish high school, continue my part-time job as a janitor in a department store, hang out at Hobo Junction. I therefore felt more overworked than lackadaisical—unlike my dropout friends who got up late, lounged all day, and carried on at night.

Guys, at least those who didn't get kicked out by their parents, were expected to stay home, get a job, pay room and board, and not move out until they got married. Unless they left for the Army or the West Coast.

Jim's father's insistent tone also came from another reality: girls were in a hurry to get married. Most were eager to leave their parents' house, others felt pressured to do so. All were looking for stability more than adventure. Except Jackie, who on that account also distinguished herself.

Jackie surpassed me in her contempt of domesticity. She had spunk. She lived at home, but even though she had quit school at sixteen, she had already distanced herself from our world. She worked as a filing clerk in downtown Chicago, commuted there by train, returned in the evening after hanging out with management and white-collar types for the happy hour. She wore nylons and high heels to work. She had decided she would not stay in lower echelon jobs, and egged me on too: "What are you gonna do later in life? You're not gonna bury yourself here like a nobody, are you?" She described a world of challenge and movement, with carpeted offices reached by fast elevators, and fantastic views from skyscrapers. I sensed that to follow her in that world wouldn't be easy: every day I'd have to move upward or forward. Granted, she would push me, pull me, prod me, but damn, that'd sure be exhausting. I didn't have the courage, talent, or imagination to deal with such a perspective. Jackie severely overestimated me.

Who was I, deep down? What was my core identity?

Compared to my three long years of malaise from fourteen to seventeen, I had just lived through a period of profound change. I had reinvented myself, found friendship again, my life had been transformed. Hobo Junction was for me a haven, a home base, in short a family.

In France, I had entered the lycée shy and lonely, and left four years later as an adventurous teenager. Then, in America, I withdrew back into my shell, before emerging again at Hobo Junction, thanks to my alter ego Roy, who introduced me to this gathering place.

Roy, who had quit school at sixteen like everybody else, lived a few houses from me. We met by chance in the street. He spoke first:

"Hi, my name's Roy, you're new around here aren't you? You want me to take you to the place where we hang out at night, Hobo Junction?"

"Yeah, that would be nice, thanks."

Toward the end of that first evening, someone asked:

"So, Red, what do you think? You wanna hang out with us?"

Uptight from my long solitude, I was startled by this abrupt question, but I answered without hesitation "Yeah. Sure." A sign that I had been adopted was the immediate granting of that very American one-syllable nickname "Red," based of course on my hair, and easier to pronounce I suppose than Milan. Nobody came up with the derivatives Miles or Milton. Nor Frenchie. And no one mentioned my foreign accent. At Hobo Junction, I suddenly felt totally American.

Although I had traveled a lot on this earth for someone my age, my new world revolved around an astonishingly small area. Jackie lived fifty yards from me, Roy a hundred, and Hobo Junction less than a quarter mile away.

During my last year of high school, I veered from nightly attendance at Hobo Junction only twice, for long and "culpable" absences, each time because of women.

For a period of two weeks, I spent every evening parked in the driveway of the most beautiful girl in town, Carol, recognized as such without question. As with Madame Legrand in Paris, it was a veritable bewitching, the irresistible call of a siren.

Carol came from a very strict family, whom I never met. She was adamant on remaining a virgin until marriage. She formally declared this at the start of our "relationship," before throwing herself on me. From eight o'clock, when she finished her homework and I was already impatiently waiting for her in my car in her driveway, until ten, when her father flashed the light on the front porch, we devoured each other, strictly above the waist, without squandering any time with talk, so precious did the minutes seem to us. The steamed up windows ensured our privacy. When the porch light flashed, she straightened out her mussed up hair, her bra, her blouse, her skirt too, which she managed to keep below her knees despite my repeated attempts to exceed the imposed limits. Then she'd give me a formal goodnight kiss like those in the romantic movies. At the end of two weeks, as strangely as we met, we parted ways. I learned practically nothing about Carol or her family, beyond her name and the taste of her skin. This total lack of knowledge about our mutual history felt both bizarre and appealing.

For my second prolonged absence from Hobo Junction, I let myself be sequestered by Gloria, a thirty-five year old woman divorced from a husband known for his brawling ways in the local taverns. She also had several brothers with a bad-ass reputation. They formed a clan really. She was the mother of a two-year old girl being raised mostly by her own mother, in a trailer park.

I had no idea of the odyssey that awaited me when this woman appeared at Hobo Junction around closing time one night. After asking for a beer, introducing herself all around, and chatting with people, she said, looking straight at me: "I'd like *you* to take me home tonight." Naive like a boy scout, whereas I thought I had "seen it all," and intimidated by the reputation of her ex-husband and her brothers, as well as by her parental responsibilities, I expected to simply drop her off at her door. The intensity of the *you* should have raised my suspicions. I woke up in her bed, and she drew me into a whirlwind of sex, booze, and joy rides that lasted three demented months.

I had just turned eighteen, but could easily pass for twenty-one. We often hit the taverns along route 66 to Joliet. They became more and more stressful for me the closer we got to the penitentiary. Everywhere, she knew people, she was welcomed, she introduced me as her new friend. Surprisingly, no one gave me trouble.

One night, in Joliet, we went into a bar where the tension was palpable. I stuck out as someone who didn't belong there. My rose tattoo, with still vivid colors after four years, seemed laughable compared to the awkward drawings etched on the arms of the people surrounding us. They looked like they had been done with sewing needles and black ink, probably in prison.

I followed Gloria to the pool table, trying not to make eye contact with anyone: I wasn't a fighter. A tough-looking guy approached her and pointed at me:

"Glo, who's this dude? Is he bothering you?"

"He's a friend of mine, leave him alone. His name's Red."

"Hey Red, welcome. A friend of Glo's is a friend of us. You can come here any time you like."

Whew! I had no taste for altercations, nor any desire to come back to that place.

In the Hillbilly joints that Gloria also frequented, the atmosphere was more on the melancholic side. Everybody in there seemed to be humming the jukebox tunes, and relating to them in a personal way. The songs revolved mainly around two variations of the same theme: "She cheated on me, she done left me" for the male singers. "He cheated on me, he done left me" for the females. I went along with the emotional flow in those taverns. My favorite tune, with a foot-stomping beat, was "Well I'll make it alright/ Monday morning to Friday night/ Lonely weekend."

I was thus happily living the fantasy dream of every eighteen-year-old male: to be kidnapped by an irresponsible, excitement loving, thirty-five year old nymphomaniac. Except that I was also at the same time (foolish me) spoiling this unadulterated fun by trying to finish high school, maintain my part-time job, and make an early morning appearance at home each day to pacify my worrying mother and change my clothes. She dared not question me regarding my whereabouts (I told her I was staying at a friend's house), but she insisted on making me eat a full breakfast, which was the last thing I wanted, hungover and exhausted as I was.

This crazy pace proved too much to sustain, and even though I had great recuperative powers, after three months the dream began to feel like drudgery.

One night, instead of showing up at Gloria's apartment, I sheepishly returned to Hobo Junction, where I was greeted with a non-judgmental welcome: "Man, it's about time you came back. You're starting to look like a zombie."

By then, I would have loved to just sleep for an entire week.

I continued to juggle my diverse identities. Among my friends at Hobo Junction I was the only one to continue attending school, or not be on probation for minor infractions that nonetheless conferred a certain status. So and so was accused of having torched an abandoned farmhouse, so and so of car theft, shoplifting, or drunk driving. The malefactors were often required to undergo psychological evaluations, which they relished telling us about: "Do you have an erection when watching a fire?" was asked of the arsonist. "No, M'am, but I have one every morning when I wake up."

Those troublemakers weren't pyromaniacs or kleptomaniacs. They had simply responded to a dare: "I bet you're too chicken to..." Banal delinquency, commonplace among bored, idle dropouts.

With my police record as virgin as Carol, the only field in which I could claim distinction was as a driver. My reflexes, nerve, and judgment were admired. I loved scaring my passengers by barreling down the Congress Expressway at full speed while weaving from lane to lane without touching the brakes; or, my specialty, passing through narrow spaces between cars with only inches on each side. Throughout these antics, I remained oddly calm and detached. I didn't go beyond a "safe" threshold I could control, whereas others crossed it deliberately, stealing a car just for the pleasure of rolling it over. I didn't have this kind of daring.

One night, however, I acquired my stripes, so to speak, while cruising along with Roy in my Oldsmobile with triple carburetors. As we were handing back and forth a quart of Bullfrog, Roy suddenly tensed up:

"Dont' look back, a cop car is following us."

"What should I do?"

"I don't know, but we can't stop, I'm on probation. If I'm found with an open bottle in the car, I'm fried."

"Throw it out the window!"

"I can't, they'll see it."

Without thinking, I made a stupid decision: "OK, hang on, I'll lose them."

I downshifted, and punched it.

Vooommmm, the carburetors without air filters seemed to suck in a huge dose of oxygen, and we were catapulted to 95, with still some acceleration remaining when I shifted up.

In the rearview mirror, the pursuers, at the wheel of a powerful car too, held on for a while, but then suddenly gave up, as if they got cold feet. The reason became obvious soon enough. An intersection was coming up at hallucinating speed, multiplied by the contrast with the slow moving vehicles I was passing. Two lanes each way. Green light turning to yellow. Roy, speechless, raises his elbows like a boxer to protect his face.

Too late to brake. A cramp in my stomach. My chest and throat in a vise.

I careened across the intersection teeth clenched, just before the light turned red.

"We made it!" Roy shouted, "We made it!"

I tried to catch my breath, but couldn't speak.

The reprieve didn't last long. A couple of hours later I was arrested from the easy description of the car, black '57 Olds two-door sedan with red wheel rims: "You're a public threat. You're going to jail and we'll throw away the key." At the police station I was allowed to call home, but was so rattled by all the stress that I couldn't remember my number and had to ask for a phone book. That memory lapse felt as scary as the arrest. My distraught mother and stepfather came to bail me out and spare me further embarrassment.

The day of the trial, Roy accompanied me to court. One of the policemen submitted his testimony in writing, the other appeared in person. All through the officer's deposition, the judge shook his head with visible indignation.

I was expecting the worst, when, unintentionally, the magistrate threw me an out I had not thought of when rehashing the event in my mind:

"You know, young man," he said, "I'm sometimes understanding, but your action was unforgivable. A police car is chasing you, siren blaring, and instead of stopping, you barrel away, and you cross a busy intersection at an unreal speed. It's clear and simple, in my courtroom anyone clocked over the century mark automatically goes to jail. At that speed a car is more dangerous than a cannon ball."

"Your honor, excuse me, but there was no siren."

The judge turned to the policeman: "Is that right, officer? No siren? Is that possible?"

"Yes, your honor, we didn't turn on the siren in order to avoid creating a panic. And we aborted the chase."

In the brouhaha that ensued, Roy, quick and clever like a lawyer, whispered in my ear:

"Tell him you didn't know it was the cops chasing you, that you thought it was some guys who wanted to beat you up."

I latched on to Roy's words, and repeated them to the judge in a plaintive voice. He reluctantly dismissed the case on technical grounds. But I learned my lesson. This marked the end of my wrongful ways. From then on I stayed on the straight and narrow.

Chapter 16

Botch Your Life: the Brutal Way

"Perdre sa vie à la gagner." ("Earn your living, botch your life.")

— A popular French slogan

*I*n June 1960, two months after my eighteenth birthday, I entered the world of permanent full-time employment with a high school diploma. In America, one has to deliberately choose to not graduate. "Seat time" is the principal criterion, and social promotion the norm. Under those conditions, dropping out is a sign of hopeless maladjustment, if not deviance.

Although I continued to attend school until the bitter end, I maintained my reputation in my circle of antisocial dropouts by never taking a book home, by blatantly eschewing the extra-curricular folklore for which the American high school is well known (pep rallies, dances and festivities, senior prom, graduation ceremonies, etc.), and by granting myself the maximum number of absences beyond which drastic consequences ensued: fifteen per semester.

Because of our successive relocations, my American education took place in three different high schools over a period of four years. Besides the bizarre swimming pool nudity scene in ninth grade—and the speech correction lessons with Miss Nelson in tenth grade—I retained only one salient memory from each of those establishments.

In the first high school, one of my teachers, apparently impressed by my ability to name the capital cities of all the countries in the world, encouraged me to take an IQ test. He perhaps thought he had discovered some kind of genius, and thereby wanted confirmation. Actually, I had acquired this knowledge in a natural, effortless way from my year-long immersion in the *Petit Larousse Illustré* dictionary in Madame Mercier's classroom. Nothing remarkable about that.

I probably shouldn't have taken the test because afterwards, without explanation, the teacher's interest vanished. He never informed me of the results, nor did I ask. Several years later I discovered in my high school record the cause of his sudden disengagement: IQ 108. Average.

In the second high school, comments by the social studies teacher about the California coast around Big Sur startled me:

"This coastline is the most spectacular I know, even more beautiful than the French Riviera," he said. He was a veteran of the American landing in Provence, a region about which he talked with much emotion.

For me, who was then suffering from aesthetic famine, and who could not imagine a more fabulous landscape than the Mediterranean coast from Menton to Hyères, where I had spent a month in summer camp, the teacher's assertion sounded like a provocation. Had I too summarily and too harshly judged America, of which I knew only the flat Chicagoland region, void of any notable geographical features except the Lake Michigan shoreline?

And of the third high school, which I attended during my senior year, my only salient recollection was of the English teacher, Mrs. Hawkins, who had because of her passion for language departed from the rule that all textbooks be free.

She insisted that we should *buy* a book to which we would become attached, and which we would forever own. She had in mind *Webster's New World Dictionary of the American Language*, a book she deemed as important as Shakespeare or the King James Bible. She had no difficulty convincing me: I held my old Larousse in the same esteem. Despite the American tendency to litigiousness, no student or parent protested.

For whatever reason, Mrs. Hawkins found me "intellectual," a characterization meant as a compliment on her part, but almost pejorative in America. She recommended that I read the *Atlantic Monthly* magazine, available in the school library. She also said I should go to college, on the East Coast, to an Ivy League institution. However, without concrete and effective intervention (scholarships, specific guidance, etc.) her well-intentioned advice seemed irrelevant. Also, I was then at the tail end of an eventful and disjointed adolescence, and often absent from class, physically or mentally. In educational matters, the combination of receptive attitude and propitious timing is of utmost importance. Had my future missed an important connection with Mrs. Hawkins?

My only objective at school had been to avoid getting expelled. Suspension, even temporary, entailed a phone call to parents from the assistant principal. It could not be hidden. I didn't want to cause Maman any distress.

As with language, culture, and social class, I was now living in two opposite worlds, high school and Hobo Junction. And as if to increase this dilemma, my strange and tenacious ambivalence seemed accepted from both sides.

By the time I graduated, I had already been working part-time for two years—fifteen to twenty hours per week—at Ollswang's, the department store owned by Maman's employer in Elmhurst. My earnings supported my first Oldsmobile, a 1953 two-door hardtop that I repainted candy apple red after a minor accident.

At Ollswang's, I was the only janitor on duty Saturdays. I washed the big display windows, swept the floors, cleaned the restrooms, collected garbage. Banal, tolerable work, allowing for stolen moments of hiding or idleness. While pushing my broom or my squeegee, I could also daydream.

What I liked best at Ollswang's was the freedom of movement. I could circulate at will throughout the store. I felt sorry for the sales people, stuck to their counters, similar in many ways to the mannequins in the clothing section.

Paradoxically, the most unpleasant part of my rounds was not the cleaning of restrooms, but the nauseating smell of dyes and chemicals in the refuse of the…beauty salon! And my most embarrassing moments were when I'd enter that place, as furtively as possible, hoping to pass through unnoticed with my garbage can on wheels and my panoply of brushes and brooms. Invariably, Ted, the most flamboyant of the hairdressers, interrupted the clicking of his scissors and, pointing at me with a languid gesture, exclaimed to his client:

"Look, dear, there goes our young custodian, isn't he gorgeous. It's as if gold had been poured on his hair. What would you give me if I dyed yours that color?"

With the end of schooling, my part-time employment at Ollswang's also came to a close. From then on I would have to earn my living for good. At eighteen, it was time to help my parents, as was expected in the working class. The best means for achieving this was to live at home and pay for room and board until one got married. By thus combining resources, it was hoped the family's standard of living would improve, at least temporarily.

What kind of employment could I obtain with my skimpy qualifications? Should I include in my applications my two other jobs before Ollswang's? I regretfully had to leave the first, at the linoleum and dinette store, after a year. And I had been fired from the second—gas station attendant— after only four weeks, although the experience remained vivid in my mind.

At the filling station, I was expected to do oil changes and lube jobs when I wasn't pumping gas or wiping windshields. I also made fast tire repairs, the house specialty. When the bell announced the arrival of a car, I was supposed to drop everything and run out to the pumps looking smart and ready. In back of the station, slogans prodded us on: "Smile"; "Remember: the customer pays your wages"; "We pride ourselves on fast and efficient service."

The boss, J.J. Jones, a tyrant with a square jaw and a crew cut, had no sense of humor. He didn't tolerate any mishap from his teenage employees, whom he paid in cash, a measly fifty cents an hour. The intersection where his business was located already had two other gas stations, and a fourth one was under construction in the last corner. Were all four going to survive? Immediate service and anonymity were replacing loyalty, with customers becoming ever more capricious and demanding. When they neared the intersection, you could see them slow down, look over the gas stations, and head without qualms to the one where they thought they would be served the fastest. J.J. Jones lived under enormous stress and anxiety from this competition.

One day, a month after I began working there, a boy about ten-years-old asked me to inflate his bicycle tire. Distracted by the surrounding activity, I forgot I was dealing with a bicycle rather than a car: the inner tube exploded in my hands. After an initial moment of consternation, before I could even apologize, I was overtaken by irrepressible laughter. The poor kid, tears streaming down his cheeks and pushing his disabled bike, left the gas station yelling threats between his sobs: "I'm gonna tell my dad, I'm gonna tell my dad."

Half an hour later, as I was cleaning a windshield at the pump, I noticed a man pointing at me and arguing with the boss. I continued to wipe, but J.J. came flying out and, furious, yanked the squeegee out of my hands:

"That's it. You're out. Wait for me at the till, I'll pay you what you got coming. I can't afford to keep employees who make me lose customers. The man said you laughed at his kid after blowing up his tire."

I didn't even protest.

The linoleum and dinette shop, the gas station, the department store: my work history to age eighteen. I now had to find a full-time job. In my mind, the stakes were high, the next step would be permanent.

I couldn't imagine any alternative other than hiring on somewhere, immediately. No experimentation, no shirking like some of my buddies, who didn't mind remaining dependent on their family until they got thrown out of the house. I felt hounded by time and duty. Why? Too long an experience of independence and autonomy? Ever since childhood, I had managed by myself, I knew no other way.

Joining the Army, a common alternative to entry into work life, didn't cross my mind nor that of my friends. We had no goals, no projects, no perspective on the future, no ambition. Without student deferment or medical excuse, I was also subject to the draft (this eventuality seemed real ever since Elvis Presley's conscription a bit earlier), but the same fatalism prevailed about the draft as about VD: something that might happen, but something we didn't think much about, sheltered as we were by a feeling of invulnerability.

Mr. Spanek having inculcated to me his hate of assembly line work, I knew I had to avoid at all cost getting a job in a factory. What other possibilities remained?

The only solution I could see was to work in one of the warehouses that were sprouting up on the other side of the tracks from Hobo Junction, close to home. Those jobs involved piling up crates from floor to ceiling with a forklift, in an immutable cycle of hires, layoffs, and sudden rehires; a sort of perpetual discontinuity that ended up looking like semi-permanent employment. That's where my dropout friends worked when they did. A high school diploma didn't serve me much in that context.

The advantage of working in warehouses was that they were air conditioned—to protect the merchandise on unbearably muggy summer days. The disadvantage was the lack of windows. One had to endure fluorescent light throughout the shift.

I was reconciled with this prospect, when fate decreed that I deserved better.

I had no idea that my patience and relative amiability would harm me. During the last week of school, as I was beginning to worry about my still unsuccessful job search, one of my teachers, acting as a recruiter and claiming he considered me a good candidate, recommended me to the owner of a very dynamic small business, Ace Metal Refinishers. The wages—$2.30 an hour for day shift, $2.40 for swing—were higher than those of the warehouses. For a new graduate without experience, this was considered "choice employment," available only with his recommendation.

I was taken aback. Reliable and serious? Was he mocking me? Had he not noticed my flagrant absenteeism, my non-conformist attitude? Had he detected that under my bravado, I was a false hoodlum? Should I have felt insulted or flattered?

The teacher was thus determining my future: I would polish brass, steel, and aluminum surfaces on the revolving doors, elevators, display windows, and facades of buildings in downtown Chicago.

When I informed Mrs. Levinson at the department store that in two weeks I would leave her employ for this full-time job, she objected that metal refinishing was too exhausting and dirty, and that I should look for something else. I told her I wasn't afraid of hard manual labor, to which she replied:

"Yes, you don't mind now because you're young, but what will you do when you're forty? Can you see yourself at that age still putting up ladders, climbing on scaffolding, raising heavy stuff, and breathing in dust and toxic fumes?"

Forty? At the breakneck pace in which I had lived my last year of high school, this perspective was too distant to ever hope reaching it. Even thirty seemed far-fetched.

Le travail, c'est la santé (Work is Health)

Training at Ace Metal took place on the job. In fact there wasn't much to learn, except apply a lot of elbow grease and fit harmoniously into a team of four workers: unload the truck, put up ladders and scaffolding, spread out protective tarps, cover windows and walls with paper and masking tape, wheel out the compressor, and apply with a paintbrush a gelatinous lacquer remover—a sort of flameless napalm, that burned the skin if not protected by thick rubber gloves. Then vigorously scrape away this gooey mixture; rinse the metal with lacquer thinner; and finally, pure chain gang labor, polish the metal with steel wool and pumice powder, in order to achieve that distinctive "Ace Metal" shine. Our team formed a smooth quatuor, led by foreman Dwight Kennedy, a kind fellow despite his overriding concern for output and efficiency.

Dwight's job was the only one requiring a special skill. Once the metal surfaces were cleaned and polished to his satisfaction, he started up the compressor and applied several layers of lacquer with a spray gun, all the while exercising great care to avoid any runs. For this phase, he disappeared under the tarps and breathed through a mask that covered his whole face. Even outside the tarps, the escaping fumes made us feel giddy.

Wintertime

Today, swing shift, in order to not disturb the public with the noise, dirt, and smell of our activities. This time we're doing the revolving doors at the entrance of the Wrigley building. Dwight is going to prod us to work at a fast clip so we can finish in eight hours; otherwise Ace Metal will have to pay us overtime. The owner, Gordon, considers overtime bad planning, although he factors it into his estimates. He is one of the few contractors offering this service in the Chicago area, and is booked up weeks in advance. He already owns four trucks, that is to say four crews of four workers each, and he lives in a splendid home in the woods, where he hosts a company picnic each year. Son of a doctor, he didn't have an appetite for long studies, so he founded this enterprise instead.

At the usual meeting place in Downers Grove, we park our cars and get into the truck to ride together to Ace Metal's central depot near Downtown Chicago. Gordon, shrewd businessman that he is, deducts five bucks from our weekly paychecks for transportation. "Don't forget, guys, you get free parking, that's already a lot." Still, he is more generous than many bosses; he gives his workers two weeks of paid vacation during their first five years, and three weeks after that.

The weather report has announced bitter cold, with blasts of Arctic air blowing in to the aptly named "Windy City." They'll be further intensified by the swirling drafts caused by the skyscrapers.

Our foreman Dwight, at thirty-five, has the most seniority at Ace Metal. He started at the very beginning of the firm, about a decade earlier. Married, he has two children. Despite his semi-management status, he is fully involved with the work and gets his hands dirty. We've nicknamed him behind his back WCH ("Working Class Hero").

Our team includes another married guy, Steve, whose wife is pregnant. Steve is worried about his increasing financial responsibilities. "Will I be able to make it?" he asks rhetorically.

"Don't bug us with that man, you screw, you pay. Get yourself a second job" gibes Bill, our fourth partner.

Steve ignores Bill's provocation.

Dwight rolls his eyes with paternal forbearance. He is of another generation, and seems put off by Bill's crude language.

Gordon favors the married guys with kids; he can count on them to stick around and be promoted. Within a couple of years, just like Dwight, Steve will also make his peace for the long haul.

After pointing the truck down the main road to Chicago, Dwight turns on the radio to his favorite station, classic songs from the thirties and forties.

Steve frowns; he doesn't dig that old stuff, Perry Como, Rosemary Clooney, and such. He likes twangy, syrupy country western songs.

Bill likes only the top forties, for the most part bubble gum music.

Me, I don't really care. My favorite station, the one from Bronzeville, would be immediately turned off if I ever dared tuning it in.

I can't believe it: in America I have to listen to the blues in hiding, no Bobby Blue Bland, no B.B. King, and nobody wants to listen to jazz, even though Dwight's classics station touches on it from time to time with tunes by Duke Ellington or Count Basie.

Since Dwight is driving and anyway he's the boss, he imposes his musical tastes, and thereby peace. He would like to please everybody, but since that's impossible, he opts for authority. A former sergeant in the army, he says it's easier to command a platoon of fifty than a group of three. "Fifty just accept an order and shut up," he says, "but three bug you no end with their discord and objections for each decision."

Soon, hunched on our seats as if we were trying to absorb the warmth of the truck to prepare for the bitter cold later, we doze off. Steve's mouth is wide open; his neck twisted, his head dangling, he begins to snore.

"We haven't even started working and already you guys are sawing zzz's," says Dwight, who momentarily interrupts his continuous whistling. A frustrated musician, he feels compelled to accompany the melodies on the radio.

In winter, we fall asleep as soon as we feel warmth. During breaks, it's enough to see the steam from the coffee rise out of the Thermos to close our eyes and check out, even if only for ten minutes. Wrapped in our parkas, we could be mistaken for hibernating bears. Sometimes, if we're not too covered with pumice powder, and if there's an open coffee shop near our work site, we trudge there for our fifteen-minute breaks, though it takes an immense effort to get going again afterwards. Once we restart, energized by the desire to get the shift over with, we endure till the next break, with an eye on the clock. We proceed like this, with four plunges of two hours each.

The shift at Wrigley Building has gone on in routine fashion, except for twenty minutes of overtime at the end. The only other discrepancy entered by Dwight in his daily report is an incident with a vagrant. Attracted by the smell, he crawled under the tarps to inhale some lacquer fumes. When we found him, he asked to stay there, but Dwight shooed him off.

Past midnight on the return trip to Downers Grove, we convince Dwight to take the toll-way, for which we all chip in. We're eager to get home and shower...before crashing to bed so we can recover and start again the next afternoon. That's how the days, the weeks, the months pass by, about two-thirds on day shift, one-third swing. Fortunately, no graveyard.

I find my car frozen and scrape the windshield. Okay, one last effort, ten minutes from now I'll be home. Will I have the energy to shower before hitting the sack? Yes, it's an absolute necessity. I have pumice powder in my ears and on my eyebrows; despite the mask, some of it has found its way into my nostrils too, and I can feel the grit between my teeth. Sweat mixed with pumice powder has formed vertical grooves on my cheeks, like hillsides streaked by erosion. Impossible to keep that abrasive dust from burrowing inside the socks, in the sleeves, down the collar, all the way to the underwear. Through the stitches of the knitted cap, my hair has taken on a dull grayish color. I have to wash all this out. What about the lungs? They must have absorbed a heavy dose too. And what's worse when working outside in Chicago, the brutal cold of winter, or the broiling heat of summer, when one can't stand to wear a mask?

Between my green uniforms with yellow "Ace Metal" lettering covered in pumice, and the welding overalls of my stepfather impregnated with fire, dirt, and grease, Maman has an enormous laundry task. The Maytag, pulse of our household, runs on and on tirelessly in the basement.

No such thing as pointless work?

I beg to differ, I protest, there *is* such a thing as pointless work. Mine at Ace Metal, for instance. With apologies to the victims, I hereby insist on truth telling.

After a long year with my nose literally to the grindstone, having subjected my perseverance to a daily trial, I began to seriously question the nature and validity of my work. This concern was a taboo among my co-workers. They preferred not to think about such things: denial, their only protection. The weekly paycheck—a cruel drug, as toxic as the worst addiction—held us in its claws.

Was it socially useful and necessary that I sacrifice my health to make metal shine? To pay for the cosmetic maintenance of those surfaces with silicosis of the lungs? I was burying myself under layer upon layer of pumice powder, lacquer spray, gritty steel wool, smelly paint removers. Were our efforts even appreciated by those good-looking secretaries, those lawyers, those bankers, those businessmen, always in a hurry, bothered by our noise, our dust, our fumes, preoccupied with more important things than to admire our results? Did they even so much as notice them?

At the end of the shift, Dwight inspected our endeavors with a spotlight. His eyes glowed with pride: "Kudos, guys, you did good work. This brass is beautiful."

Adios Chicago

From time to time, when my work schedule allowed, I still roamed around Hobo Junction, but the former atmosphere had changed. The old group was disintegrating.

The coupled life was claiming its rights, most often voluntarily, sometimes due to accidents: abortion was nonexistent, contraception haphazard, pregnant girls seldom abandoned. Their male relatives saw to that.

I was tired of the aimlessness of hanging out, but the thought of a home life horrified me even more. And with whom? The plethora of girls from the previous year had disappeared. My on and off relationship with Jackie was also falling apart. As a file clerk, probably soon to be secretary, in an office on the 15th floor of a downtown building, she led a white-collar life that she had earlier sought to draw me into. Ambitious, energetic, and bold, she was losing patience with my passivity and lack of commitment.

Hobo Junction started to be frequented by an older crowd, people who had already pulled time, real gangsters who spent the evenings planning new jobs. The trend was for burglaries of country clubs, those haunts of rich people, in good conscience, like Robin Hood. Under cover of darkness, crawl close to the building, throw a few rocks to break some windows and wait to see what happens. If everything stays quiet, go in and help yourself. Then sell the stuff to a fence.

Pressed to participate as getaway driver in an expedition, I recoiled and sensed that the time had come for me to start a totally new life and leave

Chicago. San Francisco, where our friends the Spaneks had moved earlier, seemed like a natural destination.

A determined nineteen-year-old, I raced across the continent in the heat of summer at the wheel of my only consolation, my raging black '57 Olds. I headed out of Chicago on mid-latitude route 30, more direct than 66, which I already knew down to the Ozarks (an uncle of my mother's, retired from the Southern Illinois coal mines, lived in a small town near Saint Louis). Although I had barely enough money for gas, food and, if necessary, lodging—the car could be my home on wheels—I was buoyed with hope.

The journey West proved as exhilarating as I had imagined, with stretches of two-lane road interspersed with completed segments of the epic interstate highway system. My only disappointment was that I didn't encounter any hitchhikers for conversation.

Nebraska, with a landscape still as relentlessly flat as Illinois, simmered in the wonderful fragrance of alfalfa. In Laramie, lean weathered cowboys breakfasted on enormous stacks of pancakes. At the Great Salt Lake, when I removed my shirt for a roadside plunge to check how buoyant the waters really were, I noted that my left arm had turned a deep shade of brown. And after the Nevada border, a joyous young couple in a white Thunderbird marked "Just Married" challenged me to reckless pursuit on the desert highway, past Winnemucca, and on through Reno. Our vehicles careening in sacrilegious screeching succession into the passes of the majestic California pine mountains (at last, Eldorado!), I broke off from the chase for another swim, this time in the cool waters of Lake Tahoe, and waved my tenacious road companions on to their Carmel honeymoon and a happy future.

After this refreshing pause in paradise, as I continued towards Sacramento on the last leg of the journey, a deep serenity enveloped me: I had undergone a conversion of sorts and lost my infatuation with speed and powerful machines. I was now repelled by their brutality, reminiscent perhaps of the Chicago I left behind.

In San Francisco, I endured for three seemingly endless weeks the anguish of unemployment, the only time in my entire life I found myself dangling in this unbearable predicament. I sold the car I could no longer afford—nor wanted, aspiring instead to a Volkswagen Bug for basic transportation—and had the good fortune of being taken in at the start by the ever hospitable and generous Spaneks.

Finally, thanks to my "cousin" George, I found work as a baggage and freight handler for Trans World Airlines at the San Francisco Airport—an immeasurable improvement over my former job. I enjoyed the physical labor of throwing sacks of mail into the cargo pits in the bracing evening air, and basked in the euphoria of a new beginning in a city that dazzled me nearly as much as Paris, the hometown that I still pined for after five difficult but chock-full years in America that felt like an eternity.

DETACH BEFORE CASHING CHECK
STATEMENT OF EARNINGS AND DEDUCTIONS
FOR EMPLOYEE'S RECORD

ACE METAL REFINISHERS
DOWNERS GROVE, ILL.

PERIOD ENDING _____ 7-18 19 61

EMP. NAME _Milan Kovacovic_

29²	REGULAR HOURS	2 40	70 80
8	NIGHT HOURS	2 50	20 00
11¾	REGULAR OVERTIME	3 60	42 30
1¾	NIGHT OVERTIME	3 75	6 56
	GROSS WAGES		139 66
	FICA TAX	4 19	
	FED. INC. TAX	22 40	
	GAS	5 00	
	UNION		
	TOTAL DEDUCTIONS		31 59
	NET PAY		108 07

A week in the life at Ace Metal.

Chapter 17

Botch Your Life: the Gentler Way

The workplace is no longer only a center of professional activity;
some seek in it the social environment they're otherwise lacking;
all agree it constitutes the major framework of their life."

— *Sudreau Commission Report: Reforming the Workplace, France, 1975*

*I*n 1963, two years after arriving in San Francisco, I was twenty-one, losing my hair, missing five teeth. In the image of my teetering psyche, my body too was falling apart. This at the peak of my possibilities.

What had I done to so upset the gods? Why did they inflict these ordeals on me? To strengthen or destroy me? It was imperative that I reconstruct myself. But how? Broke and broken, at a dead end, I saw no way out.

I couldn't console myself for having left Paris and my irreplaceable sponsors. Despite my having good friends at the airport, and a relationship both intimate and independent with an attractive stewardess, Liz (a pattern I seemed to be falling into), I felt alienated at the far end of the North American continent, for no clear reason. Was it the breathtaking scenery and wonderful climate that made my dissatisfaction all the more acute? Or the emotional and physical distance from Paris, or from New York, the only U.S. city in which I felt I might be most at home? Worst, I was imprisoned in a job that was killing me, not with brutal aggression like Ace Metal before in Chicago, but with slow suffocation.

"Work, Love, Health:" Of the three main dilemmas of life, the first tormented me most. The other two seemed to depend largely on its resolution.

My two years of seniority at TWA enabled me to avoid the only unacceptable aspect of working conditions at the San Francisco airport: graveyard shift, from midnight to eight-thirty. After an earlier stint of three months on that unbearable schedule, reassignment to it would have justified quitting on the spot. Otherwise my job was quite tolerable, even in many ways pleasant, and certainly addictive—endless people watching, my favorite pastime. Considering my social origins, I should have been content with my station in life. Instead, I felt stuck and miserable. At the same time, as a consequence of the "duty to succeed" inherent to emigration, I repressed those negative sentiments, and felt shame and guilt for harboring them. I envied people my age, namely students, who had a perspective on the future along with seemingly achievable projects or goals. I hungered for employment that would allow me some measure of self-direction and autonomy. This aspiration seemed unrealistic and unattainable for "people like me."

At TWA, I enjoyed exceptional advantages compared to the then prevailing norm in the American workplace. I would have three weeks of paid vacation after five years with the company, four weeks after ten, five weeks after fifteen, and then a maximum of six weeks after twenty years of service. Upon reaching that milestone at the relatively young age of 39 (but distant for my mindset), I would also be granted a "4-1" pass entitling me to free *unlimited* high priority space available travel on the worldwide system, with a token fee of ten dollars for first-class upgrade if desired, and fairly similar conditions for parents and dependents.

With patience and perseverance, I would eventually reach this appealing horizon, eighteen years distant. I was both proud and ashamed to feel capable of such fortitude. But could I trust myself to not foolishly quit along the way? Some of my co-workers buried themselves even deeper. Although still young like me, they openly pined for their ultimate goal: retirement at sixty-five.

I was distressed, and at the same time resigned. Monster of passivity or paragon of stoicism? Servile slave or working-class hero? As always, both. For whatever reason, perhaps inherited from my father who allegedly lacked ambition, I wasn't interested in career advancement within the company. My lateral transfer after a year from baggage and freight loading to passenger service, generally considered a promotion, had occurred at the invitation of a supervisor, not from any resolve or striving on my part.

I forgave TWA for its outrageous letter reminding me that during the preceding year, I had been absent *2 days* [sic], and that it was hoped my attendance would improve in the future. This message had been automatically sent by an overzealous new human resources manager, to all employees who had more than zero absences during the previous year. He was soon enjoined by his superiors to apologize for his lack of judgment.

Except for some annoyances of this type, working conditions at TWA were certainly bearable. No matter how hectic the situation might be at the gates or the ticket counter, the supervisors saw to it that we got our two fifteen minute coffee breaks and half-hour lunch. In passenger service we received the same wages as the unionized ramp workers, from the ranks of whom most of us had come, but we no longer had to punch a time clock—although I for one would have gladly traded this "perk" for continued union membership. Every six months, we could bid for shifts and days off by seniority. The company also provided half the cost of two custom-made uniforms, plus ten shirts (either white or pale blue) every two years.

My existential malaise, though indeterminate, was real. Still, the memory of Ace Metal prevented me from making any rash decisions. The contrast served as a cautionary frame of reference. In comparison, I was now privileged, I did not have a right to lament. Nonetheless...

The anguish of unemployment while I searched for a job when I first arrived in San Francisco had traumatized me. This experience prevented me from entertaining any notions of quitting or aspiring to change in a cavalier manner. I had to hold on at all cost. I couldn't imagine starting over once more from scratch.

I had arrived in California without any money, like a refugee. The Spaneks, in their tradition of hospitality, put me up while I looked for work. I thought the search would be easy, but I was mistaken. Since I had no skills or specific training, I cast a wide net, I was open to anything. But after three weeks, I still hadn't found a job and was beginning to despair. To avoid making payments, I sold my car for what I still owed, a bad idea that I regretted immediately. By this hasty decision, I was losing my final line of defense. In case of last resort, I would be in the street. I no longer had the ultimate option of living in a car.

Sensitive to my plight, George Spanek, who had previously worked at TWA, intervened personally with one of his former co-workers to push through the job application I had left there. A few days later, I was hired for what I considered a dream job: freight and bagage handler. At nineteen, finally *casé* (all set), I was embarking on a new life.

I secured lodgings within my means, a small studio on the upper floor of a two-story apartment building that looked like a cheap motel, at 721 Bayshore Highway. The interior, freshly painted, looked nice and clean: no moldy spots, no gas smell leaking from the vertical wall heater, no rusty stains in the bathtub. At the foot of the outside staircase, a scraggly eucalyptus tree sheltered under its sparse and dusty leaves a dazzling oleander whose roots pushed through the cracks in the cement walkway. Paradise, lodgings of my own.

The first night, when I returned "home" from work around 1 a.m., I understood why the apartment had remained vacant and relatively affordable. Height of irony for a now carless pedestrian, thirty feet under my vibrating windows eight lanes of cars and trucks roared by in a perpetual thunder: my door opened directly on the Bayshore freeway.

During the initial visit to the apartment, in order not to spoil my euphoria, I had deliberately closed my ears and ignored the noise problem, and opened my eyes only on the wonderful sunlight painting stripes on the floor through the Venitian blinds. The manager, a gruff man with arms covered in tattoos, his beer belly protruding from under a washed out T-shirt, his hair cut short, probably a retired sergeant from the military, had not even escorted me to inspect the place. He lived in the last apartment in back, somewhat better shielded from the freeway. He simply threw me the keys and told me to go see for myself if the digs upstairs at the opposite end suited me. Too happy to have found a place I could afford, I enthusiastically accepted the studio. I didn't think about furniture either: only the blinds, the fridge, and the stove were provided.

That first night, optimistic and tired, I laid down on the floor in my ramp service parka whose hood served as pillow. Numbed by a good dose of whisky, I reluctantly accepted the necessity of acquiring at least some basic furniture. That's when I became fully aware of the deafening din of the freeway, magnified by the stream of headlights pouring down four lanes on each side. My nostrils too were assailed by the nauseating smell of exhaust fumes, mixed at low tide with the stench of the bay just across. The unrelenting flow of traffic barreling in both directions on this main artery between San Francisco and all points South looked and sounded like absurd multiple tracks of trains whose individual wagons were each pulled by their own locomotive.

With the rattling of my nerves by the noise, it became even more difficult to sleep on Sunday mornings, the only period of calm during the week. The silence was then deafening too, like an anomaly, as if in the aftermath of a nuclear attack. This was not so far-fetched a notion: batteries of dazzling white Nike anti-ballistic missiles pointed their vigilant heads toward the sky at the crest of the hills ringing the Bay. In 1961, we were at the height of the cold war with the Soviet Union.

My neighbor below, Chuck, took pity on me and lent me a few cooking utensils and two chairs, one of which I used as a table. Since he owned an old car—automobiles didn't rust to junk in California—he took me around the San Mateo liquor stores, where he seemed to be a familiar figure, to stock up on cardboard boxes. We cut them up to make a bed, actually fairly comfortable. I was turning into a sort of derelict in the company of this drinking buddy. A TWA mechanic, to whom I had mentioned the intrusion of the freeway in my lodgings, lent me his extra set of Mickey Mouse earmuffs, impervious to sound. But I found them too uncomfortable to wear during sleep.

Divorced and about fifty, Chuck shared his apartment with his fourteen year old daughter, who was getting ready to go live at her mother's, about a mile south from us in San Mateo, on the other side of the no man's land of the freeway. Rare occurrence at the time, Chuck was a native of the region. A handyman and Marine Corps veteran, he lived from odd jobs paid in cash.

Three months later, as I was settling in with furniture gleaned from the Salvation Army, Chuck offered to pool our resources so we could split the rent of a more comfortable apartment, bigger and quieter, with two bedrooms, away from the damn freeway. He would provide the furniture. I accepted without hesitation.

Until then, I had not contemplated the option, common in America, of shared housing. These arrangements are often problematic, but despite the age difference, there seemed to be no incompatibility between Chuck and me, such as I had observed among other people. Thus, for instance, two of my airport co-workers shared an apartment: one was a neat-freak, the other brought his big Harley motorcycle inside to work on it over newspapers spread on the floor at the foot of his bed.

The association with Chuck lasted nearly a year, during which my friends from Chicago traipsed through for visits of varying durations. My place served as their California crash pad—the voyage to the West Coast then being a quasi-mandatory rite of initiation, often with the vague intention of remaining in the Golden State. But none of these new pioneers succeeded in finding work. They returned to Chicago, and after a while we fell out of touch.

California exerted a powerful attraction, justifiably so considering its spectacular scenery and pleasant mosquito-free weather ("Climate Best by Government Test" read the sign at the entrance of Redwood City, just south of the airport). Its residents, old and new, dismissed the frequent earth tremors as an inconsequential oddity.

Chuck was a likable fellow, but "the drink" got the best of him. One day, he disappeared with my half of the rent, leaving no trace except a note: "I'm ashamed, I'm a drunk, I hope you won't be too angry at me, I blew away the rent money. I leave you all the rest of my stuff to atone for my sins. Farewell and good wishes. Chuck"

In the hodgepodge of his room, in a cardboard box, I found a porcelain set, probably purchased in some garage sale. The country of origin engraved on the back of each plate "Made in Czechoslovakia" had been lined through but was still legible, and replaced, in an incredibly blatant way, with "Germany." I was holding in my hands artifacts illustrating the arrogance of the Nazi regime.

The down-and-outness of my beginnings on the West Coast held retrospectively dramatic yet strangely humorous memories, including remembrances of hunger and intense emotions, which I recalled fondly, but did not wish to repeat. Difficult living conditions sharpen the senses. I had never before, nor have I ever since, tasted anything so scrumptious as the daily stack of buttermilk pancakes that I survived on for several weeks.

My feelings of alienation at TWA were certainly not due to the human environment, extraordinarily rich and varied, with a high proportion of originals and eccentrics among my co-workers, as well as among passengers. The fabled San Franciscan tolerance made all forms of lifestyles and behaviors acceptable. A congenial atmosphere prevailed at work, especially on the swing shift.

The most "normal" TWA employees, the heads of households, were condemned to two jobs: "That's the only way you can make it, Babe. If you have kids, you're done in, you have to eliminate from your budget cigarettes, booze, even the daily paper. You have to bring in a lunch bag, and coffee in a thermos. You can't afford to buy food at the cafeteria, it's a luxury for single people."

And it was true. I had under my eyes Fred Mower's daily meal: bologna sandwich, with a carrot cut in fours, and a celery stick, in a paper bag that he carefully folded and put back in his pocket after use, and which bore his name penciled in, so that his princely feast in the fridge of the employee's lunchroom wouldn't be confused with Mike Williams's peanut butter and jelly sandwich.

Personally, after the total destitution of my beginnings in San Francisco, I didn't count my money. I spent it all, without incurring any debts. In other words, I lived within my means. In hindsight, I look wistfully on this period of my past when I didn't have to rely on credit and its stressful consequences. But I led a very narrow, skimpy, small-minded, humdrum life in the middle of what should have been the exciting razzmatazz vanguard world of California, the Golden State.

I was earning it meagerly, this little life of mine, from one weekly paycheck to the next. I had at first drawn some pride from my self-sufficiency and resourcefulness, but I now felt only a lingering malaise. The stagnation of my existence revolted me. I suppose I suffered from a syndrome whose imprecise contour has since then received the more scientific name of "situational depression." Likewise, my difficult adaptation to boarding school when I was ten would today probably be called TSD, Traumatic Stress Disorder.

Although I had considerable energy, I wasn't able to summon it to productive ends. I wasted my time (a crime!), in a sterile, deplorable, damaging way, especially in endless drinking, the plague for swing shift people needing to unwind after work. Notwithstanding the lessening of my recuperative powers since the heroic days of Hobo Junction, where I literally burned the proverbial candle at both ends, I remained astonishingly resistant. I usually made do on only four to five hours of sleep. If only it had been for some worthwhile purpose!

I entertained some notions of enrolling at San Francisco State College, but these vague impulses came to naught. Like an errant soul, I would join the registration line that stretched for blocks on Holloway Avenue in a blanket of fog rolling in from the ocean. I enjoyed the feeling of being part of the crowd, slowly moving forward under the eucalyptus trees. I had no specific goals, because in truth I understood nothing about the system. The bureaucracy seemed so opaque, the fees so dissuasive, the schedules so problematic, my motivation so fragile, that I gave up at the slightest hurdle. And I managed to find many such snags, real or imagined, sometimes before even reaching the registration windows that marked only the beginning of the labyrinth, and not its end. I lacked the patience and perseverance needed to negotiate an obstacle course whose results seemed so distant.

The capital of stamina that I possessed needled me towards temptations of adventure and wanderings contrary to my temperament. I traveled a lot, to be sure, but in depth rather than breadth, by burrowing in a fixed itinerary that reproduced the decisive stages of my life: Saint-Aquilin and Slovakia for childhood; Paris and Chicago for adolescence; and now San Francisco for adulthood.

I replicated my migrations in reverse on free airline passes. First, I reconnected with my sisters Eva in Slovakia and Olga in Paris. Then, after several returns to Chicago, I crossed out that destination. It held painful memories that I preferred to forget despite some exhilarating times there. Furthermore, Maman and her husband had followed me to the West Coast. The America that I now flew over consisted of only two cities: San Francisco and New York. No dispersion. I wasn't interested in imitating the exploit of a co-worker who had gone around the world on TWA first class space available by hardly getting off an airplane, and by extending slightly on his days off: San Francisco-New York-Cairo-Nairobi-Bombay-Hong Kong-Honolulu-San Francisco. I couldn't see the point of that, although given my age and situation, it should have been an appealing prospect. This was predictable. In the village of Saint-Aquilin already, Paris had monopolized all my interest, to the detriment of other cardinal points.

Among the "normal" people at TWA, several surprised us. They were apparently well adjusted, found time to bowl, or play golf on the lawn of the Bay Meadows horseracing track, drank with moderation, married charming compatriots, fathered beautiful children, and then suddenly...committed suicide: the Irish. Where did their hidden gloom come from? Nostalgia for their island home? An incurable wound afflicting their people? They were the life of the party, until this one hanged himself from a tree in a public park, this one fired a gun to his head, this one swallowed a vial of sleeping pills. We worked side by side, joked together, drank together, felt connected, at least by our jobs and our schedules. At the funerals, the mourners pondered over the unfathomable mysteries of the human condition.

Many immigrants, like the Irish, ended up working at the very airport where they first landed. The appeal of free travel passes proved irresistible; it was the only way an expatriate could remain connected to his roots. To work at TWA was a haven and a cocoon for those people, myself included. Like them, there remained for me only to wait for retirement "without wishing for it nor fearing it."

Outside this not very enterprising world of the airport, as I settled into my job in passenger service, I nonetheless met an immigrant who embodied the American dream, a Czech engineer named Jarek.

Jarek hardly knew any English at the time of his arrival in California, when I helped him translate his résumé. I thought he was destroyed by the upheavals of immigration, and took pity on him. Soon afterwards though, the situation reversed.

The Czechs are somewhat similar to the Germans. They have a tradition of apprenticeship, craft, competence, work well done. These qualities are prized in America, where speed of execution is more often the norm in blue-collar endeavors.

To make a living, to learn English, and to adapt to his new country, Jarek hired on with a Porsche dealer, as a tune up specialist. He didn't get his hands dirty; he worked in a white lab coat, with a screwdriver hooked in his chest pocket like a pen. He was a pro, he had the right touch, his ear and his screwdriver were enough. His employer, in a clever marketing move, exploited the latent snobbism of his clients: a personalized tune up by a genuine European expert who, for authenticity, spoke only minimal English. What cachet!

However, Jarek had higher aspirations. He wanted to work again as an engineer, but it wasn't easy for him to land a first job that would enable him to show his worth. Americans, ready to admit their inferiority next to the label "imported," were paradoxically imbued with a superiority complex regarding credentials; they looked down on his résumé with its unpronounceable consonant-laden Slavic names: Brno University, Plzeň, etc.

Finally an engineering firm hired him. He couldn't believe what he discovered in American state-of-the-art industry:

"It's crazy, everything is based on the short term. You're hired only for definite projects. As soon as your part is done, you're out. The company where I work is like a revolving door, except for me."

"Except for you?"

"Yes, because I've figured out the system. I make myself indispensable."

"How?"

"I withhold information. I'm the only one among the managers and engineers in my firm who has survived any length of time. In a company like ours in L.A., they brought in an engineer from England with his family, all expenses paid, and he was laid off six months later. The guy can't believe it. He is thinking of writing a book about his experience."

Jarek was on a roll. With a compatriot like me, he could vent and be candid. He continued his rant, hardly catching his breath:

"Another thing about the U.S., it's a predatory country. It lets others take care of education, and then it attracts their scientists, their engineers, their ballet dancers. Still, I love California, there's a kind of raw energy here. I sense I'm going to make it big in this country."

Jarek was telling me that, me who earlier had translated his résumé and thought my efforts on his behalf useless. Meanwhile, he has taken off, and I'm the one who has remained stuck on the ground, at the airlines no less. He tells me stories of wide import, but I have nothing to contribute in return, except trivial observations from my stagnant life. It's not his fault if the gulf is widening between us, he can't do anything about it. I still like him, but I feel humiliated when he arrives at the ticket counter and hands me his ATP card with unlimited credit to pay for his travels. He is now part of the establishment, he is not glued to a fixed place or schedule, but me, I'm still and always planted here at TWA-SFO. He says "Let's go have a cup of coffee," but I can't leave my position. Now, the roles are reversed. It must depress him to see me standing there at each of his trips. If this continues, we'll end up trying to avoid each other, me because I'm envious and ashamed, he because my presence reminds him of his less glorious days.

I'm forgetting one thing, which should be a consolation: the game is not equal. Although Jarek has come here as a refugee from communism, he arrived with credentials, whereas me in America, no studies, no project, no nothing. I barely manage to meet my basic needs.

After my two trips to Czechoslovakia, in the middle of winter because with my low seniority that was the only time of year I could bid for vacation, I was beginning to know the country of origin of my parents.

The reconnection with my sister Eva took place with great emotion: despite our lack of a common language and the seventeen-year separation, we "communicated" as if that long hiatus hadn't occurred. We were intuitively on the same wave-length, and thus all the more frustrated about our linguistic limitations. She had chosen to study German at school, instead of French or English, thus confirming her sense of abandonment, and my Slovak proved adequate only for basic conversation. She was six years older than I, but someone joked that if I put on a wig of thick red hair, we could easily pass for twins. In facial features and a number of other aspects, we seemed to have inherited our mother's genes, and Olga our father's.

In the village of Bzince pod Javorinou, I was a lightly dressed Californian who negotiated—in polished shoes and a raincoat—the muddy paths that froze at night and turned to muck during the day. But I thanked the biting cold that cleared up my head after the many toasts with Slivovitz plum brandy, and the buffets of cold cuts and pastries that had to be honored at each stop among our numerous relatives.

Accompanied by Eva, I felt as if the village belonged to me. I was received like a prodigal son. My disconnection and my inept murdering of the enchanting Slovak language were accepted. In the street, we'd run into family members who greeted us warmly and invited us to visit, before disappearing with their grocery bag, their milk can, their "schnitzel satchel." A comforting smell of burning coal rose from the chimneys.

When leaving one the houses, I noticed under the misty street light the silhouette of a tall, vigorous elder installed very straight on a moped, wearing a long overcoat and a fur hat. What a figure, this unknown man, I thought, just as Eva waved him to stop. She nudged me, whispering "Go say hello to our uncle Tomáš." Under the features of the old man, I imagined my father. I had heard that in their youth they looked alike. I stared at him for the longest time.

Among my aunts, the eldest, childless widow Pavla, was beginning to obsess about her brood of chicks and ducklings. To protect them from the cold, she brought them inside her one-room house. Pressed against each other, they covered the entire floor, which appeared to be moving in different directions. The cackling didn't bother Aunt Pavla: she was deaf. Someone from the family, generally Eva, stopped by from time to time to straighten things out, expel the menagerie, scrub the stone floor.

After the death of her husband, relatives had whitewashed this aunt's room and painted on the wall, instead of the traditional decorative fringes of the peasant houses, a red circle from which several lines fanned out, like a stylized Japanese rising sun. Was my toothless aunt Pavla aware of the surrealist esthetics of her interior? At the end of my visit, she reached under her mattress and handed me a fistful of Czechoslovakian Crowns, banknotes inconvertible in the West, insisting that I quickly store them in a safe place for the rainy days of my life back in America.

In this rustic Slovakian village an observation struck me from the standpoint of work: I was one of the "losers" of my generation. To undertake long studies giving access to the professions seemed commonplace for the sons and daughters of the peasants of Bzince, but inconceivable for me in the United States. Aunt Anna, who had raised Eva, wanted her to study medicine, but Eva couldn't stand the sight of blood; on the other hand she loved poetry, so she became a high school teacher of Slovak literature. Late, at 40, she married Stefan, an oncologist with the same family background as ours, and she enjoyed a rewarding career in Bratislava, the capital city. One cousin became an agronomist, another an engineer, who married a pediatrician, and so on. All within a single generation!

In comparison, my life was completely static despite its apparent movement. During my trips to France and Slovakia, I feared above all the disturbing question: "Well, what's become of you in America?" Significant achievements were expected of me after the hullabaloo of the French national scholarship. I disappointed mightily, and was even more embarrassed myself. My interlocutors sensed that I avoided the subject. I answered them in nebulous terms like "I work...for...an...airline," without specifying in what capacity. At least my hands didn't betray me, as they would have if I had stayed at Ace Metal. Despite the misleading appearance of my travels, I lived very modestly. Indeed, a San Francisco-New York trip on pass meant, among other things, saving the cost of a meal.

A nephew of my old aunt Pavla from Bzince—she whose chicks and ducklings had invaded her house—even came to California, to participate in a research project in theoretical physics at Stanford University. In Palo Alto, he missed his family. He had no car, no money, he wore the slinky navy-blue nylon raincoat characteristic of the rare Eastern European travelers allowed to leave their country during the Communist era. But aside from the temporary separation from his wife and children, and his lack of convertible funds, it was hard to feel sorry for him. Like Jarek, he possessed an impressive intellectual capital. Notwithstanding the aberrations of daily life in his country, he had risen to a prestigious professional status. My anguish of "earning a living while losing my life" was unknown to him.

The world of Stanford, a short distance from where I lived, beckoned to me as an interesting place to visit, but merely as a tourist. Below the surface, the campus was as impenetrable as if surrounded by an invisible Iron Curtain. Yet this cousin, raised in a distant peasant village, was invited there as an honored guest. Strange paradoxes...

The descendants of the Czech bourgeoisie who had fled to America and complained about deprivations or exclusions in their native country after the advent of communism, also managed to do quite well in the West. They were equipped, as if by enchantment, with advanced degrees quickly transferable in their host country. Stanford University even organized a free re-conversion program for medical doctors from communist countries.

In Eastern Europe, the pie had visibly enlarged, and been shared more equitably. The American self-satisfaction in the East-West competition seemed to me odious. I wouldn't have traded places but, disgusted by inequalities, I discerned some positive nuances in the overall balance sheet of communism, which was painted all dark in the West. An intermediate social democratic system such as Western Europe's seemed to me the most attractive option.

I was anguished by the question of work and my destiny ever since an innocuous remark made me aware that I had irrevocably botched my life. At the downtown airline terminal in Paris, after arriving from San Francisco on the nonstop Polar Flight, I had taken a taxi to the north side of the city to catch a suburban bus to Arnouville-les-Gonesse, where Olga, now recovered from her downfall, lived with her husband and their daughter, in a small house with adjoining workshop where he sharpened saws from morning to night, one of the last artisans to ply this trade in the Paris region.

I was making a quick round-trip of four days, including nine hours of jet lag each way, thanks to a complicated exchange of time off with two co-workers. This switch had been reluctantly approved at the last minute by our supervisor, who didn't like these arrangements, nonetheless necessary if we were to use the free and reduced rate transportation available to us.

In the usual crush of the great international departures, with throngs of friends and relatives seeing off passengers, I worked until the last moment at the boarding gate of my own flight before changing jackets and heading out on the tarmac as a final standby, holding an umbrella to ward off the rain whipped up by the already screaming engines. Soon after take-off, the stewardess calmed me down from all the gate room stress with champagne and hors-d'oeuvres, followed by the renowned Royal Ambassador first class service, including knitted red booties for foot comfort and a satin blindfold to help defuse the crossing of so many time zones. Still, I arrived in Paris's downtown terminal totally exhausted, with just enough strength to hail a taxi to the bus station.

But the vibration of the tires on the pavement of the beloved city revived me. When we left the Invalides esplanade, across which I had so often kicked a tennis ball during my pre-teen years, the driver looked back through his rear-view mirror and asked:

"Where exactly do I drop you off?"

"Rue Ambroise Paré, in front of Lariboisière hospital."

"Ah, so you're in Paris for a medical conference?"

His error saddened more than flattered me. Under different circumstances, I might well have been that doctor the driver imagined me to be.

Chapter 18

U.S. Army

Man is free only in the military, away from the constraints
of civilian life, away from numbing civilian life.

— *Charles Péguy*

The U.S. Army saved me from the morass of "earning my living while losing my life" at TWA. It saved me by shaving my head, à la now fashionable Michael Jordan or Zinédine Zidane style; by fixing my teeth; and by granting me an opportunity to breathe, pause, and take stock of the future, away from the unyielding servitudes of civilian life. The Army enabled me to reinvent myself, by granting me a margin of "freedom" non-existent elsewhere for someone of my social class, except for two much less attractive options: religious orders or prison.

Paradoxically, I owed my personal emancipation to a situation I had not sought, and which might appear at first glance constraining. But without support from family or any other source, I could progress only under an institutional umbrella, in my case the military. Whether due to lack of imagination on my part, or lucid perception of reality, I saw no other possibility. "America the land of opportunity" had become for me a myth, a cruel hoax.

This apparent conundrum is not as strange as might appear. The economy of America—the homeland of vigorous risk taking, individual initiative, entrepreneurship, and free markets—is in large part financed by capital generated by the most cautious private motivation: insurance. Liberate a man and his first concern will be to protect himself. Protect him, and he will opt for bold emancipation. Such at least was my personal truth.

In the carefree atmosphere of the military, I transformed myself: From irresolute and indecisive, I became determined and persevering. Freed from the constraints of daily life—these predators of time and energy—I finally embarked on a project, "Get an Education," without immediately giving up as before. Neither the distant horizon for completing this goal nor its imprecise contour dissuaded me. I felt my mental and physical powers multiply. I was getting hold of myself, constructing a future. To test my intoxicating newfound will power, I made myself stop smoking.

Ironically, I owed my salvation to the Vietnam War, to which I was opposed. Johnson, who had been president for a year following Kennedy's assassination, ordered a massive troop buildup soon after his "reelection" to the U.S. presidency in 1964, despite his campaign promises to the contrary. I voted for him, thus supporting his purportedly pacifist views and ambitious "Great Society" social programs. His opponent, Goldwater, unflinchingly evoked the most terrifying weapons to "stop communism" in Southeast Asia.

Without the military escalation, I would not have been drafted. Almost twenty-three, I had registered as prescribed five years earlier, but the military had seemingly forgotten about my existence. Suddenly I received a notice to report for induction on January 17, 1965, in the first wave of conscripts for the Vietnam War.

The order reached me as I was returning to San Francisco from Slovakia, where I had spent my two weeks of annual vacation at my sister Eva's. There, after the joy of reunion and the rounds of visits to the houses of all my aunts and uncles, I was shocked to witness again the difficulties of daily life in communist countries.

I had already caught a glimpse of those problems during a previous stay, and blamed them on endemic corruption, or the weight and stupidity of the bureaucratic management of communism. However, I still sympathized somewhat with the broad lines of the doctrine.

An incident in particular disturbed me this time: one morning shortly before lunch, my cousin returned home empty-handed from the grocery store, after having stood in line for a long time to get bread. His nerves already frayed by an accumulation of similar annoyances, he exploded. "No bread today" he thundered, as he kicked open the door, his hand deep inside his coat to calm the flare-up of his stomach ulcer. His anger and shortness of breath convinced me of the worthlessness of the regime, indefensible when it showed itself incapable of solving even the most elementary problems of food distribution. In view of the intense circumstances, I refrained from expressing disappointment that I would be missing out on the scrumptious Slovakian rye, or from evoking similar frustrations with health insurance in the U.S.

Returning West, I felt great relief when I crossed the Iron Curtain—that sandy strip of no man's land surrounded with barbed wire, and watched over by sentries scanning the border from their lookouts. The forbidden zone was also patrolled by German Shepherd dogs accompanied each by two soldiers, one presumably guarding the other, Kalachnikov at the ready across their chest. The ritual baggage search, the interrogation about the origin of the items transported and the identity of the persons visited, then the inspection of the bus's underside with mirrors on wheels shaped like long shoe horns, all this police rigamarole, this lockdown of a border, allegedly to "intercept Western spies and saboteurs attempting to enter or leave the country." To this official interpretation, I much preferred the joke being told inside Czechoslovakia, where humor flourished as an antidote to oppression:

The president of Czechoslovakia tells his mistress that he wants to fulfill her three fondest wishes:

"What is your first wish, dear?"

"Buy me a fur coat!"

"No problem, my love. We'll stop at the store for Communist Party cadre. It's well-stocked, you'll have many coats to choose from. Now, what's your second wish?"

"Take me to Acapulco!"

" No problem either. I'll arrange to have the presidential plane take us there whenever you want. And your third wish?"

"Open up the borders!"

"Ah, I get it, naughty, naughty. You want us to be alone for a romantic tête-à-tête."

However, absurdity pertained to both sides of the frontier. It oozed as much in the West on the Austrian side, with private Shell Oil ownership of an immense petrochemical complex, as in the East on the Czechoslovakian side, with state ownership of a minuscule umbrella repair shop.

Despite my indulgence toward the theoretical aspects of communism, and my aversion to some aspects of American capitalism, I brought back from this visit a remnant of my cousin's exasperation. When I returned to San Francisco— where the draft notice awaited me—the memory of his anger lowered my resistance to American propaganda, and triggered my first reaction: "Since there's no other choice, let's go, we have to fight communism, and stop it in South Vietnam, or else all the countries in that region, and then the whole world, will fall under the enslavement of totalitarianism like a series of dominoes."

I informed TWA of my draft call, obtained the necessary leave, and prepared to appear as ordered in Oakland on January 17. But on the evening of the 16th, like a condemned man struggling at the last moment, I demurred. My recoil wasn't ideological, but merely spontaneous, irresponsible. "Do I go or not go?" My draft notice stood on a shelf next to a pile of unpaid parking tickets. Since I had for so long neglected the latter, why not ignore the former? Which I did.

Several days went by until I realized the seriousness of my infraction. AWOL? Deserter? Anxiety seized me. What to do?

Panicked, fearful, alone, I sent the military authorities a terse letter stating that I had not shown up because of illness. Then I mailed a cursory reply to the threats of arrest for the unpaid parking fines: "Drafted by the U.S. Army on 17 January 1965; insolvent." (semi-true on both counts). In order not to complicate the situation further, I said nothing to TWA, and waited for what would come next.

I decided meanwhile to look for work as a "*bracero*," a field hand, and showed up one morning at the designated hiring place. But I retreated quickly: these jobs seemed destined solely for Mexicans. The only Anglos around were the foremen. Someone looking like me could only be a journalist poking around or an agitator, and therefore unwelcome.

I probably intended to do some reportage or gain documentation to write later about that experience, but all this was only in a latent state in my mind, a muddled combination of social indignation, anthropological curiosity, and literary interest. The notion of writing was, like all my intentions at the time, a vague objective that I gave up on soon after having contemplated it. I had neither perseverance nor confidence enough to set a goal and try to reach it.

Passive, but not lazy. I found a boring job, for minimum wage: preparing the interiors of newly built apartments for their first tenants. I scraped paint spots from the floors and windows and removed debris from the premises. I worked alone and anesthetized myself listening to talk shows on the radio, to which I was sometimes tempted to call despite my bad conscience and semi-clandestine status.

Evenings, when she was in town, I joined my girlfriend Liz in her San Francisco apartment whose balcony overlooked Union Street, lively center

of a neighborhood for rising young executives and professionals, a social category foreign to me. The roof of Liz's building offered a fantastic view of the
San Francisco Bay and the Golden Gate Bridge. The apartment, the roof, the
balcony were a sufficient universe for me, but not for her, who understandably, wanted to go out and have fun in the city. The Jacques Brel song nettled
me: "*Faut pas jouer aux riches quand on n'a pas l'sou.*" ("Don't act like you're rich
when you don't have any dough"). I continued my pattern of illegal parking in
her neighborhood, there being no other solution for my visits.

One evening I had an unfortunate reaction. As I was arriving at her
apartment, which she shared with another stewardess on more or less alternate schedule, Liz said: "The cleaning lady just left." I was unable to repress
the reflex of a domestic's son, or of a cantankerous husband: "What? A cleaning lady? You're kidding? Can't you do that yourself?"

Once expressed, hurtful words can't be taken back. She replied in the
same vein:

"What mentality! Once poor, always poor." Then, in a teasing tone, sting-
ing in this context: "If you're so smart, why aren't you rich?"

What hurt me in her reply was that, although I liked to read, and could
therefore perhaps be mistakenly perceived as having higher aspirations, I
never ever claimed to be "smart." Sufficed to look at my life to see how ridiculous such an assertion would be.

Given my background, I couldn't imagine employing someone for household chores. The distance between us after two years of an episodic relationship widened. I sensed I was becoming less and less interesting.

I heard nothing more about my stack of unpaid parking tickets. Had the authorities, in a patriotic gesture, granted me amnesty without informing me,
so as not to devalue their clemency?

February went by, then March, without any news from the military, without any threats. I began to think that I had disappeared from Uncle Sam's
radar (how had the draft board in Illinois tracked me down to California in
the first place?), and that my state of limbo might remain permanent. In early
April, though, I received a second notice, neutral in tone, with an order to
report for induction on the 22nd of the month. It made no reference to my
previous defection.

In my isolated situation, I could think of no alternative other than to submit.
Since my return from Czechoslovakia, my hostility to communism had waned;

I was now impatient only to escape civilian life. I gave no thought to the lethal dimension of the military. I was taking a reconstitution leave, my passivity unchanged. A conscript, my induction wasn't the result of *my* decision.

Basic training took place at Fort Ord, on the Pacific coast about a hundred miles south of San Francisco, where we were sequestered for two months in order to contain a meningitis epidemic that had spread throughout the base. Several recruits had already died from it. The only remedy was to maintain the temperature inside the barracks at 55 degrees Fahrenheit. Easy. All we needed to do was leave the windows slightly open. The perpetually cool ocean breeze took care of the rest.

The first shock, traumatizing, was the restroom arrangement, in the barracks of fifty-seven recruits in bunks superimposed in threes. The commodes afforded no privacy. They were not even set against the wall, but right in the middle of the washrooms, where people shaved, showered, and brushed their teeth. Ouch, the beginnings of dehumanization.

Everyone protested against this situation to the drill sergeants, who yawned at our complaints. And everyone grappled with the same question: How to preserve a modicum of dignity?

Soon, no more embarrassment. Humans are extraordinarily adaptable. Seated side by side on the five thrones at each end of the barracks, some read the newspaper, others meditated, others took advantage of this time to cut their nails, reread their mail, sew a button. The only code, in order to maintain some serenity: no conversation beyond a simple greeting.

The mixture of races and regional origin in the Army did not extend to social class. At the bottom of the ladder, the volunteers: Whites from Appalachia and other impoverished regions, Blacks, Latinos, Native Americans. Then us draftees from the working class, almost exclusively Whites. And that's all. Other levels of society weren't represented. They enjoyed waivers or deferments of various kinds, they benefited from counseling and support systems that helped them find ways to avoid the draft; or, through connections, they joined the National Guard, which guaranteed a cushy stateside assignment. Later, in 2003, some of these draft dodgers of the 1960s who subsequently reached positions of power and launched the war in Iraq, came to be called Chickenhawks (Bush, Cheyney, Wolfowitz, etc.).

Abstracting the missing college students, we were considered the best and the brightest, those of us deemed mentally and physically fit for military service. In Washington, the U.S. Congress, alarmed by the huge rate of disqualification of potential soldiers, enacted the Great Society nutrition and education programs, to bring the future "defenders" of this country up to acceptable standards. What has since been forgotten is that those programs, derided as social engineering by conservative critics, were implemented largely as a national security rather than a "welfare" measure (dixit Daniel Patrick Moynihan, a man in the know).

During basic training, my rope climbing ability gained me some recognition. Whereas everyone was struggling up by mere strength of arms, I reached the crossbar with astonishing ease, hardly getting tired. No big deal, I helped myself with the legs, as Madame Mercier had taught us with her printed guidelines in the Saint-Aquilin schoolyard. The drill sergeants admired my technique, discussed it among themselves, suggested an eventual modification to the training manuals. But then, on second thought, no, they gave up before even trying: it was too complicated, their suggestion would have to go all the way up the chain of command to the Pentagon. So recruits continued to needlessly exhaust themselves and risk falling.

We marched everywhere in formation, the only way large groups could move to the firing range and other destinations with any sense of order. We lined up by decreasing height. At six feet, I ranked at about the seventy-fifth percentile, and usually fell in behind Maceo Smith, whose stride I unconsciously imitated. One time, our drill sergeant Roosevelt Burns yelled out: "Kovic, you're supposed to march, not diddy bop like Smith. You can help it. He cain't."

My unconsciousness (or nihilism?) in 1965 was astounding. To my surprise, I obtained a high score in "leadership" in the battery of tests administered during induction, as well as a GT number (the military version of IQ) considerably better than my mediocre result back in high school. So I decided to make the best of my new situation by applying for OCS, the Army school that trains soldiers in six months to become second lieutenants—promoted from the ranks instead of the military academies. The interview was conducted by three spit-and-polish officers. They must have judged that I didn't really possess the required gung-ho attitude, even though, in addition to the test scores, a certificate attested that I had "satisfactorily performed duties as a Squad Leader." To my profound dismay, I was rejected. This unexpected setback did not bode well for the convalescence of my will and energy. But the rejection probably saved my life. In 1965, the war escalated wildly, and second lieutenants suffered the highest proportional death toll. Their role, it turned out, was to lead the infantry attack. Many of them were "fragged" by their own men.

Since I had not been a very serious student in high school, I had learned basic skills in typing, a class reputed easy for shammers. This "talent" as well as my results in the various orientation tests led to my being directed during the more advanced part of training toward personnel administration rather than infantry. At least I wouldn't kill anyone with my stapler, and I would provide only an indirect target for an eventual foe. I was ready to accept anything.

In order to fill my idleness during the ensuing "holdover" period, I followed the lead of a fellow soldier, Jack Kean, by registering for an English course one evening per week at Monterey Peninsula Community College, a few miles south of Fort Ord on the Pacific Coast Highway.

At Fort Ord, the barracks were grouped near the main entrance, but the maneuver grounds extended for miles in the midst of Steinbeck country, the Salinas valley and its immense lettuce and artichoke fields, cultivated by families of Mexican *braceros*: men, women, children, bent to the earth all day under broad sombreros. The lettuce was placed in crates piled up at the edge of the fields, and bearing the stamp of a multinational corporation diversified in agribusiness: "Made in U.S.A. by Tenneco."

A few miles to the southwest, one could see the Monterey peninsula jutting out in the ocean behind the wails of sea lions. The perpetually cool breeze made Fort Ord the only military base on the North American continent where the same uniform could be worn in all seasons.

A bit further south along the coast, the tourist and honeymoon mecca of Carmel beckoned, followed by the majestic hills of Big Sur overlooking the ocean—this time Henry Miller country. I liked his writings about his California retreat and his ribald earlier days in Paris.

To get to the college, Kean and I hitchhiked near the post entrance, in front of the sand dunes lining the coast highway. When we wore our uniforms, we never had to wait. "Respectable" people sometimes felt guilty to have hesitated to pick us up, and turned back to give us rides in their sparkling clean automobiles.

On the other hand, when we wore civilian clothes, the drivers who stopped for us were mostly down-and-outers from the Midwest and elsewhere on their way to L.A. in their rusted out clunkers.

Kean had a gift for making people talk. The roadies subjected to his interrogations shamelessly aired out their tales of woe. Kean, turning the wheel of an imaginary Barbary organ, nicknamed these confessions the "Ballads of the Unlucky Ones." They were stereotypical enough to justify his cynicism. One of them I still recall:

"I lost my job in Dayton, Ohio. I was working there in a tire factory but they laid off a lot of people. A while after that my girlfriend left me. She wasn't interested in living with an unemployed guy in a trailer park. To live as a poor person, it's sad, but two living together like that, it makes no sense, she said. She left for Cincinnati. Me, I headed out to the West Coast, but I didn't find a job in Frisco, so I'm pushing on down to L.A., where I heard it's easier to find factory or warehouse work. I took the coast highway 'cause I wanted to see Carmel and Big Sur, I heard it's worth a look. I hope my car holds up. The tires and brakes aren't in the best shape. Say, don't you guys think it's crazy, a few weeks ago I was making tires in Ohio and now I'm in California driving on bald treads. If I don't find a job in L.A. or Diego I don't know what I'm gonna do, I can't go any further West than that. Would you guys have any leads? Any kind of job, I don't care. You all are lucky, you found a niche, three squares and a bunk courtesy Uncle Sam, but me I'm already done with that, I don't have this option, unless I re-up. But I don't know if they'd still want me, I'm twenty-five, and the first time I didn't do so hot, I got two article 15s."

"Yeah, you envy us," Kean replied, "but it won't be a hideout if we're sent to 'Nam, like it seems sure and certain. We were drafted because of that, no other reason. For the time being we're twiddling our thumbs, but before long the shit's gonna hit the fan, you watch and see."

"Yeah, but you know what, war would be a hell of a lot more exciting than where I'm at right now, dragging my ass from one end of the country to the other to find a job, any job. What would I have to lose?"

I felt embarrassed by the candor of the statement, in part because I identified with it to some extent. The three of us then withdrew into our thoughts and the contemplation of the passing scenery.

"Don't worry," Kean said after a while, breaking the silence, "with the war coming on, your tire factory in Dayton is gonna rehire, or if you're fed up with the civilian world, you can try to re-up and be a lifer. Last time were you U.S. or R.A., draftee or volunteer?"

"R.A."

"So, they might count your three previous years of service, and you'd have only seventeen to go for retirement. You'd be only forty-two, and scot-free after that. Not bad, eh?"

"Yeah, that'd be great. Just thinking about it makes me feel better. Thanks, guys, you cheered me up, I'm gonna make it, I'm sure, one way or the other. I wasn't lucky 'til now, that's all. It's also probably my own fault if I'm in this fix, unemployed and all. I probably messed up somewhere, but I'm gonna start over. Where do I drop you off at in Monterey?"

"At the college, just before getting into town, we'll tell you where." Kean spoke, I stayed quiet on the back seat.

"Oh yeah, go to school," replied our driver, "I should try that too one of these days. For the time being it looks too complicated, I don't have the guts, or the means, unless I re-up."

As we were approaching the college, Kean the rogue launched a last question at our host, as an epilogue to the conversation.

"By the way, you for or against labor unions?"

"Against, man, for sure. All this mess we're in is 'cause of them."

At Monterey Peninsula Community College, I felt as if I was aboard an airplane which, racing along a seemingly interminable runway, finally leaves the ground: I discovered for the first time, nine years after arriving in the U.S., that I felt at home in English, without having learned or studied the language in any conscious way, except by osmosis through reading. Until then, I had no idea whether or not I wrote correctly, having had no real occasion during my schooling or afterwards to use this skill or test myself. The strangest thing was that this discovery, pertaining to an intellectual activity, was strictly a feeling.

Except for the instruction I received in grade school and the lycée, I had acquired most of whatever I learned in the same way as my self-taught English; my competencies therefore remained narrow and limited. I had acquired them by imitating the rich, for politeness and good manners; on-the-job, for metal refinishing in Chicago; poorly, regarding swimming, in which I made no progress; and not at all in tennis, skiing, or any activities requiring training, schedules, or equipment.

To be an autodidact is a laudable achievement, but the extreme form it took for me had obviously imposed drastic limits on my knowledge and abilities. Thus, for instance, having when I was about twenty entertained some notions of "making movies," I nonetheless never considered the necessity nor the possibility of *learning* to make films, either in a school for such things or on-the-job, and this chimera left me like so many others before and after. Yet my friends accomplished ambitious projects, under my eyes, simply with the required training and persistence. For instance my TWA co-worker Bill Mayfield, who had taken me on board his first solo flight in a little Cessna over the Golden Gate and the Bay Bridge, was now piloting a Boeing 707 to exotic destinations for the Flying Tigers freight company.

The only time I was tempted by some sort of training, I checked off on a matchbook cover an offer for information about correspondence courses for the following trades: welder, typewriter repairman, bartender. But, having no stamp handy, I never mailed the request.

The self-reliance to which I was accustomed since childhood had become for me a reflex, a permanent attitude, a veritable handicap. I was ignoring the fundamental injunction: "Ask, and you shall receive. Knock, and the door will open."

For the English class at Monterey Community College, we needed to write a vignette of about three pages, and I had for an entire week, in feverish exaltation, tweaked a text that I anxiously presented to the teacher. I remember only that it dealt with a pastoral scene featuring some brooks and meadows. The intense concentration, the permutations of nuances and words appearing even during sleep, had exhausted me.

The following week, the teacher announced to the class: "I want to read you something." It was my text.

I was happy my three pages received some notice, but I would have preferred to remain anonymous. Although he didn't reveal my name, the teacher, stating that the piece was written by someone "whose native language is not English," identified me to the class as if he had been pointing at me. I felt embarrassed.

After hitchhiking back to Fort Ord that night, squeezed like in a bumper car aboard a Corvette whose inebriated driver insisted on showing us what his machine could do, I tore up the text, despite Kean's protestations. My psychological convalescence was progressing in fits and starts. I wasn't yet fully healed of my neuroses.

Just about everyone in our basic training company had already left for Vietnam. As I was pondering over the next assignment for the English class and expecting to be sent to Saigon too, Kean received orders for Korea, and I for West Germany.

The puzzling military postal code listed on my documents, APO NY 09168, signified in civilian terms the city of Würzburg, Leighton Barracks, Headquarters Company, 3rd Infantry Division. I ran to the post library to consult some maps and encyclopedias. What luck, every entry described Würzburg as a city of art and history, in the heart of Europe. Paris was about a ten hours' drive to the west, and the border with Czechoslovakia less than three hours to the east.

Following the long holdover at Fort Ord, I experienced another typical U.S. Army "hurry up and wait" period of limbo, this time on the opposite side of the continent, at Fort Dix, New Jersey, where I was sent in December to await transportation to West Germany.

At Fort Dix, we didn't know until reveille each morning whether or not we would be scheduled for departure that day, but we had to be ready to go. Shipboard transportation overseas had been completely phased out the previous year, and now everybody went by air charter, possibly with TWA. Maybe I would even know the crew?

If our name wasn't called out from the flight roster in the morning, it meant we had another day to kill as we saw fit. But first, immediately after breakfast, we had to report for "police call," which consisted of fanning out by the dozens, each of us armed with a stick and a nail on the end, to clear the grounds of cigarette butts and other garbage.

Some of my fellow soldiers were bored out of their head, but I didn't mind the idleness. And I didn't have to think about anything practical: I was a draftee, property of Uncle Sam's worldwide operation for another sixteen months. Room-and-board until then. All my belongings were stuffed into a tightly packed duffle bag weighing 70 pounds, and I was provided with a bunk, copious meals, and same-day laundry service.

Actually, I relished this life of complete freedom and lack of responsibility. I didn't even have to decide what clothes to wear: we were not allowed out of uniform while in transit.

Did I have it in me to become a lifer? Liz recoiled when I mentioned to her that if I could have a regular-size bed with her in it, and a private room with bath instead of a 57-bunk barrack with open showers and latrines, I'd be tempted to re-enlist for twenty years: "Imagine, at 43 I'd be eligible for retirement."

That prospect didn't seem appealing to her. She believed in me, she said (whatever that meant?), but she also deplored that I had no ambition, echoing reproaches I heard earlier from Jackie in Chicago. Until I was drafted, I had absolutely no idea what her higher expectations might be. Unlike some of my co-workers at TWA, I had no desire to become a lead agent or a supervisor. So, what else was left besides plodding along? I had to earn a living, and my job at the airport was for sure a hell of a lot better than Ace Metal Refinishers in Chicago. That was *my* frame of reference. *Hers* probably consisted of the "successful" people she routinely met in the course of her work up there in the stratosphere. I sensed she was beginning to give up on me. However, she transferred from San Francisco to the New York international route, which meant that maybe we could meet when feasible during her layovers in Bad Homburg, near Frankfurt.

Actually, thanks to leisure time in the military and the off-duty educational opportunities provided by the Army, I felt like I might now finally be able to accomplish something worthwhile. Maybe I could acquire credentials to become a high school teacher of French, a subject that would enable me to skip over some hurdles, hasten the process, and give me a "competitive advantage"? Or was that too far-reaching a goal? And what would I do without the free travel passes from TWA? To be stranded on the West Coast without periodic trips to New York and Paris would feel like a form of exile.

So, what to do at Fort Dix while waiting for the flight to Frankfurt, besides read? The daily shuttle to Philadelphia through endless suburban sprawl is starting to get tedious. Once you've seen the Liberty Bell, there's not much else to discover. The Christmas cheer in the department stores rings false. And on the Army post I can't stand the board games and other activities organized by USO. I'd rather do nothing, *farniente*, than kill time playing dominoes, checkers, or darts in the rec area. There's even a large assortment of puzzles. What's next? Shuffleboard?

I shouldn't be so hard on USO people. They're well-intentioned civilian volunteers who work diligently to enhance the troops' morale. They even staff booths at the major airports to help homesick or lost GIs. Occasionally, they organize big shindigs abroad, for instance the Bob Hope Hollywood tours to far off military bases. But at home, it's usually small stuff.

Or so I thought, until the morning when posters appeared all over the base: "Dance. Fort Dix gym. The Duke Ellington Orchestra. Free. Brought to you by USO."

What! I couldn't believe my eyes. Duke Ellington! Was it a joke? No, it couldn't be, the posters bore official stamps. But how could the legendary Duke Ellington, whom I would expect to hear in a venue like Carnegie Hall, be appearing at Fort Dix? In a gym no less! On a weeknight! And at a dance! A dance with whom? There weren't any women on base, except for a few WACs.

While mulling over these mysteries, I decided that if my name was called for a flight before the announced date, I would find an excuse to stay behind. I simply couldn't miss such a unique event.

Seven p.m., the awaited night. I head out to the gym, the air cold and clear. I still can't believe this is real. Maybe it will be the Duke Ellington Orchestra minus the Duke?

The athletic area is all lit up. A bus and a truck marked "The Duke Ellington Orchestra" are parked near the building. Military policemen stand by for crowd control. Groups of GIs in uniform are milling around, but everyone has to filter in single file through a narrow entrance. I join the line into the huge hall. No chicks in sight, yet this was billed as a dance. There is no seating, the bleachers remain folded. On the stage, everything seems ready, with the bandstand shields installed, and a grand piano set up to the side. No musicians though. They must be in a huddle in the locker room.

With fifteen minutes to go, and still no sign of females, the MPs start to push the soldiers to the far side of the gym. The line coming in has dwindled, so I decide to go back out to escape from the crush. An MP at the door says "Make up your mind, troop, you might have to wait to get back in."

Outside, an unbelievable sight: The MPs have formed a cordon to the street, where a line of buses marked YWCA awaits to unload its passengers. So, that's where the girls are coming from! As each bus pulls up to the entrance, a matronly woman disembarks with a counter in her hand, which she clicks for each passenger getting out. Last to come down the steps is a second chaperone. The busload gathered on the sidewalk then proceeds inside, and so on with the next batch, under the surveillance of two overseers each time, assisted by the MPs.

The girls are attractive, seemingly in their late teens or early twenties, well dressed, wearing high heels and nylons. They look as much out of place in a lowdown joint like Fort Dix as the Duke Ellington Orchestra. It makes you wonder why they're here. Is it because they want to meet guys, or because they're jazz buffs? The second eventuality seems unlikely, and the first makes no sense: we're all transients, passing through Fort Dix on the way to distant places. The girls look like they might be office workers or such, high school graduates for sure, unattached I assume. The net result is depressing. I have an aversion to organized fun.

The MPs let me back in after the last busload has entered, and I make my way to the far corner of the gym, near the piano. A few moments later, the musicians file in, like a sports team, to loud applause—and take up their positions on the bandstand. They're middle-aged black men, dapper in their coordinated outfits, confident, experienced.

Last in line is the Duke himself. Right then, I understand his nickname. The guy has class written all over him, he *is* nobility, all the way to his patrician name: Edward Kennedy Ellington! I looked up his career in the World Book Encyclopedia at the Fort Dix library. Born in 1899, which makes him sixty-six years old, he still has a lot of spring in his step. You can tell he is clothed by an Italian tailor. Undefinable style. A detail: his suit coat is on the shorter side, giving it a jacket look one wouldn't find in a regular store.

The base commander does a spiel on the public address system to welcome Mr. Ellington and his musicians to Fort Dix. He tells them how honored we are to have them perform for us (I'll say!). He then extends greetings to the Philadelphia young women and their chaperones and thanks the YWCA and USO for making the event possible.

Next he hands the mike over to the charge officer, a captain, who looks directly to the soldiers' side of the hall and lays out the ground rules for the evening with this overflow crowd and the tension rising: "Listen up, men. We expect you to conduct yourselves like the fine soldiers you are. We want as much mingling as possible. No monopolization. This means no more than three dances between partners. There will be one ladies' choice. Return to your respective sides during the brief orchestra breaks. No smoking in the gym, and the restrooms are on this end for the men, and this end for the women. Is that understood, troops?"

All the soldiers yell out "Yessir!" in unison.

And with a grand gesture, the captain motions to the Duke that the evening now belongs to him.

Rather than get engulfed in the mob scene and the frantic jockeying for partners, I stay in my spot near the piano to enjoy the music while observing the band close-up. I'll be a wallflower and if I'm lucky I'll get picked when it's ladies' choice. Fat chance though. One of the sergeants has reminded us that with our shaved heads and olive drab fatigues, we pretty much all look alike. No snazzy West Point or Annapolis uniforms around here to make the ladies swoon.

The Duke hits a key several times, while the musicians tune their instruments. When they're ready, he raises his index finger, and pure satin comes out of their horns. It's as if a ship had just been launched with full sails, free to set its own course. The director abandons the rudder, ambles nonchalantly across the stage, returns to sit at the piano, caresses the keyboard. He surveys the crowd on the dance floor with a magnanimous expression, and leads the musicians with only the slightest glance or gesture. It all looks extraordinarily smooth and effortless. Unlabored perfection. The ensemble produces a sound so gorgeous it almost brings tears to the eyes. And the up-tempo numbers swing with exhilarating drive and passion.

At 10 p.m., after the last set is finished and the applause has ended, the musicians start to pack up their instruments. I haven't moved from my spot the whole time, and I debate whether to go up to the famous composer to tell him how much I enjoyed the music and ask for his autograph. But I don't have a photo or program he could sign, so I give up on this notion, thinking he has probably heard thousands of trite compliments before. I settle for simply watching him banter and unwind with the band. It's clear they genuinely like each other. Looking at the group, I finally understand why Duke Ellington, described in the encyclopedia as "generally considered the most important figure in the history of jazz," has accepted this somewhat demeaning gig: It's to provide work for his seasoned musicians. And my unbounded admiration for Duke Ellington the musical genius is further heightened by this realization.

Out front, the YWCA buses are wrapped in clouds of steam from their engines running at idle to generate some heat inside. They're in the final phase of loading, after a bit of last-minute "monopolization" has taken place anyway, under the resigned glare of the various authorities. The chaperones stand at the door of each bus with their clicker in hand, making sure everyone of their charges is accounted for. The caravan then disappears in the distance, headed back to Philly.

I return to the barracks in the silent night, Duke Ellington's "Mood Indigo" playing in my head.

The reassignment to West Germany held particular interest for me. It seemed to bring me closer to Vera, a young woman in Prague with whom I had begun corresponding. Just before getting drafted, I had obtained for my parents a pass on TWA that they used for their first return to Czechoslovakia in twenty years. My stepfather reconnected there with a cousin of his, whose daughter Vera was employed as a costume assistant in the Barrandov film studios in Prague. Since Vera was studying English, my mother, not so subtle matchmaker, suggested to her that she might develop her language skills by writing to me in California: Imprisoned as I was at Fort Ord, I would be glad to correspond with her.

This went without saying. For my first mailing, I chose a beautiful postcard of the Pacific coast at sunset, and marked on the picture the exact place from which I was writing.

My unexpected assignment to Würzburg, so near to the Czechoslovakian border, intensified the relevance of those written exchanges, suddenly "real." Fate seemed to have a hand in this.

However, despite the proximity, a major obstacle remained: the Iron Curtain. I could not cross it before being discharged from the military. Meanwhile we continued to write, thanks to the courage and generosity of a German friend of mine, who worked as a mechanic in the motor pool of Leighton Barracks. He offered to receive my mail at his home. I had discovered that I was being watched by the U.S. authorities. They frowned on "fraternization" between GIs and people on the communist side of the Iron Curtain.

At Leighton Barracks, located on top of a hill overlooking the beautiful town of Würzburg, I devoted my abundant spare time to studies, or rather credit-gathering through an insane system of cramming. In addition to the counter-espionage people, the staff of the education center watched me closely, suspecting some kind of cheating. But I was only cheating myself, by getting an education on the cheap. I registered for correspondence courses, one at a time, and shortly afterwards requested the prescribed final exams. A couple of days before those exams, all multiple choice, I concentrated my mental powers on preparing for them, and passed handily. The next day I emptied my mind completely, and two or three weeks later went on to the next course and exam.

My perseverance, formerly so fragile, became amazingly strong. One course after another, I would reach my goal. I was entirely available, my military duties being negligible. The essential thing for me was not so much to learn, as to catch up on wasted time. During my sixteen months in Germany, I completed two years of college for free, through this aberrant system, and through University of Maryland extension courses in Würzburg and Frankfurt. Not much of an "undergraduate education," but so favored by luck, and under such privileged circumstances, how can I complain?

My beginnings in Würzburg were marked by a regrettable rift with Sergeant Wright, who led my section. I wanted to expand my horizons beyond the then prevailing GI equation: "One quarter=Ein Mark=Ein Bier, a real one with a thick head of foam, not the sloshy stateside stuff." I was also struck by the newly discovered beauty of the German language and its melodious sound on the radio ("*Meine Damen und Herren, die Nachrichten*"). I therefore decided to enroll in an intensive three-week conversational course offered at our division headquarters. For this I needed Sergeant Wright's authorization.

"I knew it, another shammer!" he said when I presented my request. "No, I'm not signin' this. Ain't English good 'nough fer yew?"

Instead of arguing with Sergeant Wright, which I sensed would be useless, I talked about my application to our company commander, Captain Edwards. He approved it immediately with great enthusiasm. "Learn, Private, always learn, it's the most important thing."

Sergeant Wright didn't take my end run kindly. He swore that I would never be promoted beyond the lowly rank of Private as long as he was there.

A short time later, I won the "soldier of the month" competition, based mostly on knowledge of current events. As winner, I obtained an automatic promotion out of the cellar to the next rank, E-4, and savored this victory over my nemesis. I normally should have reached E-5 before the end of my tour of duty, like most of my friends, but Sergeant Wright was successful in preventing me from attaining further steps on the ladder. From my standpoint, the stakes were strictly financial.

Since I had access to all the personnel files for enlisted men and officers of the 3rd Infantry Division, I checked on his background and discovered that he had not graduated from high school. And like many lifers, he drank milk during the day, but hard liquor after 5 p.m. Alcohol was a safety valve tolerated by the Army.

I also overheard him agonize over an important decision he needed to make in the near future. He was asking for advice all around:

"My brother-in-law says he can get me a job as a salesman in the tool department of a Sears store in Little Rock, Arkansas. But I'm up for reenlistment right now after seventeen years, so I only need three more for retirement. Should I re-up or leave the Army? Will I be able to get used to the outside world?"

He re-upped.

That said, I respected the "room and board" mentality among some of the other lifers. I recognized myself in them.

As a strange coincidence, I was confronted with a dilemma somewhat similar to Sergeant Wright's. My brother-in-law, one of the last saw sharpeners in the Paris region, a disappearing trade, wanted to purchase the tool store of an elderly client of his, Rue de Lappe, in the heart of the Bastille/Saint-Antoine woodworking district of the city. He wanted to hire me, I think mainly for moral support; he worried about the future of these decrepit buildings that seemed destined for demolition.

The temptation to accept my brother-in-law's job offer was great, especially the prospect of living in the colorful Bastille neighborhood, but after mulling over his proposal for some time, I turned it down. I could not in good conscience abandon Maman so far away on the West Coast of America.

Ever since Pépère's stories of the artillery battles of 1914-18 in Eastern France, I had heard that the Army was an important form of education, and found that notion a bit questionable. But my experience in the military caused me to change heart, though for another reason. It is in the Army that my lucidity awoke, as a result of "working" in a cavernous hangar in Würzburg amidst mounds of personnel files. Like an illumination, I suddenly saw and understood the class structure of American society. A topography of injustice appeared before my eyes, clear as a road map, uncannily predictable: scandalous overrepresentation of Blacks in infantry, rotating worldwide between the rice paddies of 'Nam, the mud fields of Germany, the barren hills of Korea; shocking incidence of dental deterioration among Appalachian

Whites (myself included); high rate of recidivism in discipline problems among volunteers, compared to draftees; conspicuous absence of college students; disproportionate number of Southern sergeants ("Now listen up, men. Y'all report ri'chere at seb'm o'clock fer nucular warfahr trainin', y'hear").

In processing OERs (Officer Efficiency Reports) sent yearly to the Pentagon, I also saw the huge degree of conformity required for a career in the Army, as I assume is true of all bureaucratic organizations. Better not rock the boat or have an unsupportive wife if you aspire to promotion.

On April 22, 1967, I was released by the Army that had reconstructed me while it destroyed so many others. I couldn't help but harbor feelings of guilt about my luck. Under the terms of this "European Discharge," I was allowed a period of two months before having to return to the States.

With money saved from replacing other soldiers on guard duty, I bought a used Volkswagen and made arrangements to have it shipped from Bremerhaven to San Francisco prior to flying back. The savings on the purchase price more than made up for the transportation costs.

I finally met Vera in a cafe in Plzen, the first major town in Czechoslovakia after the Iron Curtain. I brought flowers from Nürnberg, the last city in West Germany, to make sure I wouldn't have to deal with shortages on the communist side of the border.

In what language were we going to speak? Czech/Slovak, German, or English? With our lopsided abilities in any of those alternatives, communication seemed daunting, but the two-month clock for my return was ticking, and it must have accelerated our linguistic progress and decision-making. Six weeks later we were married.

Married, yet I returned to the States alone. I resumed working at TWA in San Francisco, and immediately sent Vera a first-class pass so she could join me as soon as she obtained her visa. We thought the process might take a few weeks at most. Seven months later, we still had not received any news, despite repeated inquiries, including a trip I made to the State Department in D.C. To no avail. No response, no information, nothing. Why the delay? We had a clear conscience. Neither of us was a spy. We both began to despair.

One day at lunch in the airport cafeteria, I happened to be sitting across the table from a customs and immigration officer I knew by sight. When I put down my tray, he said "Hi, how are you?" Instead of replying "Fine, thanks, and yourself?" as I normally would, I was unable to mask my feelings: "Not so good."

"Oh, what's wrong?"

I proceeded to describe my hopelessness regarding Vera's visa.

The officer must have taken pity on me, because when he left, he said he couldn't promise anything, but he would see what he could do.

A few days later, I received notification that the visa had been issued. Before my shift started, I dashed to the Customs and Immigration area to thank my Good Samaritan and ask him what he had done to bring about this miracle. "Not much," he said, "I just rummaged around the downtown office and put your wife's file on top of the pile."

Chapter 19

San Francisco Airport, Summer '67

If you're going to San Francisco
Be sure to wear some flowers in you hair.

— *John Phillips/Scott McKenzie hit song, Summer 1967*

He who enjoys crowds will experience feverish delights of which the
egotist, closed like a coffin, and the lazy, interned like a mollusk, will be
eternally deprived. He who enjoys crowds will adopt as his own all the
professions, all the joys, all the miseries that circumstance presents.

— *Baudelaire, "Crowds"*

*M*y return to work at TWA and the endless wait for Vera's visa coincided with a period of chaos in American society: the 1967 "Summer of Love." Thousands of young people from throughout the nation, mostly students, were pouring into San Francisco to "tune in, turn on, drop out." At the same time and in the same place, thousands of GIs were transiting to and from Vietnam, many in caskets: *peace, love, and body bags*. In the midst of all this turmoil, the Silent Majority remained mired in the conformism of the 1950s, and a year later would elect Richard Nixon. The working class of which I was a part didn't know what to make of the contradictory slogans erupting simultaneously: *Flower power; America, Love it or Leave it; Hell No, I Won't Go; Make Love not War; No Shirt, no Shoes, no Service; Burn Baby Burn; Get a Haircut.* From my vantage point at the airport I experienced culture shock about all those new developments, among which the emergence of drugs. Even as a fairly street-wise teenager in Chicago, I had never encountered any. They were strictly for jazz musicians. But now they seemed to be everywhere. Inhaled, injected, ingested too, in scary pill form—barbiturates, amphetamines, reds, blues, greens. To think that I cringed at my mother's three to four daily Bufferins for her arthritis!

"Hey man, wanna go toke up during coffee break?"
"What do you mean, Eddie?"

"Yeah, well I parked my car in Pay Lot Number One near the baggage claim area, and I got me some hash in the glove compartment. Great shit, man, it'll help us float through the shift."

"Well, Eddie, after work maybe, but right now I'll pass. I'd like to keep a clear head."

Actually, I'm scared of that stuff. In this new more responsible phase of my life, a clear head looks to me like the ultimate high.

There's even a rumor about some of the mechanics on graveyard at the hangar smoking pot. In truth, come 3:00 or 4:00 a.m., you don't need to smoke anything to feel giddy. I know, from having worked that ungodly shift myself. By the time 8:00 o'clock rolled around, I was a zombie. But at 3:30, watching flight 15's landing lights emerge from the dark above San Mateo Bridge and descend softly over the hushed San Francisco Bay, I always felt lightheaded. In the silence, from a mile away, you could hear the screech of the tires as the plane touched down on the runway. An instant later, the deafening roar of reverse thrust. The bleary-eyed passengers who deplaned from that late-night sweep across the continent from New York to San Fran via Chicago and L.A. always seemed super-mellow, even when we lost their baggage. Never ran into any irates at that hour.

Eddie is one of the new employees, some with a few college credits, some women, some blacks, all hired while I was gone in the Army. Up to 1965, blacks could only be skycaps and women weren't assigned to physical jobs at the gates, but now most of the heavy push-stairs have been replaced by power-driven jetways that anyone can drive.

Still, progress toward social equality is not as deep as might appear. The director of Selective Service, General Lewis B. Hershey, has stated publicly that only the poor and the uneducated need be concerned about the draft.

In fact, the poorest and most ignorant don't even wait to be called. They enlist! Beats the rat race of working in a factory, or being unemployed, or aimless, or struggling to barely survive. The military can be a laid-back cocoon, so long as the civilians keep the peace. But right now in Vietnam things are unraveling out of control. "Escalation," they call it, "with no light at the end of the tunnel."

Another new employee, Bill, works at the position to my right on the ticket counter. He hasn't slept for a couple of days. He has been taking LSD, grass, uppers, downers. He is a very unusual individual, to say the least. First of all because he is an *educated* family man; the walls of his apartment are lined with paperbacks. Second, because he has become some sort of psychedelic mutant, with his wife's apparent cooperation. He thinks cigarettes and alcohol are "awful," and he is horrified by the sugar we put in our coffee. He calls it "white death." He is also a strict vegetarian. That's why we have to bring our own supplies for the occasional post-swing-shift breakfasts at his place, when, for us, only ham and eggs will do.

Bill is strung out on drugs and he sometimes hallucinates, but he always comes to work on time. His dutiful entrance at exactly 3:30 p.m. at position 4 on the ticket counter is his sacred—and only—anchor in life. He can't get his mind off his recent visit to the San Francisco Zoo, across the street from his apartment. There, he tripped on acid in front of the tiger cage while the beast was devouring a slab of meat. A vision of carnage has since then been obsessing him.

At 6:00 p.m. early lunch in the cafeteria, I bring up an incident for discussion: Two returning soldiers created quite a ruckus when they were denied a beer at the airport's Ishi Bar, for being underage. But I'm ignored. Nobody wants to talk about the war, even though San Francisco is the nearest airport to Travis Air Force Base, and the main point of transit for thousands of servicemen each day.

What's odd about the military this time is that because of the new system of rotation devised by the Pentagon, there are no collective troop movements as in past wars, only a multitude of individual soldiers facing their destinies alone. You jet to 'Nam by yourself, and if you survive you return to the World the same solitary way, 365 days later, with no decompression time, no common experience to share, no camaraderie to soften the shock of reentry. Less than 72 hours after being plucked out of the mosquito-infested southeast Asian jungle in the chaos and fury of combat, you're bumping into indifferent if not hostile civilians at the San Francisco Airport, alone, disoriented, jetlagged.

The topic of conversation among the family men at the cafeteria has to do with house-fixing, as usual. Today, the relative merits of gravel or wood chips instead of grass as maintenance-free cover for garden lawns.

Another interesting change that took place in the two years I was gone is the new ecological awareness, non-existent before. Fred Mower, who used to be considered a cheapskate because he saved his brown paper bag after lunch for reuse the next day, is now viewed as a trailblazing environmentalist. San Francisco has also discovered smog, which previously was thought to exist only in L.A.

I'm thankful when our co-worker Chen enters the cafeteria. He breaks up the tedious homeowner talk with a report on his latest adventures in the Customs & Immigration area. His job, because of his knowledge of Asian languages, is to assist passengers from the Orient who hold connecting flights on TWA. In the process, he tries to steal some ongoing travelers from United and American, who do the same to us: the three airlines have flights leaving simultaneously for the same destinations. But the people most in need of his assistance, especially the elderly, often resist his attention. They have been warned before departure by their wary relatives back in Bangkok, Manila, Hong Kong, or Taipei *not* to follow anyone offering help.

When I return from lunch to the ticket counter, I run into Mike Alsope. He makes do with only one job, even though he has a wife and an infant daughter. My generation of guys is apprehensive about the two-jobs sentence looming for us on the horizon if we have kids, along with Volkswagen commutes to cheaper housing in distant no-money-down subdivisions, past San Jose to the South or Fremont to the East. Mike, for his part, has opted for nearer but permanently fogged-in Pacifica. That cotton shawl wrapping the hills along the coastline is a spectacular sight from a sunny distance, and fun to drive through, but unfit to live in, as far as I'm concerned.

Mike is twenty-four, a year younger than I, full of contradictions. He is one of the most intelligent people I know, yet he married right out of high school. Unlike most of us, he never uses foul language, but he talks incessantly about retirement, forty-one years away. Already he fears he will not see his daughter grow up. The best he can hope for, when he gets some decent seniority, is swing shift with Sundays and Mondays off, or day shift with Tuesdays and Wednesdays.

Mike never smiles, but he has a biting sense of humor. A few days ago, he got me good, when I asked him triumphantly upon returning from break:

"Mike, guess who I just saw in the latrine? I was standing right next to HIM at the pisser!"

"There you go again, eh, celebrity victim. Who is it you saw this time? If you keep this up, one of these days you'll be like that former ticket agent

George Spanek who was planning to write a book titled *Famous People Who've Met Me.*"

"Come on man, try to guess."

"Come on, don't be stupid. There are thousands of people in this airport. How can I possibly guess?"

"Okay, I'll give you a hint: two first names in a row."

"Thanks, that helps a heck of a lot. Look, I have no idea. Tell me who it is you're talking about."

"Ray Charles, man! That's who I just saw, Ray Charles, The Man hisself. I was standing right next to HIM!"

"So what. I bet he didn't see YOU.

At least with Alsope I can talk about things. For instance the slick "up up and away" brochure put out by the company for its public contact employees. It's part of a marketing campaign concocted by the new crop of executives with business degrees, who are displacing the old-line aviation pioneers. A passenger is now called a customer, and a flight is a product. The airline seeks to achieve a youthful, dynamic, friendly corporate image, through a strict uniform and grooming code. "The difference between airlines becomes less and less each year. What makes the difference is people."

Nothing is left to chance in this extraordinarily detailed 21-page document. Reality does surpass fiction: "All females are required to wear a brassiere and underpants... A girdle may be required to correct stomach, seat or thigh problems... Bald men will not be required to wear hairpieces... Beards are not permitted, as their acceptance by the general public is questionable... All shirt buttons must be buttoned... As a general rule, such deviations from standards as overweight, poor hygiene or grooming habits, minor skin problems, teeth irregularities and overall neatness are considered correctable." The brochure addresses weight problems with utmost precision: according to the chart, at 6 feet, my maximum allowable weight is 189 pounds, in uniform, without shoes. "If the employee agrees to take corrective action, a reasonable time will be established by the manager to correct the deficiency. If the standard is not achieved within the prescribed time limit, the matter will be referred to Industrial Relations for consultation on appropriate disciplinary action."

Anything to beat out United and American! Our services are similar, so we compete with gimmicks. A while back, our strategy, since discarded, hinged on "foreign accent" flights. After takeoff, stewardesses donned disposable paper costumes over their uniforms during meal service. Thus, a white Roman toga when lasagna or spaghetti were on the menu; a fraülein outfit for sauerkraut and wurst; cowgirl attire when serving hamburgers on U.S.-bound flights; and so on.

Another creative edict thought up by our clever marketing strategists to personalize service and enhance TWA's "competitive advantage": "You must use the customer's name at least three times in the course of a transaction. It's music to his ears." We comply, because we can be monitored through the squawk box on the counter.

The employees at the Airport Bank have apparently received the same orders. When I go in to cash my weekly check, the tellers feel compelled to greet me by my name, and usually proceed to butcher it, solicitude giving way to embarrassment and stuttering. I am used to it, and have at the ready a smart aleck reply: "In Serbo-Croatian, Kovacovic means 'smith', so please just call me Smith." Whew!

Americans have, sometimes deservedly, the reputation of being nice to a fault. They're capable of saying anything. Once, a teller who had panicked at midpoint with my moniker, stopped, and not knowing what to do, blurted out:

"Oh, you have such a pretty name!"

Couples checking in at the airport. It's interesting to try to figure them out in these new times, when gender roles are being reassessed and nobody knows what to do anymore.

Usually, the husband takes charge, walks up to the counter, puts the baggage on the scale, digs into his pockets for the tickets or the passports, while the wife stands by passively in the background.

Sometimes, in a slightly modified version of the same scenario, he turns towards her: "Honey, give me your purse, would you." Under that arrangement, she carries the paperwork, he lugs the suitcases and makes the decisions.

In the least frequent but most interesting variation, the husband places the baggage on the scale, then steps back, lights up a cigarette and stares around idly while his wife handles the hassles, including excess baggage charges, which can flare up out of nowhere to explosive proportions. No responsibilities, no involvement: he sees himself simply as a porter. Times like that, my co-workers make snide remarks: "We know who wears the pants in that family, don't we."

Let them snicker, I take his side. In my view, this is a lucky dude. He has a "wife," a real one, as sarcastically defined by the feminist movement. But damned if you do, damned if you don't. His fate might be that because he's so adept at avoiding stress, he'll live too long and become one those rare widowers wasting away to decrepitude in a nursing home. And concerning excess baggage, my policy is to close my eyes most of the time, unless provoked by some irritating detail, such as the impatient tap-tapping of a credit card on the counter. Sometimes I charge for 3 pounds excess, sometimes I don't for 50. Depends. To alleviate my guilt feelings about playing God so capriciously, I never ever charge the Basque sheepherders who return home to Spain loaded with gifts for nieces and nephews after their shopping spree in San Francisco at the end of their solitary two-year stints on the ranges of Nevada.

Next in the check-in line is a boy, about 9 years old, escorted by his mother, who looks high class, judging from her clothes and jewelry. She informs me that this is Jimmy, who will be flying by himself to Boston, where he'll be met on arrival by his father. I ask her to fill out the form for unaccompanied children.

We get more and more of these kids of divorced parents criss-crossing the country each summer (the expression "from broken homes" has also disappeared from the lingo). All I know is that she is extremely good looking. Down the counter, I hear some appreciative, not so discreet "Yes's" cast in my direction. It's the code hoot among our co-workers to signal that an exceptionally attractive female has appeared on the radar.

A line of passengers is building up behind Jimmy the unaccompanied minor. His bag is already checked in on the conveyor belt, but he clutches a half-gallon carton of milk.

"You don't have to carry this on board," I tell him. "The stewardesses will give you milk if you want."

"It's not milk I have in there," he answers. "It's my friend. Wanna see him?"

Without waiting for my reply, Jimmy pops open the top of the carton and places it on the counter under my eyes.

"Don't worry, he's harmless," he says. "Take a look."

I peer inside the carton; at the bottom, under a loose eucalyptus leaf, a tiny garden snake folds into a coil.

"Well, Jimmy, I wish I hadn't seen him. Okay, I'll pretend I didn't. But you have to promise that you won't open the carton during flight. You can make a few holes in the sides for air. Promise you won't open it?"

"Okay, I promise."

"By the way, what's your friend's name?"

"Slick."

"That's a great name. Slick the slithering slender snake!"

His mother winks at me. I think she liked the alliteration, but we all have to move on. Wahjo (Roger) Wilkins, who has observed the proceedings from his position further down the counter, and who is hep to everything that's going on, calls me aside to the conveyor belt and, pretending to check some baggage labels, whispers in my ear: "You low life reverse pervert, hitting on kids so you can get to their moms, eh."

Jimmy and his mother gone, my peripheral antennae turn to the position to my left on the ticket counter, where a passenger has just begun a transaction with my friend Max. I overhear the passenger say to him "I'd like *you* to write up my ticket instead of that queen over there." He points to Pete, working at the next position down from Max's.

Ouch! He should have said that in a softer voice, because Pete heard it too.

Pete is in his late forties, a creature of habit, very fastidious in all he does. He comes to work an hour early each day to primp for his shift. At the last moment, he applies a splash of cologne to his face before entering the "arena," as he calls the terminal, with the mindset of a torero facing the bulls. He often engages in altercations with passengers, whom he likes to berate when they show up late and out of breath for check-in. (Don't ruin my day, don't have an icky stroke or heart attack in front of me, is what he really thinks.) A former sailor from the merchant marine, he lives in San Francisco with his long-time partner from Spain, Manuel.

Pete is known for his quick repartee. He steps over to Max's position and tells the passenger: "You know mister, I heard what you said, and it wasn't very nice. I wish you had called me a princess, instead of a queen. It would have made me feel younger."

Speaking of which, another new appellation has popped up while I was gone in the Army: "gay." It used to mean "happy."

Next! Next! Next! Lines are backed up more than ten passengers deep in front of each position. It's easy to get caught up in a routine, ride a rhythm, and stop thinking when checking in so many people.

I used to space out like that all the time when I worked down below on the ramp. Loading mail inside the cargo holds of the 707's was my favorite duty. My partner on the ground would call out the load balance instructions from the weight sheet: "Green Air Mail sacks forward, yellow First Class aft! Let's go!" And he'd hurl the sacks on the conveyor belt at a furious pace to keep them charging up into the cargo pit. The idea was to overwhelm the guy inside and bury him under a mountain of mail. Great fun. Blam! Blam! Blam! Yellow! Green! Green! Yellow! Green!

The higher seniority ramp servicemen didn't look kindly upon those games: "If youse assholes don't slow it down, we're gonna kick the shit outta youse in the parking lot after work. Unnerstand?"

Otherwise, in the invigorating San Francisco Bay breeze, which always startled the lightly clad summer tourists—"*This* is California? Hell, it's cold out here"—, the only thing that could disrupt our mindless synchronic rhythm in loading mail bags was the starting up of jet engines at nearby gates.

Those were mailbags, but people induce the same kind of lobotomized trance when they keep coming at you relentlessly. The next passenger in line asks for a ticket to L.A.:

"Last name, please."
"Brando."
"First initial?"
"M."
"N? like... euh... euh... Nancy?"
"No, not N, M! M, like Marlon."
"Oh, yes, of course. I'm sorry, Mr. Brando."

I have barely recovered from this unfortunate lapse of attention—in my defense it must be recognized that, on screen, movie stars loom larger than life and I'm not used to looking *down* at Marlon Brando—when I sense that people are beginning to avoid my line, as happens when an intimidating presence such as a Hell's Angel or a Black Panther checks in. Something's wrong. When the last passenger in queue reaches the counter, I discover the reason: standing in front of me is a broad-shouldered individual whose face is covered by a grotesque mask of dingy-grey papiermâché, topped by a cotton rain hat. There are lots of outlandish characters in San Francisco these days, sightseers even come out to the airport to watch the rock bands board the notorious PSA "Midnight Special" flight to L.A., but what's this? Couldn't be a holdup, you don't wait in line looking like that to pull a robbery.

Writing the ticket gives me an excuse to look away from the guy. I can't bear even glancing at him. His eyes are scarcely visible through the slits in the mask.

Good thing I didn't smoke with Eddie during break. I'd have a fit of pothead paranoia at this point. Still, I'm paralyzed. Small talk with this passenger is inconceivable. He begins to hit the counter lightly, with contained force, his fists clenched, his knuckles bursting white. A distorted, muffled voice comes through the mouth hole in the mask. I listen with total concentration, aware that I don't have the option to say: "I'm sorry, I didn't understand, could you please repeat."

"I suppose you wanna hear what happened to me?"

"Euh, yes, I do."

"Look, man, I'm wearing this mask 'cause I don't have a fucking face anymore."

And he proceeds to tell me, with understandable rage, that he was a victim of friendly (Ha!) fire in Vietnam, a glob of napalm searing into his face.

When the transaction is over, the hapless veteran slips away from the counter, collar up, hat pulled down to shield himself from the world. His flight doesn't leave for another hour. I call the ramp control agent to have the three seats in the front row blocked for him so he can be alone if the plane isn't full. That's the least we can do...

All this Vietnam aftermath is seriously rattling me. I lucked out, in spite of myself, being sent to Germany after the rejection from Officer Candidate School. Fate? A benevolent computer at the Pentagon? Almost everyone in my basic training unit ended up in 'Nam. Which means I'm left with a bad case of survivor's guilt confronting me daily at the airport. That disfigured guy could easily have been me.

Just two weeks ago, I visited my old TWA swing-shift buddy Steve at Letterman Hospital. He got drafted a year after me, and was being repatriated stateside from 'Nam for mental disorders. On the way in to his psychiatric ward, I had to pause and go outside for air, so sickened was I by the sight of all those crippled, mutilated guys lying around. Immediately upon greeting me in his hospital garb of T-shirt, boxer shorts, and shower thongs, he told me that he was faking it, that he had the shrinks buffaloed, that he was sure he would be getting out soon on a medical discharge. But he couldn't wait to press into my hand a couple of glossy black-and-white photographs stashed away in his night stand, showing a squad of GIs drinking beer and holding up decapitated heads of Vietcongs, like trophies. I didn't muster the courage to ask him whether he had taken those pictures himself. His voice took on a feverish tone, though, when he insisted on telling me that before he arrived in 'Nam, it was common to "cut the gooks' ears off" to get accurate body counts.

At the airport, it's difficult not to think of Vietnam, there are reminders of the war everywhere, yet life goes on as if that faraway hell didn't exist. Nobody wants to disturb the civilian routine. A while later during my shift, I'm reassigned to the concourse, to meet inbound flights and help close out outbounds.

Pandemonium and wails at the arrival gate of the Rome-New York-San Francisco flight. Entire clans of Italian-Americans spanning several generations await the appearance of the Mammas, the old and frail black-scarved matriarchs from Sicily, here on their once-in-a-lifetime visit to their descendants in the New World. The tumultuous crowd provides a warm respite from the ambient militarism and decadence. As if distracted by the turbulence inside the terminal, the pilot overshoots his parking spot, and is waved around again by the signalman. He angrily revs up the 707's turbofan engines, unleashing a hurricane of fumes against the buckling gateroom windows. I put on my earplugs, drive the jetway up to the plane and abandon my position before getting engulfed in all the shrieks and the mayhem.

No sooner has the Italian crowd dispersed than delegations of long-haired barefoot hippies in flowing psychedelic garments descend upon the airport from their haunts in the Haight-Ashbury. They dance to the sound of tambourines and tinkling bells, and they sing, burn incense, throw flowers at the startled disembarking businessmen who exude competing scents of freshly-applied breath sweeteners and after shave lotions. Holding their briefcases up like shields, their stocky frames ensconced in the armor of three-piece suits, the salesmen and executives in hard, cleated Florsheim Imperial wing-tip shoes cut a sharp swath through the gambolling herd, and brush off the floral offerings with hostile grunts: "Get away from me, creeps."

On the sidewalk out front, a pack of dogs cavorts under the exasperated watch of the airport police while their masters frolic inside. My only regret is

that this is not a presidential election year, with throngs of Republican del-
egates arriving at the airport for their national convention like they did three
years earlier, in 1964, when they nominated arch-conservative hawk Barry
Goldwater. He was creamed by Johnson, who promised "No 'Merican boys
in Vitnem" but promptly cranked up the war once he was elected.

Though the hippies are great fun to look at, we working stiffs have a nagging suspicion that they're simply privileged brats on a temporary lark. How
else can you explain their contempt of employment? Somebody's got to feed
them. Or maybe we're just jealous?

The Washington flight returns from the runway to its departure gate. Bomb
scare. Most likely a crank call, but we have to take all threats seriously. "All
passengers deplane, please! Baggage inspection." Everybody complies calmly,
except one: Dr. Edward Teller, father of the H bomb, who thought that the
A's dropped on Hiroshima and Nagasaki were too puny for the Russkies, so he
devised one that had *a thousand times* more explosive power. His thick eyebrows
quiver: "Zis is terrible. Zese people voo make phone calls like zat are sick. Pro-
paply kommunists, or hippies on druks. Zey don't even vash." His own thermo-
nuclear business must be booming. Our Albuquerque, Las Vegas, and Washington flights are heavily patronized by his Lawrence-Livermore Nuclear Weapons
Lab people, regular fellows in short-sleeved shirts and corduroy jackets with
patches at the elbows, smoking pipes, wearing turquoise and silver Navajo string
ties and comfy Hush Puppy shoes, doing what they call "interesting science."

Dr. Teller's rants continue, by now he sounds like an old-testament tyrant spewing out incoherent fire and brimstone about TWA in a thick Hun-
garian accent. I decide he has gone over the edge and can be classified as
"irate." Following standard operating procedures, I offer to let him speak to
our Passenger Relations Representative, Mr. Owens. Usually, a mere change
of interlocutor works wonders to defuse tense situations like this, transform-
ing raging lions into embarrassed, apologetic lambs. Not so with Dr. Teller-
Strangelove. "I don't vant to talk to any other jerk," he replies, killing two
birds with one stone.

In the ramp office, the flight information coordinator, who has no sense
of humor and readily admits he loves chess but hates people, stares at his
planning board, one hand scratching his brow, the other unconsciously
reaching into the jar of Tums. He doesn't worry about bombs, conventional
or nuclear, only his messed-up gate assignments for the rest of the evening.

With all the confusion, I screw up real bad and forget my assignment to the Polar flight arrival at the international concourse. The supervisor lashes out at me: "Look, Kovic, I told you more than twony minutes ago that he was cleared to land. Now he's been waiting at the gate with no stairs. You better get over there quick, 'cause if the captain writes us up, you've had it."

Just what I need, now that they're evaluating my application to work Saturdays and Sundays only, with continued seniority rights, health insurance, and pass privileges. With my two years of college credits gleaned in the Army, I'm contemplating to go on with my studies under the GI Bill. Our veterans' entitlements are pretty measly compared to earlier periods, but California tuition is reasonable, and I think completing a degree might be feasible if I can keep my job two days per week at TWA. The full-time employees are supportive of this arrangement, which will free someone up on the week-ends. These intricate negotiations, now possibly jeopardized, race through my mind as I tear across the ramp toward the international concourse.

The Polar flight, TWA's flagship run from Paris non-stop to the West Coast, sits on the tarmac, its red and white fuselage glistening in the crisp night air against the backdrop of the San Bruno hills lapped by the usual blanket of fog that stretches in from the ocean, and suddenly stops at the crest. I'm glad to hear the engines still running, because that way I can ask the captain to blame the delay on ground traffic. I'll tell him I got sidetracked by the Washington flight's bomb scare. He'll understand, I hope.

An Australian mechanic getting ready for the Qantas arrival from Sydney at the next gate helps me shove our push stairs into motion. "Bloody heavy, mate, aren't they! Cheeeeers!" Emerging out of nowhere, a Philippine Airlines ramp serviceman flings his wiry bantam frame into the opposite side of the stairs to straighten our crooked trajectory. "What happen, TeeWAy? Your plight been here pibe minutes already."

My plight! How correct he is! The big Aussie and I lumbering on one side, the agile Pilipino shadowboxing on the other, I'm assailed by a disturbing premonition: **WE WILL LOSE THE VIETNAM WAR.**

The Polar flight's front cabin door pops open after my knock.

"Well, it's about time, San Fran. Oh, Hi, Red. How you doin'. Long time no see."

It's Moms, TWA's highest seniority stewardess, a legendary figure at the airline, the mother of us all, survivor of two crashes, the first one in a DC3. Nobody
knows or cares about her age. She's always ready to extend herself, do errands,
help out with red tape procedures, shop on your behalf for items, frivolous or not,
at the other end of the world. She has spent most of her life aboard airplanes,
and done the TWA round-the-globe route. After work she commutes "home,"
either to Hawaii or Bermuda, depending on whether she happens to be based
at the time in San Francisco or New York. Her skin is permanently tanned and
leathery, from the sun at the beach or the ozone at 33,000 feet.

Mom's longevity is exceptional. Like with the ground personnel, the situation with stewardesses is changing radically, from an adventuresome, even
glamorous bachelorette profession, to just plain waitressing. They used to work
on average a couple of years before getting married to a passenger or crew
member, and then had to quit, but now there's talk they'll be able to continue
flying even after marriage. The "coffee, tea, or me" image is beginning to fade.

A glance down the long cabin tube confirms my fears: the aisle is jammed
with passengers itching to get out through the single front exit. Moms makes
an announcement on the P.A. system to get everyone back in their seats so
the health inspector can conduct his walk-through with a spray can of disin-
fectant. A French passenger in the first-class lounge grumbles: "Zis country
is like a fortress. Not only do ze Americans require a visa and all kinds of ze
papers, but zey also treat us like if we have ze plague or some horrible disease.
This is worse than the Union Soviétique."

I recognize this passenger from a previous encounter and acknowledge
his mutterings with a nod of agreement. He is some sort of high-level trade
representative who travels all over the world to explore potential markets for
French products. During a flight delay a while back, I had an opportunity
to chat with this chronically impatient complainer who actually had all the
time in the world. Mistaking me for a genuine American, he asked me what
products from France I thought might have a future in the United States. I
half jokingly answered "wine and bicycles."

"Non, non, my friend, impossible" he replied, "I know ze Amérique well,
and in zis country ze wine is only for ze winos, Thunderbird or Silver Satin in ze
paper bag from ze liquor store you know, and ze bicycle are only for ze children."

I almost added a third product, bottled water, to my list of promising
French exports to the United States, but held back at the last moment from
this too blatantly ridiculous notion.

After the interminable full load of passengers has deplaned, and I have obtained the captain's assurance that he won't file a discrepancy report, Moms
briefs me about the leftover first class Ambassador Service goodies, which
are supposed to be dumped in the garbage by ground personnel on arrival—
violations punishable by immediate firing.

"All right, I've got some filet mignons in the oven for you guys, and I
left three Rémy Martin cognac miniatures in the pocket behind seat 2C. The
cheese tray has hardly been touched, the Camembert is fantastic, and there is
an open bottle of really great Château Something in the galley to go with it.
There are also two baguettes, but they're pretty crusty now after the twelve-
hour flight. For God's sake, don't get caught."

She then launches into her predictable tirade from the past: "By the way
Red, when are you gonna listen to me and go to college? You got a good start
already with all them languages you speak. Education is so important!"

"Yeah Moms, I know, I know."

"Don't vegetate like this too long! I've seen it happen to so many people
at the airlines, myself included. Do something with your life! Either get married and have kids, or else go to college."

"Come on Moms, give me a break, let me breathe, I just got out of the
Army. And I'm now married but my wife can't get her visa."

Moms is so categorical in presenting only two options for my future, that I
don't have the heart to tell her there's a third alternative: Per Moe's. It doesn't
apply to me anyway, I don't have the required perseverance or discipline, I live
for the moment. But if he can bring off his project, wow!

Moe is an immigrant from Norway who works as a baggage and freight load-
er on the ramp. For whatever reason, he is not threatened by the draft. He is now
in the middle of his five-year plan to retire at thirty. Meanwhile, he accepts to have
no life. He doesn't own a car, he rents a room in a boarding house near the airport
in South City, he is available for duty around the clock. His paychecks must be
astronomical, with all kinds of overtime and double-time, and he invests it all. The
Wall Street Journal is always sticking out of his back pocket. Nobody knows how
much he has managed to accumulate so far, but his mellow, confident attitude
indicates he's on track. His determination is phenomenal. We all root for him.

My next assignment is to process the half-fare youth standbys on the New
York flight. Most of them are college students on draft deferments of one

kind or another. Why not! More power to them. Unlike us from the working class, students have goals, a vested interest in the future. They're allergic to the military. But they waited too long to protest effectively against the war, thinking they were sheltered from conscription. Their lack of class solidarity has come to bite them. The draft has run out of proletarian cannon fodder and is now starting to grab them too. My conclusion: The only way to prevent disastrous military adventurism of the Vietnam kind in the future is to have an *equitable* draft and/or an immediate war tax, in order to focus everyone's attention right from the start, while it's still feasible to stop the juggernaut.

This summer, the students are traveling light. Their baggage consists of a cardboard box with a sleeping bag in it and a few odds and ends. They've had their fling in San Francisco and now they're returning home to their regular life. The only outrageous thing they haven't done during their summer binge is to get tattoos, because that's low class and permanent. I'm there to check I.D.s and make sure everybody wears shoes and a shirt before boarding the plane. The engines are already running, and there is much pushing and jostling. "Can I get on? Can I get on? Please, I gotta get back to New York before tomorrow."

Two other foreign-born agents are handling the flight with me. They're from countries where *backshish* is a way of life. They can't get over the lack of corruption in America in situations like these. In their former countries, they say, a standby would not implore and beg, but simply point to a $20 bill discreetly tucked in the envelope under his ticket, and ask the agent to see what he could do for him. I confirm to them that in the U.S. low-level transactions are indeed clean, but that on the other hand, Lockheed has been known to buy up half of the Japanese government.

The student standbys look unkempt and unwashed, but I know for a fact that they take good care of their teeth. Along with no tattoos, that's where they draw the line on neglect and self-abuse. I took the same flight to New York on pass a few days back. As soon as the "fasten seat belt/no smoking" sign went out after take-off, and everybody lit up their cigarettes, you could see through the haze the standbys lining up for the restrooms with toothbrush and dental floss in hand. What a contrast with basic training in the Army! There we had to sit through a series of horror films about gum disease and tooth decay, too late for many of us, especially the Appalachian guys.

Moms is right about school and learning. It's amazing how much confidence a little education can bring. When I first arrived in Germany, in the middle of winter, we had to put up with all kinds of harassment, such as standing outside in the bitter cold for useless reveille formation at 5:30 every morning. A year later, we barely managed to get out of our bunks at 7:00 to eat breakfast. We stopped making our beds or shining our shoes, FTA—Fuck The Army—became our motto. This transformation was brought on by an influx of new draftees with some college background (still no real students). The semi-literate sergeants were easily intimidated by the magical threat, suddenly credible: "You fuck with me, Jack, and I'm writing my congressman." The Vietnam returnees, many of them addicted to drugs including heroin, also contributed to this defiant new attitude.

Meanwhile, below the boarding gates, the evening's complement of Human Remains from 'Nam continues to accumulate on the tarmac. Near the massive crates trucked in from Air Freight and lined up ready for loading into the cargo pits, a ramp serviceman engages in loud protest with his supervisor:

"Fuck man, I already loaded three tonight. I'm tired of always getting stuck with the backbreaking stuff. Put me on mail or baggage and assign these H.R.s to somebody else."

"Are you refusing to do work I'm assigning to you, Jones?"

"Fuckin-A right, man. Get somebody else."

"Why do you have to be so foul-mouthed about it?"

The uniformed soldiers on Human Remains escort duty pretend not to hear the exchange. They shuffle nervously, diligent to keep track of the individual casket for which they are responsible. If it is loaded on the wrong plane, they will be court-martialed.

The supervisor's reproachful tone transports me back two years earlier, to basic training at Fort Ord. All the platoons in Company B-1-4 have been assembled for a sermon by the post chaplain: "You troops WILL clean up your act! The way you talk is disgusting! All I ever hear from you is F this, F that, F this, F that. Don't you know any other words? A good soldier is not foul-mouthed! If you want models of proper military conduct, follow the example of your officers and NCOs."

Moments before, during bayonet practice, a drill sergeant had been exhorting us to yell "Kill! Kill! Kill!": "Listen up, men! You gotta scream and lunge with all your might or else you won't stick it in, the blade will be deflected by the rib bone. You troops had better learn this right, 'cause it ain't no make-believe no more. You're probably all goin' you know where at in a couple months, and when you're nose to nose with Charlie in the jungle, it's either you or him. Once you stick in your bayonet, you'll have to pull it out with all you've got if you want to retrieve your weapon. Use your feet to yank the body away. Any questions? OK, take a short break. Smoke 'em if you got 'em."

Maybe Jones swears because that's the only way he can express his anguish at the prospect of spending another half-hour inside a cramped cargo pit, alone with a casket, tugging it to its proper tie-down position, packing smaller items around it, imagining the contents, probably dismembered parts of a human body in a plastic bag. Those remains could be his own in a few months. Being young and unmarried and not a student, and lacking connections to be assigned stateside in the National Guard, he'll get drafted anytime.

Off in the distance on the airport tarmac, a similar scene unfolds at American and at United Airlines. During my two-year absence, airfreight revenue at TWA has increased by 400 per cent. Several passenger planes and crews have been leased to Military Transport Command to fly troops directly out of Travis to Saigon. We have new openings in Guam and Honolulu. Many of the employees who weren't drafted have been promoted to management.

In the showrooms of the land, compact cars are making way for large automobiles again. No more austerity. The American economy is going up, up and away, just like TWA.

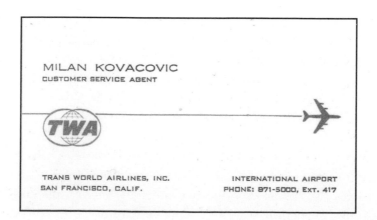

Sole use for this card: In case an irate passenger demands my identification.

Chapter 20

Oxford-by-L.A., the Oasis at Claremont

"In France, we don't even know such places could exist."

— *Jean Malaurie, visiting scholar, speaking of Oxford University, England.*

One a.m. Loud banging at the apartment's front door. Vera and I bolt out of bed. It's probably the neighbors, reacting to our repeated three knocks on the wall—an old European custom meaning hey, it's late, cut the noise.

Towering in the entrance is a black guy, about 6'5", 250 pounds, shirtless, looking mighty peeved. A long-toothed comb is planted like a pitchfork in his hair puffed up into an Afro. He says to Vera, "Move over, I wanna talk man to man wit' your husband."

Then, glaring at me: "Say, what's with the knockin' on the wall?"

"Well, euh, just trying to get you to turn down the stereo."

"Look man, I work swing shift at the warehouse down the road, and when I get home I like to cook me up some chow and listen to music. You got a problem wit' that?"

"Well, your music's fine, in fact I like it a lot, especially your James Brown records, but this time of night it's not music, it's noise."

"Then get yourself some earplugs, man, or somethin'. Look here, I work hard, I pay my rent, I got a right to kick back and relax when I come home from my job. So cut that shit out and let me be, dammit!"

Whew! A confrontation for sure, but not as drastic as could have been. If things had turned physical I wouldn't have stood a chance.

Unexpected neighbor trouble in Claremont Village, the low-income housing project where we've just moved in. Vera is five months pregnant, and our son Paul two and a half years old. It's September 1973, the start of my final year at Claremont Graduate School—a beautiful oasis nestled less than a mile from the "Village" in the midst of the Los Angeles suburban sprawl, but worlds away in all other respects.

We've just returned from a year abroad for my studies in Nice, on the French Riviera, with the same Mediterranean climate as L.A., and we're renting a two-bedroom apartment for a blanket rate of twenty-five percent of our income, as are all the families in the compound. A godsend really, not only from the financial standpoint, but also because it's difficult to find rentals that accept children. Owners and managers turn you away as soon as they see a kid or a pregnant woman. Some ads even state "No children, small pets OK." What a contrast with Nice, where Paul, dubbed "*le bébé américain*," was doted on everywhere like a prince.

Except for the shortcuts on soundproofing, Claremont Village is in my mind a successful example of the Great Society housing programs started by the Johnson administration and continued under Nixon. No high rises, two-story max, with leafy grounds and play areas for the kids. However, the apartments are not appreciated enough by everyone who lives there, according to the manager. He doesn't hide his displeasure concerning the tenants. He treats us differently, maybe because we're graduate students, the (hopefully) temporary poor living among the real poor.

I can support my family at a frugal level with my stipend, and the astronomical university tuition is taken care of by a fellowship. We qualify for MediCal, a great comfort what with the forthcoming childbirth. We're also eligible for food stamps, but they're not worth the hassle for what you get, so we haven't applied for them.

Personally, I love living in the Village. It suits my "room and board" mentality and reminds me of the lively atmosphere in the Black neighborhoods of Chicago when I first arrived in America. Bobby Blue Bland's gritty songs were my lifeline back then, on the Bronzeville radio station that I tuned in to nurse my wounds from having left Paris. I owe a big debt of gratitude to Black culture. But the fracas at Claremont Village in the wee hours is too much to bear. What to do? My neighbor has a valid viewpoint, and so do I.

The confrontation that night led nowhere, the noise continued. What to do? As the only Whites in our section of the Village, we wanted to avoid any racial tension. The demographic makeup had radically changed from our previous stay there two years earlier, when the compound was brand-new, and a fairly equal Black and White distribution prevailed. That year our neighbors were a young White couple, barely above their teens, with a baby, and I marveled at how soundproof the buildings were, until one day, toward the end of our stay, I heard someone retching in the bathroom next door, as if that awful scene was taking place in our own apartment. It turned out that these young parents had simply been very quiet all along. They liked above all to smoke pot and meditate. They hated the "sterile" environment of Claremont Village, where deviance from the beige color scheme in interior decor was prohibited, and no exterior touches allowed. They wanted to paint their living room purple. As soon as they could, they moved to nearby Pomona into a rundown boarded up house, of which there were many in the area. It had a magnificent palm tree and a lot of junk in the front yard. They promptly decorated their dream home inside and out in brilliant psychedelic colors.

Had we during the intervening year become uptight "honkies" with a low threshold of tolerance for noise? Was this a clash of two cultures (there had been some racial tensions over the same issue in the Claremont campus dorms), or was it just boorish behavior on the part of our neighbor? And what about his family? How did they manage to sleep in the tumult, when the TV sometimes vied with the stereo full bore into the night?

Finally, at wit's end, we found a solution without resolving the problem. Toddler Paul slept in the bedroom located at the opposite end of the apartment, sheltered from the noise. Nothing seemed to disturb him once his head hit the pillow. So, we simply switched rooms with him. And though the noise continued, it ceased to bother us.

In February, after our daughter Laurie's birth (we nicknamed her Rosebud for her complexion), Vera moved for two months with the children to my mother's place near San Francisco, so I could concentrate on finishing my dissertation. Reduced to pedestrian status and undistracted except for a survey course on familiar French authors that I taught twice a week at Scripps, one of the Claremont colleges, I was able to simplify my life to the extreme and devote my undivided time and attention to meeting the June deadline. Papers and notes littered the floor of the apartment, and I lived on a routine fare consisting of a Swanson TV Dinner in the evening, and for lunch a California Burger that I fetched on foot, between cars lined up at the *In-N'-Out* drive-through shack located across a vacant lot from the Village compound—the epitome of "barbarian" L.A. carefree living, which in these circumstances appealed to me greatly.

Several times each day during those two months of intense concentration, I'd step out to the grassy area in front of the apartment to stretch my legs and clear my mind. More often than not I'd find there my neighbor Ike, walking around barefoot too, or doing push-ups like in a prison yard, killing time until his afternoon shift at the warehouse. On each occasion he greeted me with an eager "Was happenin', man?" to which, cloistered as I was, I could offer no interesting reply. We did engage in some banter, though, mostly about our favorite soul singers, or occasionally about weightier subjects, for instance the police harassment that sometimes occurred at night, when a helicopter hovered above the Village, and illuminated it with powerful floodlights for no apparent reason.

Unbeknownst to me, during our year in Nice, seemingly peaceful Claremont Village had gained a reputation for crime and vandalism, although my family and I never experienced anything untoward in the compound. Shortly after Laurie's birth, my main professor Mr. Leggewie and his wife, sweet people both, came down one afternoon from their beautiful house with swimming pool in nearby Padua Hills, to bring a baby gift. They acted somewhat nervous, though, as if they were visiting a dangerous place. Was it safe to leave the Mercedes in the visitors' parking area, they asked, to my surprise.

Once, I mentioned to Ike that Vera's parents, during their visit with us from Czechoslovakia, had admired the spiffy way in which the black women and their children primped up for church every Sunday, and how sloppy we looked in comparison, and how we should emulate them. That got quite a laugh from him. He said, "Man you guys don't even go to church, and besides I can't imagine your boy wearin' a starched white shirt and bow tie, or your baby girl one of them frilly outfits, or your wife gettin' up at five on Sundays to have her hair done up."

Ike and I became good friends, abstracting the midnight R & B concerts that continued daily. This annoyance was never evoked in our conversations, nor did it need to be: the problem had been solved. And toddler Paul apparently wasn't damaged by the unfair sleeping arrangement during his time in the Village, judging from his adult career as a pianist and composer noted among other things for his excellent sense of rhythm.

Living in the compound was fine with me. I had to pinch myself, though, to make sure I wasn't dreaming every time I entered the utopian world of the nearby Claremont Colleges.

The Graduate School sits at the center of a gorgeous campus consisting of six independent yet affiliated private colleges (Pomona, Scripps, Claremont-McKenna,

Harvey Mudd, Pitzer). Although not well known by the general public, these colleges are considered the "American Oxford" in academic circles, for their unique mode of organization based on shared resources and distinctive identities, like the British model. The campus forms an enclave at the foothills of snow-capped Mount Baldy, on the northern edge of the L.A. megalopolis that stretches eastward all the way to the desert amidst a jumble of orange groves, car washes, shopping malls, freeways, subdivisions. Sheltered from this urban sprawl, the Claremont Colleges are a tranquil oasis of fountains, lawns, Mediterranean tile roofs, and slender coconut trees reaching high into the sky above chubbier palms and fragrant eucalyptuses. Flowers bloom everywhere in breathtaking displays, my favorites the hibiscus and the bougainvilleas aflame on the facades of beautiful buildings. Paradise! Southern California as it once was, except for the smog, which after a while people choose to ignore. Things are never totally perfect...

I ended up in this school through sheer luck. At registration time, I couldn't believe what people paid for tuition. They had to be either rich or deep in hock. Or else like me on fellowships. My miraculous access to this heaven on earth warrants some explanation:

I came from a social class reluctant to incur debt, especially for something so intangible as "education," which in my world could only be conceived of as free, or at least affordable—certainly not the case at Claremont. Later in life, I developed a more relaxed but not necessarily wiser middle class view of credit. Whereas the heroic tale of success up until my generation had been "I started out with nothing...", the emerging version became "I started out with big student loans to repay, like a mortgage, and I married my college sweetheart, so now we owe double."

After release from the Army, with my two years' worth of college credits gleaned while in the service, I could envisage completing a degree. Prior to that, it had seemed too long a haul for my patience, my perseverance, and my wallet.

Eligible, like all veterans, for the GI Bill, I returned to work week-ends at the San Francisco Airport, with top pay scale and full benefits acquired through six years' seniority (how things have changed in part-time employment since then!). I enrolled at reasonably-priced California State University, Hayward, which I chose over equally distant San Francisco State because there was no ocean fog and less traffic for the seventeen-mile commute.

Even if for the wrong reasons, it was a fortunate choice. At Hayward I met a professor, Élie Vidal, who offered me guidance and became a lifelong mentor and friend. He lived in the Berkeley hills overlooking San Francisco Bay, was originally from Algeria, Jewish, seventeen years older than I, and married to a brilliant and beautiful California native, Mary. I admired him among other things for his powerful intellect, his proficiency at sports, his ability to repair the exotic DS Citroën car ("engineer's dream, mechanic's nightmare") he had brought back from France. He taught courses on the medieval poet François Villon, the sixteenth century essayist Michel de Montaigne, and the 20th Century writer Albert Camus. Studying Camus with Elie in Hayward in the summer was like being transported to the Mediterranean coast of Algeria where both he and Camus had grown up. In his retirement, he wrote a fabulous memoir, *Adieu Béni-Saf*, describing the rich multicultural world of his childhood.

When I told Élie that my goal was to become a high school French teacher, he recoiled and said that in that case I should stay with my job at the airport. He described secondary school teaching in the U.S. as an honorable but backbreaking underpaid endeavor, with 25 hours of classroom duty per week plus a bunch of other responsibilities. "Don't even consider it," he said, with such conviction that I felt obliged to take note.

To alter a destiny, a few words, so rare, are sometimes sufficient. His were clear, committed, decisive: "You must get a doctorate."

Following up on this seemingly far-fetched notion, he informed me that Claremont Graduate School had received a prestigious grant to develop a new interdisciplinary terminal degree, the D.A. (Doctorate of Arts), designed to provide better preparation for college teaching than the traditional Ph.D., deemed too narrowly focused. "You should apply," he said. I did.

Lo and behold, I received an invitation to fly down to L.A. for an expense-paid interview. I was tremendously impressed by the campus and the personalized attention I received, including lunch in the Dean's house, and I hoped I had likewise made a good impression. A few days later I received a letter offering me free tuition, a stipend for living expenses, and, in view of my impending fatherhood, a family supplement.

I consulted my co-workers at TWA. They advised me to turn down the offer: "Stay at the airport, go back to full-time. With your college credits you might get promoted to lead agent or supervisor. And what about the travel passes? Can you imagine living without them?"

Also, whereas my view of a teaching career was that it would keep me young by maintaining contact with young people, the pessimists opined that on the contrary, teaching would make me feel old because the age gap with students would widen each year.

The naysayers' reactions made me hesitate. Upon this, I received a follow-up letter from the associate dean of Claremont. He expressed surprise that I had not yet accepted his school's generous offer, especially since I was the only candidate from a public institution among the four who had been selected.

From a public institution? Naive and unaware of the topography of American higher education, I felt slighted. I had had great teachers at Cal State Hayward.

After anguishing for several more days, Vera helped me decide: "OK, we go."

How disconcerting to have dithered so long to accept such a fabulous offer! Levels of consciousness can be sorely deficient, and it's important to choose advice wisely. My mother, whom I also consulted, gave me her usual recommendation: "Do what you think it be best."

I discovered at Claremont a world and a set of attitudes completely different from what I had encountered until then in America. One of the participants in the D.A. program almost became physically ill when we visited the Cal State L.A. campus for an overview of higher education institutions in the region. She was accustomed to a more aesthetic, more genteel, less crowded environment.

In Art and Architecture class, a student unwittingly insulted me when she made the following remark: "I can't imagine how people can live in homes that don't reflect their personality." If she had visited my apartment in the housing complex, she would have concluded I had *no* personality.

In that class, not surprisingly, I launched into a impassioned defense of the "tyrannical humanist" French architect Le Corbusier when I learned he had found a way to completely soundproof each unit in his apartment buildings. Would that he had been heard by other builders and architects!

The seemingly relaxed environment of the Claremont colleges—with sunbathers lounging on the grass and others throwing frisbees—belied a different reality. I was surrounded by extraordinarily driven high achievers. A Pomona student from Wyoming, heavy pot smoker who roomed with one of my classmates, whipped out an eighty-page senior project for his honors B.A. degree in three days. And at Harvey Mudd, the college that focused on science and engineering, the average SAT score was 750 for math and 700 for language, with just about everyone also participating in musical ensembles—junior Einsteins and their violins. I frequented Harvey Mudd because it had the best outdoor swimming pool, with a vaguely Aztec design.

Students at the Claremont Colleges lived either on-campus or nearby, without burdensome external employment to take them away from their academic or recreational pursuits. A far cry from the Cal State Hayward commuter scene, where students often faced jobs on the night shift, along with transportation problems and unfavorable living conditions. When I taught there as an inexperienced and insecure graduate assistant, a student once complained to me that I assigned too much homework. To my response that I would consider lightening up the load, but that first he should improve his attendance, he replied matter-of-factly "I wasn't here last week 'cause my uncle stabbed my dad."

I thoroughly enjoyed the Claremont Doctorate of Arts program and its personalized transdisciplinary perspective. It was a perfect fit for me. I don't think I would have fared so well in a more conventional and restrictive Ph.D. setting. My enthusiasm about the school even made me lose my San Franciscan condescension toward Los Angeles. I began to appreciate many aspects of life in the often disparaged Southern California city.

Although there's much more I could say about the Claremont Colleges, all with everlasting gratitude and admiration, I will single out one anecdote to complete the circle of my formal education.

One day, Mr. Leggewie had lunch at the faculty club with Professor Johnson, a colleague of his from the Salvatori Center—a noted conservative think tank housed on campus, and at that time, 1973, laying the groundwork for a Reagan presidency. They discussed various national school systems, and in the course of their conversation, Mr. Leggewie mentioned that he knew someone who had experienced one-room primary schooling in France under the Fourth Republic. Apparently, his colleague's ears perked up on hearing this, for he expressed the desire to interview me about my experience in Madame Mercier's classroom.

As I walk to the faculty club for my lunch invitation with Professor Johnson, I regret I'm not accompanied by Madame Mercier, now retired at the other end of the world in her charming home near the hospital where I was born. She wouldn't believe we're talking about her little one-room schoolhouse!

After comparative studies bearing on several industrialized nations of fairly similar economic level, Professor Johnson is troubled, justifiably so, by the aberrant rate of criminality and incarceration in the United States. He is eager to devote his efforts not only to the study, but also the solution to this shocking disproportion that seems to humiliate him personally. Among other things, he is advocating a controversial project, which raises hackles in the United States: The formal teaching of moral conduct in grade schools.

"Reactionary brainwashing," claims the Left.

"Threat to family prerogatives and values," says the Right.

Where does the professor stand ideologically? On the conservative side, I presume. In the United States, "right-wing sociology" exists, though elsewhere the juxtaposition of these two terms is an oxymoron.

But since I'm here to bear witness, and not to analyze motivations or political agendas, I simply describe Madame Mercier's classroom to my host.

"And what are your most vivid remembrances?" he asks.

"The morals lessons!" I answer without hesitation.

"Ah, that's what I'm interested in" he says. "Even if you didn't apply these teachings, but don't worry, I'm not accusing you of anything, at least you *heard* them, they were formally *taught* to you. That's not the case with American children today. Because of the collapse of family, school, and religion, kids no longer *learn* morals. Yet we could argue that distinguishing right from wrong is as much a cognitive as an ethical problem. But do you think the personality and character of your teacher were important factors?"

"Yes, for sure. Don't forget that I spent a full five years under her tutelage, at a very impressionable age. We called her our *maîtresse*, and families had complete confidence in her. This hallowed perception of the primary-school teacher has since considerably eroded in France, and is radically foreign to the American tradition, where schooling has always been placed under strict parental oversight. That's too bad for your project..."

"Yes, but did you detect any potential danger in this experience which seems very positive to me, and to you too?"

"Well, as an adult, I have sometimes wondered whether this teaching of morals, this indoctrination, hasn't had some negative consequences, for instance blunting my critical sense. Prominent among the list of vices was the injunction to not speak ill of people: 'Unless you can say something nice, keep quiet.'"

"Yes, I see there a risk of conformism or submission."

I had often thought about this problem myself and come to the conclusion that just as individualism doesn't exclude solidarity (As anarchist songwriter Georges Brassens quipped "Listen, if in the village someone falls in a well, it's clear that everyone must immediately come to the rescue"), similarly the allergic to ill-speaking must denounce the despot or the swindler.

"You know, Professor Johnson, when all is said and done, what is meant by the avoidance of ill-speaking is not so much criticism, but systematic denigration, a waste of time and energy to sterile ends, a negative stance unfortunately too prevalent."

"Anything else?"

" Yes, a detail. We should use the term "primary school" and not "elementary school" to designate this sector of the educational system, in order to underline its essential role. The rest, including Claremont, with all due respect, is somewhat secondary."

When I returned home to the Village after the interview, I found my neighbor Ike doing pushups as usual in front of his apartment. He couldn't wait to let me hear a new Bobby Blue Bland record he had just bought. He went in, opened the windows, and turned on the stereo full blast. I thought to myself *"Man, am I living in an interesting world or what!"*

Part V

Fast
Forward

"Reflections," a black-and-white photograph by D.S.

Chapter 21

Disentangling the Psyche

"Know Thyself"

— *Socrates*

*H*i Milan, nice day isn't it?"

Psychotherapist Kelly R. welcomes me into her office. She invites me to have a seat on the sofa, then rolls out her chair from behind her desk to remove any barrier between us. This is our second session. She's trying to make me feel at ease. But I'm tense. I don't know what to expect.

"Yeah, nice day," I reply nervously, looking around at the children's toys—anatomically correct dolls, crayons, felt pads, kid-size table and chairs—making up the rest of the furnishings in her office. Those objects don't look so cute in this setting. They've probably witnessed many sordid tales of abuse or neglect, a reminder that the child is the "parent" of the adult.

The clock on the wall is ticking. Time rules here as everywhere. At the beginning of our previous session I wondered how we were going to fill the hour, but then got rolling and by the end felt cut short. During that meeting Kelly asked me about my "family of origin," and she merely listened and jotted down some notes. I assumed that "family of origin" meant parents and siblings, and since my story is rather complicated, I told her I was writing a memoir, hinting I could let her see the synopsis to save time, but she showed no interest. All this effort for naught, I thought. I suppose she wanted to hear me talk so she could decide for herself what was important, from inflections of voice or other signs of emotion.

"Cup of coffee, Milan?"

"Yes, thanks. With cream and sugar please."

"Non-dairy creamer okay?"

"Yeah, fine."

She rummages around the countertop for the supplies, leaves the room to look for a swizzle stick. I wish I could simply drink my coffee black, instead of being so persnickety. How banal can things get? Here we are ready to plunge into the deepest recesses of my psyche and instead we're bobbing around in small talk. First the weather, then coffee. What's next, cats and dogs?

I'm here reluctantly, at the insistence of my wife of twenty-five years, Vera, from whom I am separated, with a divorce on the horizon. My chronic over-work was probably a major factor in the collapse of our relationship, an all too common situation. Ironically, I thought the reverse would happen, that she would be the one to leave the marriage, as occurs in the overwhelming majority of cases, with men plodding along and women taking decisive ac-tion. I'm fifty, our son Paul is twenty-one and in his last year of college, and our daughter Laurie, eighteen, recently graduated from high school. Lots of milestones occurring simultaneously. Vera wanted me to honor our long mar-riage by undergoing couples therapy, but I can't do that in good conscience because I'm seeing someone else. However, I've accepted to do individual counseling, in order to find out whether I'm as confused and messed up as she suggests, and as I myself suspect. A mutual friend of ours, saddened by our split, has expressed perhaps the most objective, least blameful interpreta-tion of our breakup: "Maybe you accomplished everything you were meant to do together. You raised two wonderful children, traveled a lot, and probably shared many good times and memories over the years."

Kelly specializes in child psychology and she is in great demand, but on the basis of a recommendation by a former client of hers, my writer friend Bart, she has agreed to see me. Himself recently divorced, he has through that expe-rience become familiar with the world of psychotherapy, self help books, AA meetings, men's groups. I tease him that he has, with surprising enthusiasm for a curmudgeon like him, become addicted to…addiction and therapy. I admire his writing, his words are chiseled on the page in a strong, decisive way, like on an anvil, as befits a former typesetter, but in conversation he sometimes lapses into the lingo: "Kelly will help you work through your *issues*."

My own stance is more skeptical. After all, what can anybody tell me about myself that I don't already know?

The psyche has an aura of depth, danger, and mystery associated to it, sometimes mixed with ridicule. I once heard an eminent scholar categorically state that anyone who has not undergone psychoanalysis is not worth talking to. But I also heard a sarcastic insider view, conveyed by a psychiatrist at a party, after a few drinks had loosened up his tongue: "Psychoanalysis is lengthy and expensive, but it is well worth the time and cost. It will transform your life. At the end of the process you'll be able to say **FUCK** in front of **M-O-T-H-E-R**."

I had some doubts about psychology, was drawn to Marx more than Freud. I had been invited to join a men's encounter group once, and had gone out of curiosity, but my participation didn't last long. My "issues" at the time didn't mesh with the group's focus, which was based on, what else, feelings and relationships. But those emotions are contingent on individual circumstances, so the sessions turned out to be mostly vehicles to vent personal anger and frustrations, from which it was difficult to extrapolate further. Useful for the protagonists, yes, and interesting in a voyeuristic way, and universal to some extent, but not really applicable beyond those individual situations.

The group's facilitator had given us a cautionary, half-jocular definition of a dysfunctional family: "A family of more than one person." Most of us were facing latent or overt midlife crises, characterized in some cases by a panicked search for meaning, in others nearing depression. To the lament "I'm too old to work, too young to retire, and too tired to have an affair" voiced by one of the participants, another retorted "I would have an affair, except I don't have the energy to retell my whole life story to someone new." When my turn came to initiate the discussion, I said I had been traumatized, at thirty-four, by the purchase of a washing machine, by the realization that if I ever moved in the future, I would have to lug this appliance along, that I was now a bourgeois homeowner, the very role I had up until then disdained in my unrealistic and immature counter-cultural phase, when everything had to be "alternative." I was clearly out of synch with the group's concerns.

At another meeting I brought up my theory, based on personal observation and scattered readings, that one becomes an adult at thirty-seven. "Why thirty-seven instead of eighteen or twenty-one?" asked a participant. "Because at thirty-seven you have to stop blaming your parents," I replied, with maybe too much of a patronizing tone. My remark did not sit well—most of us were past that age, and the group's recriminations often had to do with parents, in addition to wives, girlfriends, and siblings. To my surprise, rarely with bosses or co-workers. During a particularly vehement session beating up on parents, I cast a pall in the room by wondering out loud how our own children perceived us as fathers. Yikes! Everything about sex, money, family of origin, religion and innermost feelings was fair game, but here I was touching a raw nerve, a taboo. After a long silence, someone said, "Let's not go there."

Interestingly, the genesis of the encounter group—whose membership evolved over the years—was that two prominent alpha males in the community had been left by their wives for... other women, after seemingly stable long-lasting marriages. A new trend seemed to be emerging, very damaging to the male ego already struggling to redefine itself in the wake of the feminist revolution. Another man could be considered a rival, and the situation dealt with accordingly, but a woman?

Kelly's return with the swizzle stick snaps me back to the here and now of our session: "Before we go on to new stuff, Milan, I'd like to give you my thoughts on something you told me last time, okay? The episode when you were four years old, and you viciously bit your sister on the wrist, because you thought she was going to hit you in order to make you stop a tantrum directed at your elderly caretaker. The vividness of your recollection and your insistence on it definitely mean it's an important event. You described how all the yelling and crying led to a sudden transformation in your behavior, from unbearable brat to good boy eager to please and do chores and so on. That radical change still mystifies you, and as is typical for an orphan, you attribute it the moral influence of your deceased father from on high. You said you saw yourself through his eyes and were overcome with shame. Have I got it right?"

"Yes, that's pretty much how I see it, except I'm not an orphan. My mother didn't die. And I know my father had a huge influence on me, but only in the abstract. I have no concrete recollection of him, only vague images, and I don't know whether they're from my own memory or from stories I've heard about him. The first remembrance of which I'm certain is of being in an underground storage cave during an American air raid against the Germans in our area in July 1944, eight months after his death. I know for sure I was there because I can still smell the moss and lichen from the walls of that bomb shelter whenever I'm in a cellar or a damp basement."

"Yes, smell is the most primitive of our senses, and therefore the best trigger for involuntary memory, which can't be imaginary. But you *are* an orphan, not only because orphanhood is defined as the loss of one parent, but also because you did in fact loose both of your parents, one after the other. First you were abandoned by your father through death; then by your mother when she had to board you with the elderly peasant couple, so that she could continue to work and earn a living. Plus this is further compounded by all the linguistic complications you mentioned last time, and the upheavals caused by your failed installation at age four in Slovakia. You perceived that place as paradise, but you were yanked away from it and returned to France with your older sister, who until then had been raised by relatives. I don't think you realize how much baggage you're carrying from your childhood."

"Isn't *abandoned* too strong a word, regarding my parents? After all, they had no choice in the matter. And I really don't remember my father, so how could I feel *abandoned* by him?"

"Come on Milan, think of your own children. If you were to vanish from their lives in their infancy, don't you think that emotionally they'd feel that loss as an abandonment, even if later they couldn't remember the trauma from a cognitive standpoint?"

"Yes, I guess you're right."

"OK, last time you also said your major issue was that you hunger for ir-responsibility because you didn't experience it in childhood, and that instead you're stuck in caretaking roles. Paradoxically, you bring those on yourself but later resent them. And you wonder why you spontaneously make these choices. You initially feel good about them, altruism and empathy being your genuine second nature, which is amazing to me given your background, but eventually you come to chafe under those obligations because they turn out to be the opposite of what you really want and need. You told me you were burned out on diligence and responsibility, you dream of a simple life, within you means, using cash only, in twenty-dollar bills stored in a shoebox."

"Yes, I'm not interested in power or prestige, what I want is carefreeness, like my childhood mentor Pépère. I think this hunger comes from never hav-ing lived in my own home until my mother remarried when I was sixteen, and then sharing the place with her husband, who wouldn't teach me how to drive. Like everything else, I learned that by myself, by taking his car from the parking lot while he was at work. I was fortunate in many ways, given the wonderful people who took me in at various times—Pépère and Mémère, Madame Kapferer, the Spaneks—but living in somebody else's house en-tailed expectations and restrictions, self-imposed I'm sure, because I never got any hint I was unwelcome or anything like that. The same with my scholarship to attend boarding school at ten. It made me feel like a chosen child of the Republic, and that was great for my self-esteem, but it implied obligations as well, apparently more imagined than real. My calamitous academic results during the first year were met with a forbearant "Can do better," not the condemnation I feared. At any rate, I grew up with the notion, skewed or not, that wherever I happened to tread, I should do so lightly and leave no trace of my passage."

I was trying to help Kelly understand that what one lacks in those circumstances is a sense of unquestionable belonging such, for instance, as I have observed in the attitudes of two long-time friends. One comes from a very large family and has had in the course of his life frequent falling outs with his siblings. But their quarrels always turn out to be temporary, until the next reconciliation and the next dispute. This pattern, hard to imagine outside blood relationships, has had negative implications for his personal friendships—most have gone badly because he has treated his friends as if they were kin, but that cavalier attitude about disagreements, insults, misunderstandings, or slights isn't tolerated outside the family bond.

The other friend was "banished" from her conservative Jewish congregation because of her militancy in radical left-wing causes followed by marriage to a gentile blue-collar union activist. Bad choices in the eyes of her upper-class parents and their community! Yet she scoffed at this rejection and told me she knew she could go back any time she wanted, because no matter what, she was, is and always would be an M.O.T. "What's that?" I asked. "A member of the Tribe," she replied as I marveled at the confidence and security this sense of belonging had provided her.

"You know Milan, " Kelly continues, "your father's imagined reprobation may help explain your sudden change of behavior after the biting episode, but I think there's another aspect, even more important. It sheds light on your dilemma regarding responsibility and caretaking. In psychotherapy, once you identify a founding event, everything else follows from there in a logical pattern. Now keep in mind I'm not being judgmental, only trying to propose an explanation."

"Okay, go ahead, I can take it." At this point, notwithstanding my bravado, I'm downright scared. What has Kelly discovered about me that I didn't know? The child-size chairs and table suddenly take on an ominous dimension.

"Well, Milan, caretaking can be a control mechanism. It works this way: by making yourself indispensable, you protect yourself from rejection. I think that's what happened in the biting episode. In the midst of all the shrieking, you realized that you'd gone too far, and you suddenly felt in danger of being abandoned again. So you became a nice boy, eager to please, and you reversed roles with your guardians. You became their caretaker. And this has been your pattern ever since. Does that make sense?"

I feel totally bared by Kelly's revelation. I had no idea. The room blurs. She hands me a Kleenex. I'm unable to speak. There are still twenty minutes left in the session but I can't continue. I see no point in going any further, either now or later. I'm wrung inside out, finished with therapy.

As I leave her office, Kelly invites me to make another appointment, though she senses I won't be back. She tries to comfort me: "Don't be too hard on yourself, Milan. Given all the traumas in you childhood, you had only two alternatives: caretaker or psychopath. I'm glad you chose the first."

Chapter 22

Workin' at the U.

"My mother was a seamstress, my father a laborer. Thanks to the
meritocratic tracks of the Republic, when the French school system
still worked, I found myself catapulted into the University.
There, I made my way through the cracks of a schizophrenic system
that simultaneously nurtures the good and its opposite. I now find
myself among those who are very critical of the University; in itself,
the institution is a highly respectable spiritual principle,
but its temporal incarnation is rather regrettable."

— *Marcel Gauchet, editor of the French journal Le Débat*

As a tenured faculty member at a university, I am extraordinarily privileged. Not in income, for I earn only a modest living. To defray the cost
of their college studies, my children fall into the vast American quasi-middle-
class that does not qualify for financial aid yet cannot afford higher education,
except on loans, scholarships, or disruptive concurrent employment.

No, my privilege derives from another source, more important than income: my matchless working conditions. Furthermore, I'm able to appreciate
them fully and not take them for granted; prior to ending up in my present
enviable situation, I also experienced the opposite, on what I expected would
be a permanent basis. A proletarian background gives you a perspective on
things.

Hubris aside, and knock on wood, I enjoy solid employment security
and, according to Teachers Insurance and Annuity Association actuarial
tables, decent odds for longevity, although these historical characteristics
of the college teaching profession are eroding; the first, under budgetary
retrenchments and repeated assaults on tenure; the second, following the
intrusion of pathological levels of stress in this previously genteel occupation.

While I deplore a number of aberrations in the recent professional trends, particularly the new "productivity" expectations for tenure-track faculty, and the grossly unfair three-tier (tenured, tenure-track, temporary) stratification that prefigured the disturbing evolution in the general economy towards marginal employment—it's not always honorable for universities, where half of the teaching is now done by temporary or part-time people, to play a vanguard role—I have nonetheless benefited greatly from the climate favoring writing and research, which I enjoy fully as much as teaching. The problem is how to make those activities compatible, because, notwithstanding facile rhetoric to the contrary, they aren't. Perhaps the solution lies in providing alternating periods of full engagement in each, rather than simultaneous divided attempts at both.

But personal complaints seem unbecoming at this point. Tenure, which I was fortunate to obtain in 1980, before the full onslaught of the current insanity, gives me the option to determine my activities freely, and thus maintain my self-esteem and integrity, at some tolerable cost to my career. And my working conditions are truly incomparable. To wit: no boss, no dress code, no shift work, no week-end or holiday duties; summers off, plus semester breaks; a private office (what a luxury!) in a clean, quiet, well-heated building (no air conditioning needed in my "cooler by the lake" region), with parking nearby in case I forgo the twenty-minute walk from home; a direct telephone line, voice mail, e-mail, the Internet, the latest technology, and training opportunities galore to learn how to use all these gizmos; in my office, a wide window which opens for fresh air on a vista of sky, lawn, and foliage, with Kitchi Gammi, a.k.a. Lake Superior, in the background; swimming pool and recreational sports facilities, if I care to use them; university letterhead and mailbox; secretarial support, and use of a sophisticated photocopy machine for whose maintenance and repairs I am not responsible; a captive audience of bright young people and interesting non-traditional students presumably eager to hear me think aloud; social if not financial status, allowing access, if desired, to all levels of society; last but not least, a readily available community of well-traveled colleagues, some of whom have "nevertheless" become friends, as we facetiously say in the profession.

Or perhaps not so facetiously, as intimated by the quintessential—hence revealing—joke about academic mores, regarding the professor who receives a get-well card in the hospital following a heart attack: "The Department wishes you a speedy recovery. Signed: Five for, three against, two abstentions."

In the strange mix of cantankerous individualism and groveling submis-
siveness that characterizes the culture of academe and the temperament of
its denizens, one finds little evidence of working class solidarity. In fairness,
though, it must also be recognized that the instinct to organize has dimin-
ished if not disappeared in society at large.

It is well known that academic politics are particularly vicious, because
the stakes are so...small! Thank God professors are not physically brutal, or
else most campuses would erupt into warring mini-Balkans. This doesn't necessarily mean that *homo academicus* is a gentler subset of the *homo sapiens*
species. I haven't sorted out whether delayed dismissal of tenure-track faculty
during or at the end of their six-year probation period ("You don't measure
up to us, you're fired, one year from now") is a humanitarian gesture or a
sadistic act.

In my long and indecent enumeration of advantageous working conditions at the university, I have overlooked several important additional ones:
the possibility of obtaining sabbatical leaves every seven years at half salary; competitive travel or research grants; and the unparalleled freedom
of scheduling and movement that faculty enjoy in the accomplishment of
their duties. I am restricted to a specific place, the classroom, only a limited number of hours per week and even there I can sit, stand, or walk as I
please. My regular office hours are likewise hardly burdensome, and the rest
of my activities largely self-defined. Utopia! Much better even than being
a member of the idle rich.

Indeed, I am given the conditions, if not the monetary means, to lead a
privileged life, free from the relentless dehumanization that so many people
endure to simply earn a living. And as regards to my relatively enfeebled
purchasing power, considering the enormous length of training required
for this profession, I am sheltered from embarrassment or ridicule by a
tradition of tolerance for eccentricity in the absent-minded professor. Thus
if my shoes, sweater, or bicycle (I can hear my exercise-averse blue collar
friends, who get enough of a workout on the job, snicker "At his age and
with all his schooling, can't he afford a car?") are not of the latest fashion,
or if they are somewhat ragged at the edges, it is not because I am a pauper
to be pitied, but because I have no time or interest for such trivial concerns;
my mind is preoccupied with much more important intellectual matters,
for instance pondering over the seventeenth-century French author La Ro-

chefoucauld's curmudgeonly maxim: "Contempt for riches was among the philosophers a hidden desire to avenge themselves from the injustice of fate, through scorn for the very things of which they were deprived; it was a secret way to protect themselves from the humiliation of poverty; it was a devious means of obtaining the consideration they could not get through riches."

Truly, I have no right to complain, when I think that so many people earn their living as I once did, in unhealthful if not outright toxic or dangerous occupations, on graveyard, swing, or rotating shifts, in freezing or scorching environments, under artificial light and deafening noise, doing repetitive, monotonous tasks, watching the clock tick away the seconds, until the first fifteen-minute coffee break, until the thirty-minute unpaid respite of lunch, until the second fifteen-minute coffee break, until quitting time or mandatory overtime, until retirement decades away, and death shortly thereafter.

The only industrial injury I face as an academic is the risk of contracting tennis elbow from excessive or improper keyboarding (how embarrassing to hear this diagnosis from an orthopedist specializing in sports medicine). OSHA seldom finds the need to intervene in the university, although lack of complaint is not necessarily a good indicator of satisfaction. Americans, notoriously litigious in most other realms, feel they have no rights in the economic arena and are therefore surprisingly tolerant of substandard working conditions. "Take it or leave it" is the most widely accepted principle of U.S. labor relations. In that context, grumblings about windowless offices or foul-smelling labs are viewed as frivolous.

While tendonitis or torticolis are extremely painful, debilitating, even disabling ergonomic ailments afflicting numerous sedentary employees lashed to their computer screens, myself included, and while it can be argued that all suffering is real, those ailments are not "qualitatively" comparable, as an occupational hazard, to the threat of silicosis that I endured at Ace Metal Refinishers in Chicago—often on the night shift, so as not to inconvenience the nattily dressed office workers. And, supreme humiliation, this was not even a heroic, essential blue-collar undertaking, like coal mining or steel beam riveting, but simply cosmetic work, to make the metal surfaces shine brightly, at the expense of my and my co-workers' lungs.

Nor is any academic ever required to ask permission to go to the restroom, and then have to endure the boss's snide remarks adding insult to indisposition—"Come on, shammer, what's the matter wit' you, you already went twony minutes ago"—as I did in my job at the San Francisco Airport.

Not a single day goes by that I don't count my blessings, that I don't treasure the wonderful working conditions that I enjoy in my cherished second home, the cinderblock Humanities Building, whose 1950's architectural blankness I no longer notice, much less bemoan ("My God, they tried to do the Bauhaus" a new colleague exclaimed when first seeing the building).

Not a month passes that I don't retrieve my doctoral degree from its storage place between the pages of a large atlas, like a veteran digging out his bronze star periodically from a shoebox for reminiscence or inspection. I gaze with disbelieving and grateful eyes at this parchment of genuine sheepskin, which I own only because it came free with my generous 1971-1974 fellowhips at Claremont Graduate University. I contemplate the beautifully calligraphied document, similar in importance, for me, to a union card for a journeyman bricklayer, and I give thanks for this miraculously-acquired passport into the paradise of academe, where I belong like a fish in water, although my integration to the professional class has been far from seamless, the proverbial square peg in a round hole. An example: it took me quite a while to accept to delegate to a secretary work that I didn't want to do or couldn't do myself—a bit like the dilemma facing upwardly mobile lower-class people suddenly too preoccupied with their professional responsibilities to wash their own dishes or clean their floors, hence in need of a housekeeper, with all the guilt, damage to self-esteem, and invasion of privacy this entails.

Once poor, always poor, i.e. self-sufficient, it's in your genes. I have fun in French class torturing students with the idiomatic uses of the verb *"faire"* (to do, to make). To nail my point, I ask for a contrastive translation between *"laver les vitres"* (to wash the windows) and *"faire laver les vitres."* It usually takes quite a while before someone comes up with the correct answer ("to have the windows washed"). This distinction elicits chuckles from the class. Once, though, a student got in the last word with a perceptive observation: "Who cares about clean windows, anyway?" His remark made me feel dated and called back memories of Monsieur Allais, the concierge at the Kapferers'. One of his main duties was to endlessly polish the front windows, so they would look like mirrors to the gentry riding their thoroughbreds on the equestrian lane in the middle of the avenue.

Slightly ill at ease in the professional class (but not in the university), I continue to see myself simply as an intellectual *worker*. Some obscure atavism still compels me to inscribe a (w) instead of an (o) before my campus phone number. Similarly, I am uncomfortable with the somewhat pompous generic title of *Professor*.

At the same time, my more precise in-house title of *Associate Professor* is beginning to feel tarnished after thirty years in rank, the equivalent of terminal Lieutenant Colonel in the Army—that disgruntled caste fomenting coups in developing countries. My treasured *Webster's New World Dictionary* from high school days even has a listing for that title, upon which I happened accidentally: "Associate Professor: a college teacher ranking above an assistant professor and below a full professor." Lite Bird, Full Bird, Lite Prof, Full Prof, no longer junior faculty, not yet senior (i.e. didn't jump through the right hoops—a situation again similar to the military, where I had fun poring over countless Officer Efficiency Reports).

And *Dr.* seems appropriate only for medical people in white, who receive serious salaries commensurate with the gravitas of their title. A friend of mine once scoffed that if ignorance hurt as much as a toothache, teachers would be paid the same as dentists.

So I'm left with the title of *teacher*, or perhaps *college teacher*, or better yet, *educator*, although the latter sounds a bit jargonny, and I'm well aware that I'm only tertiary in this realm. I couldn't withstand the crushing workload and confinement of secondary school teaching in the U.S., and I haven't considered working in the most important level of all, primary school.

I'm not alone in experiencing discomfort with the elevated connotations of academic titles. My friend and former political science colleague Paul Wellstone made it a point to eschew "Professor" and to refer to himself instead as "Teacher" during his many years at prestigious Carleton College in Minnesota, thereby deliberately grating the sensibilities of some of the more status-conscious faculty and administrators. When he was elected to represent our state in the U.S. Senate, the supercilious people (fortunately few in numbers, but unfortunately powerful) whom he had antagonized at Carleton with his social justice activism, breathed an audible sigh of relief at his departure. I first met Paul on a picket line for striking cafeteria workers at his college, during the year I taught there on visiting appointment.

I know academe is my place, I belong there, I claim ownership, I'm not an impostor, even if I got in through the side door, at the right time—as a former student, now locked out from similar opportunities, likes to remind me. I feel totally at home in the university, at all hours, unlike many of the front-door-entrants, who are either more normal than I or else less enamored of the campus.

Despite my having the strong attachment characteristic of a convert, I don't make a fetish of the institution, where one can simultaneously find "the good and its opposite." I have never, never, even fleetingly, subscribed to the second part of the most cynical insider definition of institutionalized education—"Feeding false pearls to genuine swine"—but I have often found myself in agreement with the first.

My indulgent wallowing in two seemingly antithetical values, freedom and security, should not be misconstrued. As a privileged academic I work hard, very hard, damn hard, incredibly hard, much harder than imaginable. I work all the time, as do most of my colleagues, who lament that they feel caught in an ever-accelerating treadmill.

Just as self-censorship is the most insidious form of control, self-imposed work is the most demanding. Fortunate are the few tenured academics who jump off the treadmill; possessing limited financial resources but much leisure time, they become adept do-it-yourselfers, or notorious hobbyists with exquisite skills in woodworking or other crafts. At the campus club dining room, they describe their latest home improvement projects, and elicit exclamations of awe, sighs of boredom, or glares of envy from their less handy colleagues. I have no time, patience, or inclination for such distractions. I stand resolutely at the other extreme. The rain gutters on my house will forever remain unsightly, and I have no garage in which to tinker, nor any plans to build one. My only hobby is reading, active semi-recreational reading which then becomes part of my work, itself void of boundaries. I make no attempt or pretense at "balance." If anything, I want to focus my life even more and eliminate all remaining annoyances. And instead of imploring the clock to make the interminable minutes tick by, as I did at Ace Metal, my eyes are transfixed on the calendar and the avalanche of faraway deadlines that suddenly loom close as I anguish over the scarcity of Time and the realization that I will leave a number of projects unfinished, or even unstarted, in this go round on earth. I have come to the radical but serious conclusion that in order to tame the deadline beast, the frequency of everything should be halved, through systematic placement of a "bi-" prefix before yearly conferences, quarterly irritations, monthly reports, weekly meetings.

I have survived for years on a regimen of five hours' sleep per night, my personal and professional life have melded. I interpret this lack of boundaries as evidence of absorption in a very satisfying occupation, not workhaholism, although my family and friends might disagree. One thing is certain: I cannot possibly work more than I do.

I live in a frenzy. Or maybe I don't live at all. Still, I wouldn't trade my present existence for my former one, when "work" stopped the instant I punched the time clock. I fantasize that when my current writing projects are completed, I will teach and do nothing else. Enough of this demented pace; "Teach well and be kind" will be my humble goal, the initial one I had when I entered this venerable profession. Or perhaps I will only write, and not teach at all. That prospect sounds appealing too, although I would miss the social interaction and the ready forums for my musings. Trying to juggle writing and teaching and doing neither fully is what drains me; the most exhausting work is the work not done, the work postponed. At any rate, I will do considerably less, and soon; my current pace is not sustainable.

But even this reduced level of activity would entail much effort and energy. Serious teaching is consuming; it is by definition always incomplete, imperfect; it is one of Freud's three "impossible occupations," along with healing and governing. Yet, paradoxically, this lack of finality, this need for constant reevaluation, is also what makes teaching such a fascinating and rewarding endeavor, like a performing art, or parenting. Only the teacher is aware of the shortcuts taken, and what could have, should have, might have been done, even when the evaluations look good (said evaluations being a veritable obsession in the United States. I once gave a public lecture at which, as I filed into the room with the attendees, I was handed a blue sheet of paper, like everyone else. I casually looked at it on the way to the podium, and to my dismay, discovered that it was an evaluation form for...my talk! It was hard to concentrate after that, seeing the audience down there fidget with their blue sheets, sizing me up, wondering how they should rate my performance on the various numerical scales and open-ended questions).

In the meantime, caught in the treadmill, I try to accomplish too much, and experience mainly exhaustion and frustration. A friend once admonished me: "You cannot be a good husband, father, friend, teacher, writer, scholar, engaged citizen, and homeowner. You have to choose. You have to accept being mediocre in some areas, you have to neglect or drop some roles."

At the time, unbeknownst to him, I was also trying to be a dutiful son to my invalid mother.

Through luck and some wild quirks of fate I have thus become a member of what John Updike calls the "international race of teachers and artists...people who are at home with pencils and paper, with the tools of education and art...peaceable, reasonable people, who value civilization and trust it to offer them a niche."

That I would seek, much less find, such a niche, is utterly astonishing to me. The academic profession is exceedingly difficult to enter, and the sacrosanct "terminal degree" a daunting prospect for a self-supporting, isolated working class person with dependents, such as I was.

Earlier, I could not have imagined undertaking such a journey, nor did I even aspire to. I had set out into the world of work with only one expectation: To lose my life while earning it.

Sometimes, I wish I were Jewish, Armenian, Palestinian, or a member of the other diasporas who, because of the vicissitudes of history, consider *knowledge* as the only worthwhile possession. All my overwork would be appreciated, even revered, in a milieu where education and culture are valued for their own sake. But I am marked by my roots and my environment. My European peasant origins and the anti-intellectual atmosphere of American society inhibit me from accepting intellectual validation easily.

I remember my otherwise beloved peasant mentor Pépère vituperating in a populist mode about politicians: "Those people don't know what it is to work. All they do is make speeches, go to banquets, and get us into wars. They need to learn what it feels like to do real labor, they need to dig ditches with a pick and a shovel. That would straighten them out." The literary critic Roland Barthes was not far off the mark when he wrote in a celebrated essay that authoritarian regimes, reflecting a sizable segment of public opinion, would reserve for the "idle, lazy, harmful" intellectuals the ultimate concrete, quantifiable work: digging holes and piling rocks.

Given my background, I am often assailed with doubt about the validity and usefulness of my endeavors. Not a trivial dilemma. The universally admired Mahatma Gandhi gave great importance to the cleaning of latrines.

Unlike a plumber, a mechanic, or a surgeon, I do nothing truly concrete or immediately visible. My principal activity, teaching, is even less tangible than my parallel one, writing, which at least produces words on paper. Granted,

I'm fortunate to be able to earn my living in an occupation that is not, to the best of my knowledge, harmful to others. But my efforts, directed at college students, are expended helping a social and demographic category arguably least in need of my intervention, somewhat like a physician ministering only to relatively healthy patients.

I know that my concern about the concreteness and tangibility of my work is ill-founded and excessive. I was reminded of this while showing my then four-year-old son Aaron a busy construction site near our house. He was admiring the bulldozers, backhoes, pneumatic drills, and other equipment chewing up the asphalt. A worker, noticing the child's spellbound attention, walked over so his voice could be heard above the din. He removed his hard hat to wipe the sweat and dirt from his face, and yelled out "Make sure you go to college, kid, so you don't have to do this kind of work when you grow up."

But Aaron's enthrallment didn't flag. Soon after, another worker stepped up to our vantage point and admonished him: "Better go to college kid because by the time you're my age if you do this kind of work I'll be your boss, and by then I'll be pretty damn crabby."

I have now presumably "arrived." But during moments of self-doubt or vulnerability, instead of considering myself a teacher/writer/scholar who has attained statistically singular achievement against forbidding odds (i.e. a terminal degree and a tenured position), and notwithstanding the French Communist Party's preemptive defense of intellectual work as equally legitimate and useful as manual labor, I feel a bit like a fraud or a class traitor. In addition to my populist baggage from the past, the attitude of society at large contributes to this occasional malaise of mine. Americans basically disdain education: "Those who can, do; and those who can't, teach." Or: "If you're so smart, why aren't you rich?" Academic work is often derided as "not real work," and universities are described condescendingly as ivory towers removed from the "real world."

Three personal anecdotes come to mind to illustrate the "I don't get no respect" syndrome that intellectuals face in this country.

The first is an experience that occurred a few years after I began teaching. I returned to Chicago and was visiting a blue-collar tavern with a friend who introduced me as his "now successful" buddy from old metal refinishing days.

He asked people standing around with us at the bar if they were able to guess my new line of work. Someone suggested I put my hands up so they could be examined. No sooner had I done so than a derisive voice piped up: "Hey guys, look it, with smooth hands like that, this dude can't be doin' diddly shit, he doesn't work *at all*."

For a brief moment my embarrassment was greater than my recoil from the stupidity of the statement.

The second episode in this vein had to do with my daughter Laurie and her friend Ann Maiolo in their Suzuki violin group lesson. Seated in the parents' row in the classroom, I was doting on the blissful sounds coming out of those children-sized instruments, and reflecting on the casual comment I overheard from Annie on the way to the lesson: "I wonder what musical instrument my sister Lottie is going to learn when she turns six like me."

While pondering over the social implications of Annie's statement, coming as it did on the heels of Laurie's deadpan question to her the preceding week "Does your daddy have tenure?", and while trying to absorb the distance between those comments and my own childhood, I noticed among the group of parents a former student of mine.

"How are you doing?" I asked the now suddenly thirty-something young woman, in a tentative voice.

"Great!" she exclaimed as she moved to the chair next to me, "I brought my niece here, and guess what, I have a FAN-TAS-TIC job! I'm a buyer for a department store!"

"Congratulations!" I replied enthusiastically, relieved that she had not joined the ranks of the underemployed college graduates, as often happens these days, to the point that I feel uncomfortable going to franchise restaurants or shopping malls, for fear of encountering former students working there.

But the situations are sometimes reversed. After a long silence, the successful alumna turned to me and asked, like an afterthought: "And what about you? You still workin' up there at the U.?"

Finally, in a third consciousness-raising episode, I was invited by a student of mine to speak to her fifth-grade class, where she was doing an internship. She introduced me as her university professor, and asked the children if they had any questions they'd like to ask me, about French culture or any other topic.

Unlike at the U. at question time, a wall of hands immediately shot up. Forgetting my newly learned gender-sensitive pedagogical principles, I pointed to the pupil who had lurched forward the fastest, pleading with both arms raised "Me, me, me, please."

"OK, you're first," I said.

"How many hours do you teach each day?" asked the boy, about eleven years old, wriggling on his chair.

I gulped, unable to believe what I was hearing. Was this an innocent question, or his family's topic of choice at the dinner table? "Those damn profs up there, all Commies, teaching so little, eating up our hard-earned tax dollars."

"Well, euh, it's hard to give you a clear number, because I also work a lot outside of class on campus, and at home too, often late into the night."

Why am I so defensive, why this bad conscience? I will match any highly paid business executive with the mental energy I expend, what with the study abroad programs I have developed (and which were deemed useless if not detrimental to my career by a former dean), the international exchanges, the new courses, the independent studies, my long-in-progress memoir in two languages, the committee meetings (so taxing on patience and so wasteful of time and energy), the countless requests for crucial letters of recommendation. All this in addition to the never-ending work of preparing, correcting, editing, grading, advising. Not to mention the professionally related "why-don't-you-mind-your-own-business" controversies, such as trying to save the beautiful Old Main building from demolition, or, during the early Reagan era, embarrassing the University with the overlooked fact that some full-time faculty members were eligible for free government surplus cheese distributed from the back of trucks, or for reduced rate lunches at school for their children—I myself having narrowly missed the qualifying mark.

My work has by no means been only of a contemplative nature; much of it has entailed entrepreneurship, organizational skills, international negotiations at ministerial and foundation level. Still, I cannot satisfactorily explain what I do, nor can I expect anyone to understand how hard or how much I work, short of spending an entire day at my side; and that would amount to outright punishment, for it is not in the least interesting to watch an academic at work—unlike a welder, a cook, or a gardener: "Wanna come over and see me think and write?"

Two

> "I often have this strange and revealing dream..."
>
> — *Charles Baudelaire*

If I could relive my life, I wouldn't change a thing. Too much imagination is required to alter the "what if" chains of events ordained by fate. How could I come up with a more far-fetched itinerary than the journey from the archaic village of Saint-Aquilin to the Kapferer mansion in Paris, and on to the Midwestern American town of Duluth, via Chicago, San Francisco, and Los Angeles, with a French or Czecho-Slovakian backdrop throughout? Or lurching haphazardly from the peasantry to the professional class? Or raising two sets of children more than twenty years apart?

Regarding my work at the U., however, I sometimes harbor a fantasy, born of "end-of-career radicalism," when one has nothing to prove and nothing to lose, and when one can therefore be free, bold, and truthful. Whenever I feel defensive about the intangibility of what I do, or get upset about the morass of grading and other administrative rigamaroles required by the educational system, I fantasize that there is on the university campus a job that would assuage my need to do something unquestionably concrete, useful, and necessary, and at the same time allow real teaching to take place, in the ancient personalized Athenian tradition of mentorship, as opposed to the bureaucratic instruction now being dispensed. And that job would not be professor, but...janitor!

It is well known that physical movement activates the mind. The sixteenth century essayist Montaigne claimed that his best thinking occurred while he rode his horse. More universally, walking has a similar effect. This was true for Jean-Jacques Rousseau, eighteenth century author of *The Reveries of a Solitary Walker*, and it is the case too for my poet friend Louis Jenkins, who heads out daily with a small notebook in his pocket, catching thoughts as they come to him, at random, like butterflies, while he nonchalantly puts one foot in front of the other. In ancient Greece, teachers were called peripateticians, precisely because they walked with their students and engaged in discussion at the same time.

As always, singularities occur, exceptions confirming the rule. The French writer Marcel Proust, for instance, liked to think and write while lying in bed. I share the same predilection for supine reverie, which I view as complementary to the mobile kind.

Writing obviously requires remaining still, and so does reading, unless one is willing to risk being run over by a car, or falling into an open manhole cover, but all in all, consensus has it that mindless movement is good for the intellectual or creative process. "Mindlessness" is crucial in this respect. The concrete activity should not in itself require thought or concentration, lest it become a "zen," which totally absorbs one's attention on the task at hand, here and now. For this purpose, then, clearing brush is okay, woodworking not.

Ironically, this shift to janitorial work of an intellectual nature could occur only towards the end of a career, after standard recognition has been received—because earlier on, it would pose problems of credibility. For example, the main character in Louis-Ferdinand Céline's novel *Voyage to the End of Night* is a man who, after a number of years knocking about in Africa and working at odd jobs including a stint at an automobile factory in Detroit, decides to make something of his life by returning to his native France to study medicine so that he can become a doctor ministering to the poor. A worthy goal! After finishing his degree he sets up his office in a run-down suburb of Paris. But patients reject him. They suspect he is not a competent doctor. They think he works with them only because he's not good enough to have a rich clientèle. "Why else?" they wonder.

Similarly, I'd have to prove that I am a good traditional teacher before I could claim to teach as a janitor. And by the time that reputation was established and I had gained sufficient credibility, I would probably have lost some of the drive and energy required to implement my goal.

The eminent educator representing France at UNESCO's founding, Jean Guéhenno, said that the most important subject teachers teach is...who they are. I would use the cover of his authoritative statement to give myself license for spontaneity and improvisation. Rather than adhere to any kind of predetermined program or syllabus, I would share my current passions with the students, who in turn would bring me theirs. In education, as opposed to training, timing is essential. The moment must be seized. In the adventure of the mind and spirit, there is nothing worse than knowing in advance where one is going to be three weeks hence.

In my janitorial incarnation, I could also act as a consultant. For instance, I was once hard at work at home digging a hole to get at a cast iron sewer pipe that had cracked during the previous winter because of permafrost. A student of mine stopped by to ask if I could look over a crucial letter of application he was sending to an ultra-selective M.D./Ph.D. program, at the last minute of course, a situation I understand only too well, being myself an habitué of under-the-wire deadlines. I handed him the pick and the shovel to take over the digging while I sat on the porch to look over his writing. I read slowly and carefully, and I think he enjoyed working up a sweat to unearth the broken pipe entombed at a depth of six feet. This was a fair exchange which put us both at ease, rather than a service rendered, with its inevitable consequence of obligation or gratitude. He was admitted to the program and, with the help of a local philanthropist, he is well on his way to making important scientific discoveries.

Similarly, students who might want to consult with me about a piece of writing during my janitorial hours could take over my duties while I looked at their work; or, if they just wanted to talk, I would hand them a broom or a squeegee so they could help me as we conversed. No tests or grades. Just real stuff. And in the process, exercise with a purpose. Come to think of it, in addition to his fixation on the symbolic value of cleaning latrines, Gandhi advocated precisely this kind of approach, mixing humble manual labor with lofty intellectual pursuits.

Dream on, Miles. Like the French songwriter Georges Brassens, who identified with the medieval outlaw poet François Villon and dreamt like him of a spectacular death on the rack or the gallows, but realized that in fact he would probably die in bed just like "any old jerk," I too will likely one day collapse face down on my keyboard—and miss out on a grand exit, sprawled on the floor of the Humanities Building, with my students in white togas hovering over me, as I float down the River Styx back to my starting point in Saint-Aquilin, and thank for a last time on the way there all the people and institutions to whom I owe so much.

Acknowledgments

Although writing is often viewed as an individual endeavor, I would have been unable to complete this book, over nearly three decades, without the help and encouragement of the friends and colleagues listed below. I apologize in advance to those whose names may have been left out. They are not forgotten; I will no doubt at some point suddenly recall these omissions with great dismay.

I would like to thank (sadly, in several cases posthumously):

Patricia Hampl, for setting me on the path of memoir, and for her support throughout.

Florence Trystram, for her unwavering commitment to the ill-fated French version of the manuscript in her *Mémoire Vive* collection at Editions Seghers; and, along with Jean-Marc and Hélène De Leersnyder, for generously hosting my family in Paris all summer 1990.

Mara Kirk Hart, distinguished scholar and practitioner of the art of the memoir, for her expert and sensitive editing, including, at my request, suggestions on how to cut nearly one-fourth of the English manuscript.

Andrea Sande and Patricia Weaver Francisco, for likewise expert and sensitive editing.

Jane Fleeson, for translations of several chapters from French to English; and Milan Bajmóczi, for translations from English to Slovak. Their talented interpretations in this experiment gave me an opportunity to see my work through their eyes, a fascinating experience for a writer.

FOR INVALUABLE ASSISTANCE WITH THE PROJECT: Jean-Raymond Audet, Carmel DeMaioribus, Hannah Dentinger, Tony Dierckins, Katie Frantes, Sadie Green, Gendron Jensen, Sharee Johnson, Vera Kovacovic, Josette Le Bon, Carrie Lundell, Joe and Julie Maiolo, Nitya Malik, Freddy Muñoz, Joel Ness, Anna Owens, Mark Paschke, Marly Rusoff, Hélène Sanko, Tony Trimarchi, Elie and Mary Vidal, Josh Williams. And especially George Spanek, for steadfastly prodding me forward in both the French and the English versions. And Bart Sutter for his generous advocacy on behalf of his friends.

FOR FORMAL REVIEWS OF SECTIONS OF THE MANUSCRIPT, OR LETTERS OF RECOMMENDATION: James Day, Zara Kinnunen, Roger Lips, George O'Brien, Christopher Pinet, Roland Simon, Alan Singerman, Charlie Sugnet, Nicole Vaget, Paul Wellstone, Ann Williams, Cathy Yandell.

FOR INVITATIONS TO READ/DISCUSS VARIOUS CHAPTERS IN THEIR HIGH SCHOOL AND UNIVERSITY CLASSES: Tom Bacig, Julie Ball, Kate Basham, Jim and Linda Belote, Aydin Dirdingoglu, Jeffrey Hole, Bob Kosuth, Mike Linn, Linda Miller-Cleary, Greg Mischel, Cherie Pettersen, Margi Preus, Marty Thompson, Joan Varney, Janelle Wilson, Richard Woodward.

FOR INSTITUTIONAL AID: Arrowhead Regional Arts Council; Editions Seghers, Paris; Lake Superior Writers; Minnesota State Arts Board; University of Minnesota Duluth College of Liberal Arts and Chancellor's office.

FOR INFORMAL YET CRUCIAL ENCOURAGEMENT: Nick Albertson, Michel Barrère, Lisa Buljan, Jake Cáceres, Max, Christiane and Isabelle De Paz, Terry Hanson, Blake Hendrickson, Dick Hudelson, Jean Jacobson, Mike and Annette Jaros, Louis and Ann Jenkins, Tadd Johnson, Judith Kachinske, Dana Lindaman, Jean Malaurie, Michel and Janice Monnot, Ariane Ostier and Cécile and Vincent, Jean-Baptiste and Veronica Quillien, Henry and Terry Roberts, Anne Royko, Shar Sivertson, Denis and Shirley Spanek, Pat Stoddard, Thom and Cindy Storm, Eric and Claudine Vincent, Peter Wakefield, Matt Ward, Jacques Yvart. And many students over the years.

FOR MEDIA INTERVIEWS/ARTICLES: Jean Feraca, Stephanie Hemphill, Melanie Keveles, Micky McGilligan, Deborah Peterson.

Early drafts of several chapters appeared in the following publications, whose editors are gratefully acknowledged:

"Ma's Dictionary," in *Boundaries of Twilight*, New Rivers Press, 1991.

"Laundry Day," in *The Wolf Head Quarterly*, Spring 1995.

"Payday at the Village Tavern," in *The Wolf Head Quarterly*, Autumn 1995.

"San Francisco Airport, Summer '67," in *The Clinton Street Quarterly*, Summer 1988.

"Workin' at the U.," in *This Fine Place so Far from Home*, Temple University Press, 1995.